Building Supportive Communities for At-Risk Adolescents

It Takes More Than Services

Martha R. Burt
Gary Resnick
Emily R. Novick

American Psychological Association • *Washington, DC*

Published by
American Psychological Association
750 First Street, NE
Washington, DC 20002

Copies may be ordered from
APA Order Department
P.O. Box 92984
Washington, DC 20090-2984

In the United Kingdom and Europe, copies may be ordered from
American Psychological Association
3 Henrietta Street
Covent Garden
London WC2E 8LU
England

Typeset in Century by EPS Group Inc., Easton, MD

Printer: Edwards Brothers, Inc., Ann Arbor, MI
Cover designer: Berg Design, Albany, NY
Technical/production editor: Valerie Montenegro

Library of Congress Cataloging-in-Publication Data
Burt, Martha R.
    Building supportive communities for at-risk adolescents : it takes more than services / Martha R. Burt, Gary Resnick, and Emily R. Novick.—1st ed.
        p.   cm.
    Includes bibliographical references (p.   ) and index.
    ISBN 1-55798-466-2 (pb : acid-free paper)
    1. Teenagers—Services for—United States.   I. Resnick, Gary.   II. Novick, Emily R.   III. Title.
    HV1431.B84   1998
    362.7'083—dc21
                                                                    97-32411
                                                                    CIP

British Library Cataloguing-in-Publication Data
A CIP record is available from the British Library.

Printed in the United States of America
First edition

Contents

Preface

All adolescents need good friends, caring families, and supportive communities that provide them with constructive activities. Young people who live in environments or engage in behaviors that put them "at risk," either for violence, substance abuse, school dropout, or pregnancy, often suffer from a lack of adequate supports. This book explores the challenges involved in creating and sustaining supportive communities for at-risk youth. The first section provides an introduction to the concept and history of service integration and comprehensive-service models, a thorough review of the literature on risk and adolescence, and a new paradigm for thinking about adolescence and risk. The second section presents case studies of nine programs that serve youth and their families. The third section identifies the program elements that are critical to meeting the complex needs of adolescents and their families and discusses the challenges of funding and evaluating youth programs. The book concludes with a summary of themes and issues raised by the previous chapters.

This book began as a research project sponsored by the Office of the Assistant Secretary for Planning and Evaluation, U.S. Department of Health and Human Services (HHS) in 1992. It was inspired, in part, by the Carnegie Council on Adolescent Development's (1989) influential report entitled *Turning Points*. *Turning Points* identified the age span of 10–15 years old as a critical point of intervention in the lives of young people, reviewed the attributes that young people will need to succeed as contributing adults in our society, and made a number of recommendations concerning school reform that would affect this age group. The HHS-funded project was designed to learn more about existing programs or strategies to improve outcomes for young people and their families and to review the issues involved in designing and evaluating such efforts. Emily Novick (of HHS) initiated and supervised the project; Martha Burt (of the Urban Institute) directed the project under contract to HHS, working with Gary Resnick (of Westat, Inc.) and Nancy Matheson (of Pelavin Associates).

The HHS-funded project differed from the Carnegie report in several ways. It involved a review of the literature on adolescents and risk; the development of a model for identifying risk factors in young people; an in-depth description of a number of youth-serving programs' experiences with comprehensive services, collaboration, service integration, funding, and evaluation; and a summary of issues that were common to all of the programs. Burt, Resnick, and Matheson conducted site visits to nine programs in six different cities in 1992, and Burt and Resnick updated their information through telephone interviews in 1996. Burt revised and updated chapters on risk in adolescence, the conceptual framework, service integration and other cross-cutting issues, and evaluation issues. Novick assisted with the New York site visit in 1992 and wrote new chapters for this book on the history of integrated services initiatives; current efforts to promote integrated services on the federal, state, and local levels; innovative methods of funding youth programs in 1996 and early 1997; and conclusions and recommendations.

Our ideas on risk prevalence among youth and the need for integrated and comprehensive services to help youth avoid serious risk (presented in Chapters 3 and 4) guided the selection of programs to visit and the design of our site visit procedures. We were interested in the achievements of service integration in programs directed toward at-risk youth. We wanted to learn about the structure and experiences of programs that try to treat youth holistically in enough detail to understand the issues that might arise in doing evaluations of comprehensive programs for this population. To do this, we considered it essential to visit a variety of programs that try to deliver comprehensive services, using service integration as at least one mechanism for increasing comprehensiveness. Thus, site visits were included in the study design to achieve several of the study's objectives:

- To understand the full range of program configurations and options for 10–15 year olds, including the programs' sense of their mission or purpose;
- To understand the reasons behind these programs' choices among certain program design alternatives (e.g., whether to emphasize "activities" or "services"; whether to concentrate on prevention or on treatment; whether to adopt a focus on youth, on youth and their families, on families in general, or on the total neighborhood; whether to strive for comprehensive service delivery);
- To understand the relationship of these programs to their larger community, including both the program's role in the service delivery network and network of supports for youth, and the program's role in relation to other community institutions, such as churches, businesses, and civic organizations;
- To learn what programs believe are the benefits of a more comprehensive range of services and what they believe are the benefits and drawbacks of service integration through collaborative arrangements with other agencies; and
- To gain a sense of the readiness and willingness of programs of this type to participate in evaluations and what types of evaluations they might be open to (or have already been involved in).

We consulted with several experts in the field of youth and youth services to guide our selection of programs that provide comprehensive, integrated services to at-risk youth. We looked for programs that met the following five criteria: (a) serving clients between the ages of 10 and 15 years old; (b) conducting comprehensive, individualized needs assessments for individual youth; (c) using the needs assessment as the basis for service planning and case management; (d) developing formal, institutionalized interagency linkages (e.g., resource sharing, case management); and

(e) conducting standard follow-ups with agencies to which referrals are made to ensure accountability.

In addition to these five formal program criteria, final program selection was based on a desire to have the final set of programs represent a good mix across geographic regions and serve youth of diverse racial or ethnic backgrounds. We also wanted the final group of programs to represent a variety of program models, including variety in the program's configuration (residential, school-based, or community-based); in its primary activities (case management, treatment, or activities/enrichment) and in its length of involvement with youth (crisis, medium-length, or long-term). This process generated a list of nine programs in six different areas of the country, each of which serves individual youth, youth and their families, or a whole community.

To ensure a depth of perspective, each site visit included interviews with program directors, directors of individual program components, line workers with direct youth contact, youth clients, families of youth, mentors or volunteers where relevant, representatives of agencies with which the program has formal or informal linkages, and members of the program's board of directors. We also collected and examined a variety of program documents, including descriptive literature (e.g., brochures, newsletters, newspaper articles) and internal documents (e.g., budgets, program evaluations, and recent intake forms). This wealth of material was examined and analyzed to produce program descriptions (Chapters 6 through 14) and our summary of the ways that different programs meet the challenges of serving at-risk youth and their families (Chapter 15).

Acknowledgments

We are deeply indebted to the staff and administration of each of the programs featured in this book. Regarding those programs represented in Part II, we are grateful for the invaluable information, feedback, and access provided during the original site visits in 1992 and for additional input during the update interviews in 1996. We wish to acknowledge the following individuals according to their respective programs: Lydia Muñiz, Executive Director (1992 site visit and 1996 update interview, Big Brothers/Big Sisters of Greater Miami) and Judy Smigel, Director of Public Relations (1996 update interview; see Chapter 6); Myrnia Bass-Hargrove (1992 site visit, New York City [Bronx] Teen Connections) and Bernice Humphrey, Director of Health Girls Initiative, National Resource Center, Girls Incorporated (1996 update interview; see Chapter 7); Yvonne McCullough, Executive Director (1992 site visit, Belafonte-Tacolcy Center, Inc.) and Sabrina Baker-Bouie, Executive Director (1996 update interview; see Chapter 8); Mary Jane Dewey, Executive Director (1992 site visit, Oasis Center), and Ronnie Steine, Executive Director and Sherri Allen, Director of Crisis Services (1996 update interview; see Chapter 9); Gerard Veneman, Executive Director, CHINS UP (1992 site visit and 1996 update interview, CHINS UP, Joint Initiatives; see Chapter 10); Cynthia Clay-Briggs, Executive Director (1992 site visit and 1996 update interview, Houston Communities in Schools; see Chapter 11); Dr. Lorraine Williams Greene, Deputy Director (1992 site visit, I Have a Future) and consultant (1996 update interview; see Chapter 12); Debbie Wilde, Executive Director (1992 site visit and 1996 update interview, Garfield Youth Services; see Chapter 13); and Sister Mary Geraldine, Center Director, and Sister Mary Paul, Director of Clinical Services (1992 site visit and 1996 update interview, Center for Family Life; see Chapter 14).

We would also like to thank the following individuals for their substantive contributions to the book: Marty Blank (Institute for Educational Leadership), Jerry Britten (U.S. Department of Health and Human Services), Judy Chynoweth (Foundation Consortium for School-Linked Services), Glenda Cochrum (Kentucky KIDS), Laura Duberstein Lindberg (Urban Institute), Eric Friedlander (Kentucky Cabinet for Families and Children), Lisa Gilmore (U.S. Department of Health and Human Services), Mike Herrell (U.S. Department of Health and Human Services), Glenn Kamber (U.S. Department of Health and Human Services), Roberta Knowlton (New Jersey School Based Youth Services Program), Connie Roberts (New Beginnings), Nancy Matheson (Pelavin Associates), Lisa Newmark (Urban Institute), Lorraine Reilly (Urban Institute), Michael Resnick (University of Minnesota), Connie Roberts (New Beginnings), Freya Sonenstein (Urban Institute), Charles Terrett (Kentucky KIDS), and Amos White (East Bay Asian Youth Center).

Finally, we are grateful to the following individuals and institutions for their support during the course of this project: Barbara Broman, Ann Segal, and Richard Silva (of the U.S. Department of Health and Human Services); Andrea Phillippi (of American Psychological Association Books); Josh Morganstein, Sonya Ouelette, Vernonica Nieva, and Cecilia Cervantes (of Westat, Inc.); and Robert Lerman, Mildred Woodhouse, Christina Card, and Karen Foley (of the Urban Institute).

Part I _____

Service Integration, Adolescents, and Risk

1

An Overview of Integrated Services

There are many ways to create supportive communities for youth. One important way is to improve the functioning of the existing social services network so that it more closely meets the needs of young people and their families. In recent years, the term *integration of services* has been used to describe innovative ways that agencies work together to improve social service delivery. The ultimate goal of integration is often described in terms of *comprehensive* or *wraparound* services. To create a context for this study of youth-serving programs, in this chapter we review the existing social service landscape for adolescents, present a working definition of service integration, discuss the difference between integrated and comprehensive services, and provide some examples of the many ways in which service integration can occur.

The Rationale for Service Integration

Adolescence is a challenging stage of life, but most young people navigate their way to adulthood without going seriously off course. Some proportion of adolescents, however, engage in behavior that seriously compromises their chances of charting that course successfully. According to Dryfoos, 25% of America's teenagers are in this category, and another 25% may be engaging in behaviors that put them at moderate risk (Dryfoos, 1990). Although there are differences among groups of adolescents, whether grouped by age, race, sex, or socioeconomic status, most adolescents will experiment with behaviors commonly considered risky, such as the use of illegal drugs (Dryfoos, 1990). It is important to view this experimentation, and more serious involvement in high-risk behaviors, in the context of young people's interactions with family, school, neighborhood, and peers. It is difficult to understand or prevent high-risk behavior without considering these contextual factors (National Research Council, 1993).

The view of adolescence has recently begun to change in the literature and in the design of programs and policies that concern young people. In recent research and practice, adolescents are seen as whole people with strengths and resiliencies, whose actions should be viewed in the context of their family, school, neighborhood, and peer group. This perspective differs from the traditional view of teenagers as rebellious and unpredictable beings whose problem behaviors must be corrected, controlled, or punished (National Research Council, 1993). The new philosophy posits that providing certain basic opportunities and supports will build on young people's strengths and will ultimately be more successful than intervening after a crisis has already occurred. The positive youth development approach is a by-product of recent research on adolescent development and the experience of practitioners in the youth services field (National Research Council, 1993; Pittman and Cahill, 1992).

In general, the social services system that serves young people and families is not in step with the current thinking on contextual and comprehensive approaches to risky behaviors and negative outcomes. Over the years, a number of studies and reports have described the fragmentation and lack of coordination in the human services system, which includes both governmental and nongovernmental programs (Fishman & Dolson, 1987; Gardner, 1994; Kagan, Goffin, Golub, & Pritchard, 1995; National Commission on Children, 1991). Fragmented services, typically defined as a large number of uncoordinated programs with different rules, requirements, and administrative structures, has led to delayed or inadequate services, no services at all, and little accountability to the target population (Fishman & Dolson, 1987). The National Commission on Children (1991) described the problem in this way:

> The present system of human services generally fails to meet the needs of . . . seriously troubled families. Service providers in separate programs serving the same family rarely confer or work to reinforce one another's efforts . . . . [F]amilies seeking assistance often encounter a service delivery system that is confusing, difficult to navigate, and indifferent to their concerns. For many parents and children, these obstacles appear at a time when they are least able to cope with additional stress or adversity. (p. xxxii)

The combination of fragmentation and lack of coordination among programs and services is linked in the public's mind with waste and inefficiency, and evidence of wasted resources is found in the duplicative record keeping and reporting requirements imposed on state and local agencies and nonprofit recipients of federal funds (National Commission on Children, 1991; National Performance Review, 1993a). Gardner (1994) has noted that state and local human services officials spend between 20% and 40% of their time seeking, reporting on, and reviewing federal and state grant funding, which translates into millions of dollars diverted toward administrative functions. In addition, grant recipients often have limited ability to customize social services through service integration or other approaches because of competing federal program rules (National Performance Review, 1993b).

Critics often place the blame for the fragmentation of social services on the proliferation of categorical grant programs. The term *categorical programs* is usually used to describe discretionary grant programs that funding agencies award to single agencies, community-based organizations, or coalitions of such groups for specified purposes. Categorical grant programs that serve adolescents are usually focused on alleviating or preventing a narrowly defined problem, such as school dropout, juvenile delinquency, running away, substance abuse, or teen pregnancy (Burt, Resnick, & Matheson, 1992). Most of these programs have tended to follow a "deficit model": They focus on preventing or treating specific problems or risky behaviors rather than addressing the context of at-risk behavior or following a positive youth development model.

Although narrowly defined discretionary programs are often the focus of discussion, most federal funding for social services in the United States takes the form of formula grants, entitlement programs, and block grants. Each of these types of funding streams are also "categorical" if they are designed to address a narrowly defined issue or problem. *Formula grants* are funds awarded to states on the basis of population characteristics, such as poverty or the percentage of children under a certain age; *entitlement programs* (such as Medicaid) allow any person who meets certain eligibility criteria to participate; and *block grants* give states or local governments funds with very little restriction on how funds are to be spent. Some block grants are "earmarked" to require that the grant recipient use a fixed percentage of grant funds for a target population or problem; most give recipients a great deal of flexibility. Most block grants for social services (such as the Social Services Block Grant administered by the U.S. Department of Health and Human Services) do not earmark funds specifically for adolescents.

The categorical nature of the American social service system results from a number of factors. Gardner (1994) has noted that one of these is state and federal legislators' concern that program dollars reach only those people who are truly in need. Another is social service programs' requirements for professional and technical expertise, which has led to the creation of cadres of experts in particular problem areas. These experts are often joined by advocates in lobbying for continued or increased funding for narrowly defined programs. A third factor is the practice of giving legislators and philanthropists credit for creating new programs. The committee and subcommittee structure of the U.S. Congress reinforces this situation by creating "fiefdoms" for legislators who retain their popularity with particular advocacy groups by establishing and reauthorizing narrowly focused programs. Some believe that significant reform of the categorical social service system will not occur without parallel reform of the congressional committee structure (Gardner, 1994).

The proliferation of narrowly defined social service programs is only part of the explanation for fragmentation in the human service system. Among other factors are (a) the expansion of local governmental structures, such as city and county agencies and planning commissions, which has led to a diffusion of roles and responsibilities in the social services sector; and (b) the complex array of public- and private-sector social service funders and providers other than the federal government (Fishman & Dolson, 1987). Kagan et al. (1995) have suggested a number of reasons for the fragmentation in services for young children in the United States, many of which apply to services for adolescents: an ideological emphasis on family privacy; crisis-oriented public policy; an emphasis on means-testing programs, which leads to segregation of children by income; and sporadic government intervention in the service of larger goals, such as war or economic recovery.

A Definition of Service Integration

In recent years, social service providers have reached an informal consensus about what works best for troubled youth and their families. The ideal approach can be described as "integrating" services across different service domains to improve the delivery of services to and outcomes for vulnerable or needy populations. Although social service practitioners have been working on this problem for many years, the term *service integration* did not come into use until 1971. In that year, the Secretary of Health, Education, and Welfare (HEW), Elliott Richardson, described integrated services as "ways of organizing the delivery of services to people at the local level" (Fishman & Dolson, 1987, p. 3). A more recent definition of the term describes service integration as "procedures and structures that help several service agencies coordinate their efforts to address the full range of service needs presented by youth and families in an efficient and holistic manner" (Burt et al., 1992, p. 41).

Discussions of service integration are often confused by the use of different terminology to describe various ways of approaching the same goal. The names or catch words change with the times, the actors, and the locus of activity. Among the terms that have been used are *coordination*, *collaboration*, *interagency cooperation*, *service integration*, and *integrated services*. *Service integration*, also known as *integrated services*, was described earlier. A *cooperative relationship* is one in which organizational partners help each other to meet their respective organizational goals but do not make any substantial changes in the basic services they provide or in the rules and regulations that govern their agencies and do not establish common goals (Melaville & Blank, 1991). These activities can also be described as *coordination*. *Collaboration* refers to the establishment of common goals in order to address problems that lie beyond the exclusive purview of any one agency but concern all agencies. In collaborative arrangements, partners typically agree to pool resources (either funds, personnel, or both); jointly plan, implement, and evaluate new services and procedures; and delegate individual responsibility for the outcomes of their joint efforts (Melaville & Blank, 1991).

Although the two terms are often linked, an integrated service system is not necessarily a comprehensive one. *Comprehensiveness* is the existence in a community or service agency of the full range of services that are required to address the needs of the target population (Burt et al., 1992). A comprehensive system may not be integrated, as when a single agency has the resources to provide everything that its clients need. An integrated system may not be comprehensive, as when an agency serving at-risk youth and their families negotiates arrangements to provide those services that meet only the most common needs of its clients, such as income maintenance, child care, recreation, and education. The agency may not have similar well-established relationships with agencies providing less frequently needed services. Finally, a community may have the entire array of services and have established interagency arrangements for ensuring that clients can access the services but still not have enough of some services to serve all the people who need them. The last circumstance probably characterizes most communities and is a limiting condition for any integrated service effort (Burt et al., 1992).

Goals and Objectives of Service Integration

Why should an agency or group of agencies at any level undertake the often arduous process of integrating services? Three of the overarching goals of integrated services are to increase the efficiency and effectiveness of human services delivery systems and to improve outcomes for target populations. These goals are often pursued simultaneously. Improved social service systems can and should lead to positive changes in outcomes for children and families, but this is not an automatic process. Kagan et al. (1995) have noted that external factors, such as economic change, may intervene to prevent positive outcomes and that system change undertaken without attention to the quality or relevance of services may have little or no effect on outcomes.

Although the broad goals of integrated services are common to most social service organizations, there is more variation in the specific objectives of integrated-services efforts undertaken by particular agencies. As Elliott Richardson noted in 1971, the objectives may include improved coordination of services, developing a more holistic approach to serving individuals and families, providing a comprehensive range of services at the local level, and making the allocation of resources at the local level more rational and responsive to local needs (Fishman & Dolson, 1987). In addition, integrated service networks can perform a number of particular functions. They can bring together previously diffuse services, change past practices or policies, create mechanisms that will sustain or promote integrated services, and change relationships among people and institutions (Kagan et al., 1995).

Integration of services can be undertaken in different ways, and there is some debate over which method is preferable. One approach, known as *general service integration*, attempts to bridge the gulfs between different social service systems such as health, mental health, and child welfare. This was the approach pursued by HEW in the early 1970s. Another is *within-field* or *single domain* service integration, which attempts to integrate services across funding streams but within a particular field or discipline. Although some believe that within-field service integration should precede general service integration, others maintain that the within-field approach perpetuates the categorical approach to social services and stands in the way of true service integration (Kagan et al., 1995). There is also debate as to whether integrated services should focus on the client, program, policy, or organizational level. In the view of Kagan et al., one approach can facilitate another, and the synergy between the different approaches is more important than the causal relationships between them.

Service integration can also occur at different levels of government or outside of government altogether, and there are arguments in favor of and against each approach. The federal level is a popular target, because federal funding is a critical factor in the social service delivery system and federal dollars can often serve as a catalyst for improving service delivery and outcomes at the state and local levels. State-level service integration is important because states often provide funding of their own, control the use of federal funds, and oversee the implementation of human services programs. Local-level integration is also significant because it addresses the individuals, families, and service providers that are most directly affected by the fragmentation of services. The recent literature on integrated services emphasizes the locally focused, community-driven, or "bottom-up" approach (Kagan et al., 1995, citing Bruner, 1991, Marzke et al., 1992, and Morrill, 1991).

Overview of This Book

This book is intended to provide a new paradigm for analyzing risky behaviors and outcomes among adolescents. It is also intended to highlight some programs that are creating supportive communities for troubled young people and to identify the characteristics that make these programs effective. The "communities" created by these programs may be as large as a county or as small as a teen discussion group. The book is divided into three parts. The remainder of Part I provides a history of service integration efforts, a discussion of theories related to adolescence and risk, prevalence rates for risky behaviors and their antecedents, and a description of recent service integration initiatives. Part II presents descriptions of exemplary youth programs. Part III examines the service-integration, cultural, and community decisions that faced all the programs we visited, looks at evaluation and funding issues for youth-serving service integration programs, and presents key factors to consider in the development of supportive communities for troubled youth.

Chapter 2 provides a history of efforts to improve conditions for vulnerable children and their families in the United States. This chapter reviews the development of the social service system in this country, including private charitable societies, settlement houses, the New Deal, the Great Society, and the War on Poverty; the creation of block grants; and the recent welfare reform. Chapter 3 reviews the literature on risk and adolescence, including the philosophy of positive youth development, a currently popular approach to designing interventions for at-risk teens. Chapter 4 presents a conceptual framework for analyzing risk in adolescence that defines the key antecedents and markers for identifying risky behaviors and outcomes in adolescents, and it reviews available evidence related to each element of the framework. To conclude Part I, Chapter 5 reviews a number of initiatives for young people that are occurring at the federal, state, and local levels, including "reinvention" of federal agencies, devolution of federal programs to the state and local levels, and state and local efforts to promote collaboration and cooperation among service providers.

Part II, Chapters 6 through 14, presents a wealth of information on nine programs that serve troubled youth in five areas of the United States. Each chapter uses information gathered from site visits, program documents, and telephone updates to summarize the program's mission, goals, and objectives; configuration of services; current clientele; type of service integration network; funding sources; involvement in evaluation activities; and methods of integrating services.

Part III includes a summary (Chapter 15) of decisions, issues, and factors that cross-cut all of the nine programs we analyzed, such as the age range to target, the mix of treatment and prevention services to offer, the breadth and depth of services and activities to offer, and how to incorporate the cultural context of the community and youth served into the program's format. Chapter 16 addresses issues involved in evaluating these complex youth programs. This chapter discusses the difficulties of identifying appropriate participants to include, identifying the services and activities received, and identifying appropriate outcomes to measure. It also addresses the challenge of developing outcomes that are focused on service systems and on communities, in addition to those that occur for individuals. Chapter 17 reviews traditional approaches to funding social services for children and families and describes some innovative approaches, such as the creation of special taxing districts for children. Finally, Chapter 18 reviews the major themes of the book, identifies trends in the provision of support services to at-risk teens, and restates the critical elements of effective programs and service integration networks.

We hope that this book will be a valuable resource for anyone who works with or cares about adolescents, who could include teachers, social service practitioners, researchers, policy analysts and policymakers, foundation staff, neighborhood and community leaders, and youth and their parents. We will consider the book a success if it helps to shift the dialogue away from a debate about whether or not to invest in our nation's youth to a discussion of how we can best support them in their sometimes circuitous journey toward adulthood. Also, we hope it ultimately will inspire adults to think about the supports they enjoyed as adolescents and endeavor to provide the same assistance to all young people.

2

The History of Comprehensive Service Integration

The history of integrated services in the United States is the history of public sector involvement in the life of the poor. The level of government responsibility for social services has fluctuated from a minimal level in the late 19th century to significant levels from the 1930s through the 1980s, when the pendulum began to swing back in the direction of state and local responsibility for needy populations. This pattern reflects the tension between centralized and decentralized government power that has characterized the American political scene since the founding of this country.

This chapter traces the changes in the federal and state roles in caring for the poor from the late 19th century to the present. It includes a discussion of the private charitable societies that flourished after the Civil War, the rise of the settlement houses and the creation of the Charitable Organization Societies, the agitation for greater state and federal involvement that characterized the Progressive Era, the Depression and the New Deal's creation of a federal social insurance system, the expansion of that system during the 1960s Great Society and War on Poverty, the 1970s era of experimentation with integrated services through demonstration projects, the focus during the 1980s on decentralizing social services through the use of block grants, and the focus in the 1990s on "reinvention" of the federal government and devolution of federal responsibility for a number of social insurance programs to the states.

The Late 19th and Early 20th Centuries

The government role in human services emerged after the Civil War, when emancipated slaves, orphans, and displaced families were in critical need of housing, food, and medical services. At the same time, immigration and industrialization were swelling the numbers of people in need of basic

---

This chapter is indebted to Sharon Lynn Kagan's excellent volume, *Integrating Human Services: Understanding the Past to Shape the Future* (Kagan, 1993) and Bernard Frieden and Marshall Kaplan's book, *The Politics of Neglect: Urban Aid from Model Cities to Revenue Sharing* (Frieden & Kaplan, 1975), among other sources.

services and assistance to survive. During the postwar period, state boards emerged to oversee human services institutions and provide advice to state legislatures on the needs of the disadvantaged. Some state boards recommended centralization of services at the client level; others recommended it at the administrative level—an issue that is still the focus of debate. As state legislatures struggled with the best way to provide aid to the poor and dependent, they raised issues that are still relevant today: coordination, economy, professionalization, specialization, centralization, and integration (Kagan, 1993).

During the period from Reconstruction to the end of the 19th century, private charities and mutual aid societies emerged as the primary mechanism for aiding the poor. Kagan (1993) has traced the development of an American upper class, the emergence of American noblesse oblige, and the role of industrialization and immigration as factors in this process. This period also saw the emergence of the settlement houses, which were organizations based in the community and designed to provide advocacy and a wide range of services to poor families. According to Kahn and Kamerman (1992), settlement houses were colocating services as diverse as day care, primary health care, citizenship classes, and language instruction before the terms *colocation* or *wraparound services* had come into common usage.

Created as a counterweight to the large, impersonal public institutions for the poor, settlement houses such as the Henry Street Settlement in New York City and Hull House in Chicago were seen by their founders as vehicles for mobilizing communities as well as for providing personalized services to the poor. Although they pioneered the concept of multiple-service organizations, some found fault with their tacit belief that poor families were hopeless, inadequate, and in need of "moral uplift" (Kagan, 1993). Nevertheless, because of their community focus and orientation toward helping children and families whatever their specific needs, the image of the settlement house is often touted as a model for integrated social services today.

In an attempt to streamline and rationalize the wide array of private charitable organizations that had developed by the mid-1870s, the Charitable Organization Societies (COS) was established in 1877. COS was created in the belief that improved organization of charitable groups would reduce poverty, in part by reducing duplicative services and payments to the poor and thereby removing disincentives to employment. The themes of eliminating duplication and increasing efficiency and administrative flexibility were all part of the rationale for COS and continue as powerful arguments for improving the organization of social services today. Another contemporary issue that surfaced during the establishment of COS was the need for methods of providing multiple services to the same client. Although the goal of COS was to reduce duplication, Kagan et al. (1995) have noted that it actually worsened the fragmentation of social services because its focus was on reform of private charities and on those persons who could be rehabilitated by them, thereby relegating others to the public institutions for the poor. This greater fragmentation reinforced the idea of the state as the provider of last resort and widened the gulf between public-sector "relief" and private-sector "charity."

In the early part of the century, the Progressive movement and the increased professionalization of social work were both factors in the greater role that state and federal governments took in providing services to the poor. In contrast to the earlier view of charity to reform or ameliorate individual behavior, the Progressives focused on two issues: eliminating the root causes of poverty and providing a social safety net for older persons and widows with dependent children, whom they saw as the most vulnerable sectors of the population. In their view, the federal government was not a provider of last resort but rather a "guarantor of individual opportunity and equity" (Kagan, 1993, p. 10). Kagan has cited a number of events as evidence of the increasing federal role in disseminating information and directly funding social services during this period: the 1909 White House Conference on Children; the creation of the Children's Bureau by Congress in 1912; and the 1921 Shepard-Turner Act, which authorized federal matching grants to states for their efforts to reduce infant mortality. (The Act expired in 1929 and was not reauthorized.)

The New Deal to the 1950s: Dual Federalism

The Social Security Act of 1935 formalized and extended the federal role in the provision of human services. The federal relief programs created to alleviate the effects of the Depression were the backdrop for this groundbreaking legislation. They established the states' role as conduits for and overseers of federal dollars and set the stage for an evolving state–federal relationship in this area (Kagan, 1993). The Act itself authorized federal support for dependent children, older persons, and blind persons; maternal and child health programs; child welfare services; and vocational rehabilitation and public health services. Its importance stemmed from its creation of a "permanent state structure with primary responsibility for social welfare" and its requirement that state governments become significantly involved in categorical social programs (Kagan, 1993, p. 11 citing Vasey, 1958). In 1939 the Federal Security Agency was established to administer and coordinate the new array of federal human services organizations. The agency was designed as an intergovernmental partnership and included the Social Security Board, the National Youth Administration, the Civilian Conservation Corps, the Public Health Service, the Office of Education, and the U.S. Employment Service.

With the exception of the New Deal programs, most federal assistance programs created from the 1930s to the 1950s did not have an articulated national purpose; rather they retained the role of the states as sovereign entities. The practice of providing federal assistance to the states to accomplish their own objectives, and providing those funds on a formula basis, has been described as *dual federalism* because of the clear division of responsibilities. A slightly different version of the same relationship was *cooperative federalism*, in which the federal government and states operated as separate sovereign entities with clearly defined spheres of activity. In the 1960s, both of these relationships gave way to *coordinated federalism*, which was characterized by states' acting as conduits for attaining clearly defined national objectives. According to Kagan (1993), this new relationship was the result of advances in communication, transportation, and the development of a national economy, as well as social issues (such as civil rights) that demanded national solutions. At the same time, states were engaging in efforts to consolidate and reorganize their human services programs (Agranoff, 1991).

The 1960s: Coordinated Federalism

The 1960s was a period of dramatic expansion in the number of federal categorical grant programs designed on an ad hoc basis to meet specific needs and the beginning of a movement to improve the organization of social services. Between 1962 and 1966, the number of federal categorical programs increased from 160 to 349 and by 1971 had reached 500 (Kagan, 1993). Some programs transferred federal dollars to the states (e.g., Title IV of the Social Security Act); some programs transferred funds to local grantees (e.g., Head Start). Other programs transferred state dollars to local recipients (Title I of the Elementary and Secondary Education Act). The panoply of funding formulas, types of grants, and levels of administrative responsibility led to confusion and fragmentation for service providers and clients alike (Agranoff, 1991; Fishman & Dolson, 1987).

As in the Progressive Era, service providers were aware of the multiple responses needed to address complex social problems and began to undertake efforts to improve the organization of services (Agranoff, 1991). A parallel effort was occurring on the federal level. In 1961 President Kennedy established the Advisory Commission of Intergovernmental Relations, the formal successor to a commission on intergovernmental relations appointed by President Eisenhower. The new commission documented the fragmentation of federal programs at the state and local levels and blamed a lack of coordination at the federal level. The commission was motivated by a concern about waste, duplication, and misuse of federal resources and a general desire to improve efficiency at the federal level. Its work led, in 1965, to the establishment of the U.S. Department of Housing and Urban Development (HUD). HUD was created to serve as a focal point for all federal policies and programs related to urban problems (Frieden & Kaplan, 1975).

A concern for improving conditions in slum neighborhoods and preventing juvenile delinquency and crime resulted in several new programs and activities during this period. In 1961, the Ford Foundation began its "gray areas" program, which awarded grants to city governments and community agencies in New York, Oakland, New Haven, Philadelphia, Boston, Washington, DC, and the state of North Carolina. In the same year, President Kennedy established the President's Committee on Juvenile Delinquency and Youth Crime to review and coordinate federal activities related to juvenile delinquency and to stimulate innovative and experimental programming (Frieden & Kaplan, 1975). The year 1961 also saw the passage of the Juvenile Delinquency and Youth Offenses Control Act, which authorized the award of grants for "experimental community projects" that focused on changing institutions; integrating and coordinating existing programs; involving local leadership and residents; and funding activities in the areas of education, vocational training, youth employment, legal aid, and community service. By 1965, this program had spent $20 million, with some of the funds going to cities that were also gray areas grantees (Frieden & Kaplan, 1975).

Frieden and Kaplan (1975) have noted that the gray areas and juvenile delinquency projects had limited impact on communities but did highlight two important issues that are relevant to a study of integrated services programs: that many of the existing services and programs directed at the poor were not reaching the poor and that those that did were offering the wrong services. In addition, these efforts influenced the design of later antipoverty programs.

One of the most significant legislative developments during this period was the Economic Opportunity Act of 1964, which launched President Johnson's War on Poverty. The Act was motivated by several ideas that still drive efforts to improve outcomes for poor children and families: correcting the causes of poverty, coordinating efforts, relying on developmental services, using local initiative, and involving the poor in solving their own problems (Agranoff, 1991). The Act broke new ground by appropriating funds for the express purpose of reducing poverty. Despite its lofty ideals, the emphasis on involving the residents of poor neighborhoods in the local planning and decision-making process was reduced by President Johnson in 1965 after an organized protest by a group of mayors (Frieden & Kaplan, 1975).

The Act established the federal Office of Economic Opportunity and authorized the creation of 500 Community Action Agencies (CAAs) around the country to improve coordination among local human services programs such as Head Start, Legal Services, Job Corps, and VISTA (Volunteers in Service to America) and to operate some of these programs directly. CAAs were designed as community-based, nongovernmental entities that could work across agencies and service sectors to mobilize public and private resources (Kagan, 1993). They operated outside of the local political system of elected officials; were required to include the poor in their governance structure; and received their funds from the federal government directly, without the involvement of state or local intermediaries (Edelman & Radin, 1991). According to Frieden and Kaplan (1975), the CAAs were one of the most distinctive characteristics of the War on Poverty.

Although designed to promote coordination and integration of services, CAAs were not very effective at this task, for a variety of reasons. According to Kagan (1993), they lacked local political support and were viewed as duplicative of existing community planning entities, radical, confrontational, and poorly managed. Local officials were successful in pressuring Congress to reduce the power of CAAs, so that by the early 1970s they were reduced to small local agencies working outside the organized social service delivery system (Edelman & Radin, 1991). Some CAAs still exist and receive federal funding through the Community Services Block Grant, but many have chosen to affiliate with the local social service delivery infrastructure so they can gain access to additional funding sources (Edelman & Radin, 1991). Most rural areas still have CAAs.

In the mid-1960s, the Model Cities program was launched, with the twin goals of helping the poor and reforming and coordinating the federal grant system (Frieden & Kaplan, 1975). HUD funded the effort, which was designed to avoid the mistakes of the CAAs by encouraging the development of locally driven planning processes that would precede community action (Kagan, 1993). In its original conception, the effort was designed to focus on three cities, but the number grew steadily as the program moved from task force recommendation to legislative proposal. Although the Johnson-appointed task force had called for 66 cities, Congress doubled that number to ensure political support for the effort. At the same time, Congress reduced the proposed authorization amount and limited program operators' ability to draw down funds from agencies other than HUD (Frieden & Kaplan, 1975). Model Cities could no longer be described as a program that concentrated resources in a few target areas.

The Model Cities program had some success in medium-sized cities, with a record of success at coordinating services, the support of the local chief executive, and an ability to engage a number of public and private agencies in the process. Overall, the program was judged to be less than completely successful for several reasons: It was underfunded (in part because funds were diverted to fund the Vietnam War), did not make it easier for communities to coordinate different federal funding streams, and did not adequately concentrate its efforts (Edelman & Radin, 1991; Frieden & Kaplan, 1975). Model Cities has been described as a "lesson in the dissipation of limited resources" (Edelman & Radin, 1991, p. 7) and a victim of the belief that the President could change not only the federal government, but also the world beyond Washington. It is also a cautionary tale for policymakers of today.

The 1970s: New Federalism

In the 1970s a significant federal interest in service integration emerged, but efforts were more modest than those undertaken in the 1960s. In addition, President Nixon shifted the focus from direct intervention to reduce urban poverty to coordination and reform of the federal grant system, shifting power from federal to local government and improving the situation of all citizens (Edelman & Radin, 1991; Frieden & Kaplan, 1975). A number of demonstrations and legislative initiatives were launched during this period as part of the Nixon administration's new federalism. This approach emphasized state and local control over most tasks of government and led to the creation of standardized federal regions, decentralization of federal programs, simplified federal grant procedures, and revenue sharing (Kagan, 1993). Two major block grants were also created as part of the new federalism, the Community Development Block Grant (which consolidated a number of urban programs created during the Johnson administration) and the Comprehensive Employment and Training Act (CETA; which consolidated 17 categorical training programs and was replaced in 1982 by the Job Training Partnership Act; Peterson et al., 1986).

The term *service integration* came into use during this period to characterize efforts designed to counteract the "categorical excesses" of President Johnson's Great Society programs. It also described efforts to meet the needs of the whole person, an approach that reflected new thinking in the field of developmental psychology. HEW was the lead agency for service integration efforts and developed an ambitious agenda of research and demonstration projects, proposed legislation, technical assistance efforts, and internal reforms. Other federal agencies also became involved in the new federalism: The Department of Labor's CETA program (1973) and HUD's Community Development Block Grant program (1974) typified this approach with federal funding, local agencies performing planning functions, and nongovernmental entities delivering actual services through contracts (Kagan, 1993).

HEW launched three major service integration efforts in the 1972–1975 period to overcome the fragmentation created by categorical programs, but the findings of these demonstrations were not conclusive due to weak evaluations and the diversity of the projects. The Services Integration Targets of Opportunity (SITO) demonstration, begun in 1972, focused on forging interagency program linkages in the areas of budget, personnel, planning and programming, administrative support, core services, and case coordination on the local level (Agranoff, 1991). Forty-five project grants were given to agencies and groups with diverse approaches and goals, with the idea of testing approaches to integrating services in preparation for the introduction in Congress of an Allied Services Act. Because the projects collected information about the process rather than outcomes of service integration, they were of limited use for future efforts (Kagan, 1993). Although the projects did not demonstrate any improvement in the accessibility or availability of services, they did document the high cost of service integration (Fishman & Dolson, 1987).

HEW launched the Partnership Grant Projects (PGP) in 1974 with the goal of helping local governments improve the planning, management, and accountability of human services programs. The PGP emphasized innovative program design. Like the SITO projects, PGP projects were difficult to evaluate because of the wide variety of objectives undertaken by grantees. Although the PGP projects did not provide any data that were generalizable, they did build on the findings of SITO to provide more information about contextual issues such as the importance of the political environment for the success or failure of service integration efforts (Agranoff, 1991).

In 1975, HEW funded five sites to participate in the Comprehensive Human Services Planning and Delivery System project (CHSPDS), an attempt to develop and test the effect of several different models of local comprehensive management and planning on the efficiency and effectiveness of human-services systems. The initial evaluation indicated that improved management techniques could reduce clients' waiting time and improve agencies' accountability and efficiency, but funding cuts prevented the project's full implementation, and a planned third party evaluation was never carried out (Kagan, 1993).

During the 1970s several attempts were made to pass federal legislation that would institutionalize service integration on the local level. These laws were either proposed and never enacted or enacted and seriously undermined by reduced funding or other obstacles (Edelman & Radin, 1991). An example of these legislative proposals was HEW's proposed Intergovernmental Cooperation Act of 1972, later amended to become the Allied Services Act of 1972. The Allied Services Act was intended to improve state and local planning and administrative capacities by waiving federal requirements and allowing the transfer of funds between programs, concepts that are very much alive in today's policy debates. The legislation was eventually withdrawn from consideration by Congress for several reasons, including inadequate funding and perceptions that the bill gave too much power to governors and too little to local communities. It was revamped and reintroduced as the Allied Services Act of 1974, which authorized HEW demonstration grants and allowed the transfer of up to 30% of funds from one HEW program to another. The bill did not pass because of opposition from supporters of categorical programs. The Act was reintroduced again in 1975 with a number of changes, but it did not pass for reasons that included a loss of White House support during the Watergate scandal (Kagan, 1993).

A major legislative change did occur in 1975 with the passage of Title XX of the Social Security Act (renamed the Social Services Block Grant [SSBG] in 1981). Title XX, which became the first title of this historic social welfare act to fund services, was intended to facilitate states' development of comprehensive, integrated human service delivery systems. Title XX replaced parts of two categorical social service funding streams with a block grant that gave states significantly more flexibility to use the same level of funding (Kagan, 1993). SSBG is still an important source of funding for human services programs; it was funded at $2.8 billion in FY 1995.

After the failures of the demonstrations and legislative proposals of the early and mid-1970s, initiatives undertaken in the late 1970s took the form of more modest coordinative partnerships between state, city, and federal agencies and state-level service-integration efforts (Edelman & Radin, 1991; Kagan, 1993). HEW supported the efforts of several states to develop "umbrella" human services agencies with centralized management of the major social services and public assistance agencies and at least three other major human services programs to encourage service integration. One of the efforts that received HEW support was Florida's Department of Health and Rehabilitative Services, which the state legislature had given the authority to act as an umbrella agency and to exert more control over categorical programs than social service agencies in any other state (Kusserow, 1991a). Umbrella agencies declined in the 1980s as governors became more concerned about cutting social service expenditures than with finding ways to improve social services administration.

The 1980s: Block Grants and Local Experiments

During the Carter administration, HEW became the Department of Health and Human Services (HHS) and it oversaw some modest efforts to identify barriers to coordinated services and to outline national strategies to improve planning and service delivery. By the early 1980s, however, formal efforts to initiate service integration on a large scale had begun to fade and federal initiatives in this area came to a halt (Agranoff, 1991). The Reagan administration launched reforms intended to reduce the federal role in social service provision, ease the burden of federal regulations on the states, and significantly reduce funding for human service programs. The Omnibus Budget Reconciliation Act of 1981 (OBRA) epitomized this approach; it created nine new or revised block grants, decreased funding for social services and other programs by 25%, reduced federal reporting requirements on states, and gave states more discretion in the use of federal dollars (Kagan, 1993; Peterson et al., 1986). In contrast to the approach taken in the Nixon administration, in which block grants were seen as a mechanism both for cutting unnecessary costs and improving service delivery by using state and local expertise, the OBRA block grants were seen simply as a way to reduce spending and shift more responsibility to the states (Kagan, 1993; Peterson et al., 1986). Overall, funding for social services programs declined significantly during the years of the Reagan presidency, 1981–1988 (Kagan, 1993).

Experiments with integrated services continued in this period, partly as a response to congressional interest in welfare reform. The Deficit Reduction Act of 1984 authorized the Services Integration Pilot Projects (SIPP) with the explicit goal of reducing social welfare costs, in contrast to the focus during earlier efforts on improving management and delivery of human services as ends in themselves (Kagan, 1993). This reduction was to be accomplished by increasing the accountability of the social service system and the economic self-sufficiency of the individuals served by that system, primarily through the use of case management to link all the relevant services and providers in the community (Agranoff, 1991). Five states—Arizona, Florida, Maine, Oklahoma, and South Carolina—participated in SIPP, and all included measures of client and system outcomes in their evaluations (Fishman & Dolson, 1987; Kagan, 1993). The evaluations revealed that successful service integration required support at every level, including state and local policymakers, in-house "power brokers," employees, case workers, clients, and community leaders (Kagan, 1993).

In contrast to earlier attempts to overhaul the social service system, recent efforts have been more modest, and concentrated and targeted on particular sets of problems or populations (Agranoff, 1991). During the mid-to-late 1980s, federal agencies and foundations began to fund community-level attempts to overcome fragmentation at the point where clients receive services, an effort made more urgent by increasingly complex social problems and a less cohesive social service system. Because there was no overarching theme guiding these interventions, this period has been described as one of "unplanned variation" (Kagan, 1993, p. 26).

The 1990s: Reinvention and Devolution

Efforts undertaken in the early 1990s have continued to emphasize local system reform. Several federal initiatives have included an integrated services component, including the reauthorization of the Head Start program, the creation of the Child Care Development Block Grant (CCDBG), and the passage of the Family Preservation Act. During the last 2 years of the Bush administration, HHS funded a National Center for Service Integration to disseminate information and provide technical assistance to local governments and nonprofit organizations, but the center's funding was not renewed when the Clinton administration arrived in 1992. In the education arena, the first of the national education goals established by President Bush and carried forward by President Clinton emphasized the establishment of family, school, and community partnerships (Kagan et al., 1995). On the state and local levels, the use of federal CCDBG dollars as a catalyst for collaborative planning, integrated training, and coordinated service referral; the popularity of "one-stop shopping" for multiple social services; and community-based planning for comprehensive and coordinated service systems are all examples of integrated service efforts (Kagan et al., 1995).

The most recent federally sponsored effort to promote the integration of services is an outgrowth of the "reinventing government" effort begun by the Clinton administration. Vice President Gore has overseen a process, the National Performance Review, that among other things called on HHS to design and implement improvements in the delivery of services to children. This effort is described in more detail in Chapter 5. In addition to the efforts undertaken by HHS as a part of the National Performance Review, the 104th Congress (1994–1996) focused on reinventing government more directly by block granting and eliminating or reducing funding for a number of social service programs, including welfare, food stamps, and Supplemental Security Income (SSI). These changes have shifted the responsibility for serving vulnerable populations to the state and local governments and the private sector. The role of integrated service approaches in this new landscape remains to be seen.

The history of government involvement in the provision of social services to the poor does not follow a linear pattern. The federal role in this arena has shifted and changed, from one of minimal involvement (from the late 19th and early 20th centuries), to one of significant involvement (from the 1930s through the 1960s), and then to a gradual reduction in federal responsibilities through the mechanisms of block grants and reduced funding for social programs (from the 1970s to the present). The election of President Clinton in 1992, and his reelection in 1996, have not reversed the trend toward reducing the federal role in providing for the most vulnerable sectors of our population. In fact, the passage of welfare reform legislation, which significantly increases the responsibilities of the states, local governments, and private sector in caring for the poor, signals a continuation of the pendulum swing back to the minimal federal involvement of the 19th century.

3

Defining Adolescence and Risk

This chapter examines the underpinnings of risk in adolescence, bringing together the state of knowledge of adolescent development across the diverse fields of psychology, sociology, criminology, social work, education, and health. It looks at current definitions of adolescence and risk. It also explores the implications of different definitions for identifying youth with varying levels of competencies and protective factors as being "at risk." We pay particular attention to the situations relevant to younger adolescents because we are interested in understanding the early development and onset of problems as well as the later consequences of these problems. In Chapter 4 we consolidate this information into a conceptual framework that provides a unified approach for all adolescents, taking into account strengths and protective factors as well as dysfunctional elements and vulnerabilities of development. Because this book focuses on adolescents and not on life span development, we cannot give equal attention to childhood risk factors, but we do take them into account as part of our overall conceptual framework.

Currently held beliefs regarding services for adolescents focus on the concept of risk, but the term is used in different ways. The idea of *risk* ought to imply a probability, not a certainty. There should be at least some chance that the risk will not materialize, that the undesirable behavior or outcome will not occur. When speaking of youth behavior, the idea of risk conveys that a youth may display problems, but it does not convey that the event has already happened, nor a certainty about the future course of events in a young person's life.

The processes leading to problems in adolescence are not completely predictable. In addition, specific problems are rarely linked to a single cause. Instead, the pathways leading to an end point of major problem behavior or of successful transition to adulthood involve many factors in the environment interacting with the capabilities and endogenous characteristics of the individual. A child may arrive at the cusp of adolescence already handicapped by familial neglect, abuse, or other circumstances rendering a parent incapable of offering needed support and guidance. In addition societal institutions, most notably the schools, may fail to create conditions that assure success for every child and may compound this failure by labeling and isolating the very children who need the most help. As a youth displays initial negative behaviors, the environment's response to the behaviors will positively or negatively influence the chances that further problems will occur (Lorion, Price, & Eaton, 1989). At multiple points in a child's or youth's development, the environment's response can increase or decrease the likelihood that serious and long-term problems will occur. The research literature documents many examples of individuals whose obvious vulnerabilities, or risk factors, were overcome by a nurturing or responsive environment (Rutter & Rutter, 1993; Sameroff & Fiese, 1989; Werner & Smith, 1992). Factors in a nurturing environment, including parents, other adults, and neighborhood or community resources, may modify the individual's response to a negative situation that, under most circumstances, would lead to a maladaptive outcome. For example, acquiring an important skill, such as social competency, may help the adolescent avoid an escalation of problem behavior or, better yet, attract supports and guidance that will promote healthy development.

We look first at the different ways that experts have viewed adolescence. We then turn to an examination of different ideas of risk found in the literature. We conclude with a discussion of two relatively new approaches—youth development and children's rights—that have the potential to change much of the way we think about services and supports for youth.

Adolescence

Many analysts believe that structural changes in North American and other urban–industrial societies have contributed to the "invention" of adolescence (see, e.g., Fasick, 1994). According to this view, if it were not for changes in technology producing greater affluence in society, as well as demographic transitions that occur with increasing wealth, adolescence as a clearly marked stage in development might not have emerged within the 20th century. In earlier eras young people began working at or before the onset of puberty, and at that point their childhood was over. This condition still prevails today in many parts of the less developed world.

Although the start of adolescence is most frequently identified as puberty, the end of adolescence is less clearly defined. Some experts and organizations are beginning to increase the upper age limit to 24 years (World Health Organization, 1989). Today, in the United States adolescence typically is thought of as covering the years from 10 to 19, although girls usually mature earlier than boys (Tanner, 1972). The end of adolescence is less well-marked, but it typically involves milestones in cognitive and emotional development (e.g., graduating from high school or college, getting married) as well as socioeconomic independence (getting a full-time job; World Health Organization, 1989).

There is an increasing tendency to view adolescence as comprising two relatively distinct periods; early adolescence and late adolescence. *Early adolescence* includes most pubertal change and roughly corresponds to the middle school or junior high school years (usually ages 10–15), whereas *late adolescence* includes the range from 16 through 19 years (Santrock, 1991). Research results may not apply to adolescents of all ages, and many studies do not provide separate breakdowns for the two age groupings (Hamburg & Takanishi, 1989). When reports do make such a distinction, frequently they do not do so consistently; sometimes the cut-off age between early and late adolescence is 14, sometimes it is 15. For the purposes of this book, we follow the dominant trend in adolescent research and define early adolescence as the age range from 10 through 15 years.

Adolescence involves the task of forming a sense of identity accompanied by a cohesive set of personal values (Erickson, 1968). During early adolescence, the young person forms a separate identity by negotiating relationships with parents and peers. This often happens at the same time that rapid physical changes are occurring, typically between the ages of 13 and 15 (Steinberg, 1981). One view in the literature holds that conflict between parents and adolescents reaches its peak during this early adolescent period, when the process of pubertal maturation is at its apex, and then declines by later adolescence (Clark-Lempers, Lempers, & Ho, 1991; Steinberg, 1981, 1988). This view has led many theorists to see early adolescence as a time of turbulence and emotional stress in which conflict is characterized by parent–child disagreements over everyday issues such as adolescents' personal appearance and choice of friends (Smetana, 1988).

It was initially believed that identity formation was facilitated by the child breaking the parent–child bond during this period of stress (Grotevant & Cooper, 1986). However, recent thinking sees much less *necessary* difficulty with the process of identity formation in adolescence and much more continuity between the child who was, through the adolescent who is, to the adult who will be. This view, expressed by Offer and colleagues (Offer, Ostrov, & Howard, 1989; Offer & Schonert-Reichl, 1992) and others, is that normal adolescents negotiate this period of life transition with relatively little major disruption or sustained high-risk behavior, maintaining and developing their own identity and their relationships with parents as well as adding elements of identity and building new extrafamilial relationships and skills. This view of "normal" adolescence suggests that those teenagers who do experience major disruptions and who do persistently engage in problem behaviors are in trouble now and have a significantly greater chance of being in trouble later in life (Hamburg & Takanishi, 1989). Therefore, successful interventions with these youth are likely to have important payoffs in terms of preventing future health problems and promoting satisfying and productive lifetimes.

Recent evidence supports the view of adolescence as a gradual renegotiation of the parent–adolescent relationship (Bulcroft, 1991; White, Speisman, & Costos, 1983; Youniss & Smollar, 1985). Adolescents are now viewed as transforming rather than abandoning their relationship with their parents while becoming more closely connected to a peer group (Smetana, 1994; Youniss & Ketterlinus, 1987). As teenagers assume more independence in decision making, strains naturally occur in the parent–child authority relationship (Grotevant & Cooper, 1986). From early- to mid-adolescence, the legitimacy of parental authority declines, particularly over issues of choosing friends (Smetana, 1994). If parents do not begin to grant greater independence to their child, the parent–adolescent relationship can be negatively affected (Bulcroft, 1991). However, adolescents still generally need and want adult support when they are faced with important decisions, issues, or choices (William T. Grant Foundation, 1988).

There is even some disagreement in the literature as to whether parent–adolescent conflict increases during early adolescence (Galambos & Almeida, 1992). Levels of parent–adolescent conflict may be affected by the family's economic situation, and conflict may increase when the family experiences job loss or other forms of economic instability (Flanagan, 1990). Regardless of whether such conflict is at a peak or not, it is clear that adolescence is a period of stress in many arenas of a young person's life. Adolescents in the 1990s face many problems heretofore not considered part of "normal" adolescent development. For example, adolescents are at greater risk for either becoming victims of violence or being the perpetrators of violence in comparison with all other age groups (Centers for Disease Control, 1992; Osgood, O'Malley, Bachman, & Johnston, 1989). The contrast between adolescents and other age groups in their risk of being involved in violence also seems to be increasing over time, even as the modal age of perpetrators of violent crimes is decreasing (Tracy, Wolfgang, & Figlio, 1990). There is a similar trend toward increased use of drugs and alcohol by young adolescents, according to data from the 1995 National Household Survey on Drug Abuse (Substance Abuse and Mental Health Services Administration, 1996) and results from the University of Michigan's (1995) Monitoring the Future surveys.

A question many people ask is whether adolescents differ greatly from adults in terms of their values and attitudes. Widespread generalizations about the existence of a "generation gap" between most adolescents and adults have been fueled primarily by information about a limited number of individuals (Adelson, 1979). Surveys have reported that few or no differences actually exist between the attitudes of adolescents and their parents on issues such as self-control, hard work, the law, long-term planning, and expectations for quality of life (Yankelovich, 1974), and many of high school seniors' personal and social goals have remained stable or show increases in commitment to conventional and community values between the mid-1970s and the mid-1990s, as reported through the Monitoring the Future project (Office of the Assistant Secretary for Planning and Evaluation, 1996).

Despite significant areas of agreement, parents and adolescents differ in how much autonomy adolescents should have over these issues (Smetana & Asquith, 1994). In a recent study, styles of parenting (permissive, authoritative, or authoritarian) were related to how much autonomy adolescents received concerning certain issues (Smetana, 1995). Whereas permissive parents gave adolescents more leeway in some areas of decision making than did other parents, authoritarian parents were restrictive in treating almost all issues as subject to parental authority. These conceptions of parental authority and parenting styles were useful in explaining differences in adolescents' emotional autonomy and adolescent–parent conflict (Smetana, 1995).

Although adolescence often involves some degree of experimentation, most adolescents experiment in positive ways by trying out a variety of potential work and recreational identities before making a commitment to vocations, a career choice, or a given set of values (Marcia, 1987). The development of a firm sense of identity during adolescence forms the groundwork for success as a fully integrated member of society, which means being productive in work, meeting commitments to family and friends, and assuming the responsibilities of citizenship. However, adolescents also receive mixed messages from the culture at large. They are told that if they play by the rules they will get ahead, and this message carries the implicit assumption that they will be able to do better than their parents. This message now engenders increasing skepticism even among economically privileged adolescents. It seriously conflicts with the realities for youth from households at the bottom of the income distribution, many of whom perceive that prosperity is out of reach and that even a steady job paying enough to rise above the poverty level may not be on the horizon. Among youth with the fewest economic opportunities, the opinions of peers may reinforce a turning away from legitimate options and a turning toward problem behaviors (Majors & Billson, 1993).

Some adolescents may experiment with negative role identities involving such risky behaviors as gang membership, criminal and violent acts, early unprotected sexual intercourse, drug or alcohol abuse, or truancy from school. For those who do engage in risky behaviors, some still manage to become productive and successful adults, whereas others remain marginal members of society and become mired in welfare dependency, low levels of employability, drug addiction, or criminal and violent behavior. The problem is how to identify adolescents who are likely to develop problems that prevent them from becoming useful and productive citizens. Lately, attention has been focused on the notion of "risk."

The Meaning of Risk

Three important trends in child development and prevention theory within the past 15 years have contributed to the current interest in definitions of youth at risk. First, there has been acceptance and strong empirical support for "ecological theories" of human development since Bronfenbrenner published his comprehensive model for portraying the environment's role in child and adolescent development (Bronfenbrenner, 1979). Empirical evidence continues to substantiate the influence on the individual's development of family processes, the peer group, social supports and community resources, neighborhood safety and quality of life, as well as the larger key social institutions such as the schools (Baruch & Stutman, 1994; Kreppner & Lerner, 1989; Lerner, 1993; Pence, 1988; Wozniak & Fischer, 1993).

Second, findings from early intervention research conducted over the past 10 years have influenced current definitions of risk. Research from the Perry Preschool Project (Berrueta-Clement, Schweinhard, Barnett, Epstein, & Weikert, 1984), the Yale Early Intervention Project (Seitz, Apfel, & Rosenbaum, 1991), and Project CARE (Wasik, Ramey, Bryant, & Sparling, 1990) shows that early childhood interventions are able to reduce the negative effects of poverty and disadvantage on children's school and social competencies, producing impacts still measurable after 10 to 20 years. New findings indicate that the benefits of continuous educational interventions over the first 5 years of life last as least until early adolescence (Barnett, 1995; Ramey & Ramey, 1992) and in some cases into adulthood (Schweinhart, Barnes, & Weikart, 1993). One recent review of evidence accumulated from 40 early childhood education programs makes apparent the long-term impacts of these programs on antisocial behavior and delinquency (Yoshikawa, 1995). Broadly stated, these results suggest that the value of prevention and child–youth development work extends well beyond the childhood years.

Finally, the last decade has seen a shift toward viewing specific problems of adolescence—delinquency, substance abuse, pregnancy or parenthood, and school failure—as having common, rather than distinct, antecedent causes (Dryfoos, 1990). For example, there is now ample evidence that antisocial, sexual, and drug-using behaviors tend to correlate (Hawkins, Catalano, & Miller, 1992; Jessor, 1987; Resnick, Harris, & Blum, 1993; Steinberg, Mounts, Lamborn, & Dornbusch, 1991). There is also some evidence that antisocial behavior tends to precede substance abuse, so that interventions that aim to prevent antisocial behavior and its correlates early in adolescence may reduce the advent of more serious problems by middle adolescence (Dishion & Andrews, 1995). The co-occurrence of such problem behaviors as delinquency, unprotected sexual intercourse, and drug use appears to come from multiple pathways of influence, in which "probabilistic interactions of multiple factors" (Gollin, as cited in Sameroff & Fiese, 1989, p. 26) now are linked to a syndrome of problem behaviors in adolescence (Allen, Leadbeater, & Aber, 1994; Fergusson, Horwood, & Lynskey, 1994; Paternoster & Mazerolle, 1994). Over the past 5 years, much adolescent research has shifted from a focus on individual problem behaviors to a new emphasis on clusters of problems that constitute a syndrome. This marks a significant shift in understanding the causes and correlates of adolescent problem behaviors.

These three factors—the ecological movement in child development, early intervention research, and the overlap among risk factors for problems of adolescence—have led to an increased focus for researchers, service providers, and policymakers on the need to assess levels of risk for future problems.

The perspective taken in this book is that all adolescents have a certain mix of vulnerabilities and protective factors that ultimately determine the likelihood that they will experience problems. This likelihood or probability is *risk*. In this view an adolescent need not—in fact, should not—already have behaved in problematic ways in order to be classified as "at risk." However, this view differs from many ways in which the word *risk* is used in the literature and in practice. Researchers and service providers often assess the degree of risk by identifying current dysfunction, so that the term *at risk* or *high risk* is made synonymous with already having serious problems.

The difficulty with defining risk on the basis of existing problems is twofold. First, it rarely starts early enough in the lives of youth and hardly ever goes back to childhood. By the time problems come to the attention of service providers, it is too late to consider the youth at risk. If problems are already evident, then in the absence of an effective intervention or response, a near-certainty exists that the problems will persist in the future. Hence risk is no longer a probability; it becomes a certainty, and a tautology results when such a definition of risk is used to determine which adolescents need services.

Second, because the assessment fails to take into account existing strengths and competencies, there is no understanding of protective factors that might moderate the vulnerabilities. By considering risk only from the point of view of past or present problems, interventions will not build on the positive factors that may protect against the occurrence of future negative conditions. Furthermore, the certainty is usually attached only to a particular negative behavior or "single issue." Service providers or policymakers may fail to consider all potential pathways of future risk, just as they may also fail to appreciate how often the same family and environmental factors, often dating from childhood, precede many different adolescent problems.

We think it is more useful to define *risk* as the probability that future problems will arise given the youth's current balance between competencies and vulnerabilities. The task is to define it in terms that are concrete enough to be the basis for effective service delivery decisions. For greatest effectiveness, these decisions should be based on a consideration of the individual's full developmental potential, the interplay between risk and protective factors, and the interaction between the different ecological levels in which the adolescent is embedded. Using this perspective, we summarize in the following section the variety of risk definitions found in the adolescent research literature, discuss the ways they have been used, and examine what implications they may have for service delivery. We look at several different approaches, ranging from those of (a) theorists who see most adolescent behaviors as a phase of experimentation, or sensation seeking, that will pass rather than as problems in themselves and the precursors of future more severe problems; (b) theorists who try to lift the onus from individual youth by focusing on their larger environment (e.g., poor neighborhoods); (c) theorists who focus on factors that predict future problems but are not the problems themselves; and (d) theorists who use the behavior itself as part of their definition of risk.

Risk as Sensation Seeking

Some theorists of risk in adolescence see the behaviors of youth as part of the normal developmental process. They focus on the interplay between cultural norms and adolescence as a time for seeking new experiences, including some that carry a certain amount of risk or societal disapproval. These are characterized as sensation seeking, which as a personality dimension is thought of as the degree of novelty and intensity of sensation and experience an individual prefers (Zuckerman, 1979). When considering the entire life span, sensation-seeking behavior typically occurs most frequently in adolescence (Zuckerman, Eysenck, & Eysenck, 1978). Dangerous, risky, or illegal activities are high in novelty and intensity, which makes them very appealing to many youth. At the same time, cultures vary in their tolerance for risk behaviors, and adolescents who live in cultures characterized by "broad socialization" practices (as opposed to "narrow" practices that emphasize obedience and conformity to community standards) are more likely to be at risk because their sensation-seeking behaviors are not constrained by socialization practices in the larger culture (Arnett & Balle-Jensen, 1993).

This approach is useful to keep in mind when considering adolescent problem behaviors because it focuses on the normative or adaptive aspects of engaging in risk behaviors. Many service providers have broadened their continuum of preventive services to include programs that enable youth to take risks in a supportive environment, such as making Outward Bound or other wilderness experiences available. Furthermore, this approach to thinking about risk encourages taking a broader view of the service delivery continuum to include preventive strategies and supports to "normal" adolescents.

The "risk is only sensation-seeking, they will grow out of it" approach may fail to distinguish truly problematic behavior from behavior that youth indeed will drop as they mature. A recent study testing various theories of adolescent risk taking (as a behavior problem, as normal and adaptive for adolescents, as a sign of adolescent egocentrism, and as a decision-making mechanism) found that much risk-taking behavior is not normative and adaptive but is instead a sign of social maladjustment (Lavery, Siegel, Cousins, & Rubovits, 1993). By arguing that adolescents who display risky behaviors are "just going through a stage," we may fail to identify early enough those who need intensive intervention.

Living in a Risky Environment

A second theoretical approach to understanding risk focuses on the environment that surrounds the youth, rather than on the youth's behavior. Part of the underlying motivation for this approach is to take the stigma off specific youth and identify the intervention point as the environment. Youth are not seen to be at risk because they personally engage in problem behaviors but because they live in risky situations or environments. Such environments would include neighborhoods with high levels of familial and community violence, drug abuse, crime, unemployment, inadequate housing, and the like; communities with many negative peer and adult role models and few positive ones; little or no parental support and monitoring; and few opportunities for future employment. This approach to the concept of risk hypothesizes that living in such circumstances predisposes adolescents to behave in ways that place them at risk of serious negative consequences (National Network for Youth, 1991; Schorr & Schorr, 1988). It offers a compelling counterpoint to definitions of risk based on individual behavior and emphasizes a primary prevention strategy aimed at the neighborhood and community levels.

There are problems with the "risky environment" approach to defining risk, to balance its advantages. First, by focusing on poorer communities, it could potentially stigmatize all teenagers living in the target environment and fail to offer help to youth who are having problems despite coming from "better" neighborhoods. Also, the "risky environment" viewpoint downplays the fact that many risk factors and problem behaviors can be found among people of all income levels and communities. It overlooks the fact that some youth from even the worst neighborhoods manage to avoid problem behaviors and that some youth from the best neighborhoods get into serious trouble. Research documents the existence of factors promoting resilience in children exposed to substantial environmental risk, including having personal characteristics such as higher intelligence, personal charm, or optimism; being firstborn; coming from a smaller family with wider birth spacing; having a supportive relationship with a caring adult (not necessarily a parent); and having access to social support outside the immediate family (Baruch & Stutman, 1994; Farrington, 1983; Garmezy, 1991; Garmezy, Masten, & Tellegen, 1984; Mulvey, Arthur, & Reppucci, 1990; Rutter, 1979, 1985, 1987; Werner, 1986, 1988, 1989; Werner & Smith, 1992; West, 1982; West & Farrington, 1973).

Antecedents and Markers

A third approach to understanding risk focuses on personal characteristics and aspects of an individual's background to predict the likelihood of a future occurrence of negative behaviors and outcomes. Common antecedents of problem behaviors include economic and neighborhood factors. In addition, a child's own family may constitute a risky environment through physical and sexual abuse of the child, neglect, or parental drug use or mental illness. System markers such as school performance or a child abuse or neglect report could be used to target early and intensive interventions to children when they need it most (e.g., by choosing the children who cannot read by the end of first grade or those who have had initial involvement with child protection but have not yet been removed from their home and offering them real help).

The use of antecedents and system markers to define risk has long been popular. In the past its proponents have tended to focus on predicting each type of negative behavior separately, looking either at substance abuse, teenage childbearing, school dropout, or delinquent behavior. Most of the predictive models developed from this approach to risk have not proved very robust at predicting any *single* outcome with a high level of precision. This has implications for service delivery when it is structured as a traditional single-issue program. Such programs cannot reliably use the models to pick out the youth who will exhibit the particular problem that the program is designed to prevent or treat. A program addressing only drug abuse would waste a lot of program resources if it used such a model to target the youth it wanted to serve, because the model would identify many youth who would never become drug abusers. However, the single-problem focus is not a necessary aspect of the "antecedents and markers" approach. We adopt this basic approach for the risk model we present in Chapter 4, with only slight modifications to indicate that it can be used quite well to predict the occurrence of *some* problems without having to be specific as to *which* particular problem will arise. The service implications of this approach are that programs need to be prepared to respond with preventive and treatment interventions for a variety of issues that might arise in the life of a youth.

Risk as Certainty

The final approach to understanding risk in adolescence is to wait for youth to engage in problem behaviors, after which they are identified as "at risk" and (possibly) offered services. This approach cannot deal with risk from the perspective of primary prevention because it focuses on behavior that has already occurred and not on behavior that might take place in the future. Furthermore, by the time youth are identified as "high risk" using this approach, they may be well beyond the point of responding to simple preventive interventions that do not stigmatize and that promote self-determination. Programs will have to offer more intensive treatment, often with less hope of averting continuation of the behaviors and their consequences for the future.

The attractiveness of this approach is that we usually have more sources of data to document actual problem behaviors of specific youth than we do to document risky environments or familial and personal characteristics indicative of risk. It is also attractive from the perspective of service planning and delivery, because agencies can limit their activities to youth who have already exhibited a negative behavior or experienced a negative outcome. This limitation assures that scarce resources will not be used for youth who are not truly at risk. However, it also means that the youth who do receive attention from service systems will be harder to help because their behavior patterns will be more ingrained and that no efforts will be made to discourage other youth from taking the same path.

Youth Development and Rights-Based Approaches

Many of the approaches to risk just described focus on problems, not on strengths, although some of the later studies have broadened their scope to include a consideration of personal, familial, and community protective factors (e.g., Ginzberg, Berliner, & Ostow, 1988; Resnick et al., 1993). When viewed from the problem focus, either the adolescent or the context in which the adolescent develops is seen as dysfunctional in some way, thereby exposing the developing youth to risk for engaging in problem behavior and experiencing negative outcomes. Alternative, and potentially complementary, approaches to thinking about youth include youth development and children's rights. The youth development approach emphasizes the individual's competencies and strengths, with the underlying belief that building skills and competencies is the key to the prevention of dysfunctional behavior. This approach promotes the idea that all elements in society should be centered on supporting normal child development (Barker, 1996; Connell & Aber, 1995; Gambone & Arbreton, 1997; Pittman, O'Brien, & Kimball, 1993). These societal elements include societal institutions (schools, religious congregations, businesses, government), the laws and polity, the communities in which families live, and the families themselves in which children are socialized.

Cross-cultural studies provide useful reference points for considering a model of risk based on competencies and functions rather than problems and dysfunctions. For example, using a stratified sample of 101 different communities representing different social systems around the world, Rohner (cited in Bretherton, 1985) distinguished societies according to whether or not they are child-centered. Child-centered societies are those in which there is greater acceptance of children and all institutions in the society are focused on providing children with the skills to develop normally. Societies that are not child-centered are those that emphasize individual rights over community obligations and react to problems rather than planning proactively to prevent difficulties in development. In societies that are not child-centered, there is more rejection of children, less sympathy given to people in need, and more aggressive behavior and hostility on the part of adults. Rohner's results revealed that children living in high-acceptance societies are more self-reliant and achievement motivated, whereas children living in high-rejection societies are more emotionally unresponsive, more dependent, less emotionally stable, and more aggressive.

The parallels between characteristics of child-centered and non-child-centered societies and what we know of child rearing in the United States are inescapable, although not explicitly noted in Rohner's study. Our society has a tendency to focus on problems and to react by punishing those who have them rather than focusing on preventing difficulties from occurring by being more proactive and competency-based. Incorporating the youth development approach into our understanding of risk in adolescence helps us develop a broader approach that encompasses strengths and competencies and refocuses attention on creating the conditions for healthy development rather than blaming individuals when they fail to thrive in difficult circumstances.

The promotion of youth development includes not only the content of an intervention but the context in which that intervention or support is given (Pittman et al., 1993; Pittman & Zeldin, 1992). For service provision, a youth development approach emphasizes providing adolescents with appropriate content within the optimal context in order for them to develop normally. Contexts can include schools that allow education to occur safely and with support and commitment and neighborhoods and communities that have resources to nurture constructive relationships (Pittman et al., 1993; Pittman & Zeldin, 1992).

A youth development approach will certainly target for assistance many more youth than are likely to develop problems without its intervention. This is not a problem from the perspective of youth development advocates, who feel that current problem-centered approaches will never stimulate the types of environments that children and youth need to prosper. It also might be faulted for gearing services at a level of intensity too "low" to be effective for the adolescents who have serious problems. Indeed, if the youth development approach is thought of as identifying "at-risk" youth, it will overidentify. But that is not its goal. Rather, advocates of the youth development approach want no less than a fundamental change in systems that serve American youth. Pittman and Zeldin (1992), for instance, want the approach to shift from thinking about treatment interventions to thinking about how to interact with youth; from concentrating on fitting people into programs to being willing to meet people's needs, however that can be done; and from focusing exclusively on problems to focusing on the entire context of a youth's environment. The youth development approach is probably on the right track, theoretically, but current systems in the United States have a long way to go before they will be able to make the conditions advocated by the approach into a reality.

The paradigm shift proposed by youth development advocates fits very well with the international movement to secure the rights of the child in every country throughout the globe. This rights-based approach is best exemplified by United Nations documents signed by the United States and many other countries, such as the United Nations' Declaration on the Rights of the Child (see, e.g., Knaul & Flórez, 1996). These documents set forth the basic conditions that children need to develop into healthy, productive adults and responsible participants in their society. Signatories to these accords have agreed, in effect, that their countries have some obligation to create these conditions for children and youth if they do not already exist (as indeed they do not in most of the world's countries, including the United States). Youth development theorists and the children's specialists who developed the international consensus on the rights of the child are in substantial agreement about these basic conditions. Many youth-oriented programs try to provide some of these conditions for their participants, including relationships with nurturing adults, successful learning experiences in which youth can acquire needed skills as well as an improved sense of competency, and practice with responsible decision making.

Concluding Thoughts

The conceptual framework we propose in the next chapter incorporates the views on adolescence and risk just reviewed, as well as elements from both the youth development and the rights-based approaches. These elements have important implications for rethinking the entire approach to delivering services for youth and adolescents. At this time, services, which usually do not deserve to be called a system, may justly be described as being limited primarily to those adolescents who are either in crisis or deviating from the "normal script for adolescent maturation" (Whalen & Wynn, 1995) and are involved in behaviors that threaten either their own health and safety or that of others. However, if we want to reach youth for *preventive* interventions before these behaviors become a certainty, we have to start much earlier. To start earlier, we need a framework that directs us toward those children and youth most in need of early intervention, or who are most likely to benefit from it. The conceptual framework presented in Chapter 4 offers this guidance. It suggests a shift in our paradigms of risk by pinpointing antecedent conditions and system markers that occur early enough in a child's or youth's life so that trouble is only a probability but not a certainty. Furthermore, by starting earlier in the developmental sequence, the conceptual framework acknowledges that even "low risk" children and adolescents need support and guidance to bolster strengths, protect against vulnerabilities, and foster positive development. These key features of the conceptual framework provide the basis for innovations in service delivery that maximize the probability of normal development for all adolescents. Later chapters offer suggestions for innovation that have some track record of success.

4

A New Conceptual Framework for Understanding Risk

This chapter shapes the material presented in Chapter 3 into a conceptual framework for understanding at-risk youth. It also summarizes the research literature pertaining to each element of the framework, providing estimates for the prevalence of each element among today's youth. Where possible, prevalence among younger adolescents (those 10–15 years old) is highlighted, in keeping with our interest in early intervention before problem behaviors become entrenched and negative outcomes inevitable.

Our conceptual framework integrates different perspectives currently held by social workers, policymakers, and researchers in different disciplines about how best to meet the needs of youth through services and activities, rather than presenting a completely new approach. A central premise of this book is that traditionally oriented services for adolescents that focus on a particular problem in isolation have had difficulty addressing adolescent needs because they start after problems develop and end before problems are resolved (Barker, 1996); do not consider the larger context in which youth live; and focus on preventing negatives rather than on developing strengths (Pittman et al., 1993). In our conceptual framework of risk and resiliency, we have tried to resolve problems people may have with existing definitions of risk. The conceptual framework should also be useful for researchers, social workers, and policymakers in identifying youth with different levels of risk for whom services from different points along the treatment–prevention–development continuum would be appropriate.

The Framework

The several approaches to thinking about youth and risk reviewed in Chapter 3 are not incompatible; a synthesis of these definitions is possible within an ecological perspective. Bronfenbrenner's comprehensive model for portraying the environment's role in child and adolescent development (Bronfenbrenner, 1979) has gained strong empirical support for viewing the child as developing within multiple contexts of family, community, and larger social institutions. An extensive body of research has substantiated a host of influences from each level on individual development (Baruch & Stutman, 1994; Kreppner & Lerner, 1989; Lerner, 1993; Pence, 1988; Wozniak & Fischer, 1993). These influences include family processes (direct, as in parent–adolescent relationships, and indirect, such as the marital relationship); the peer group; social supports and community resources; neighborhood safety and quality of life; and the larger key social institutions, such as the schools.

The ecological perspective suggests that high-risk youth are more likely to come from those environments that heighten their vulnerability, communities with scarce social resources, high levels of stress, and inadequate institutional support (Belsky, 1981; Garbarino & Crouter, 1978; Garbarino & Sherman, 1980). Factors in the youth's early experiences and current family, school, community, and larger societal environment influence his or her physical, mental, and social health and lead to greater or lesser degrees of risk for developing problems (Office of Technology Assessment, 1991). This perspective considers the predictors of problem behavior, the problem behavior itself, the broader environment and socialization practices in which the behavior occurs, and the consequences of the behavior. It lays the groundwork for a risk model that includes factors on the institution, community, family, and individual levels. Furthermore, an ecological perspective on risk also considers the strengths and competencies of the individual and the protective factors in the environment that mitigate against potential difficulties.

A comprehensive approach to risk requires a conceptual framework that integrates assumptions about cause and effect and the nature of the associations between environment, individual behavior, and outcomes. We propose a conceptual framework that synthesizes the diverse literature on adolescent development, problems of adolescence, and theories of prevention. It takes into account the common antecedents of many adolescent problems in childhood. Also, it allows for an assessment of risk geared specifically to younger adolescents, 10 to 15 years of age, that emphasizes the balance between competencies, protective factors, and vulnerabilities in assessing early signs of dysfunction rather than waiting until the onset of negative or destructive consequences. Finally, this conceptual framework considers factors at multiple ecological levels (macro-, family, and individual). The framework we propose involves four components—antecedents, system markers, problem behaviors, and negative outcomes—and can be stated as follows:

> The presence of harmful existing conditions (antecedents) in the absence of sufficient protective factors create vulnerabilities. These vulnerabilities, combined with the presence of specific early signs of difficulties (system markers), institutional inabilities to help children and youth who show the markers, and the absence of positive behaviors or competencies, may lead in time to problem behavior that will have more serious long-term consequences (negative outcomes).

Exhibit 4.1 presents a schematic representation of this conceptual

Exhibit 4.1. Risk Antecedents, Markers, Behaviors, and Outcomes: A Conceptual Framework for Thinking About Youth

Antecedents	Protective factors	System markers	Problem behaviors	Positive behaviors	Negative outcomes
Family dysfunction	Individual competencies/abilities	Poor school performance	School-related problem behaviors (truancy, absenteeism, violence)	Good school attendance, attachment to school, good performance	Dropping out of school, poor credentials for economic self-sufficiency
	Parental competencies, resources	Child protection/out-of-home placement	Early sexual behavior	Postponing sexual behavior	Pregnancy, too-early parenthood, poor pregnancy outcomes
					Sexually transmitted diseases, including chlamydia and AIDS
Poverty			Use of tobacco, alcohol, other drugs		Abuse of or addiction to alcohol or other drugs, and associated health problems
Neighborhood and local institutions	Other adults Neighborhood resources Effective schools and other institutions with responsibility for children and youth		Running away from home, foster home Associating with delinquent peers	Positive interactions with family Participation in community and religious institutions Social, problem-solving, and peer skills High self-esteem and achievement motivation	Homelessness Physical abuse, battering Prostitution Sexual abuse, rape, incest Death or permanent injury from guns, knives, and other violent behavior; automobile accidents; other accidents Other morbidity/mortality outcomes (e.g., hepatitis, tuberculosis, pneumonia, AIDS complications) Depression, suicide Criminal convictions

framework. Risk antecedents are those macro- and family-level environmental conditions, such as poverty and family dysfunction or lack of parent involvement and support, that consistently predict subsequent negative outcomes for youth. Most begin to exert their influence in childhood; continued exposure sustains and may increase the risk. These antecedents create vulnerabilities when protective factors are not sufficient to moderate their effects. Protective factors in parents, other adults, the neighborhood, institutions (e.g., a committed teacher or social worker), and individual competencies may act to promote resilience in children and youth who are vulnerable due to their exposure to the preexisting conditions. System markers are situations reflected in official records that, in the absence of effective intervention by communities or institutions to help children and youth achieve positive behaviors, often signal impending dysfunction. At this point, positive behaviors that signal and may also promote resilience would include school attendance and performance; participation in community and church activities; positive interactions with family; postponing sexual behavior; social, problem-solving, and peer skills; high self-esteem; and achievement motivation. Negative outcomes are the result of problem behaviors and are more likely to occur among youth with more (or more severe) antecedents or among those who leave markers in formal systems at younger ages (e.g., early childhood involvement with protective services, failing performance in first grade, or significant health problems).

This conceptual framework is meant to reflect the prevailing view in the recent literature suggesting a confluence of factors, including increased vulnerability, multiple causation, and the transaction between the environment and the individual (Sameroff & Fiese, 1989). The framework suggests that elements to the left in Exhibit 4.1 are generally associated with elements further to the right and that positive elements function to moderate the link between adjacent columns of negative factors. For example, the protective factors are considered potential moderators of the link between the existing conditions (antecedents) and the system markers. Similarly, youth who display system markers are more likely to show the problem behaviors listed in the fourth column. However, these behaviors may not result in the more severe outcomes listed in the last column if the youth also displays some of the positive behaviors listed or if the systems develop effective ways to help children and youth when alerted to their need by one or more markers.

A number of caveats about the framework are required. It is not strictly causal because research has not fully documented the actual causal linkages. Furthermore, including protective factors and positive behaviors in the framework implies that it is possible to find strengths and competencies even in the face of adverse conditions or problem behavior. Certainly the literature indicates that youth are more likely to have system markers if they have risk antecedents without the accompanying protective factors, but markers may appear in youth with no antecedents, and youth with antecedents may display no markers. Furthermore, the framework represents an oversimplification of the links between constructs, mainly because the research literature has tended to use relatively blunt analytic tools, such as linear modeling. Research using advanced modeling techniques will undoubtedly find that the causal linkages are complex and multidetermined. Many researchers have identified clusters of adolescent high-risk behaviors that appear to stem from a complex interplay of multiple variables (Botvin, 1986, 1990; Paternoster & Mazerolle, 1994; Resnick, Chambliss, & Blum, 1993). Furthermore, available multifactor predictive literature often does not model either the ameliorative or the destructive actions of institutions. These actions are hard to include in our framework as they could occur at every point along the way.

Elements of the Framework: Prevalence Estimates

Estimates of the prevalence of at-risk youth in the population of 10–15 year olds using all of the components of our conceptual framework would ideally be based on data revealing how many youth experienced each antecedent condition, marker, problem behavior, or negative outcome. However, no single source provides prevalence data for the entire range of possible problem behaviors among adolescents, the covariation among problems, or the likelihood of outcomes arising from specific behaviors or circumstances (Office of Technology Assessment, 1991). There are, however, some data sets that cover several of the variables of interest. Here we present the available survey-based or population-based data indicating the prevalence of particular circumstances in the population of 10–15 year olds. We use these data to make some determination of the extent to which adolescents nationally may be located within high-, medium-, or low-risk groups.

Risk Antecedents or Existing Conditions

Risk antecedents consist of those forces operating at the community and family levels that have a negative impact on the developing individual by producing an increased vulnerability to future problems in the family, school, or community. From our review of the literature, three critical risk antecedents appear to be linked consistently to adolescent problem behaviors: family environment, poverty, and neighborhood (including institutions such as the schools, protective services, and the health care system).

The following discussion of the rationale for considering these factors as antecedent risk conditions is organized according to the ecological perspective presented initially by Bronfenbrenner (1979), in which different levels of the environment are represented as concentric circles emanating outward from the individual (in this case, the adolescent) at its center. Accordingly, the environment closest to the individual is that of the family, followed by the community or neighborhood, followed by the larger societal institutions (such as schools). In our conceptual framework of risk in early adolescence, these concentric rings are represented by the three "risk antecedents" that appear most consistently in the literature. Family dysfunction operates at the level closest to the adolescent; followed by poverty, which typically operates at the level of both the family and the neighborhood; and finally, the neighborhood environment itself. When a neighborhood is characterized by a very high poverty rate and a density of associated problems (an underclass neighborhood), and when its institutions do not offer effective compensation for neighborhood influences, the neighborhood and institutions themselves add to the risk.

However, there are also protective factors at each ecological level that may interact with the existing conditions to promote positive development. For example, secure attachment, which for a child is the sense of confidence and trust in its emotional connection to a parent figure, is a basic building block of healthy development (Wolin & Wolin, 1993). With sufficient social supports to provide child-rearing information and respite, children of poor, disadvantaged single mothers can develop a secure sense of attachment, which is much harder for them to achieve when their mother lacks such support (Crockenburg, 1981). For children in less disadvantaged circumstances, such support does not have such a strong effect. Similarly, some studies of child abuse show that neighborhoods characterized by high levels of poverty and family dysfunction also produce high rates of child abuse, but this association is significantly lessened (children are better off despite the neighborhood stress) when the neighborhood also provides parents with sufficient supportive resources (Garbarino & Sherman, 1980). In both cases the protective factor operates more strongly in the high-stress situation than in situations of less or no stress, producing an interaction effect in the presence of stress. In the following discussion we focus most on negative antecedent conditions, but protective factors within these conditions also play a role in moderating the deleterious effects of neighborhoods, poverty, and family dysfunction.

Family dysfunction and lack of parent support and involvement. Empirical research from an ecological perspective has consistently affirmed the importance of parental support and involvement as a critical mediator of child and adolescent development. The parent–child relationship provides the necessary structure for a child's social and intellectual development, including emotional support, modeling of socially appropriate behaviors, methods for dealing with conflict, and enhancing the child's intrinsic motivation to learn (summarized by Baruch & Stutman, 1994; see also Belsky, 1981; Lamb, 1981). Parents also exert an indirect influence through their behavior within the marital relationship, their relationships with other children in the family, their extrafamilial relationships (with relatives and acquaintances), and their interactions with societal institutions such as work and school (Bronfenbrenner, 1979).

Family dysfunction, defined as the inability of the family to adapt to change, combined with lack of closeness between family members (Epstein, Bishop, & Baldwin, 1982; Moos & Moos, 1976; Oliveri & Reiss, 1981; Olson et al., 1983), has been linked empirically to adolescent problem be-

Exhibit 4.2.   Prevalence Estimates for Family Dysfunction

The symptoms of family dysfunction are often what brings a particular adolescent or family to the attention of social and community service agencies, including the juvenile authorities, courts, treatment agencies, shelters, and child protective services. Data are available on several indicators of dysfunction: parental substance abuse, woman battering, and physical abuse of children. In 1988, there were 28 million children of alcoholics, 25% of whom, or approximately 7 million, were under the age of 18 (Office for Substance Abuse Prevention, 1989). Repeated severe violence appears in 1 of every 14 marriages (Dutton, 1988), and to approximately 2 million American women annually (Council on Scientific Affairs, AMA, 1992). The results of national surveys (Straus & Gelles, 1986) indicate that all forms of parental violence against children ages 3–17 years remained relatively stable from 1975 to 1985 at 6.2 per 1,000, with a prevalence rate for child physical abuse of 2–4% of the population ages 17 years and younger.

haviors in many studies (Office of Juvenile Justice Programs, 1995; Paternoster & Mazerolle, 1994; Patterson, 1976; Sroufe & Rutter, 1984; see Exhibit 4.2 for prevalence estimates). It compromises goals for individual growth; has involved problems in family processes, parenting styles, and, at the extreme, family violence (Minuchin, 1977), and is characterized by less-than-optimal parenting styles. Authoritarian, permissive, or neglecting parenting styles are associated with adolescents who are less competent socially, have lower levels of self-esteem, and are more likely to display negative behaviors (Baumrind, 1991). Conversely, parents who are "authoritative" and "democratic" tend to have adolescents who are more socially competent, responsible, mature, and independent (Baumrind, 1991).

Maltreated adolescents come from families across a range of socioeconomic strata. In the National Center on Child Abuse and Neglect's national incidence studies (Sedlak, 1991; Sedlak & Broadhurst, 1996), low socioeconomic status was significantly related to all child maltreatment but did not predict adolescent maltreatment. Families characterized by violence or adolescent maltreatment have been reported to show poor cohesion, family disorganization, and a lack of parental involvement and support (Baumrind, 1991; Garbarino, Schellenbach, & Sebes, 1986). Violent families have been differentiated from nonviolent families primarily in their handling of the 5–10% of parent–child interactions that are conflictual and negative. Violent families are less able to terminate these interactions quickly and thus are prone to an escalation of conflict (Reid, 1986). Incidents of abuse, particularly abuse of young adolescents, typically arise from the adolescent's testing or acting-out behavior, which is met with overwhelming and punitive force by parents (Pelcovitz, Kaplan, Samit, Krieger, & Cornelius, 1984). Alcoholism and abuse of illicit drugs by an adolescent's parents or siblings have been shown to increase significantly an adolescent's vulnerability to becoming an alcohol or drug abuser (Springer, Phillips, Phillips, Canady, & Kerst-Harris, 1992; Thorne & DeBlassie, 1985). Parents who abuse alcohol or other drugs spend less

Exhibit 4.3.   Prevalence Estimates for Poverty

According to data from the Bureau of the Census compiled by the Department of Health and Human Services (OASPE, 1996), 28% of all American youth under 18 years of age lived in poor or near-poor families in 1993. These same data show that certain groups of racial and ethnic minority youth are more likely than White, non-Hispanic youth to live in poor or near-poor families. In 1993, 17% of White youth lived in families with incomes below the poverty line, compared with 46% of African American youth and 40% of Hispanic youth. In addition, the chance of a child living in poverty is strongly related to the type of family in which the child lives. In 1993 22% of children under 18 years of age living in poverty (9.3 million families) came from female-headed families (U.S. Department of Commerce, Bureau of the Census, 1993). The number of two-parent families with children living in poverty declined from 25.8 million to 25.2 million from 1970 to 1993, but the number of female-headed families with children living in poverty nearly tripled from 3.4 million to 9.3 million families (OASPE, 1996).

time positively reinforcing their children for good behaviors (Kumpfer, 1989), and the risk for family violence is greater in families with alcoholic parents due to the parents' failure to deal effectively with child discipline, which creates coercive interaction patterns that teach another generation aggressive behaviors (Patterson, as cited in Kumpfer, 1989).

Poverty. Youth living in poor or near-poor families are at increased risk for a variety of health and behavioral consequences. According to the 1993 National Health Interview Survey (NHIS), youth ages 5 through 17 years living in families with incomes under $10,000 are less likely to report their health as excellent than are youth from nonpoor families (Centers for Disease Control, National Center for Health Statistics, 1994). Youth living in poor families are more likely to lose days from school because of illness or injury, which affects their school performance (Centers for Disease Control, National Center for Health Statistics, 1994). Living in poverty is associated with an increased likelihood of early sexual activity and teenage pregnancy (Brown & Eisenberg, 1995; Office of the Assistant Secretary for Planning and Evaluation [OASPE], 1996; Moore, Simms, & Betsey, 1986) and reduced likelihood of using contraception (Emans et al., 1987; Brown & Eisenberg, 1995; Hogan, Astone, & Kitagawa, 1985; OASPE, 1996). Youth living in poverty who become pregnant are less likely to have an abortion or to give their child up for adoption compared with youth from less disadvantaged backgrounds (Jaynes & Williams, 1989).

A variety of factors are related to the greater likelihood of being poor or near-poor for youth, including African American, Hispanic, or Native American ethnicity (U.S. Department of Commerce, Bureau of the Census, 1990, 1993); living in the South (Office of Technology Assessment, 1991, citing Kronick, 1990); and living in female-headed families (Bane & Ellwood, 1989; OASPE, 1996), particularly when children are born out of wedlock (National Center for Health Statistics, 1991; see Exhibit 4.3). Despite the stereotype of poverty being predominantly an inner-city problem, a substantial percentage of poor families with children live in rural or suburban areas (Bane & Ellwood, 1989), and only one in five poor African Americans actually live in a "ghetto poverty area," defined as a neighborhood that has a poverty rate of 40% or higher (Jargowsky & Bane, 1990).

Neighborhood. The concentration of poverty in central cities has created "underclass" areas characterized by high levels of many social problems (Jargowsky & Bane, 1990; Ricketts & Sawhill, 1988; Wilson, 1987). Youth who live in these neighborhoods are inevitably affected through peer example, influence, and opportunity structures (Wilson, 1987). Youth living in poverty are more likely to live in neighborhoods with inadequate schools and other institutions and are more likely to be victims of crime (Gibbs et al., 1988). Some of these youth have to drop out of school because of family economic problems, academic difficulties, disciplinary problems, or pregnancy (Gibbs et al., 1988; National Center for Educational Statistics, 1990). Schools and other institutions in these neighborhoods often cannot offer children and youth supports adequate to overcome these difficulties.

The factors just cited—family dysfunction, poverty, and neighborhood and institutional inadequacy—are considered antecedents of risk for youth because they exist prior to problem behaviors or negative outcomes in any given youth, and empirical studies document their association with a higher likelihood that youth will have problems. Many researchers have identified clusters of adolescent high-risk behaviors that appear to stem from a complex interplay of these multiple antecedent factors (Office of Juvenile Justice Programs, 1995; Paternoster & Mazerolle, 1994). This view is also consistent with the literature on the origins of developmental psychopathology (Sroufe & Rutter, 1984), as well as with the transactional model of development in which the child and the environment mutually influence developmental outcomes (Sameroff & Fiese, 1989). The evidence strongly supports the idea, common to several theoretical orientations, that the same outcomes may arise from different combinations of risk factors; one cannot predict risk without considering both the individual and the larger family, community, and institutional environments within which the adolescent develops.

System Markers

System markers are events that "register" in formal public systems such as schools, child welfare offices, or health care institutions. They are not the only signs that indicate a youth is on a trajectory of impending trouble, but they are readily visible ones that can easily be used to identify children who need help and for whom preventive interventions could yield high payoffs. Research evidence indicates a relatively consistent and robust relationship between these markers and the antecedent conditions just described. The research literature also shows a strong link between the markers and the later onset of more serious behavior problems. Thus,

Exhibit 4.4.   Prevalence Estimates for Poor School Performance and
Grade Retention

Census Bureau data from the 1993 Current Population Survey show that enrollment below modal grade (the grade one should be in for one's age if one follows a normal school enrollment pattern) varies by a youth's age and race/ethnicity (Bruno & Adams, 1994):

- For adolescents ages 9–11, 27.2% of Whites, 33.3% of African Americans, and 29.2% of Hispanics were enrolled below the modal grade.
- For adolescents ages 12–14, 29.2% of Whites, 38.8% of African Americans, and 32.7% of Hispanics were enrolled below the modal grade.
- For adolescents ages 15–17, 29.7% of Whites, 43.3% of African Americans, and 38.3% of Hispanics were enrolled below the modal grade.

another way to think about the meaning of system markers is as the individual youth's behavioral "symptoms" of living in dysfunctional families or stressful neighborhoods and as early warning signs identifying which youth need help.

Two system markers show consistently strong relationships with the later occurrence of all problem behaviors of adolescence. These are (a) poor school performance and (b) involvement with child protective services due to reports of abuse or neglect, including out-of-home placement in the foster care system. Dryfoos (1990) has calculated that poor school performance, including functioning well below grade level (whether a grade has been repeated or not), is the single most important marker for identifying those at high risk. For some children this marker is evident even before the end of first grade. A second risk marker is whether a child is involved with child protective services or out-of-home placement as a result of abuse or neglect. Both services to children and families to eliminate abuse or neglect and, as a last resort, out-of-home placement, may be considered consequences of the antecedent conditions of family dysfunction and lack of parental involvement and support. The research literature suggests that they are good predictors of future negative outcomes.

Poor school performance and grade retention. For young adolescents, being retained in grade is the single most important predictor of school dropout, after controlling for ability (Bruno & Adams, 1994, p. 30; Feldman, Stiffman, & Jung, 1987). In 1993, 31% of 12–14 year olds were enrolled below the modal grade for their age. The majority of retentions appear to have occurred between the ages of 9 and 11, when 27% were enrolled below the modal grade (Bruno & Adams, 1994; see Exhibit 4.4). Boys are more likely to be retained in grade than girls, and for most age and sex groups, the probability of being two or more grades behind is at least twice as high among minority children as it is among White children (Bruno & Adams, 1994).

According to data from the National Assessment of Educational Progress, which compared reading ability of students from 1971 to 1992, students in general were better readers in the 1980s than they were in the

1970s, but in 1992 the mean reading profile of African American and Hispanic *17 year olds* was very close to the mean reading profile of White *13 year olds* (Smith et al., 1995). Having a high school diploma, even with a poor achievement record in school, makes a significant improvement in labor market participation over many years (Lerman, 1996; Young, 1983).

A number of correlates of poor school performance appear to make the difference between staying in or dropping out of school for young at-risk adolescents. Dryfoos (1990) has estimated that the children at highest risk are those who live in disadvantaged families in impoverished neighborhoods and communities, get little support and encouragement from parents or other family members, and belong to a peer group whose members are also at risk for dropping out and serve as negative models. At the same time, the schools in these communities are under considerable stress and do not have sufficient resources to assist these children. In addition, they have relatively low expectations of success for these students and thus may not offer effective help even though there is some evidence that early interventions can succeed (see Sonenstein, Ku, Juffras, & Cohen, 1991, for a review of programs to prevent school failure during children's first years in school).

Involvement with child protection. One of the first signs to register in a public agency that children might be in serious trouble is a call to child protection that someone suspects abuse or neglect. Local public child protection agencies report these calls and their resulting actions and determinations to states, who in turn send the data to the National Center on Child Abuse and Neglect. The data contain duplications, as when more than one report is taken on the same child or family, but are the best available in the United States. In 1994, the latest year available, child protective service agencies received almost 2 million reports that were referred for investigation as potential cases of alleged child abuse or neglect. These calls involved approximately 2.9 million children, or approximately 4.3% of children under 18 in the population (see Exhibit 4.5). Investigations determined that maltreatment definitely or likely was occurring in approximately 37% of the reports, involving 38% of the children (National Center on Child Abuse and Neglect, 1996). Rates for victims in the 10–15 age range hover around 11 or 12 per 1,000 children of the same age, which is slightly lower than the 14 or 15 per 1,000 children of the same age for 0–8 year olds (older teens have the lowest reported rates, which may simply be an artifact of greater tendencies to report when the person involved is a younger child). The number of children found to be victims of maltreatment has risen sharply in recent years, going from approximately 800,000 to slightly more than 1 million children between 1990 and 1994 (an increase of almost 27%). Most of the jump occurred from 1990 to 1992, with steady figures since that time (National Center on Child Abuse and Neglect, 1996).

When family dysfunction reaches the point of child maltreatment or neglect or when an adolescent is considered uncontrollable or engages in criminal behavior, temporary or permanent placement for the adolescent

Exhibit 4.5. Prevalence Estimates for Involvement With Child Protection

In 1994, the situations of approximately 2.9 million children, or approximately 4.3% of children under 18 in the population, were investigated for possible abuse or neglect. Maltreatment was confirmed or likely in approximately 37% of the investigations, for 38% of the children (National Center on Child Abuse and Neglect, 1996). For victims ages 10–15, rates were 11 or 12 per 1,000 children of the same age; for victims ages 0–8, rates were 14 or 15 per 1,000 children. Victims of child maltreatment have increased almost 27% in recent years, from around 800,000 in 1990 to 1,011,628 in 1994. Most of the increase occurred from 1990 to 1992 (National Center on Child Abuse and Neglect, 1996).

Approximately 15% of the approximately 1 million children annually with confirmed situations of child abuse or neglect are placed in foster care (General Accounting Office, 1995). Between 1984 and 1990, the number of out-of-home placements increased by 65%, from 270,000 to 445,000—higher than at any time in the previous two decades. Estimates for 1994 show a further increase, to 462,000 (Tatara, 1994).

in an alternative family or group home environment is often the next step. This occurs for approximately 15% of the children with confirmed cases of abuse or neglect, although the rate varies greatly by state (Child Welfare League of America, 1996). From 1984 to 1993, the number of children in out-of-home care (including family foster care, kinship care, or care in residential facilities) increased by 65%, from 270,000 to 445,000. The American Public Welfare Association (APWA; Tatara, 1994) has estimated that the number of children in out-of-home care rose again in 1994, to 462,000. Finally, APWA estimates that between 1983 and 1990, the proportion of children in foster care who were 12 and older dropped from 47% to 32% (General Accounting Office, 1995). Calculations based on these figures suggest that approximately 128,000 adolescents spent some time in foster care in 1990.

Involvement with child protection at any level, and certainly foster care or alternative custody placement, can be a precursor or marker for more serious consequences, such as homelessness, delinquency, or substance abuse. A 1990 study reported that adolescents with a greater number of foster care placements tended to show greater difficulties in later life (Family Impact Seminar, 1990). A significant number of adolescents in foster care placements are abused physically or sexually by the foster parents (Fanshel, Finch, & Grundy, 1990), and there is a high likelihood that the adolescent will run away from foster care.

Problem Behaviors

Problem behaviors are defined as youth actions that can have negative consequences for the youth, the community, or both. In our conceptual framework, these are more than just indicators of problems, they *are* problems in and of themselves. Previous models of risk in adolescence have considered these behaviors as indicators of risk. But our conceptual framework focuses on the fact that adolescents displaying these behaviors certainly are troubled and thus are beyond early identification. If early sexual activity, drug use, and school dropout are to be thought of in any way as risk indicators, it can only be in relation to the range of serious consequences that are highly probable outcomes of these behaviors.

From a youth development perspective, most youth have some positive behaviors or competencies, even when they also show some problem behaviors. Our conceptual framework suggests the importance of highlighting both competencies and problem behaviors when assessing overall risk. The following positive behaviors have been found to moderate levels of risk among youth who are also engaging in risky behavior:

- School attendance and performance;
- Connectedness to school, independent of performance;
- Participation in community and church activities;
- Family connectedness;
- Religious/spiritual connectedness;
- Postponement of sexual behavior;
- Use of social, problem-solving, and peer skills; and
- High self-esteem and achievement motivation.

In the following review of literature, positive behaviors or competencies such as those just listed will be discussed within the context of their role, if known, as moderators of negative outcomes. In many respects we know much less of their role than we know about the multiple impact of problem behaviors, because the literature on the protective effects of positive behaviors tends to be more recent and thus sparser relative to that on negative behaviors.

Behaviors most consistently identified in the literature as indicating serious problems and as having the potential for future, more serious developmental consequences for youth include the following:

- School-related problem behavior such as truancy, absenteeism, and behaviors leading to suspension or expulsion;
- Early initiation and practice of sexual behavior;
- Running away from home (or from an out-of-home placement);
- Early use of tobacco, alcohol, and other drugs; and
- Associating with delinquent peers, gang membership, and involvement in crime and violence.

School-related problem behavior. Poor school performance figures in our conceptual framework as a system marker, and dropping out of school is considered an outcome. In between these two are problem behaviors associated with school, such as truancy, chronic absenteeism, and behavior problems that can lead to suspensions and expulsions. These might include getting into fights with other students, using or selling drugs on school grounds, carrying weapons on school grounds, or attacking a teacher. Many antecedents of poor school performance, described earlier

Exhibit 4.6.   Prevalence Estimates for School-Related Problem Behaviors

In-school drug and alcohol use by high school seniors fell dramatically during the 1980s. In 1980, 21% of seniors reported having used marijuana at school during the previous year, compared with only 5% in 1992. In 1992, 8% of 12th graders and 4% of 8th graders reported that they were under the influence of alcohol while at school at least 1 day in the previous month; 7% and 3%, respectively, reported the same likelihood of being under the influence of marijuana or some other illegal drug while at school during the previous month (Bruno & Adams, 1994).

One study of urban adolescent boys found 32% reporting all-day truancy and 40% reporting truancy from some classes (Resnick, Chambliss, & Blum, 1993). Resnick et al. (1993) have reported that school absenteeism was a problem strongly associated with other acting out behaviors (polydrug use, pregnancy risk, delinquency risk, and risk of unintentional injury).

Data from the 1988 National Survey of Adolescent Males indicates that 36% of nonpoor and 42% of poor boys ages 15–19 had been suspended from school at least once. In the 1990 follow-up, 6% of nonpoor and 13% of poor boys had been suspended at least once during the 2 years since their first interview (Chaplin & Merryman, 1996).

Data for 1993 from the Youth Risk Behavior Surveillance System show that 12% of respondents to this school-based survey reported carrying a weapon to school at least once during the 30 days before the survey. Boys were much more likely to do so than girls (18% and 5%, respectively; Centers for Disease Control, 1995a; see also Centers for Disease Control, 1991). Boys were also more likely than girls to get into physical fights at school (Centers for Disease Control, 1992).

---

during our discussion of system markers, are also associated with these school-related problem behaviors and ultimately with school dropout and failure to complete one's secondary education. Data reflecting population prevalence rates for these behaviors are not widely reported, and those breaking out data specifically for younger adolescents are even less available (see Exhibit 4.6).

Early sexual behavior. The chain of events for early adolescents at highest risk starts with early intercourse; followed by nonuse of protection at first intercourse; a long delay prior to obtaining contraception; and finally an unplanned, out-of-wedlock pregnancy (see Exhibit 4.7). Although the scope of the problem for the population of 10–15 year olds is considerably smaller than for older adolescents, the consequences are more serious. These younger adolescents are even less equipped to make pregnancy resolution and parenting decisions than their older counterparts. According to data from the National Survey of Family Growth, 82% of pregnancies among teenagers between the ages of 15–19 were unintended (Brown & Eisenberg, 1995). Moreover, pregnancies during early adolescence may signal nonvoluntary intercourse, sexual abuse, and rape (Moore, Nord, & Peterson, 1989). Age at first intercourse is strongly related to the number of sexual partners, so that youth who start intercourse

Exhibit 4.7.   Prevalence Rates for Early Sexual Behavior

The percentage of teens ages 13–17 who have had sexual intercourse has increased for both boys and girls across three cohorts; those who turned 20 in 1958–1960, 1970–1972, and 1985–1987 (Alan Guttmacher Institute, 1994). Ten percent of girls who turned 20 in 1985–1987 and 27% of boys in the same cohort reported having had intercourse before the age of 15 (Alan Guttmacher Institute, 1994). According to the 1992 National Health Interview Survey, at age 15, 58% of African American boys were sexually active compared with 19% of White boys and 27% of Hispanic boys. Among girls, 39% of African Americans were sexually active by age 15 compared with 25% of Whites and Hispanics, respectively (OASPE, 1996).

In terms of contraceptive use, 27% of sexually active girls ages 15–17 used no contraception in 1988 (OASPE, 1996). However, contraceptive use varied by race and ethnicity: 35% of Hispanic girls ages 15–17, compared with 23% of African American girls and 19% of White girls were using no contraception, according to the same 1988 data from the National Survey of Family Growth. Among boys ages 17–19, there was an increase in condom use from 20% in 1979 (OASPE, 1996) to 52% in 1991 (Pleck, Sonenstein, & Ku, 1993).

earlier are likely to have a greater number of sexual partners (OASPE, 1996). Among sexually active teens, African American boys and boys living in poverty are likely to have a higher number of partners than girls from the same groups. The earlier the age at first intercourse, the longer the delay in going to a clinic to obtain contraception, hence the greater the risk for an unplanned pregnancy (OASPE, 1996).

Factors that predict the increased likelihood of early sexual activity include being male, being African American, living in a low-income family, and lacking parental support and monitoring of the child's activities (Moore, Miller, Glei, & Morrison, 1995). In addition, children who are not involved in school activities, who have low expectations for school achievement, and who are easily influenced by friends in similar situations are more prone to early sexual activity. Early sexual activity often is also preceded by other high-risk behavior, including early substance abuse and truancy (Dryfoos, 1990).

Older White girls from higher income levels are most likely to use contraception (OASPE, 1996). Factors predicting nonuse of contraception among teenagers include (a) Hispanic minority background, (b) greater impulsiveness and lack of internal locus of control, (c) involvement in casual sex rather than being in a committed relationship, (d) low prospects for the future, low educational expectations, low grades, and (e) parents with low educational achievement and poor communication with their teenager.

Running away and youth homelessness. In our conceptual framework, running away from home is a problem behavior, and youth homelessness is a negative outcome. Because data on both are scarce and are rarely reported separately, however, we present prevalence information together for both (see Exhibit 4.8).

Exhibit 4.8.   Prevalence Estimates for Running Away and Homelessness

Little is known about unaccompanied homeless youth on a national basis. Management information system data for the nation's runaway and homeless youth shelters indicate that approximately 60,000 youth receive residential services from these facilities each year. Of these youth, in 1995 55% were female and 45% were male; approximately 45% of both sexes were 14 or younger at the time of their contact with the service agency.[1] Many more youth use the shelters' counseling and hotline services. However, street youth are the least likely to use these facilities, and their numbers remain a matter of guesswork.

Data on numbers of adolescents ages 10–15 who are homeless with their families are not available. One report estimates that 12% of homeless families include an adolescent between 13 and 16 years of age, and another 36% of homeless families have a child between the ages of 6 and 12 years (General Accounting Office, 1989). Another study found that 26.6% of families living in homeless shelters had children between the ages of 11 and 17 (Miller & Lin, 1988). In neither case is it clear whether these adolescents were with the families in shelter or had been left with other relatives. If we assume, from estimates of shelter use, that approximately 30,000 families are in shelters on an average day and have two children with them, on average (Burt & Cohen, 1989), then approximately 8,000 adolescents are homeless with their families in a shelter on an average day.

Youth become homeless on their own (i.e., without their parents) as a consequence of running away, being deserted or kicked out of the home by their parents, or their parent or guardian becoming homeless and unable to bring the youth to the shelter or welfare hotel (Office of Technology Assessment, 1991).[2] The National Network for Youth differentiates among *runaways*, who are away from home at least overnight without parental or guardian permission; *homeless youth*, who have no parental, foster, or institutional home and who may have left with the parent's knowledge; and *street kids*, who are long-term runaways or homeless youth who have been able to live on the streets, usually through illegal activities (National Network for Youth, 1991). Some youth, termed *throwaways* or *thrownaways*, have been told to leave their family or have been abandoned or deserted by their parent or guardian. Many homeless youth have run away from a foster care or institutional placement. Some studies have estimated that anywhere from 10–50% of runaways are actually throwaways (Adams, Gulotta, & Clancy, 1985). The distinction is important because throwaways are more likely to have been the victims of physical violence prior

---

[1] Data requested from the Family and Youth Services Bureau (FYSB), HHS, and supplied by Information Technology International, which administers FYSB's runaway and homeless youth management information system.

[2] Some adolescents become homeless because their families have lost their housing. Little research exists on adolescents who live with their families in shelters, and not much is known about the short- or long-term consequences of homelessness for these adolescents (Office of Technology Assessment, 1991). Our discussion concentrates on runaways and on unaccompanied homeless youth.

to leaving home and are twice as likely to stay away longer (Finkelhor, Hotaling, & Sedlak, 1990).

According to some research, homeless adolescents tend to be African American or Hispanic, to come from lower socioeconomic backgrounds, and to be from single-parent or stepfamilies (Rotheram-Borus, Koopman, & Ehrhardt, 1991). Caution should be exercised in interpreting these data, however, because much of this information is based on empirical studies of shelters for runaway and homeless youth rather than from the population as a whole. Before becoming homeless, these adolescents had moved frequently, transferred schools, and if male, were more likely to have been jailed or spent time in detention facilities.

The consequences of homelessness for adolescents include greater likelihood of physical assault and victimization, including rape or sexual assault and robbery; increased rates of drug abuse; and increased rates of depression. These youth are younger at first intercourse, have more sexual partners, and are more likely to engage in sexual risk behaviors than are nonhomeless adolescents. The consequences of these behaviors include dramatically increased risk of HIV infection and other sexually transmitted disease, as well as pregnancy and teenage motherhood (Rotheram-Borus et al., 1991). Between 50% and 71% of street youth have a sexually transmitted disease; pregnancy and motherhood are significantly higher among homeless girls; and the average age at first intercourse is approximately 12.5 for homeless youth, approximately 2 years earlier than for other adolescents. Homeless youth are also five times more likely to meet the criteria for a diagnosis of drug abuse than are nonhomeless adolescents (Rotheram-Borus et al., 1991).

Use of tobacco, alcohol, and illegal drugs. Systematically collected national data exist from household and school-based surveys to estimate the rates of tobacco, alcohol, and illegal drug use among adolescents (see Exhibit 4.9). Sources include the Youth Risk Behavior Surveillance System; the National Institute on Drug Abuse National Household Surveys on Drug Abuse; the High School Senior Surveys (HSSS), which in 1991 also surveyed 8th and 10th graders; and Monitoring the Future, which is a national classroom-based survey.

Combined prevalence. A relatively strong research literature now exists that explores the co-occurrence of multiple problems in adolescence (Allen et al., 1994; Botvin, 1986, 1990; Elliott, Huizinga, & Menard, 1989; Fergusson et al., 1994; Ginzberg et al., 1988), although no single study encompasses every possible problem behavior and negative outcome. There are also studies that look at the co-occurrence of many aspects of risk, including antecedent conditions, protective factors, and problem behaviors (Garmezy, 1991; Paternoster & Mazerolle, 1994; Resnick, Harris, & Blum, 1993; Werner, 1989). This research supports earlier findings that many problem behaviors share common antecedent characteristics, and it argues that a common dynamic probably precedes engagement in the many potential problem behaviors of youth. Therefore, different levels of

Exhibit 4.9.   Prevalence Estimates for Tobacco, Alcohol, and Illegal Drug Use

Data from the National Household Survey on Drug Abuse for 1995 indicate that 44% of boys and 36% of girls ages 12–17 have ever smoked cigarettes. Twelve percent of boys and 11% of girls had smoked cigarettes within the month before the survey (Substance Abuse and Mental Health Service Administration, 1996).

The trend in alcohol use by secondary school students has remained stable or declined in the 1990s. Alcohol use declined from 1991 to 1995, when it was 45.3% for 8th graders, 63.5% for 10th graders, and 73.7% for 12th graders (University of Michigan, 1995). A youth's age at first use of alcohol is often used as a marker for later alcohol abuse as well as for later use of other drugs (Welte & Barnes, 1985). Data from the 1993 Youth Risk Behavior Survey show that 33.6% of all students sampled from Grades 9–12 had first consumed alcohol before age 12 (Centers for Disease Control, 1995a).

Data from the National Household Survey on Drug Abuse for 1995 indicate that current use of illicit drugs among youth ages 12–17 has been increasing steadily since 1992, even though these levels are substantially lower than the rates reported in 1979 (Substance Abuse and Mental Health Services Administration, 1996). For youth ages 12–17, the current rate of past month drug use (primarily marijuana) has reached 11%, compared with a low of 5% in 1992 and a high of 18% in 1979. There has been an increase in illicit drug use among students in Grades 8–12. Data from the school-based survey Monitoring the Future show that annual prevalence rates of illicit drug use among 8th graders increased from 11.3% in 1991 to 21.4% in 1995. Similarly, the annual prevalence of illicit drug use among 10th graders increased from 21.4% in 1991 to 33.3% in 1995, and among 12th graders, the prevalence rate of illicit drug use increased from 29% in 1991 to 39% in 1995 (University of Michigan, 1995). Finally, the literature indicates that African American teens are less likely than adolescents from any other racial or ethnic group to report the use of an illicit drug (Office of Technology Assessment, 1991).

risk can be defined according to the number and seriousness of multiple problem behaviors that a youth exhibits (e.g., school failure, substance abuse, delinquency, or pregnancy).

Several recent data sources give us the opportunity to identify co-occurring problem behaviors and also to examine which factors serve to protect youth from participating in these behaviors. Resnick, Harris, and Blum (1993), using data from the Adolescent Health Survey, which was administered as a school-based survey to more than 30,000 youth throughout Minnesota, have found very high rates of participation in at least one problem behavior but relatively low proportions of youth who participate in many. A factor analysis of nine scales of problem behaviors found that the scales grouped in two clusters. The first cluster, Acting Out Behaviors (with their factor loadings) includes polydrug use (.74); school absenteeism (.68); unintended injury risk, such as drinking and driving, not wearing seatbelts, and not using a helmet on a motorcycle (.68); risk of becoming pregnant or causing a pregnancy (.61); and delinquency risk (.56). That these serious behavior problems cluster so strongly gives ample evidence that youth in serious trouble are probably in trouble in a lot of ways. The second cluster, Quietly Disturbed Behaviors, includes poor body image

(.80); disordered eating, including binging, bulimia, and chronic dieting; fear of loss of control over eating (.79); emotional stress (.69); and suicidal ideation or attempts (.51).

We can also get some idea of proportions from the information reported in Resnick, Harris, and Blum (1993), who noted that "some 80 percent of students fell into the high-risk category for at least one of the behaviors, with about 10 percent at high risk for four or more behaviors" (p. 55). Calculating proportions from their tables yields the following: 34% of girls were in the high-risk category on quietly disturbed behaviors, with 56% being at high-risk for acting out. Among boys, only 12% were at high risk for quietly disturbed behaviors, and 56% (same as for the girls) were at high risk for acting out behaviors. Four out of five girls who scored as high risk for two or more quietly disturbed behaviors also scored as high risk for at least one acting out behavior, and of those scoring high for two or more acting out behaviors, 65% also engaged in at least one quietly disturbed behavior.

The National Survey of Adolescent Males can also provide some sense of overlapping problem behaviors among young men ages 15–19 in 1991. Pleck, Sonenstein, Ku, and Burbridge (in press) have reported the following: (a) 21%, sexual intercourse at age 14 or earlier; (b) 43%, first use of alcohol at age 15 or earlier; (c) 20%, first use of marijuana at age 15 or earlier; (d) 30%, ever retained in grade; and (e) number of multiple risk markers: 0, 33%; 1, 34%; 2, 22%; 3, 10%; 4, 2%. The second panel of the same survey, interviewing another sample of boys 15–19 years old in 1995, found that 56% were sexually experienced; 37% had some involvement with criminal behavior (picked up by police, arrested, jailed); and 37% had used marijuana, cocaine, or other illegal drugs during the previous 12 months. Examination of co-occurrence revealed that 29.2% exhibited none of these problem behaviors, and 16.3% exhibited all three. Other combinations were sex only, 16.7%; drugs only, 5.0%; crime only, 5.5%; sex and drugs, 11.6%; sex and crime, 11.7%; and drugs and crime, 4.0% (Sonenstein, Lindberg, Stewart, & Pernas, 1996).

Influence of protective factors. Recent analyses of large population surveys with representative samples are beginning to reveal patterns of protective factors and the ways in which they may modulate the effects of antecedent risk factors and system markers on youth problem behaviors. These findings are very important because they identify factors that can be fostered and promoted with appropriate program designs and community organization.

Paternoster and Mazerolle (1994), using data from the National Youth Survey of 1978 with youth ages 11 to 17, have modeled a number of antecedent conditions and protective factors on delinquency at two points in time. Living in a poor neighborhood, negative relationships with adults, and negative life events (including many that we would classify as family dysfunction) were all related to delinquency cross-sectionally (at Time 1) and longitudinally (at Time 2). A youth's moral beliefs, however, served a protective function, lowering the likelihood of delinquency in both time periods.

Data from Minnesota Adolescent Health Surveys show the co-occurrence of protective factors of caring and connectedness. These data strongly support the protective effects of these relationships for youth. Data from school-based adolescent health surveys[3] indicate significant associations among youth perceptions that parents, other adults, school people, church people, and friends care about them. Correlations among individual indicators ranged from .22 to .62, with most in the .30–.49 range. Individually and collectively, these indicators of caring and connectedness are important deterrents to high-risk behaviors. Resnick, Harris, and Blum (1993) have reported that school connectedness (independent of performance), family connectedness, religious or spiritual connectedness, and low family stress strongly predict low risk for both boys and girls on a vector of acting out behaviors (e.g., polydrug use, absenteeism, pregnancy risk, risk of unintentional injury, and delinquency risk). Many of the same indicators of caring and connectedness have the same protective effects for reducing quietly disturbed behaviors (e.g., poor body image, disordered eating, emotional distress, suicidality). Data from the National Longitudinal Study on Adolescent Health show similar patterns (Blum & Rinehart, 1997; Resnick et al., 1997).

Finally, Pleck et al. (in press), using data from the National Survey of Adolescent Males for young men ages 15–19, have reported that the protective factors they examined—strict family rules at age 14 and church attendance—moderated the impact of family structure (arrangements other than a two-parent family) on problem behaviors. Strict family rules and frequent church attendance helped youth in alternative family structures achieve the same (lower) levels of problem behaviors observed among youth growing up in two-parent families.

Negative Outcomes

Negative outcomes are the final stage in our conceptual model. These outcomes are clearly injurious conditions that have negative consequences for a youth's future development as a responsible, self-sufficient adult. The flip side of the coin, positive outcomes, may be possible among youth with prior problem behaviors or system markers when protective factors and interventions to strengthen them are sufficient to counteract negative influences. These youth are termed *resilient* because they have been protected from experiencing the debilitating effects of their difficult circum-

---

[3]Michael Resnick of the National Adolescent Health Resource Center, University of Minnesota, Minneapolis, generously ran intercorrelations of protective factors from the Center's ongoing statewide surveys of adolescent health, risky behaviors, resilience, and protective factors (1986–1987 Minnesota Adolescent Health Survey, N = 36,254 7th–12th graders; 1992 Minnesota Student Survey, N = 136,000 6th, 9th, and 12th graders; 1994 North Carolina Evaluation of School-Based Health Centers; and 1992 Delaware School-Based Health Centers Evaluation, N = 2,500).

stances and appear likely to become fully functioning adults. Positive outcomes for these youth include stable jobs with adequate pay, strong family formation, childbearing delayed until parents have adequate economic and social capital, community participation, and supportive (not abusive) relationships. Furthermore, although these are the more tangible positive outcomes for developing youth, another set of less easily measured outcomes are also posited as part of positive youth development (Pittman & Zeldin, 1992), including the following:

- Interpersonal skills of communication and negotiation;
- Close attachments with mainstream organizations, adults, and peers;
- Integrity, positive personal identity, autonomy, and faith;
- Mastery of one or more "age-appropriate" tasks;
- Feelings of mastery, cognitive competencies, and strategies; and
- Appreciation of and ability to interact with culturally diverse persons.

Negative outcomes are consequences of engaging in problem behaviors and represent the endpoint for adolescents who do not receive preventive interventions to counteract antecedents, the behavior that leads to system markers, and problem behaviors. The adolescent who engages in problem behaviors for any period of time is likely to experience one or more of several long-term consequences, including the following:

- Dropping out of school, poor credentials for economic self-sufficiency;
- Pregnancy, childbearing, poor pregnancy outcomes;
- Sexually transmitted diseases, including chlamydia and AIDS;
- Abuse of or addiction to alcohol or other drugs, and associated health problems;
- Homelessness, physical abuse and battering, sexual abuse, rape or incest, prostitution;
- Death or permanent injury from guns, knives, and other violent behavior; automobile accidents, other accidents;
- Other morbidity or mortality outcomes, such as hepatitis, tuberculosis, pneumonia, and AIDS complications;
- Depression, suicide; and
- Criminal convictions.

Many of these consequences are simply more serious and chronic versions of what began as problem behaviors. The continued practice of and exposure to repeated chronic problem behaviors will increase the probability that a young person will die before reaching the age of 20—the "ultimate" and most extreme outcome.

School dropout. Failure to complete secondary school and obtain a high school diploma has serious consequences for the types of employment

Exhibit 4.10.   Prevalence Estimates for School Dropout

Of the students entering the eighth grade in 1988, 11.6% were dropouts (not enrolled in school and had not finished high school) in 1992, 4 years later. Boys and girls experienced the same rates, but rates of African Americans and Hispanics (14.5% and 18.3%, respectively) were higher than those for Whites (9.4%; Bruno & Adams, 1994).

one can get and one's earning ability both immediately and over a lifetime. Many factors affect the likelihood that a youth will fail to complete school; most have been discussed in relation to school-related system markers (poor performance) and problem behaviors (truancy, absenteeism, and behaviors leading to suspension or expulsion). Ten–fifteen year olds may be at risk for school dropout, but the prevalence of risk in this population is not fully reflected in the dropout rate because school attendance is compulsory until age 16 (see Exhibit 4.10). Younger adolescents may virtually drop out of school through repeated truancy, suspension, or expulsion, but schools will still carry them as officially enrolled until their 16th birthday. Dryfoos (1990) has argued that many expected outcomes of school failure may also function as antecedents or markers. Also, delinquent behavior, including truancy and minor offenses during early adolescence, typically occurs prior to actual school dropout or failure. But once youth leave school, they are more likely than those who remain to commit serious offenses. Little adequate prevalence data exist to indicate the numbers of truant youth, either in total or by age. Furthermore, younger adolescents may not be adequately represented in truancy and dropout statistics if they are runaways or homeless or have been suspended from school.

Pregnancy and teenage childbearing. A vast literature exists describing the antecedents and consequences of teenage childbearing (Hayes, 1987; Moore, Miller, et al., 1995). In addition, numbers and rates of teen births are routinely reported in the *Monthly Vital Statistics Report*, published by the Department of Health and Human Services; in *Facts at a Glance*, published annually by Child Trends, Inc., a Washington-based research organization, and in policy-oriented summaries of statistics and research (Brown & Eisenberg, 1995; Moore, Miller, et al., 1995; OASPE, 1996; see Exhibit 4.11).

Among sexually active teens age 17 years or younger, only 1 in 100 wanted a pregnancy to occur, and this was true for both boys and girls, and for both African Americans and Whites (Moore & Peterson, 1989). According to one estimate, there is a 90% chance that a sexually active girl age 15–19 who does not use contraception will become pregnant during 1 year (Harlap, Kost, & Forrest, 1991). For all adolescents, close to one in four sexually active teens (23%) experience a pregnancy during the year. Birth rates among girls ages 10 to 14 remained relatively stable from 1970 to 1988 (Dryfoos, 1990). Among sexually experienced teenagers, approximately 9% of 14 year olds and 18% of 15–17 year olds become pregnant each year. Of African American teenage girls ages 15–19, 19% be-

Exhibit 4.11.   Prevalence Estimates for Pregnancy and Childbearing

In 1991, 1.7% of teenage girls ages 14 years or younger became pregnant. During the same year, 7.5% of all girls ages 15–17 years became pregnant. Of all sexually active girls ages 15–19, in 1991, 20.9% became pregnant (Ventura, Taffel, Mosher, Wilson, & Henshaw, 1995). However, from 1991 to 1992 there was a slight decline in pregnancy rates for girls ages 15–19 years (OASPE, 1996).

A large disparity exists in birth rates for African American compared with White younger adolescents. For Whites ages 10 to 14, the rate was 0.7 births per 1,000 in 1989 compared with 5.0 births per 1,000 for African Americans (Dryfoos, 1990). In 1993, for 15–17 year olds, the birth rate per 1,000 for African American adolescents was 2½ times the rate for Whites, 79.8 compared with 30.3. The rate for Hispanic teens of the same age was 71.7 (OASPE, 1996). Dryfoos (1990) has estimated that 1.9 million adolescents 10–14 years of age are at risk due to their early sexual activity. Approximately 300,000 adolescent girls ages 10–14 years are likely to become pregnant each year; of these, one third will become parents.

Many fathers of the children born to teenage mothers are not teenagers themselves. According to 1988 data from the National Maternal and Infant Health Survey, for mothers who were 15 at the time their child was born, 39% of the fathers were 20 years or older (OASPE, 1996).

Nonmarital births among 15–17 year olds made up 79% of all births to this age group in 1992, compared with 65% of all births among 18–19 year olds. Increases in nonmarital childbearing have been highest among White girls ages 15–19, rising from 7% of births in 1960 to 60% of births in 1992 (OASPE, 1996).

---

come pregnant each year, compared with 13% of Hispanics and 8% of Whites (Alan Guttmacher Institute, 1994).

Particular attention is also focused on nonmarital childbearing by teens (OASPE, 1996). A large body of research indicates that the absence of a father is associated with a host of negative outcomes for children (Wilson, 1987), and studies have linked female-headed single parenting with children's lower educational achievement (Knox & Bane, 1994). In 1992, 93% of births to African American girls ages 15–19 were nonmarital, compared with less than two thirds (still high) among Whites and Hispanics; nonmarital births are more prevalent among younger teens (OASPE, 1996). Finally, younger adolescents who are likely to become teen parents fit the pattern described earlier of having low school achievement; being in a peer group that accepts parenthood; living in poor, single-mother-headed families; and having unsupportive parents who do not monitor their activities. All of the antecedent conditions and system markers included in our conceptual framework have been found to be associated with greater risks of becoming pregnant and giving birth as a teenager (Hayes, 1987; Moore, Miller, et al., 1995; OASPE, 1996).

Sexually transmitted diseases, including HIV infection. Increased exposure to sexually transmitted diseases and AIDS comes from both

Exhibit 4.12.   Prevalence Estimates for Sexually Transmitted Diseases

---

Between 1991 and 1994, the gonorrhea rate for 10–14 year olds declined from 64.6 per 100,000 cases to 50.4 cases per 100,000. During the same period, gonorrhea among 15–19 year olds declined 26%, from 1031.4 per 100,000 cases in 1991 to 763.4 per 100,000 cases in 1994. During the same time period, the syphilis rates for 10–14 year olds declined 53%, from 249 per 100,000 to 118 cases per 100,000; for 15–19 year olds the rate declined 52%, from 4,675 per 100,000 to 2,234 per 100,000 (Centers for Disease Control, 1995b).

In 1990, AIDS was the sixth leading cause of death among 15–24 year olds, although cases of AIDS among adolescents ages 13–19 represented less than 1% of all AIDS cases. Centers for Disease Control HIV/AIDS Surveillance Reports show that through June 1996, 726 cases of AIDS occurred among 13–19 year old White boys, 560 cases among 13–19 year old African American boys, and 327 cases among 13–19 year old Hispanic boys. For 13–19 year old girls, there were 169 cases among Whites, 605 cases among African Americans, and 145 cases among Hispanics (Centers for Disease Control, 1996). Overall, 1,647 cases of HIV/AIDS were reported through June 1996 among boys ages 13–19 years, and 927 cases were reported among girls in the same age group, which represents a 1.8:1 ratio of male to female cases.

The prevalence of HIV infection may give a more accurate indication of the potential AIDS problem within the youth population than does the count of reported AIDS cases, because of the long incubation period for AIDS. Data from Job Corps entrants, who are economically disadvantaged 16–21 year olds, show a seroprevalence rate of 3.6 per 1,000, which is 10 times higher than among military applicants the same age ("remarkably high . . . for a population so young and not specifically selected because of behavioral risk factors"; St. Louis et al., 1991). The high rate of HIV infection among younger girls suggests that heterosexual transmission of HIV may be responsible rather than intravenous drug use, which is higher among boys.

---

the practice of risky sexual behaviors and from environments in which high-risk adolescents live (see Exhibit 4.12 for prevalence rates). One of the more serious consequences for adolescents who develop an STD (particularly those with syphilis) is the increased likelihood of their becoming HIV-infected (Office of Technology Assessment, 1991). Because the average incubation period between HIV infection and the development of AIDS may be as long as 8–12 years, many adolescents who become infected as teenagers may not show signs or symptoms until early adulthood (D'Angelo, Getson, Luban, & Gayle, 1991). In some disadvantaged samples, the rate of HIV infection is high, particularly among younger girls, and appears to be due to high rates of heterosexual transmission, as seen among youth entering the national Job Corps program (Resnick & Giambo, 1996; St. Louis et al., 1991) as well as street, homeless, or runaway youth (Office of Technology Assessment, 1991; Rotheram-Borus et al., 1991). Needle use is a direct source of HIV infection for only a small proportion of at-risk youth, but for many other youth, it is a conduit for transmission of the virus to female sexual partners (Office of Technology Assessment, 1991).

Substance abuse. Most studies note that the use of tobacco, alcohol, or other substances by adolescents does not necessarily lead to abuse (Brown & Horowitz, 1993). High-risk behavior may be placed on a continuum of no use to excessive use according to the following criteria: those substance use behaviors that will have damaging consequences over time, prevent normal growth and development, and limit an individual's potential for achieving responsible adulthood (Dryfoos, 1990). According to these criteria, high risk of substance abuse may be defined as the high probability of frequent and heavy drug use, as measured by two indicators: current use and heavy use.

Two types of alcoholism have been identified in the literature (Cloninger, Sigvardsson, & Bohman, 1988), but only the early onset of alcohol use and alcohol problems are relevant to our efforts to estimate the prevalence of negative outcomes in adolescence. This type of alcoholism is associated with frequent impulsive and aggressive behavior among adolescents, which leads to other risky behavior, such as driving while intoxicated, unprotected sexual behavior, violence, criminal activity, and impulse-control problems (Cloninger et al., 1988).

An inherent danger exists in identifying risk factors for alcohol and drug abuse, because of the difficulties in differentiating use from abuse. A "risk factor mythology" develops in which so many risk factors are identified that practically all adolescents could be considered to be potential abusers (Brown & Horowitz, 1993). Furthermore, by considering all adolescents to be at risk, the emphasis could mistakenly be placed on illness and pathology rather than on normal adolescent development (Brown & Horowitz, 1993). With this in mind, we consider a relatively limited number of antecedent factors that appear consistently in the literature (Dryfoos, 1990; Hawkins, Catalano, & Miller, 1992; Office of Juvenile Justice Programs, 1995) as predictors of drug use in early adolescence, including (a) early initiation (ages 10–12); (b) school problems, including poor performance, low grades, and truancy; (c) lack of parental support and guidance; (d) associating with drug-using peers and being easily swayed by peer opinion; and (e) having an independent, rebellious, or nonconformist personality.

Additionally, the absence of laws and norms that prohibit or limit the availability of alcohol to young teenagers, extreme economic deprivation, neighborhood disorganization, sensation-seeking and other physiological factors, family drug behavior, family management practices, family conflict, lack of family cohesiveness, early and persistent problem behaviors, academic failure and school dropout, peer rejection in the elementary grades, and early onset of drug use are all factors contributing to drug abuse identified by the literature (Hawkins et al., 1992). Finally, some writers have suggested a "developmental sequence" to the unfolding of antisocial, sexual, and drug-using behaviors that produce a "problem behavior syndrome" (Dishion & Andrews, 1995). According to this view, antisocial behavior tends to precede substance abuse for both boys and girls, so that interventions that target antisocial behavior and its correlates

Exhibit 4.13. Prevalence Estimates for Adolescent Mortality

According to the 1993 Youth Risk Behavior Survey, in that year four causes accounted for 72% of all deaths among school-age youth and young adults 5–24 years old: motor vehicle crashes (30% of all deaths); other unintentional injuries, such as drowning and fires (12% of all deaths); homicide (19%) and suicide (11% of all deaths; Centers for Disease Control, 1995a). For youth ages 10–14, rates of death due to injuries decreased from 23.6 to 16.3 per 100,000 between 1950 and 1987, whereas the rates for older adolescents ages 15–19 increased over the same period (Office of Technology Assessment, 1991). Dryfoos (1990) has reported suicide and homicide rates for youth ages 12–17 using data from the National Center for Health Statistics. From 1980 to 1986, rates increased in each of four groups (African American and White adolescents in age groups 12–14 and 15–17), with the largest increases reported among African American 12–14 year olds. Overall, 7% of deaths in the 12–14 year old group were due to suicide in 1986 and 6% were due to homicide.

---

early in adolescence may reduce the likelihood of substance use by middle adolescence (Dishion & Andrews, 1995).

Adolescent mortality and causes of death. The 1993 Youth Risk Behavior Surveillance System indicates that in that year, the single leading cause of accidental injury deaths for 10–14 year olds was vehicle-related accidents, typically with the youth as a passenger (Centers for Disease Control, 1995a). Other causes of accidental injury deaths for this age group include other unintentional injuries, such as drowning and fires (see Exhibit 4.13). A host of factors have been found to be related to accidental injuries, including demographic characteristics (age, gender, race and ethnicity, and social class); risk-taking behavior (alcohol or drug abuse, failure to use safety belts, and failure to use bicycle or motorcycle helmets); and stressful life events (suspension from school, failing a grade level, difficulty getting a summer job, breaking up with a boyfriend or girlfriend, and the death of a grandparent). African American male teens are five to six times more likely to die from homicide than White male teens, and African American female teens have two to three times the death rate from homicide of White female teens (Centers for Disease Control, 1995a). The suicide rate among Native American adolescents is four times higher than for all other races (Centers for Disease Control, 1995a).

Delinquency and criminal behavior. In general, *delinquent* acts are either criminal offenses or status offenses. *Criminal offenses* are acts committed by minors that would be violations of criminal law if committed by an adult, such as murder, rape, assault, robbery, theft, burglary, or vandalism. *Status offenses* are acts committed by minors that would not be offenses if committed by an adult, such as running away from home, truancy, or alcohol use.

Most adolescents become involved in some level of behavior that could be considered delinquent during the course of their adolescence, but the infractions tend to be relatively minor status offenses (see Exhibit 4.14).

Exhibit 4.14.   Prevalence Estimates for Delinquency and Criminal Behavior

Estimates of delinquent behavior and delinquent youth come from a variety of sources, including rates of offenses and arrests provided through the Uniform Crime Reports, self-reported delinquency and criminal behavior from the National Youth Survey, and victimization rates from the National Crime Survey. Several data sources are required to pinpoint delinquency because no single source provides an adequate measure of delinquency among adolescents (Elliott, Dunford, & Huizinga, 1987; Huizinga & Elliott, 1986). In the National Youth Survey, 21% of youth in the sample reported having committed at least one serious offense in 1976 (Elliott, Ageton, Huizinga, Knowles, & Canter, 1983). Between 1982 and 1992, the juvenile arrest rate for murder and nonnegligent manslaughter rose 122.7% (Maguire & Pastore, 1994). According to the Federal Bureau of Investigation's 1993 Uniform Crime Reports, juvenile arrests between 1984 and 1993 rose 40% for robbery, 98% for aggravated assault, and 106% for motor vehicle theft (Federal Bureau of Investigation, 1994). According to some estimates, approximately 20% of adolescents commit muggings, robbery, or gang assaults, but only a small minority (5–8% of boys and 3–6% of girls) are responsible for most of these acts (Elliott et al., 1983, 1989; Tracy et al., 1990).

Reviews of the literature have shown that a very small minority of adolescents tend to be responsible for most of the serious offenses and that many adolescents who have been exposed to risk factors do not become offenders (Office of Technology Assessment, 1991). Chronic juvenile offenders, compared with nonchronic offenders, are more likely to begin delinquent behaviors at an earlier age, to commit them more often and at older ages, and to commit a variety of offenses rather than specializing in a single type of offense. These youth usually commit relatively few serious offenses and many minor offenses and are therefore more likely to be arrested for a minor offense. The likely causes of delinquent behavior among younger, as opposed to older, adolescents consist of those risk factors that occur earlier and that are most likely to predispose them to later delinquency. However, few risk factors for delinquency act independently, and many of the risk factors are interrelated in ways that still are not well understood.

A generally accepted perspective on the development of delinquent behavior in adolescents focuses on the convergence of social controls, personal controls, and supervision that either keep a youth from wanting to engage in delinquent behavior or fail to provide sufficient external constraints (Gottfredson & Gottfredson, 1992; Paternoster & Mazerolle, 1994). Social controls refer to the bonds of social order that youth should be socialized to follow: attachment to school, belief in conventional social rules, and commitment to conventional goals. Adolescents who have these expectations are less likely to engage in delinquent behaviors (Bynum & Thompson, 1995; Gottfredson, 1984; Paternoster & Mazerolle, 1994; West, 1982). Adolescents who are not adequately supervised by their parents, however, either because the parents are laissez-faire in their supervisory style or because parents are overly authoritarian, are more likely to engage in delinquent activities (Gottfredson & Hirschi, 1990). Association with delinquent or drug-involved peers, combined with low self-esteem or high levels of alienation as well as impulsivity and the inability to resist temptation, are also important failures in personal controls that lead to delinquent behavior (Gottfredson & Gottfredson, 1992). Finally, there is strong support in the literature for the co-occurrence of drug abuse and delinquency (Hawkins, Jenson, Catalano, & Lishner, 1988). Risk factors for both delinquency and crime include early problem behavior and conduct disorders in elementary school grades, parent and sibling drug use and criminal behavior, poor and inconsistent family-management practices, family conflict, family social and economic deprivation, school failure, low degree of commitment to education and attachment to school, peer factors, attitudes and beliefs about the social order, and community disorganization, the family's residential mobility, and finally constitutional– physiological or other endogenous as well as psychological factors (Hawkins et al., 1988).

Although it is difficult to specify the variety of combinations that will lead to delinquent behaviors, a number of likely "constellations" of factors appear consistently in the literature (Hawkins et al., 1988; Office of Technology Assessment, 1991), as follows:

- Family variables have either a direct effect, as in the case of parenting practices, or an indirect effect, such as poor marital relations or family size, by interfering with the ability of parents to properly supervise or be involved with their child;
- A child who has attention deficit/hyperactivity disorder (ADD) and is impulsive and difficult to control may be "matched" with a parent who does not have adequate personal and social resources and supports to deal with this child;
- Child maltreatment may be both a cause and an effect and is a symptom of a dysfunctional family in which family violence is legitimized and teaches the child how to behave in the larger society; and
- Neighborhood factors have an indirect effect and operate in conjunction with family and peer factors.

Finally, some children in high-risk situations (due to the multiple operation of the factors just cited) may not become juvenile offenders. Protective factors that contribute to resiliency among children exposed to risk factors include having a good relationship with at least one adult and having a supportive school environment (Garmezy, Masten, & Tellegen, 1984; Rutter, 1979, 1985; Werner, 1986, 1988, 1989).

Concluding Thoughts

This chapter has been organized according to a conceptual framework of risk containing six components: risk antecedents, protective factors, system markers, problem behaviors, positive behaviors, and negative outcomes. The framework is based on evidence showing that many problem behaviors share similar antecedents and that certain factors in the environment may serve to protect the developing adolescent from engaging in problem behaviors. Furthermore, even if the adolescent displays problem behaviors early on, if he or she can build positive behaviors and competencies, then longer term negative outcomes could be averted.

The conceptual framework is particularly geared toward early adolescence. Many points in a young person's life may be appropriate for intervention (Office of Juvenile Justice Programs, 1995), and it is quite likely that the earlier that intervention occurs, the better the outcome. Childhood might be best, but this book focuses on adolescence for those interested in that period. Our framework assumes that one can intervene to prevent later problems if adolescents likely to experience those problems can be identified when they are younger. Although few studies properly disaggregate the subgroups of early (10–15 year old) and late (16–19 year old) adolescents, it is critical that risk be considered separately for these two groups of adolescents because service needs as well as the proper mix of prevention and treatment strategies will differ. Yet we also caution against the belief that age alone is an indicator of degree of risk and hence of appropriateness for prevention activities.

Dryfoos (1990) has pointed to six common characteristics that predict high risk of the four main problem behaviors of adolescence: substance abuse, delinquency, school dropout, and pregnancy or parenthood. The adolescent at greatest risk is one who

- Initiates the behavior early;
- Has low expectations for education and school grades;
- Is antisocial, acting out, or truant;
- Has low resistance to peer influences and associates with friends who participate in the same risky behaviors;
- Has poor support and monitoring from parents and is unable to communicate with parents; and
- Lives in an urban poverty area.

The Office of Juvenile Justice and Delinquency Prevention (OJJDP) of the U.S. Department of Justice also focuses on the ways in which the antecedents and system markers we have included in our conceptual framework are strong indicators of later adolescent problem behaviors. OJJDP (1995) has summarized 30 years of research on the interaction between various antecedent risk factors and problem behaviors. Factors that predict many of the negative adolescent outcomes of substance abuse, delinquency, teenage pregnancy, school dropout, and violence include (a) community characteristics, such as extreme economic deprivation and high mobility and transience of residents; (b) family characteristics, such as family history of the problem behavior, family conflict, and family management problems; and (c) school indicators, such as early and persistent antisocial behavior in school, academic failure beginning in elementary school, and lack of commitment to school.

Discussions of risk cannot be limited to a focus on problems and dysfunction but must also consider how to promote youth competencies and protective factors in the environment. It is reasonable to assume that by accurately assessing a youth's potential for future problems and by documenting his or her current strengths, interventions can be targeted to points earlier in the developmental process to prevent problems from occurring. Preventive interventions can attempt to promote resiliency (Baruch & Stutman, 1994) or to avert the onset of problems either by modifying the environments that promote vulnerabilities or by enhancing the competencies of adolescents so they can overcome their vulnerabilities (Catalano & Dooley, 1980). In addition, anything that can be done to make the primary institutions dealing with children and youth more effective in their tasks will also help youth avoid problem behaviors and negative outcomes.

Our conceptual framework should be useful in attempts to assess levels of risk in youth. Many 10–15 year olds have not yet shown negative outcomes but could be classified as high risk if they share a combination of antecedents and markers. At a minimum, we consider a young adolescent to be *high risk* if he or she lives under any of the antecedent risk conditions, has a minimal level of protective factors or positive behaviors, and currently displays one or more of the system markers. *Moderate risk* would be assigned to those youth who *either* live under any of the antecedent conditions *or* currently display one or more of the risk markers but for whom some protective factors or positive behaviors operate to offset some of the negative influences or conditions. Alternatively, moderate risk may be assigned to youth living under any of the antecedent conditions who may not display system markers or problem behaviors but who also do not appear to have sufficient levels of protective factors or positive behaviors. For these youth, later problems may develop because they lack competencies that protect against risk. *Low risk* would be assigned to those young adolescents who do not live in negative antecedent conditions, who do not display system markers, and who have an adequate level of protective factors or positive behaviors. The conceptual framework thus allows for a definition of risk that can be used by service delivery programs to judge a youth's risk level and need for services.

An even more productive approach, but a radical one, would be to take seriously the shift in perspective described by those advocating either a youth development or a rights-based approach as described in Chapter 3. Both propose remarkably similar steps toward enhancing the well being of children and youth and promoting their transition to a successful adulthood. Advocates for the rights of the child propose that societies should, as a matter of right, provide children and youth with the conditions that will keep them free from want and able to develop in ways that will make them competent and productive adults and citizens. Youth development proponents point out that if we believe in the value of certain skills and competencies, as we surely do, then we should be developing ways to foster them because they are valuable, not just because they can protect against problem behaviors. Pittman, O'Brien, and Kimball (1993), offering a succinct summary of this view, provide an appropriate conclusion for this chapter:

> ... The differences in community commitment and community action that come from presenting problem prevention as the by-product of systematic efforts to promote development (which include education and services to avoid risk) and the commitments that come from presenting problem prevention as an end in itself are profound. If outcomes such as social skills, communication skills, community commitment, leadership, self-awareness, autonomy, sense of future are to be valued in and of themselves as key goals for youth, there is a need to rename programs, rethink strategies, and redesign evaluations. (p. 14)

5

Service Integration Initiatives

Efforts to improve service delivery and outcomes for children and families have increased in the past few years at the federal, state, and local levels. Some of these efforts have been completed and have evaluation results, and others are in the process of implementation and evaluation. Government agencies, business groups, individuals, and community-based non-profit organizations have been active in the development of effective social service systems, and privately funded foundations have also been significant players. The interplay of different levels of government and public and private involvement in integrated services follows the historic pattern described in Chapter 2. It is part of the ongoing interaction between government and voluntary sector partners that provide support and services for the poor. With the current emphasis on devolution of federal responsibility for social services to the states and localities, efforts supported by state and local governments, foundations, and even private corporations are likely to become more prominent.

There are several ways to think about the myriad of efforts to improve the delivery of social services and achieve better outcomes for children and families. Looking at these efforts by functional categories, such as school-based or community-based programs, can be useful because both schools and community agencies are important points of entry for adolescents into the health and social service systems. Joy Dryfoos' volume on full-service schools is an excellent contribution in this area (Dryfoos, 1994). This approach, however, may miss some efforts to establish linkages between functional arenas in a form of "macro-level" service integration. Looking at efforts that emerge within defined fields, such as mental health, education, or child welfare, can miss innovative efforts to integrate across service domains. Similarly, a focus on efforts targeted at particular populations, such as gang-involved youth or teenage parents, will exclude efforts to work across populations to capture youth that engage in more than one type of risky behavior. In this chapter, initiatives are grouped by the nature of the initiating sponsor (i.e., foundations and county, state, or federal government) rather than by functional area, field of service, or target population. This approach captures efforts that are engaging in a truly collaborative and multisectoral service integration effort.

The level of government has a significant effect on the way that integrated services efforts will be carried out. In general, it appears that the closer the effort is to the clients, the greater is the emphasis on service delivery to and assessment of individuals. The more remote the effort from the individuals, the stronger the emphasis on systemic change. Observations of the nine programs profiled in this volume reveal that although state and federal agencies are not as invested in service delivery to individuals, their efforts to restructure funding streams and force agencies to work collaboratively can make it easier or harder for locally driven service integration efforts to move forward. We begin with a review of county and state efforts and then examine foundation-funded and federal-level initiatives.

County-Level Initiatives

Many of the states that are pursuing service integration initiatives for children and families are working closely with their counties to support locally driven efforts with technical assistance, state funding, and evaluation support. If the devolution of federal programs to the state and local levels unfolds as expected, states are likely to put increasing pressure on counties to maximize the use of existing resources through integrative and collaborative mechanisms. Those counties that already have collaborative infrastructure in place are likely to be at an advantage if this dramatic change in the social service landscape actually occurs.

San Diego New Beginnings

New Beginnings is a prime example of using collaboration to bring about institutional change that benefits children and families. New Beginnings started in 1988 as a conversation between the school superintendent for San Diego County and the director of the San Diego County Department of Social Services about the fragmentation that characterized the social service system reaching families. As an outgrowth of this conversation, 26 high-level public officials from the city and county of San Diego, the San Diego community college district, and the San Diego county schools met to learn more about each other's services and resources; identify gaps and possible overlaps in services; and develop an integrated service delivery system to improve outcomes for children, encourage parent involvement, and improve cost efficiency (McGroder, Crouter, & Kordesh, 1994). Later the collaboration grew to include the departments of health, probation, and social services; the juvenile court; the county chief administrative officer; and other city agencies.

The project began as a school-based effort to provide services to all families with children between the ages of 5 and 12 years who live in the area surrounding Hamilton Elementary School. Each of the partners contributes staff time, support services, and leadership to the joint effort, and services include immunizations, school registration, parent and adult education, and family counseling (McGroder et al., 1994). The family services advocates, a cornerstone feature of the project, follow a case management model; they conduct family needs assessments and eligibility screenings and make referrals to additional services available in the community. Another critical aspect of the collaboration is the colocation of a number of critical school and agency services in one multiservice center; the staff for these services are paid by their home agencies (McGroder et al., 1994). New Beginnings is funded by the Stuart Foundations and state funds provided through Healthy Start and the Youth Pilot Project (A.B. 1741). California Tomorrow, a nonprofit educational corporation, provided in-kind technical assistance during the start-up phase. Healthy Start funds for planning have been a critical factor in the success of the New Beginnings experiment with promoting collaboration (interview with C. Roberts, April 23, 1996[1]).

New Beginnings is more of a strategy to promote collaboration than a program or service delivery model, and cross-site collaboration is an integral part of this process. Since its beginnings at Hamilton Elementary School, the effort has expanded to three additional communities that are each pursuing a slightly different model of collaboration and modifying it as they go (interview with C. Roberts, April 22, 1996). Two of the newer sites, in the Vista and El Cajon neighborhoods, are not school-based models. Vista is a forum for agencies to work together on particular projects (such as creating a safe house for children), and El Cajon is a school-linked multiservice center located in a high-risk area of the community. The fourth and newest site, located in the National City neighborhood, is the Family Resource Center. The center is run by parents and community members at a school site and emphasizes peer support and problem solving over case management. All of the efforts are focused on prevention and serving the whole family, and each has its own unique governance structure (interview with C. Roberts, April 22, 1996).

Shared governance is also a critical element of the New Beginnings approach. In addition to governance structures operating at each site, all sites send representatives to a citywide New Beginnings governing council that tackles cross-cutting issues of system change. New Beginnings staff attend meetings of the Healthy Start governing structure, include Healthy Start staff on their governing council, and work closely with Youth Pilot Project sites and sites funded with monies from Title V of the federal Juvenile Justice and Delinquency Prevention Act (interview with C. Roberts, April 23, 1996). The philosophy of the New Beginnings staff is to work together with other collaborative efforts on common issues regardless of the funding source. The process of evaluating New Beginnings was complicated by the uniqueness of the effort at the time it began. A private consulting firm was hired to develop an appropriate evaluation design and has conducted evaluations of the program each year since 1993. As part of the evaluation process, a management information system (MIS) model was developed that is now being used by other collaborative projects

---

[1]Connie Roberts, Community Initiatives for Children and Families, Department of Social Services, County of San Diego, April 22 and 23, 1996.

around the country. In addition, service providers are now considering a common evaluation across A.B. 1741, Healthy Start, and New Beginnings sites operating in San Diego.

A last important characteristic of New Beginnings is its emphasis on sharing what has been learned with others. The project provides an extensive amount of technical assistance in the form of model memoranda of understanding, reports, presentations, and quarterly seminars for visitors (interview with C. Roberts, April 22, 1996). Because the project is now at a more mature point in its development than many other collaborative efforts across the country, it is able to share important lessons from its failures and its successes.

El Paso County, Colorado

Joint Initiatives (JI) is a special case of service integration on the county level (interviews with T. Schwartz and G. Veneman, 1992[2]; interview with R. Izer, 1996[3]). JI is a formal collaboration of local human service agencies that strives to improve services to children and youth in El Paso County, Colorado. It began in 1989 with a meeting of five agencies that were concerned about the number of children and youth being placed in out-of-county foster homes and institutions. JI became a Colorado nonprofit corporation in 1995 and obtained tax-exempt status in 1996.

JI's membership includes public agencies and private nonprofit organizations. Its members serve on committees, recommend specific projects, and commit their agency's resources to JI initiatives. Each member has one vote and pays membership dues that support JI's office, executive director, and support staff. As of September 1996, JI comprised 19 member organizations, consisting of 8 public agencies, 10 nonprofit organizations, and 1 for-profit organization. Members include the county school district, the juvenile court, the county mental health agency, the county police department, the court-appointed special advocates organization, a residential treatment center, and a psychiatric hospital.

The El Paso Department of Human Services (DHS) was an original member of JI but recently dropped its membership after disagreements with the board over the structure and governance of JI, the pace of efforts to decategorize funds, and JI's decision to obtain nonprofit and tax-exempt status. Concerns about perceived conflict of interest with member organizations that are also DHS grantees were also a factor. Despite DHS's departure from the JI board, the two organizations share many goals and maintain working relationships both collectively and individually. In addition, DHS continues to be a major funder of many of the JI member organizations.

JI uses a multi-agency review team process to identify and meet the service needs of youth in the county. A committee of three to four members

---

[2] Terry Schwartz, Joint Initiatives, and Gerard Veneman, CHINS UP, August 1992.
[3] Robin Izer, Joint Initiatives, September 1996.

is set up and meets frequently over a 2 to 3-month period, develops a recommendation, and reports back to JI. Once JI approves, JI staff seek funding for the project from state or other noncounty funds or through state waivers that affect the use of county funds. JI then puts the new project out for bid to local service providers. Once established, each new service benefits from having a multi-agency team created specifically for the needs of its clients. The agency directors who participate in JI assure that their agency staff cooperate fully in these teams.

In early 1996, JI members articulated a number of goals for the organization, including creating alternative education facilities for youth and treatment programs for high-risk girls; supporting prevention and early intervention programs for children and families, targeting 50–100 high-risk families; restructuring the delivery of social services to children and families; advocating for funding and services for children and families; and supporting research, prevention, and intervention strategies regarding the overrepresentation of youth of color in the juvenile justice system. JI is now making progress toward a number of these goals.

A good example of the JI approach is the restructuring of the county health and human services system. State legislation passed in 1994 called for improvements in efficiency, effectiveness, accountability, and consumer satisfaction of health and human services on the local level. County planning committees were formed, and the executive director and six JI board organizations served on these committees. Their work resulted in a pilot integrated system for delivering human services that emphasizes prevention and early intervention at the neighborhood level. The pilot system is designed to be consumer-driven, outcome-oriented, and accessible through a single entry point. It also features integrated case management and management information systems. Participating organizations will sign formal memoranda of agreement regarding shared funds, staff, and technical assistance. JI has the responsibility of reviewing and evaluating the pilot project.

State-Sponsored Efforts

The American system of government is built on the belief that states should have some autonomy and decision making power, whereas the federal government should retain authority over certain key functions. An essential component of this federalist view is that states can serve as a "laboratory" for national social and economic policies. There are many examples of states leading the way with social policy reform; the Progressive Era's state child labor laws are one, and one could argue that recent state experiments with welfare reform are another. Although state social service agencies do not have much direct contact with clients, they do interact with community- and county-level social service providers through the state legislative process and the distribution of federal and state grant funds. Through these contacts, some state agencies are convinced of the need for reforms and innovations in the state-level social delivery system.

In addition to the role of state-level reformers, these agencies also play a critical intermediary role between local and federal social service agencies. A traditional function in this arena is the distribution of federal block grant funds.

States are perpetually faced with difficult decisions as they balance social services against other important investments and the pressure to avoid raising taxes. This is not a new dilemma, but the recent federal welfare reform and social service funding cuts are likely to make these decisions more difficult. Although a number of states have launched creative efforts to improve services and outcomes for youth and their families, very few of these initiatives focus on adolescents as the target group or as the point of entry to the family system. This chapter describes a few that do, plus some that have served adolescents well while focusing on a larger target group. It is important to note here that although New Jersey, California, and Kentucky are exemplary in their efforts to improve social service delivery to adolescents, other states, such as Florida, New York, and Michigan, are also investing in preventive and integrated services for this population.

New Jersey School Based Youth Services Program

The New Jersey School Based Youth Services Program (SBYSP) was developed by the New Jersey Department of Human Services to provide an integrated array of social and health services to children and adolescents, with a particular focus on at-risk young people. The program's goals are to give young people the opportunity to complete their education, obtain skills that would lead to employment or further education, and lead a mentally and physically healthy life (Knowlton & Tetelman, 1994).

SBYSP currently operates in 30 high schools and 10 elementary and middle schools throughout the state of New Jersey (an additional 15 middle schools operate feeder programs that are not funded by the state). When the program began in 1988, sites focused on providing services at or near one high school in each school district to youth ages 13–19; in 1991, three districts received additional funds to expand the program into elementary schools that feed into funded high schools (Annie E. Casey Foundation, 1995b). All sites serve young people who are not currently attending school as well as those who attend (Knowlton & Tetelman, 1994).

SBYSP was designed so that each site could adapt itself to needs and resources available in the target community and therefore would not require sites to adopt a standard program model. There are some guidelines for operation, however. Each site must operate as a school and community collaboration from the outset, as indicated by the requirement that applications for funding be jointly filed by a school district and one or more local nonprofit or public agencies. To receive funding, communities must demonstrate the support and participation of a broad coalition of local community groups, teachers and parents, businesses, public agencies, nonprofit organizations, students, and local school districts (Knowlton & Tetelman, 1994).

Each site is also required to provide core services in the following eight areas: individual and family mental health counseling; primary and preventive health services; employment counseling, training, and placement; drug and alcohol abuse counseling; recreation; crisis intervention; referrals to health and social services; and summer and part-time job development. Many of the sites also provide other services, such as pregnancy prevention and parenting programs, transportation, child care, crisis hotlines, and violence prevention. Most sites provide counseling, recreation, and employment-related services on site, whereas health services are provided on site or by referral (Annie E. Casey Foundation, 1995b; Dryfoos, 1994). Recreation activities are encouraged at all sites as a way of attracting young people and making the programs nonstigmatizing to those who use them (Knowlton & Tetelman, 1994).

The program does impose some requirements on funded sites in addition to the specified core services. It requires that sites develop agreements between schools and community agencies, use parent permission forms from the state Department of Human Services, keep the program open to all students, and create a local advisory board to guide the program's operation (Annie E. Casey Foundation, 1995b). On the local level, each program is operated by a managing agency that contracts with local nonprofit agencies to provide services. Managing agencies are school districts or community agencies and organizations that work closely with the schools. The community groups operating as managing agencies include medical schools and hospitals, mental health agencies, nonprofit employment agencies and service providers, and organizations such as the Urban League (Annie E. Casey Foundation, 1995b; Dryfoos, 1994; Knowlton & Tetelman, 1994).

SBYSP is somewhat unique among integrated youth service programs in that its funding comes through a line item in the New Jersey Department of Human Services' annual budget and the state has committed to providing ongoing support to the original sites. The program is currently funded at $7.5 million per year, which flows to the managing agencies in each SBYSP district in the form of annual grants ranging in size from $152,000 to $500,000, with an average grant size of $250,000 (interview with R. Knowlton, 1996[4]; Knowlton & Tetelman, 1994). Local communities are required to provide a 25% match, through direct funding or in-kind contributions, such as school space, utilities, and staff time (Dryfoos, 1994; Knowlton & Tetelman, 1994).

Funds are used for direct services, coordination of services that already exist in the community, and the development of innovative integrated services strategies (Annie E. Casey Foundation, 1995b). Although SBYSP was designed to foster the healthy development of all school-age youth, communities that demonstrated a high incidence of problems, such

---

[4]Roberta Knowlton, New Jersey School Based Youth Services Program, New Jersey Department of Human Services, February 26, 1996.

as school dropout, youth unemployment, teen pregnancy, youth suicide, and juvenile delinquency, were given preference in the award of funds. As a result, each program must struggle with the issue of how to allocate funds and services between general prevention and interventions focused on particular problems (Annie E. Casey Foundation, 1995b).

Although some of the SBYSP's sites report that the program has led to a decrease in fighting, school dropout, suspensions, and teen pregnancy, these data were not generated by independent third-party evaluations. The Academy for Educational Development (AED) began a 3-year independent evaluation of the program in 1995 with funding from the Annie E. Casey Foundation and has not yet reported any findings. The first phase of the evaluation describes the policy context in which the program was developed and now functions, using information gleaned from visits to all of the currently operating sites. The second phase features implementation, process, and outcome evaluation of a limited number of sites, including analysis of the program's history and community context (interview with M. Gutierrez, 1996[5]). The uniqueness of each SBYSP site's approach to serving adolescents is expected to pose a challenge to evaluators (interview with R. Knowlton, 1996).

California Healthy Start / A.B. 1741

In 1991, the California state legislature passed the Healthy Start Support Services for Children Act to encourage local-level integration of services for young people. The Act allows local education agencies (or consortia of these agencies) to apply for funds from the California Department of Education (the agency that administers California's Healthy Start program) to support the planning and implementation of support services at or near Healthy Start sites. The Act was designed to provide seed money for system change at the local level and to support the provision of primary health care, mental health services, substance abuse prevention and treatment, family counseling, suicide prevention, family support and parenting education, child care and early childhood development programs, and nutrition services (Cutler, Tan, & Downs, 1995; Dryfoos, 1994; Kahn & Kamerman, 1992; Ooms & Owen, 1991; interview with Connie Roberts, April 1996).

Only agencies or consortia serving low-income populations or populations with limited English proficiency are eligible for Healthy Start funds (Dryfoos, 1994; Kahn & Kamerman, 1992; Ooms & Owen, 1991). To receive funds, education agencies or consortia must demonstrate that they are part of a collaborative partnership with health, mental health, social services, drug and alcohol, probation, and other public and nonprofit agencies or that they are working to create such a partnership (Dryfoos, 1994). The state appropriated approximately $20 million each year from 1991 to 1995, with the exception of 1993, when appropriations fell to $13 million because of a state fiscal crisis (Cutler et al., 1995; Dryfoos, 1994).

---

[5]Manuel Gutierrez, The Annie E. Casey Foundation, January 5, 1996.

Stanford Research Institute (SRI) recently completed a $1.6 million, 3-year process-and-outcome evaluation of the Healthy Start collaborative projects operating in 40 California communities which was funded by the Foundation Consortium for School-Linked Services. The evaluation found that the biggest improvement for Healthy Start clients was the reduction in their unmet need for goods and services, such as food, clothing, child care, legal assistance, and health and dental care. Smaller improvements were seen in students' grades, emotional health, involvement in risky behavior, and general well-being. No significant changes were seen in participants' receipt of public benefits, teen substance abuse, sexual activity, gang activity, housing issues, or student absenteeism (Wagner & Golan, 1996). The evaluation noted that local Healthy Start initiatives could be strengthened in several key areas: case management, integration with schools, parent involvement, acknowledging the trade-offs involved in targeting one or multiple schools, and support for coordinators. It also raised the question of whether it is possible to achieve fundamental and lasting system change with 3-year project grants (Wagner & Golan, 1996).

In another state-level service integration effort soon after the award of the Healthy Start support services funds, eight private foundations formed a partnership with state agencies to promote comprehensive integrated service delivery systems throughout the state. This relationship began in January 1992 with a signed partnership agreement among the foundations, the governor, and the state superintendent of schools (the superintendent is an elected official in California). The partnership had three objectives: to support the development of local models of comprehensive integrated service delivery, to create a stable financing mechanism for these local efforts, and ultimately to create a statewide system with infrastructure to support these sites (interview with J. Chynoweth, 1996[6]; Ooms & Owen, 1991). The partnership agreement expired three years later and was not renewed for several reasons. Among these were state agencies' concerns about the foundations' intruding into their decision-making territory and the foundations' unrealistic expectations about how they could influence the direction of state government in this area. The Foundation Consortium for School-Linked Services, which now includes 18 foundations, continues to work on discrete projects to promote integrated services through unilateral relationships with individual state agencies (interview with J. Chynoweth, 1996).

In addition to these efforts, California has recently begun an experimental effort to change service delivery methods, with the goal of improving outcomes for children, youth, and families. In 1993, State Assembly Bill (A.B.) 1741 created the Youth Pilot Project, which gave five counties the authority to combine state funds for child and family services to change methods of service delivery over a 5-year demonstration period. The goal of the demonstration project is to test approaches that are locally

---

[6] Judy Chynoweth, Foundation Consortium for School-Linked Services, Sacramento, California, March 12, 1996.

focused and controlled, create integrated service delivery systems, and use blended funding streams. The program is also intended to test the proposition that state agencies can give local government the authority and flexibility to design and administer their own social service programs (Cutler et al., 1995). In December 1994, the state selected Alameda, Contra Costa, Marin, Placer, and San Diego counties to participate in the demonstration.

A.B. 1741 provides no funds but gives the counties the authority to transfer some or all of the allocated funds from 15 child and family programs to a county-administered child and family services fund and then reprogram the funds to serve the children and families in that area most effectively. The counties are required to combine funds from a minimum of 4 of the following 15 service areas: adoption services, child abuse prevention, child welfare, delinquency prevention, drug and alcohol services, eligibility determination, employment and training, foster care, health care, juvenile facilities, mental health facilities, probation services, housing, youth development services, and all other services that are focused on children and families (Cutler et al., 1995). The ability to pool funds in this manner gives the counties the potential for accessing large sums of money for specific uses. In addition to the authority to combine funds, the state provides technical assistance in obtaining waivers of state and federal regulations.

In exchange for the flexibility provided by the demonstration, selected counties were required to target their efforts to low-income areas, use a locally driven planning process to develop their proposals, and specify measurable child and family outcomes. The counties' progress toward achieving these outcomes will be monitored throughout the 5-year demonstration (Cutler et al., 1995; interview with C. Roberts, April 1996). Each county must evaluate its efforts, and state program staff may seek outside funding for a third-party evaluation of the demonstration as a whole (Cutler et al., 1995).

Kentucky KIDS

Another promising approach is the Kentucky Integrated Delivery System (KIDS), a joint venture between the Kentucky Department of Education and the governor's Cabinet of Human Resources, begun in 1988. The initial effort helped more than a dozen communities develop agreements to facilitate the delivery of social and health services in the schools but provided no state funding to support the pilot projects. State support came with the passage of the Kentucky Education Reform Act in 1990. The legislation authorized the creation of an interagency task force and charged it with developing and implementing a network of family resource and youth service centers throughout the state within 5 years (the timeline has since been extended for another 3 years, through December 1997). The centers can be designed as family resource centers, youth service centers, or combination centers that serve younger and older children and their families.

Funding for the KIDS program is provided by the Kentucky Department of Education, which receives the funds for the centers and transfers all of the funds to the governor's Cabinet for Families and Children (formerly known as the Cabinet for Human Resources). The Cabinet awards grants, issues regulations, provides technical assistance, conducts evaluations of the centers, and staffs the interagency effort at the state level (Dryfoos, 1994; interview with C. Terrett and G. Cochrum, 1996[7]). The task force itself has the legal authority to operate the centers. The number of centers and funding for them has increased significantly since the first year of operation, the 1991–1992 school year, when $9 million was awarded to 136 centers. In the 1996–1997 school year, the Cabinet expects to award $38 million to more than 590 centers serving 800 schools (interview with C. Terrett and G. Cochrum, 1996). Funds for training and evaluation activities throughout the state have been provided by the Annie E. Casey Foundation since 1991 (Kentucky Cabinet for Families and Children, 1996).

The family resource and youth services centers are designed to identify, develop, and coordinate the resources of existing child- and youth-serving agencies to address the individual needs of young people and their families. The centers can be located in or near elementary, middle, and high schools, and grants are awarded to schools or consortia of schools with 20% or more of enrolled students who are eligible for free school meals (Dryfoos, 1994; Illback, 1994; Ooms & Owen, 1991; interview with C. Terrett and G. Cochrum, 1996). Family resource centers must provide access to full-time child care for 2 and 3 year olds, after-school child care, parent education, support and training for child care providers, and health services or referrals to health services (Dryfoos, 1994; Illback, 1994; Kentucky Cabinet for Families and Children, 1996). Many centers also provide summer programs, employment services, and referrals for social, mental health, and family support services and sponsor activities to promote the development of community resources (Illback, 1994).

Although the family resource centers are geared to the special needs of young children and their parents, the youth services centers focus on adolescents over age 12. All youth services centers provide the following core services after school, in the evening, during school vacations and holidays, and on Saturdays: referrals to health and social services; employment counseling, training, and placement; summer and part-time job development; substance abuse counseling; and family crisis and mental health counseling (Dryfoos, 1994; Ooms & Owen, 1991). Examples of direct services are placement of public health nurses and mental health counselors at the school site on a regular (1–2 day per week) basis, which has dramatically improved access to health and mental health services for many children and enabled schools to maintain higher attendance levels,

---

[7]Charles Terrett, Fulton County, Kentucky Schools, and Glenda Cochrum, Fulton County, Kentucky KIDS Project, May 15, 1996.

which in turn enables them to receive more state education funds (interview with C. Terrett and G. Cochrum, 1996).

Like the New Jersey School-Based Youth Services Program (SBYSP), the KIDS program is available to any child and family in the target school. Although the original KIDS legislation restricted the provision of services to economically disadvantaged children and families, in 1992 the legislative language was changed to allow universal participation of children from schools with more than 20% enrollment in the free-lunch program. This change was made in response to program administrators' concerns about means-testing children and families who were clearly in need of services (interview with C. Terrett and G. Cochrum, 1996).

Like California's Healthy Start initiative and the New Jersey SBYSP, each of the centers in the Kentucky system must be created and sustained through a community planning process that includes a local advisory council. Each council must have representation in roughly equal proportions from parents, school personnel, and social service agency personnel. All centers are required to provide training for the advisory board, parents, youth, community members, the staff of the center, the school, and relevant health and social service agencies. In addition, all centers are also required to conduct evaluations (Dryfoos, 1994; Ooms & Owen, 1991).

A recent evaluation of the family resource and youth service centers, based on data from the 1994–1995 school year, indicated that health services and referrals were the most frequently used services and that parent training, child care, and counseling were also commonly used. Most services were provided by the centers themselves rather than other community providers, which could reflect success at filling service gaps or duplication of existing resources (Illback, 1996). The evaluation of changes in students' educational outcomes was not based on a controlled experiment but rather on teachers' evaluations of students on several classroom performance variables at the start and completion of their participation in the program. Elementary school students (ages 3–11) were more likely than secondary school students (ages 12–20) to show positive gains in achievement, academic proficiency, and reduced risk of dropping out of school. Both age groups showed strong positive gains in completing classwork and homework and on social and emotional variables, such as participating in activities and cooperating with others. The evaluators observed that improvements were less dramatic for children who were extensively served by the center, which is probably indicative of the severity of their underlying needs (Illback, 1996).

Foundation-Funded Initiatives

The traditional role of foundations is to test an interesting social experiment and look to the federal government to continue the investment if it proves successful. With a reduced federal role in youth programs and integrated services, foundations may have to change their orientation dramatically to play a more sustaining role in the human services field. The current landscape of foundation-funded efforts that focus on adolescents includes the limited success of past efforts and some efforts that are relatively new or just getting under way. It remains to be seen whether the foundations can pick up the sustaining role played in the past by federal social service programs.

New Futures

In 1987, the Annie E. Casey Foundation launched New Futures, a new, multisite initiative in five medium-sized American cities. The initiative's overarching goal was to improve outcomes for at-risk youth in these cities by transforming local youth-serving institutions through cross-system reform and collaboration among service providers (Annie E. Casey Foundation, 1995a, 1995b; Thompson, 1995). The specific objectives of the effort were to reduce school dropout rates, improve academic performance, prevent teen pregnancies and births, and increase the number of youth who go on to jobs or college after high school (Center for the Study of Social Policy, 1995).

The foundation awarded 10 planning grants and chose five cities to receive implementation grants averaging $10 million each for 5 years, for a total of $50 million. Target sites selected for implementation grants were Dayton, Little Rock, Lawrence (Massachusetts), Pittsburgh, and Savannah. Lawrence later dropped out and was replaced by Bridgeport, Connecticut (which had received a planning grant, Center for the Study of Social Policy, 1995). At each site, communities were given the task of forming new collaborative decision-making bodies that would develop strategies for meeting the needs of at-risk youth in more effective ways. The collaboratives were to be made up of representatives from local government, business, agencies and nonprofit organizations, parents, and other community members. They were created on the theory that new decision-making structures must be in place before changes in outcomes for youth can occur (Center for the Study of Social Policy, 1995).

According to the Center for the Study of Social Policy, which conducted an evaluation of New Futures in 1995, all of the sites were successful in establishing collaboratives with diverse membership that included high-level officials, and each collaborative was able to create a case management system to facilitate service delivery to youth across different agencies and systems. The sites placed case managers in middle and high schools, where they "brokered" services for youth, acted as mentors, and informed the collaboratives about policies and procedures that stood in the way of meeting the young people's needs (Center for the Study of Social Policy, 1995). The collaboratives obtained state and local funds to match the Casey Foundation's contribution on a one-to-one basis and used the funds to pay for special programs to further the project's goals. Among the programs sponsored by collaboratives were after-school recreation, academic enrichment for students who were functioning below grade level, teen health centers (in school and community settings), and career education centers. Some sites tried reorganizing the schools into smaller units or "clusters" to foster a sense of closeness among students and teachers. Each site developed school-based management information systems to follow changes in student outcomes as they moved through the program (Center for the Study of Social Policy, 1995).

New Futures had limited success in improving outcomes for young people. The evaluation revealed that the annual dropout rate in New Futures cities increased between the first and fifth year of the project's operation, but the number of students who scored poorly on standardized reading tests decreased. None of the sites were able to show a decrease in its rates of teen pregnancy or parenthood, but the proportion of youth who reported being sexually active declined and the number who reported using birth control devices increased over the 5 years of the project. There was no documented increase in the number of high school seniors who by spring of their senior year had been accepted for college or had full-time employment lined up (Center for the Study of Social Policy, 1995).

Despite some positive accomplishments, the New Futures evaluation noted that the collaboratives were generally unable to achieve true system reform. For the most part they continued to fund narrowly tailored interventions in a few schools and were unable to replicate these efforts (Center for the Study of Social Policy, 1995). One of the reasons for the project's limited impact is the fact that there was no good model for cities to follow as they undertook the herculean effort of institutional change. The evaluation noted that little was known about effectively restructuring social service systems in 1987, and not much more is known about it today.

Other reasons for New Futures' weak results are the lack of interim benchmarks that could have provided positive feedback, kept momentum up toward ultimate goals, and served as preconditions for more dramatic system change (Annie E. Casey Foundation, 1995c; Curnan, as cited in Thompson, 1995). In addition, the sites probably needed more time to plan and implement the type of complex system change that was envisioned, in large part to forge the consensus among various parties involved in the projects. In its own assessment of New Futures, the Casey Foundation noted that institutional and service system change is not the route to improved outcomes for vulnerable children and families in all communities. In some areas, there is a need to invest in "social capital" and economic development efforts that target an entire low-income neighborhood (Annie E. Casey Foundation, 1995c).

Community Change for Youth Development

One of the few privately funded initiatives that currently focuses on adolescents is the Community Change for Youth Development (CCYD) demonstration launched in 1994 by Public/Private Ventures, Inc., a private consulting firm that specializes in evaluating youth programs. Although this effort is more focused on positive youth development than on service integration, some demonstration sites will use service integration as one of many tools in their overall efforts to improve outcomes for low-income youth. The goals of the 10-year demonstration project are to "build an enduring system of supports, services and activities that promote positive youth development for young people 12 through 20, and expand the resources and opportunities they have to reach adulthood successfully" (Public/Private Ventures, 1994, p. 1).

CCYD is currently operating in six sites, of which three are receiving significant technical assistance and other attention from Public/Private Ventures (East Austin, Texas; Savannah, Georgia; and St. Petersburg, Florida) and three are operating more independently (New York City, Kansas City, and Minneapolis). Public/Private Ventures is providing more than $9 million for the effort, which includes funds to sites for program implementation and funds for research and evaluation, and sites are providing matching funds. In some sites, matching funds equal or exceed the amount provided by Public/Private Ventures. Other supporters of the project are the Ford, Annie E. Casey, Charles Stewart Mott, and Ewing M. Kaufman Foundations; the Commonwealth Fund; and the U.S. Department of Health and Human Services (interview with J. Greim, 1996[8]; Public/Private Ventures, 1994). The CCYD initiative is designed around the following core goals: (a) to expand supportive relationships among adults and neighborhood youth; (b) to use work as a tool for development, learning, and income; (c) to fill "gap periods" in adolescents' lives with constructive activities; (d) to create and enhance adolescents' opportunities to engage in decisions that affect them and their peers; and (e) to provide support during transition periods in the lives of young people (Public/Private Ventures, 1995). Although the initial design documents do not refer specifically to service integration as a preferred method of carrying the core concepts forward, they do refer to the history of collaboration among service providers and specifically whether or not targeted communities have operating youth-collaborative organizations (Public/Private Ventures, 1994).

Public/Private Ventures has planned a careful evaluation of the project that includes interim as well as long-term measures of neighborhood change and improvements in the lives of youth. Researchers will interview people involved in the planning and implementation process (including youth) and document increases in activities for youth during the nonschool hours, changes in the level of adult involvement in the lives of youth, and increases in opportunities for youth to assume leadership roles. They will also attempt to determine whether the intervention affected how adolescents use their time out of school, how involved adults are in their lives, whether they have more opportunities to engage in "meaningful and productive work," and whether they have more chances to be involved in decision making (Public/Private Ventures, 1994). Interim outcome measures will be particularly useful in determining whether the 10-year project is making progress toward its ultimate objectives.

---

[8] Jeffrey Greim, Public/Private Ventures, October 2, 1996.

Health and Safety of Urban Children Initiative

An example of a foundation-supported effort that is just getting under way is the Robert Wood Johnson Foundation's Securing the Health and Safety of Urban Children initiative. The initiative will support community-based collaborative approaches to improving the health and safety of children living in distressed urban neighborhoods. The effort is designed to test the proposition that bringing parents and children together with urban leaders and organizations in a focused and sustained collaborative effort will reduce levels of violence, substance abuse, mental and emotional problems, sexually transmitted diseases, teen pregnancy, and infant morbidity and mortality. Each community is expected to develop objectives keyed to the most urgent problems in that area and the potential for achieving a real impact on the overall health status of children in that community (Robert Wood Johnson Foundation, 1996).

The foundation has specified that every person who has a role to play in improving the health and safety of children in the community must participate in the collaborative process, but it does not specify how the collaborative effort should be structured. Participants must include children and parents, community leaders and service providers (from the city and surrounding suburban communities), the media, and government officials from the local, state, and federal levels. The effort is required to build on existing collaborative efforts in the community that focus on children (Robert Wood Johnson Foundation, 1996). Given that several of the sites are located in designated empowerment zones or enterprise communities, some of which have child and youth-focused activities planned or under way, there should be numerous opportunities for networking with other collaborative efforts.

Initial 2-year planning grants of $400,000 each have recently been awarded to Baltimore, Chicago, Detroit, Miami, Oakland, Philadelphia, Richmond, and Sacramento, and the foundation will provide renewable 4-year implementation grants of between $500,000 and $750,000 to as many as five of the eight cities. In effect, this means that successful sites have the potential to receive funding for up to 10 years. The foundation will provide technical assistance to the target cities, including an initial survey of children and youth to identify their health and safety concerns and information about effective approaches being tried in other communities (Robert Wood Johnson Foundation, 1996).

Despite the passage of the welfare reform law, the larger process of devolving federal social service programs to the states and the reinvention and downsizing of federal government agencies is still unfolding. It seems clear that states and communities will have to increase their activity in the social service arena as the elimination of several major entitlement programs and reductions in federal social service programs takes effect. Although it is difficult to predict the role of integrated services in this scenario, it may very well change its orientation from an innovative method of promoting collaboration and ensuring improved outcomes to a survival strategy for service providers that serve our nation's most vulnerable populations.

The Federal Level

Federal social service agencies do not actually deliver services; they fund service through block grants, entitlement programs, or grants to state and local agencies and community-based service providers. Because of this indirect role in the delivery of social services, the federal government is focused on the issues of funding, access, and evaluation of social services. The funding and access issues typically include writing regulations to more clearly define benefits and beneficiaries, creating earmarks in block grants for specific services, and setting priorities in grant announcements so that funds are awarded to certain types of service providers for specified activities or particular populations. The federal government can require that its grantees integrate services and can work to remove barriers to collaboration or integration. In general, the federal role in service integration is to make it more feasible for service providers to work together.

The National Performance Review

In March 1993, President Clinton announced that Vice President Al Gore would spearhead a 6-month review of the operations of the federal government. In September, the National Performance Review issued its report called *From Red Tape to Results: Creating a Government That Works Better and Costs Less*. The report made a series of general recommendations for improving government performance that focused on reducing the size and complexity of the bureaucracy, making it easier for citizens to access government services, empowering employees to accomplish more, and simplifying government functions (National Performance Review, 1993a).

A number of accompanying reports focused on changes in governmental systems, including one that made recommendations for improving intergovernmental service delivery. The report described the public perception that American government was not working, described "an increasingly hidebound and paralyzed intergovernmental process," and noted the proliferation of government grant programs (National Performance Review, 1993b). It documented the duplication and overlap in programs for children and families and the increase in federally imposed requirements and regulations on states and localities that prevents local communities from tailoring programs (through service integration or other means) to meet the needs of their "customers."

The report set forth four areas in which specific proposals were to be developed for each agency: (a) reduction in the number of categorical federal grant programs; (b) reduction of unfunded government (especially federal) mandates on other levels of government; (c) refocus of program rules and regulations from compliance to outcomes, from sanctions to incentives; and (d) facilitation of federal interdepartmental and intergovernmental collaboration. Finally, the report made five broad recommendations on how to improve intergovernmental service delivery, including allowing waivers of regulations that prohibit effective delivery of services, improving federal grant processes, and simplifying accounting and auditing procedures (National Performance Review, 1993b). This report, as did most of those that were finally published, emphasized improvements in administrative process rather than achieving desired outcomes.

One of the outcomes of the National Performance Review process was a work group on service integration issues that was cosponsored by National Performance Review staff and the White House Domestic Policy Council. The work group focused its efforts on a process called Partnerships for Stronger Families, which was intended to motivate all federal agencies to remove barriers to serving children and families most effectively. A conference was held on this subject in the winter of 1995, and federal staff from several agencies worked together on disseminating information, providing technical assistance, and setting up single points of contact for gaining information about government grants and services (interview with A. Segal, April 23, 1996[9]). In 1997, what remains of this effort is an Internet Web page that provides information about a number of federal programs and services for children and families.

Empowerment Zones and Enterprise Communities

In contrast to the National Performance Review, which focused on making the federal social service system more efficient and easier for citizens to navigate, the Empowerment Zone and Enterprise Community initiative is concerned with changing federal policies to empower low-income communities to improve outcomes for their residents. In 1994, the U.S. Departments of Housing and Urban Development (HUD), Agriculture (USDA), and Health and Human Services (HHS) sponsored legislation to create Empowerment Zones and Enterprise Communities in distressed urban and rural areas across the United States. More than 500 communities submitted strategic plans in an effort to be designated an Empowerment Zone (EZ) or Enterprise Community (EC), a status that entitles a community to receive targeted federal economic and social service assistance in the form of tax incentives and grant funds. In addition, designated communities can apply to the Community Empowerment Board for waivers of federal regulations that inhibit coordination and collaboration. The board has pledged to work with all communities that submitted a strategic plan, not just those that became designated as EZ/ECs, to overcome impedi-

---

[9]Ann Segal, Office of the Assistant Secretary for Planning and Evaluation, U.S. Department of Health and Human Services, June 28, 1995 and April 23, 1996.

ments to community development (U.S. Department of Health and Human Services, 1996a).

Of the 500 communities that submitted a strategic plan, 105 were designated as EZs and ECs and received a total of $1 billion in Social Services Block Grant (SSBG) funds from HHS, approximately $2.5 billion in federal tax incentives, and special consideration in many other federal agencies' competitive grant programs (U.S. Department of Health and Human Services, 1996a). The SSBG funds are divided among designated communities in the following manner: each urban EZ receives $100 million, each rural EZ receives $40 million, and each EC receives approximately $2.95 million to carry out projects identified in their strategic plans. In addition, HUD used economic development grants to create two Supplemental Empowerment Zones (SEZs) and four Enhanced Enterprise Communities (EECs). These communities have received grants of between $25 million and $125 million to finance economic development, housing rehabilitation, and other projects. A list of designated EZs, ECs, SEZs, and EECs is included as an appendix to this volume.

To be designated an EZ or EC, communities were required to develop a comprehensive strategic plan that demonstrated strong community-based partnerships, participation of community residents, integration and coordination of services and activities, commitments from the private and nonprofit sectors, and the cooperation of state and local government. The philosophy that undergirds this efforts is focused on inclusive, community-based, comprehensive, and outcome-oriented approaches to social and economic problems. Communities that are designated to receive EZ/EC funds are encouraged to work across bureaucratic divisions and disciplines to create new jobs, support and preserve families, promote public safety, educate and train residents, provide health care, and protect the environment (U.S. Department of Health and Human Services, 1996a).

Activities that fall under the rubric of integrated services for children and families are funded by the SSBG dollars flowing to designated EZ/EC communities. Although they have more flexibility than under usual program rules, communities must use their SSBG funds to meet one of three broad goals. The goals are preventing dependency and helping residents achieve economic self-sufficiency; preventing or remedying the neglect, abuse, or exploitation of children and adults who are unable to protect their own interests; and preserving, rehabilitating, or reuniting families. Allowable activities range from community and economic development services, such as job training and financial management counseling, to substance abuse treatment programs and after-school and summer programs for youth (U.S. Department of Housing and Urban Development and U.S. Department of Agriculture, 1994).

Most youth activities sponsored by EZ/EC communities are still in the implementation phase and are making use of technical assistance offered by HHS and other agencies. These activities include a youth-operated radio station in Memphis, Tennessee; teen centers to promote youth employment and leadership development in San Francisco, Oakland, and Minneapolis; and youth community councils in Albany and New Haven (interview with M. Gootman, 1995[10]). The New York City strategic plan includes plans for a family resource center that provides health and family support activities to promote the academic success of children at a middle school. The program is run by the Children's Aid Society of New York and staffed by bilingual social workers, paraprofessionals, parents, and other volunteers. Portland, Oregon, is building a family resource center that will provide offices for 15 state, county, municipal, and nonprofit service providers that will offer health care, counseling, vocational and educational training, senior services, and playgroups for mothers and infants (interview with M. Werner, 1996[11]). In December 1996, economic development professionals and staff of youth programs in 70 EZs and ECs participated in a satellite video conference on positive youth development principles and programs. The video conference was sponsored by HHS with support from USDA, HUD, the Community Empowerment Board, and several other federal agencies. It featured a panel of youth and adult experts, video clips of exemplary youth programs, and live call-in questions from participants located at downlink sites across the nation.

Concluding Thoughts

Increasing devolution of federal social service programs to states and counties, exemplified by the new welfare law, is likely to have a significant effect on both levels and locations of integrated services activities. In our view, states and counties with established collaborative infrastructures and a history of integrating services will fare best when faced with the need to use existing or reduced resources for social services most efficiently. For state and local agencies and youth-serving programs, service integration may well be a survival strategy.

States and localities have been the site of demonstration programs and federal waivers in the past; they will now be the focal point for innovations in social service delivery. If additional programs are converted to federal block grants, states and counties will also have increasing control over funding levels and allocations for such services. In this scenario, the current role of the federal agencies as facilitators of service integration on the state and local levels will be significantly reduced.

The role of nongovernmental funders in this picture is less clear. Foundations may choose to move beyond their traditional role as funders of demonstration programs and take on the ongoing support of state- and county-driven reform efforts. For this support to be meaningful in an atmosphere of reduced government funding, however, they will have to be even more selective about which efforts to fund. Given the conclusion of the New Futures and California Healthy Start initiatives that system re-

---

[10] Marek Gootman, Office of the Assistant Secretary for Planning and Evaluation, U.S. Department of Health and Human Services, October 10, 1995.

[11] Marsha Werner, Office of the Assistant Secretary for Planning and Evaluation, U.S. Department of Health and Human Services, March 1996.

form efforts need sustained funding to flourish, the foundations may need to work cooperatively with government and corporate funders to generate the long-term support that will be required to make a difference. With the shift in responsibilities for social service programs from the federal level to the states and private sector, the corporate world may have to play an even more significant role than it has to date.

Part II

The Programs

6

Big Brothers/Big Sisters of Greater Miami

Overview

Big Brothers/Big Sisters of Greater Miami is an example of a community agency that uses one intervention strategy—volunteer matching—as the basis for all of its service integration and comprehensive delivery approaches. It differs from the other programs because it has been successful in using a single, prevention-oriented program element to achieve greater integration and comprehensiveness of services to youth in the community.

Big Brothers/Big Sisters have served the Greater Miami community as two distinct organizations for approximately 35 years. They joined in 1972 to form Big Brothers/Big Sisters of Greater Miami, a full member of Big Brothers/Big Sisters of America. Big Brothers/Big Sisters has an active, committee-driven board involved in the organization's policy decisions. A new executive director, Lydia Muniz, and restructuring of the agency's board of directors helped to refocus the program's services. Within the past 5 years, the number of specialized program offerings has grown significantly and interest has increased in targeting a wider range of potential volunteer groups (e.g., older adults for the Project Wisdom, an intergenerational match program). Big Brothers/Big Sisters of Greater Miami is well known within the community and offers its clients a diverse range of mentoring or "match" services that are closely monitored by social workers. Originally the program focused solely on its "core match" program of matching interested children between the ages of 5 and 18 who live in single parent families (with exceptions based on need) with volunteers who serve as friends and role models. Because the sole criterion for participation (within specified age limits) is that the youth come from a single-parent family, the program's clientele are from diverse backgrounds and neighborhoods. Recent modifications in the matching program have enabled a wider range of youth and volunteer adults to participate, and services are given to a greater number of youth in the community through interagency agreements and community outreach. Matches are arranged for adolescent girls at risk for delinquency as well as for disabled and special-needs youth. Volunteer adults come from a more diverse group within the community, including multiple generations and among a wider range of ethnic groups.

Mission, Goals, and Objectives

The overall mission of Big Brothers/Big Sisters is to support and enhance single-parent families by providing volunteer friends and role models who will help children develop their full potential. The children served by Big Brothers/Big Sisters are considered at risk because they come from single-parent families.

The key goal of the program is to "provide concerned, responsible volunteers to serve as friends and role models to youth from one percent of Dade County's single-parent families before these children 'get into trouble'" (Big Brothers/Big Sisters of Greater Miami, unpublished program documents, n.d.). The relationships developed through Big Brothers/Big Sisters have as a major objective: providing positive adult role models through sustained companionship and feedback. The Big Brothers/Big Sisters relationship is also expected to build self-esteem and teach the youth new skills. The program has an additional goal of forging community linkages and collaborative partnerships with other organizations to meet the diverse needs of their client population.

Current Clientele

Big Brothers/Big Sisters of Greater Miami provides services to Dade County youth between the ages of 5 and 18. Youth between the ages of 5 and 16 may receive matches, which last until the participants reach the age of 18. About half of the youth are 10–15 year olds. Most come from single-parent families and have little contact with the absent parent, with the exception of some participants in the Special Needs Program, in which living in a single-parent household is not a requirement. The program's participants have diverse economic and cultural backgrounds. Approximately 50% of the youth participating in active matches during the 1991–1992 program year were African American (including many Haitian), 25% were Hispanic, and 25% were White. In 1995, the proportions from each group were as follows: 60% African American, 26% Hispanic, and 14% White.

The overall goal of the program is to provide matches to one youth from each of 1,200 families, thereby reaching 1% of the county's single-parent families. Big Brothers/Big Sisters had approximately 400 active matches during the 1991–1992 program year and approximately 300 children on the waiting list. The majority of the youth participate in the core match program, but there is also a substantial number who participate in the specialized programs, such as Project Share and TAGS (Take A Giant Step), a school-based juvenile justice prevention program. There are approximately 80 or more matches between these two programs. A subset of the children on the waiting list participate in activities sponsored by Project CARES (Children's Advancement through Recreation and Educational Services).

Clients are commonly referred to the program by a parent. Other referral sources include the youths themselves, school counselors, courts, program participants, and outside agencies. The program is well-known within the community, and potential clients often learn about the program through word of mouth. Big Brothers/Big Sisters also conducts an extensive advertising and marketing campaign to recruit participants and volunteers. Potential participants go through a structured application process, and both the child and parent must indicate their consent before the program accepts a youth.

Service Configuration

Most services at Big Brothers/Big Sisters are aimed at its mentoring function, that is, providing volunteer adult role models to youth in need. Social workers closely monitor the mentoring relationships and also provide case management to families in need of referrals for services (e.g., mental health, housing, income maintenance). All potential clients go through a comprehensive in-home assessment by a social worker assigned to the child. The assessment includes an application form (for both the parent and the child) and a home visit to gather information on the family's history, discuss the child's interests and questions, and ascertain the type of volunteer match desired by the parent. Once accepted into the program, the child is placed on a waiting list until an appropriate match is found. The amount of time an individual remains on the waiting list varies depending on the characteristics of the match participants. For example, African American boys take longer to match when African American male volunteers are best suited, because of the high level of requests for matches relative to the smaller number of African American males volunteering.

Potential volunteers also undergo extensive screening and assessment. These adults first attend an orientation at which they discuss their expectations and receive an application form. Orientations occur twice a month at either the central office or one of its satellites. Potential volunteers complete an application and undergo an extensive background check that includes a screening of references, police record, and driver's license. Big Brothers/Big Sisters of Greater Miami used to administer the 16PF psychological profile but have discontinued its use because it did not serve the purpose to which it was intended, to identify potential pedophiles. Big Brothers/Big Sisters of Greater Miami also used to have access to the state child abuse registry, but the state could no longer assist them because of increased costs. A social worker assigned to the volunteer also conducts an in-depth home visit that includes an exploration of the potential volunteer's background and past experiences. Approved volunteers are put on a waiting list until the program can match them with an appropriate youth, but most are matched relatively quickly.

Matches are made on the basis of the social worker's professional expertise and take into account the preferences, interests, and characteristics of client, parent, and volunteer. Once matched, the social worker contacts both parties to assess interest in the proposed match. If accepted, the volunteer, social worker, youth, and parent attend a match conference at the child's home to review and sign copies of the program's rules and regulations. Within 6–12 weeks of the match, the social worker convenes a goal setting conference to set goals and objectives for the match with all participants. These vary depending on the needs of the child. A typical initial goal for a match is to establish a relationship with the child.

Standard procedures also include an annual review to evaluate progress toward goal attainment, assess the viability of the match, and generate new goals. The program includes a formalized match closure process that either the parent, the child, or the volunteer can initiate. The volunteer and youth must spend between 3 and 5 hours together each week, and the volunteer must make a 1-year commitment.

Each social worker typically spends part of his or her time at satellite offices located throughout Dade County. This allows Big Brothers/Big Sisters to maintain a presence throughout the community. Social workers contact each parent, volunteer, and child on a set schedule according to the length and needs of the match relationship. Support to the volunteer is provided along with referrals for additional services, if these are needed by the parent or child. Approximately 40–50% of the caseload requires some type of referral or linkage to a community agency. Big Brothers/Big Sisters has a variety of match programs to supplement its core program and meet the diverse needs of its client population. The program offerings include the following.

Intergenerational Match Program: Project Wisdom

Since 1989, Big Brothers/Big Sisters has offered an intergenerational match program in which older adult volunteers (ages 55 and up) provide companionship and support to a child. This program is an extension of the core match program, and it evolved out of requests from parents for a mentor who is more than just a "big brother." Greater Miami's intergenerational match program is one of nine pilot sites for national Big Brothers/Big Sisters' intergenerational program initiative. It is a small program, serving 20 active matches at a time.

Teen Connection Program

Teen Connection began in 1987 and provides female mentors for 10- to 16-year-old girls who are at risk for teen pregnancy and drug use. Volunteers for this program receive additional training during their orientation and participate in quarterly support groups to discuss issues related to serving this special population.

Special Needs Program

Since 1990, Big Brothers/Big Sisters has offered a special mentoring program for mentally and physically disabled and developmentally delayed 5–18 year olds. This is the only program in which clients need not come from a single-parent family. The program currently serves 13 matches. Its major goals include independence, normalization, and the development of leisure time activities.

Juvenile Justice Delinquency Prevention Program: TAGS

TAGS began in 1992 to provide mentors to qualifying juveniles (those who are beginning to show evidence of delinquency and may have been involved with the juvenile justice system). The major goal of this program is to provide one-on-one experiences to build the self-esteem of this group of at-risk youth. The program targets teenage boys and girls from a local middle school and nearby elementary school, that is part of the middle-school feeder pattern, with many high-risk Haitian and African American youth. Each child in the program is placed in contact with three individuals: (a) a volunteer tutor from a local college or university who spends 1–3 hours each week at the school with a child; (b) a Big Brothers/Big Sisters adult volunteer, and (c) a mentor advocate to help the child deal with any difficulties within the school system (e.g., fighting, poor attendance). The Big Brothers/Big Sisters social worker also monitors each case. This program has an evaluation component that includes comparisons with a control group, a middle school with a similar profile.

Project CARES

Project CARES is an educational and recreational program for children who are waiting to receive a match. It began in 1990 in response to the program's large waiting list and provides activities three times per month to a subset of youth. In its present form the program can accommodate 150 of the approximately 300 children on the program's waiting list. All of the activities are sponsored by local businesses and community groups.

The agency's services and clientele were affected by the devastation caused by Hurricane Andrew in 1992. Approximately one fourth of their existing matches were disrupted as a result of the storm because one or the other partner was displaced from his or her home. In addition a number of satellite offices were damaged or destroyed. The community is in the midst of rebuilding, and Big Brothers/Big Sisters has become involved in new programs to facilitate this process through Project Share, which provides families affected by the hurricane with support, advice, relief, and enrichment by matching them with families who were unaffected.

Type and Make-Up of the Service Integration Network

Big Brothers/Big Sisters collaborates with other community agencies both formally and informally. The core program has informal linkages with a variety of agencies, including Dade County Youth and Family Development, school counselors, and a coalition of other youth service organizations. These agencies provide referrals, collaborate on special projects or events, and in some cases, share facilities for matches. Social workers assigned to the specialized match programs rely on a different set of informal linkages to obtain referrals or program-related services. For instance, Teen Connections deals with family planning issues and has informal linkages with Planned Parenthood and medical clinics that may serve Teen Connections clients or meet with matches. The Special Needs program has formed linkages with the state-funded developmental services, a local mental health center, and various medical service providers to make referrals for clients and their families.

The Juvenile Justice program has forged informal linkages with local universities and minority fraternities and sororities in order to find volunteers, tutor advocates, and mentor advocates to participate in the program. Project CARES actively pursues community agencies and businesses to sponsor activities to engage youth who are waiting for a match. In the past, it received support and sponsorship from private companies (e.g., IBM), churches, sports teams, retail stores, and private clubs.

Big Brothers/Big Sisters has been involved in several joint ventures with community groups to obtain funding and create some of the program's newest components. Formal linkages exist between Big Brothers/Big Sisters and these community groups to run the programs that are successfully funded. Specifically, Big Brothers/Big Sisters collaborated with Switchboard of Miami to create and run its Teen Connections component, with TROY (Teaching and Rehabilitating Our Youth) to create and run the Juvenile Justice Program, and with Parent-to-Parent of Miami to develop and run the Special Needs Program.

The program's success relies on the participation of hundreds of volunteers, and much of the agency's efforts goes toward program marketing and volunteer recruitment. The agency has forged linkages with local media representatives and has received in-kind contributions in the form of videotapes, public service announcements, and segments on television and radio shows.

Funding Sources

Big Brothers/Big Sisters of Greater Miami receives the majority of its funding from the United Way. A large portion of its total revenue also comes from in-kind donations, mainly advertising and public service announcements. In fact, in-kind contributions for advertising more than tripled from 1991 to 1992 when the agency expanded its media campaigns. Other funding sources include the following:

- Special events such as the annual Toast and Roast, fundraising activities sponsored by the Women's Committee, Inc. for Big Brothers/Big Sisters, and the agency's major annual fundraising event, Bowl for Kids' Sake;
- Support from foundations such as the Bassett, Cross Ridge, Dade Community, Dunspaugh-Dalton, Thomas J. Lipton, George B. Storer, Winn-Dixie, Wiseheart, and Southeast Banking Corporation foundations and the Mitsubishi Electric Sales America Corporation;
- Contributions collected during the annual fund campaign; and
- Bequests, investments, and miscellaneous income.

Update: 1996

Since the site visit in 1992, mentoring has become extremely popular among prevention programs for youth. This popularity has created an opportunity for Big Brothers/Big Sisters of Greater Miami to expand its interagency linkages and to develop an additional line of service provision through training and technical assistance. The primary changes since our initial site visit appear to have been in the areas of expanded training and technical assistance, as well as volunteer recruitment, and changes in administrative structure.

Training and Technical Assistance Enhancements

Despite the increased popularity of mentoring, some agencies treat it as a "cheap fix," and often it is not done properly, particularly in the screening and partnering of "bigs" (the adult volunteers) with the youth. If the adult volunteers are not screened properly, the pairing will not have enough in common and the partnership may terminate early. Big Brothers/Big Sisters of Greater Miami is seen as the "mentoring expert" and is often approached for technical assistance. Many agencies have received technical assistance from Big Brothers/Big Sisters of Greater Miami, including the Greater Miami Chamber of Commerce, local hospitals, Atlantic Gulf Communities, Switchboard of Miami, Miami Dade Community College, North Miami Middle schools, Norland Middle School, and Metro Dade Parks and Recreation. After the initial training is completed, Big Brothers/Big Sisters of Greater Miami provides follow-up and continual monitoring. The trainer also receives evaluations about the training and generally stays in touch with a contact person in agency. Over the past 4 years, Big Brothers/Big Sisters of Greater Miami developed a partnership with United Way called One to One, which funds a trainer who goes to other organizations wishing to do mentoring to share his or her expertise.

The expansion of its mentoring training and technical assistance has also paid off in terms of new partnerships with community entities, particularly private corporations as well as schools. For example, Big

Brothers/Big Sisters of Greater Miami developed a partnership with an elementary school and a corporate body (Atlantic Gulf). One of the members of the Big Brothers/Big Sisters of Greater Miami board is on the board of Atlantic Gulf and wanted to do mentoring his own way. Atlantic Gulf approached Big Brothers/Big Sisters of Greater Miami for initial technical assistance. Additionally, Big Brothers/Big Sisters of Greater Miami worked with a new school site that wanted a mentoring program, conducted the mentor training, and helped get the program started, and then the school took it over. Big Brothers/Big Sisters of Greater Miami also receives calls from local schools for help to organize agencies that will provide a range of services in their schools.

Changes in Volunteer Recruitment

Since 1992, competition for volunteers has intensified, and Big Brothers/Big Sisters now requires a full-time staff person to find adult volunteers, particularly those from culturally diverse communities (such as the African American, Haitian, Hispanic, or Cuban communities). Big Brothers/Big Sisters of Greater Miami now has a full-time volunteer recruiter. In the past, the program relied on word of mouth to recruit volunteers, but now it has to do more.

In addition to finding adult volunteers, the volunteer recruiter is responsible for a speaker's bureau, in which speaking engagements to clubs, organizations and community groups are used to recruit volunteers. This speaker's bureau also trains "bigs" to speak to other agencies. In addition to the volunteer recruiter, Big Brothers/Big Sisters of Greater Miami is currently implementing a major media recruiting campaign for the first time.

Despite having a slight increase in Hispanic volunteers this year, the agency still has a problem recruiting African American volunteers, particularly men, as mentors for inner city youth. It is not so much that successful African American men do not come back but that the ones who do are in constant demand. Furthermore, there is a general problem recruiting enough men to be big brothers. Big Brothers/Big Sisters of Greater Miami recently changed the amount of commitments that adult volunteers must provide, in order to attract more volunteers. Previously, volunteers were required to give a 1-year commitment with a minimum number of hours per month, and this has been reduced to as little as two outings per month with an unspecified number of hours per outing. Thus, Big Brothers/Big Sisters of Greater Miami is responding to the fact that people have busy lives and that the agency must compete with other community agencies for a limited pool of volunteers. It still encourages volunteers to spend as much time as possible with the youth, and many existing matches involve a high degree of commitment and time given by the volunteers.

One of the problems that Big Brothers/Big Sisters has wrestled with in relation to screening adult volunteers is the detection of pedophiles.

The program no longer uses the 16PF, because it does not test for pedophilic behavior. Program staff have been unable to find good psychological screening instruments to identify potential pedophiles, and the Florida Department of Human Services no longer provides information on individuals from its child abuse registry. Instead, Big Brothers/Big Sisters focuses its effort on background checks (primarily motor vehicle and criminal records), the interview process, and an educational intervention titled "Empower." Empower is an educational packet developed by the national office of Big Brothers/Big Sisters that provides information and education on identifying pedophiles.

The recent trend toward mandated community service work for high-school and college students has spurred greater connections with local universities and colleges to arrange for student volunteers as mentors. This is a relatively new area, and Big Brothers/Big Sisters of Greater Miami finds that students have many issues that do not always make them ideal "bigs." Students generally are only available for one or two semesters, whereas matches may require a longer investment of time. The existing screening process may take so long that by the time a student is placed with a child, the student does not have sufficient time to develop a relationship before the student's available time ends. Furthermore, students from out of town go to their homes for holidays or longer school breaks, whereas matches may need them throughout the year. Recently, Big Brothers/Big Sisters of Greater Miami completed an agreement with one of the local universities to start taking graduate-level social work student interns as social workers to assist in the matches and other programs, who will be supervised by the social worker.

Changes in Management and Administration

Organizationally, Big Brothers/Big Sisters of Greater Miami is now more departmentalized, with office support staff assigned to specific departments and the budget done by department. This change was partially due to the results of a 1993 staff survey in which staff expressed a desire for a less hierarchical style, more shared decision making, more delegation, and more decentralization.

Recently, Big Brothers/Big Sisters of Greater Miami received its 5-year evaluation from the national office. The results indicated that it must do even more extensive screenings for volunteers and children, using revised instruments for psychosocial evaluation and a thorough needs assessment for the youth and family. The results of an annual impact survey, in which questionnaires were sent out to all participating youth and families, were generally favorable, but the response rate of 22% is too low to draw valid conclusions from the population of users. Every year Big Brothers/Big Sisters of Greater Miami also conducts a telephone survey to volunteers in randomly selected matches to get a sense of service quality.

Program Changes

Shifts in community needs and changes in the Miami's social service network necessitated some adjustments to the Big Brothers/Big Sisters program. For example, in 1992 the only youth placed in matches who did not come from single-parent families were those with special needs. Recently, the program has become more flexible in identifying children and youth from a diversity of family structures for potential matches. The social service network in Miami is getting thinner, which means there are not enough social workers to provide long-term monitoring of at-risk children and youth and to provide case management and referrals to treatment services. This can have negative effects on the match as the adult volunteer ends up carrying more of the emotional load. When there are major issues in the child's life that require more intensive intervention, the lack of resources requires the increasingly overburdened volunteer to take responsibility. This can lead to "burnout" among volunteers and a higher than expected turnover rate.

Another shift in services is toward more group mentoring. The program finds, particularly for inner city areas, that there will never be enough volunteers available for all of the children and youth who need it. Big Brothers/Big Sisters of Greater Miami recently initiated a pilot program in which a group of youth are formed, usually from those waiting for one-to-one matches, and the group meets once a month for 4–5 months to provide some measure of relationship and role modeling. One social worker is placed with the group to act as a facilitator and role model. Another form of group mentoring under consideration by Big Brothers/Big Sisters of Greater Miami involves matching siblings with the same adult volunteer.

Changes in Funding

Another trend is in the area of funding. Medicaid is cutting back on services to children and youth, and schools are experiencing reductions in their own funds for ancillary services. As a result, prevention-oriented agencies such as Big Brothers/Big Sisters of Greater Miami find themselves stepping into the role of coordinating services and providing a broader continuum of services to fill these gaps. This shift in roles is accompanied by an overall reduction in public funds available, so Big Brothers/Big Sisters finds it cannot be as dependent on public sources of funds. In the wake of Hurricane Andrew, a flurry of new funds was targeted for services in South Dade (the most poorly served area hit by the storm), but since then this money has run out. The current proportion of revenue from United Way has been reduced to 40%, and Big Brothers/Big Sisters has become much more active in seeking private funds. As a result of this greater need for private money to fund a broader continuum of services, the board of Big Brothers/Big Sisters of Greater Miami had to shift its fundraising emphasis away from the more labor-intensive strat-

egies, such as special events. The board is now focusing on annual fundraising and planned giving, particularly targeting individuals in corporations. In the past 2 years, a private individual donated a major gift, which
has eased the burden somewhat.

Although Big Brothers/Big Sisters is not dependent on federal or state
funds for its core programs, it does apply for new program grants. For
example, the school-based program, TAGS, has been expanded into an
elementary school through a special grant from Juvenile Justice. Currently, Big Brothers/Big Sisters of Greater Miami is applying for a grant
in which it will partner with an elementary and a middle school. The
program involves school-based mentoring in which volunteers are placed
in the school as "tutor mentors" to spend an hour per week with a child
providing tutoring and also developing a mentoring relationship. By placing volunteers in the school, more children receive mentoring services from
a given volunteer and the children (and parents) feel better about going
to the school for services rather than working with a volunteer mentor out
in the community. One of the difficulties with a school-based approach is
the potential for turf issues. The program has discovered that it is important to develop a long-term relationship with the school and that the details of scheduling and staffing are determined with the school's active
participation as a collaborator.

Involvement in Evaluation Activities

Big Brothers/Big Sisters of Greater Miami has steadily increased its involvement in evaluation activities as its services have grown and diversified. From beginnings in board-initiated telephone surveys to random
samples of matches to assess satisfaction and recordkeeping reviews by
board members, there is now extensive documentation on each match,
match closure, and annual goal-setting process. Its annual report summarizes data collected over the year on the intake process, the number of
assessments, the number of potential volunteers requesting information,
the source of volunteer inquiries, the number of matches made by match
type, and the racial/ethnic distribution of the youth participants and volunteers. Every 5 years Big Brothers/Big Sisters of Greater Miami is evaluated by the national office of Big Brothers/Big Sisters, Inc. The 1996
results indicated that it must do even more extensive screenings for volunteers and children, using revised instruments for psychosocial evaluation and including a thorough needs assessment for the youth and family.
In addition, a survey of the community and the agency's major funder, the
United Way, to obtain feedback about its mission and activities led to
sweeping innovations in programming and service delivery, volunteer recruitment, and fund development in order to respond to the changing
needs of the community.

The centerpiece of its activities geared toward evaluating program impact consists of an annual mail survey of current and closed matches to
ascertain the perceptions of volunteers, parents, and youth in several ar-

eas, including the appropriateness of the match, helpfulness of the staff, impact of the program (for the volunteer, the evaluation targeted perceived impact on the client's grades, school attendance, teacher relations, self-esteem, peer relations, and family relations), suggestions for improving agency services, and the perceived impact of its services on the child's life. The 1996 results were generally favorable, but the response rate of 22% was too low to draw valid conclusions about the population of users. Every year, Big Brothers/Big Sisters of Greater Miami also conducts a telephone survey to volunteers in randomly selected matches to assess service quality.

There is an expressed interest in expanding the program's existing evaluation structure, but there does not currently appear to be sufficient capability within the organization to conduct systematic evaluation studies. Key management staff do not know of the availability of funds for more extensive program evaluations, but if they did have the capability, they would like to engage in more extensive evaluations, such as longitudinal outcome studies. Considering the interest of the executive director and the board in self-examination, it is only a matter of time and resources before more extensive research studies will be conducted.

Concluding Thoughts

The comprehensiveness of the Big Brothers/Big Sisters of Greater Miami program is based on the use of a team approach to fit their services to the needs of a given child and family. The team consists of the volunteer and the social worker, both of whom work on setting concrete and specific goals for services, making referrals, and doing case management. The shift by Big Brothers/Big Sisters of Greater Miami toward more school-based programs expands the comprehensive and preventive nature of the services by aiming services at a number of levels through group discussion, speakers, tutoring, and mentoring. Volunteers are central and are not there just to solve problems. Volunteers spend positive time with the youth in the real world, developing a close relationship, so they can see the entirety of the child's stresses and resources. Furthermore, many youth are matched for years at a time, so the volunteers can identify developmental trends and changes in the children's level of risk and competency as they get older.

The service integration feature of Big Brothers/Big Sisters of Greater Miami operates through the high visibility and influence of the agency in the community and the human service delivery system. The agency forms one-to-one partnerships with outside agencies and institutions for the purposes of volunteer recruitment; coordination of services for a given case or youth; or the introduction of new, preventive-based services. A form of reverse service integration occurs whereby there is two-way assistance provided between Big Brothers/Big Sisters and another agency or group of agencies. Big Brothers/Big Sisters of Greater Miami acts as a "broker," and once the services are in place, the school then takes over the day-to-day operation of the service integration.

7 _____

Teen Connections

Overview

The Girls Club of New York's Teen Connections program is part of a national demonstration designed to improve the health of early adolescent girls, especially those at high risk of developing poor health behaviors. Established in 1990, Girls Club of New York was one of four affiliates selected by Girls Incorporated to participate in the 3-year pilot project funded by the Kellogg Foundation. The impetus behind the program was a perceived decline in the health and physical fitness of adolescent girls. From its inception, the program has been prevention-oriented, and its primary activities have been a combination of providing information and participatory activities to identify those in need of more help, managing cases and referring high-risk program participants to the appropriate community agencies for treatment, and developing adolescent girls' leadership abilities through health-oriented community action.

It is important to understand the structure in which the Teen Connections program operates and the interdependence of the organization's multiple layers. Girls Incorporated is the national organization that received the Teen Connections grant and is ultimately responsible for providing each site with the budgetary support to operate Teen Connections. Girls Club of New York, the site of the Teen Connections program we visited, is an affiliate of Girls Incorporated. Girls Club of New York has been interested in dealing with teenage health issues for some time, so Girls Incorporated perceived the Girls Club of New York to be well-suited to participate in the Teen Connections demonstration. The focus of this chapter is on the Teen Connections program, specifically the one conducted in the Bronx, New York, but also generally on Teen Connections as a model of a prevention-based strategy and its evolution over time.

Teen Connections is presented as an example of a comprehensive service integration effort whose effectiveness was compromised by several factors. There was a lack of strong connection to the surrounding community and service delivery network, and there were problems within the umbrella organization supporting its work (i.e., Girls Club of New York). The 1996 update provides an interesting window into the future for programs that have a potentially effective model but that do not have sufficient levels of organizational and community support to fully achieve their objectives.

Mission, Goals, and Objectives

The Teen Connections mission is to improve the well-being of youth in the South Bronx through the application of a holistic view of each youth in the service delivery network. The program's major goal is to "train teens to meet their own health needs . . . through a comprehensive preventive approach that includes case management, peer counseling, health, fitness, nutrition, and teen directed community health projects" (Teen Connections, unpublished program documents, n.d.).

Teen Connections has a detailed set of objectives that reflect the four key program components: Health Fair, Teens for Teens, Connections Advocacy, and Body By Me (these are described under Service Configuration). The objectives consist of developing outreach and networks with a broad spectrum of service providers; providing an opportunity for teens to interact with service providers on the teens' turf; recruiting high-risk teens who would not normally come through the doors; providing supportive services through groups, one-to-one sessions, and referrals to internal and external resources; identifying gaps and inadequacies in services; increasing teens' knowledge about their health; and developing leadership skills through health-related community action projects.

The program has evolved continuously, and some of its goals and objectives have been modified and streamlined to meet needs uncovered at the Teen Connections pilot sites or changes introduced by Girls Incorporated or the demonstration's funder. For instance, although the involvement of significant others (e.g., parents) has always been an objective of the Connections Advocacy program component, the funder placed increased emphasis on this objective during the third year of the demonstration by requiring youth to be counseled to obtain parental consent for involvement in the program, particularly its case management activities. But the program's service emphasis remains on the youth. In fact, many Girls Incorporated affiliate agencies that have implemented the Teen Connections model provided related programs open to Teen Connections participants. The motto of Girls Incorporated is "Strong, Smart, and Bold," and their primary focus is on the development of programs, affiliate services, and interagency collaborations that enable girls to be strong, smart, and bold through alternative, positive-growth-focused activities.

Current Clientele

Teen Connections serves 12–18 year old boys and girls residing in the South Bronx. Its working definition of "at risk" was revised following its first operational year because many of Teen Connections' school-based referrals were high school dropouts with multiple severe problems. The program found that most of these teens needed far more support, assistance, and intervention than the program's prevention activities were set up to handle. In subsequent years, therefore, the program set up a screening process and refined its risk definition to ensure that referrals would be more appropriate for the program's prevention goals and services.

Attendance in the specific programs is limited; at any given time Teen Connections serves approximately 15–20 youth during the school year and 10 during the summer months through case management, 500 at the health fair, 25–35 with Body By Me, and 20 younger participants and several teen leaders through Teens for Teens. The program keeps groups small so staff can pay more personalized attention to each participant, but this year it is experimenting with groups of up to 50 youth. The racial composition of the Body By Me and case management components varies, but on average African Americans and Hispanics participate equally. The case management component serves individuals ages 12–15, and approximately 80% of its participants have African American backgrounds, whereas 20% are Hispanic. Most clients come from low-income single-parent families.

Youth become aware of the program through word-of-mouth or referrals by school personnel or other professionals for case management services. A concern voiced by participants and staff was the lack of widespread knowledge about Teen Connections within the community. This "image problem" is exacerbated by the fact that Teen Connections is housed in the Girls Club, which many youth do not perceive as a place to go for the type of program offered by Teen Connections. This is the first Girls Club of New York program that attempts to reach a broad-based clientele.

Any interested youth within the specified age range may participate in Body By Me. Participation in the other program components is more restricted. In the Teens for Teens component, teen leaders are recruited and must go through an application and screening process. Those teens who express an interest in health-related topics are favored. The teen leaders then work with a group of participants in designing community action projects. For Connections Advocacy, the case management service, youth must exhibit one of the risk factors specified in its intake assessment in order to become a "case." These risk factors include excessive absence or restriction from activities due to a health problem; poor appearance; being over- or underweight; and involvement in behaviors that put the youth at risk for teen pregnancy, AIDS, or sexually transmitted diseases.

Service Configuration

The program's primary focus is on the health issues facing adolescent girls, and it primarily offers prevention and case management services. The program has four distinct components: Body By Me, Teens for Teens, Connections Advocacy, and the Health Fair. Clients may participate in any of these program components and need not enter through case management.

All of the Teen Connections activities occur at the agency, and case management is also conducted at two school sites.

Connections Advocacy

Youth ages 12 to 15 have access to Teen Connections' case management services. To participate in Connections Advocacy, the case management component, potential participants, and a parent must sign consent forms. For case management clients, service delivery involves an extensive assessment, including questions about the participant's nutrition, dental care, education, drug habits, home life, mental health, health needs, and so on, and the development of a case plan. Youth must exhibit one of the specified health-risk factors to participate in the program's case management component. The risk assessment lets the case manager identify inappropriate cases, prioritize cases, and identify the clients that require immediate referral but not long-term case management.

The case manager maintains an office at the Girls Club but provides much of the case management at selected school sites. Clients are not actively recruited, and a school nurse or other staff member typically refers participants. Youth also learn about Connections Advocacy through informal contacts with other agencies and word of mouth. However, the case manager uses Connections Advocacy as a vehicle from which to advertise the other components of Teen Connections. The program has one case manager for its two school-based sites. The case manager typically sees approximately 15–20 cases throughout the school year and 10 cases during the summer. The program has had a number of longer term cases, although most clients simply request some type of health information.

Caseload clients meet regularly (every week or two) with the case manager, although the frequency of these meetings is situation-specific. The primary responsibilities of the case manager include providing health information, making client referrals, and encouraging clients to learn about health-related community resources. Although the case manager makes referrals, it is the client's responsibility to set up and attend appointments—in essence, to ensure that their own health needs are met. Attempts are made to involve parents in a child's treatment plan if the child is amenable. Participation of a child's significant others is mandatory only in cases that involve imminent danger. To obtain assurance that the youth received the service, the case workers ask the youth directly and routinely contact the referral service both before and after the expected service contact (to tell the referral agency to expect the youth, and to see whether the youth got there).

Body By Me

The 12-week Body By Me curriculum is offered twice each year to individuals ages 12 to 15. Those individuals who simply desire to participate in this health and fitness component are not included in the Connections

Advocacy caseload. The primary focus of Body By Me is nutrition, but it addresses a variety of health-related topics, including (a) communication, (b) self-esteem, (c) hygiene, (d) substance abuse, (e) stress management, and (f) teen sexuality. The program meets three times each week, and its weekly structure includes fitness, health education, and recreational activities. Participants can enter any time during the 12-week cycle if there are openings, but class sizes are limited to approximately 25–35.

This component has been modified significantly during the course of the demonstration. The program added recreational activities to the original curriculum structure as an incentive for program participation and modified the health education curriculum to include adolescent sexuality, a topic of importance to many participants.

Teens for Teens

Teens for Teens focuses on leadership development and community action. The program is structured in two 12-week phases that incorporate training of high school aged teen "leaders" and field experience. Teen Connections staff recruit high school students who are interested in health issues (there are three teen leaders this year) to participate as youth role models in the group's design and implementation of a community action project. These teens receive training (e.g., instruction in project planning and working in groups) and a certificate of leadership. The teens are then responsible for recruiting students between the ages of 12 and 16 who are interested in participating in the program. Although the primary focus is on recruiting female participants, boys are accepted into the program. The group designs and carries out community-related health projects. During the second year of the demonstration, Teens for Teens participants created a public service announcement on AIDS.

Health Fair

The annual Health Fair exposes participating teens to information about local health agencies and attempts to promote the use of the agencies' services. Teens for Teens youth participants have the responsibility to recruit youth presenters for the Health Fair, but an organizing committee of adults has overall responsibility for the event.

Type and Make-Up of the Service Integration Network

Teen Connections has no formal contracts or agreements with other agencies to exchange resources or services. Most of its activities and services are offered in-house, but it does make referrals to outside agencies. Teen Connections has formed informal relationships with key community agencies that facilitate referrals of youth to these agencies as needed. One of Teen Connections' major referral agencies is the area's adolescent sexuality clinic, the Hub Center for Change (a project of Planned Parenthood of New York City, Inc.), which provides services related to pregnancy and sexual activity. Other agencies to which Teen Connections refers clients include the Fordham-Tremont Clinic (for mental health services) and the Citizens Advice Bureau (geared toward parents who seek information about domestic violence issues).

The program also has informal linkages with two junior high schools and a number of local agencies. The case manager obtained permission of two junior high school principals to locate Teen Connections' case management function within the schools. The case manager shares an office with a school staff member while in school. Additionally, because Teen Connections does not have the capacity to perform home visits, the schools' dropout prevention programs conduct these visits and may refer some of these youth to Teen Connections.

Teen Connections also forged a relationship with Lehmann College. The college provides a number of health education interns who work with Teen Connections staff to support its programming. Teen Connections has also attempted to work collaboratively with other Girls Club of New York programs. During the 1992–1993 program year, Teen Connections were hoping to collaborate with two additional Girls Club programs: the Options Center, which offers a violence forum, sports, and fitness activities; and the Youth Employment program. Teen Connections and staff of these two programs developed a plan for how this collaboration would proceed, but it has not yet begun. The plan includes sharing staff and financial resources among the programs in order to extend the club's hours and give youth access to a broader range of services.

Funding Sources

The Kellogg Foundation is the primary funder of this demonstration project, although the city of New York's Department of Youth Services provides the financial support for the Body By Me component. The Kellogg Foundation awarded $1.8 million to Girls Incorporated for the 4-year demonstration (3 years are operational and 1 year is administrative). The national evaluation headquarters is at Girls Incorporated in New York, but the project director for Teen Connections is in Indianapolis. The national program regulates the flow of funds to the local demonstration sites, and New York's Teen Connections receives approximately $100,000 each year to administer the program. These funds are distributed fairly evenly across the sites.

Teen Connections program staff indicate that they unsuccessfully tried to obtain additional funding for their Bronx program to meet operational expenses but that Girls Incorporated's "pass through" system of allocating funds, which gave an equal amount of funding to each site, did not allow funding-related modifications in response to site-specific expenses. The Kellogg Foundation's demonstration funding ended at the conclusion of the 1992–1993 program year, and continuation funding remained in doubt at the time of the 1992 visit.

Update: 1996

When we finished the site visit in 1992, we were convinced that the Teen Connections demonstration at the Girls Club in the Bronx was destined to be terminated. The program's parent organization, Girls Club of New York, was without an executive director for more than 6 months as a result of both additional staff turnover and uncertainties within the parent organization. Teen Connections was operating in a somewhat unpredictable environment at that time.

By 1996, Teen Connections had become a victim of the internal, administrative, and financial problems at the host Girls Club of New York and was terminated. One of the problems was that the board of the Girls Club of New York was developed for influence and fundraising but not to become linked with community needs. As a result, over time, the agency became increasingly more removed from its community constituency and was not viewed favorably by the neighborhood residents. At one point, in 1994, the Girls Club of New York was considering dissolution, but instead it merged with the Citizens Advice Bureau in order to consolidate the organization, coordinate staff functions, and develop program priorities. The Citizens Advice Bureau salvaged the agency, but its future mission and structure were still in limbo as late as our interview in 1996.

Despite the fate of the Bronx Teen Connections program, our update interview with Bernice Humphrey, director of Healthy Girls Initiative at the National Resource Center for Girls Incorporated, suggested that Teen Connections lives on as a key prevention strategy of Girls Incorporated. The Kellogg Foundation research and demonstration project involved four sites, and the New York site was probably the most problematic of the four in terms of both program implementation and effects, although the Seattle site faced similar challenges and issues. The New York and, to a lesser degree, Seattle experiences contrast markedly with the two remaining demonstration Teen Connections programs, which were seen as major service providers in the communities and therefore able to make more systemwide changes to the service delivery network. Two of the program components were retained in the updated version of Teen Connections, Teens for Teens and Connections Advocacy, because these were found to have some impact, according to the demonstration project evaluation report. Changes in Teen Connections since the demonstration ended have been primarily in funding, administration, and program.

Changes in Funding

Girls Incorporated was not successful in obtaining additional funding for Teen Connections as a national program, so it adopted an alternative strategy for dissemination. Girls Incorporated decided to promote the program actively to its affiliate Girls Club agencies across the country through its National Resource Center. Although Girls Incorporated does not provide funds to its affiliates for startup costs, it encourages the affiliates through professional development, dissemination of materials, and staff training at national conferences to implement these programs as useful prevention strategies for adolescent women. The National Resource Center offers technical assistance for the development and implementation of the two key components of Teen Connections: Teens for Teens and Connections Advocacy. In 1995, Girls Incorporated gave implementation training to affiliates on the Teens for Teens, and approximately 10 affiliates participated in the training and are currently in various stages of implementing this program component. The National Resource Center is also in the process of preparing and publishing an implementation guide for Teen Connections, but this has been delayed because of a shortage of funds. As we shall see, a number of affiliates have successfully implemented one or both of the Teen Connections components.

Changes in Management and Administration

The continued growth of the Teen Connections model hinges on the ability of the Girls Incorporated affiliate agencies to implement the program components. According to Bernice Humphrey, not all affiliates have the necessary resources to implement Teen Connections successfully. Local affiliate Girls Clubs can make the transition to the Teen Connections approach for comprehensive services integration if they are strong and stable and have high credibility in their communities. All sites noted that taking on Teen Connections helped increase visibility and credibility, but there may be some conflict between the goals of Teen Connections and the primary mission of many affiliates. The Teen Connections model focuses primarily on health issues of adolescent women, whereas the mission of affiliates is to build the girls' leadership and action skills. Sometimes affiliates are not prepared to push for the health education outcomes when the priority is placed on leadership skills, especially when logistics, funding structure, or resources do not allow both goals to be developed concurrently.

There is a strong commitment by Girls Incorporated to see their affiliates evolve into comprehensive, service-integrated agencies in their respective communities by functioning as advocates and health experts on resources for the needs of girls. However, as a national organization, Girls Incorporated does not fund program implementation, with the exception of special projects to develop and evaluate new programs. Girls Incorporated primarily assists the fundraising efforts of affiliates by identifying funding sources and providing technical assistance in writing a proposal. The National Resource Center for Girls Incorporated promotes Teen Connections to its affiliate agencies through presentations at regional conferences, individual technical assistance to the affiliates to start-up Teen Connections, and workshops.

Program Changes

The National Resource Center for Girls Incorporated drafted an implementation and planning guide that identified the strategies critical to maximizing the success of the Teens for Teens component from the lessons learned from all demonstration sites. However, the recommended implementation differs from that used by the Girls Club of New York site and is based on the successful program experiences reported by the other three sites in the demonstration project. Rather than the older "teen intern" first deciding on a community action strategy and then finding a group of younger teens to implement the plan, there is now much more emphasis on the teen interns acting as facilitators for the leadership and community action skills of the younger teens. They lead the younger teens in a series of engaging, educational activities to learn about community issues, facilitate a discussion of potential solutions that would make a difference, and then help their younger peers to choose and develop a project that could have an impact. The program now emphasizes the ongoing process of leadership building and community awareness. A group of teens may do several projects over the school year, or they may just study a problem or series of problems without arriving at an "action-ready" plan. There is no pressure for the group to develop a project around every issue they study.

A recent example of a successful Teens for Teens project gained media attention for an affiliate of Girls Incorporated located in South Dakota. A Teens for Teens workgroup identified smoking among teens as an important issue. The workgroup, led by a teen intern, generated and carried out a number of plans to get the message out that teens should not begin smoking cigarettes, including inviting police department speakers to discuss the laws regarding the sale of cigarettes to minors, surveying peers to find out how easy it was for teens to obtain tobacco products, educating merchants about selling to minors using a "sting" operation (they received a great deal of press for this activity), and lobbying school boards to change the school smoking policies for teens and school staff to provide a consistent message about the harmful effects of smoking.

Originally a case management component, Connections Advocacy has been reconfigured so that it integrates the coordinating council and the Health Fair within an overall case management strategy. Girls Incorporated found this component a challenge for agency affiliates to initiate because it moves the agency from the original prevention-oriented focus of most of its programs to one that deals with the real life issues and problems that many of the teens have, including serious problems with substance abuse, sexuality, violence, or school dropout. For teens to become involved in the program, they must show some degree of risky behavior. That is, the girls must have some identified difficulty or problem. Students are referred to the program by school counselors, nurses, or teachers; program staff who have day-to-day contact with the teen in the prevention programs; and other organizations that have contact with the affiliate program. For example, the Girls Incorporated affiliate in South Dakota has a strong connection with the juvenile justice system, and this system is the source of many referrals. Girls needing the intensive support of this component are also found through the case manager's own outreach activities. Once the youth is referred to the program, an assessment is conducted in which the case manager interviews the adolescent.

An important lesson learned from the use of assessment in Connections Advocacy is that teens at this age do not volunteer information about their current problems. The case manager has to probe for risky situations that need attention. This reticence may initially cause difficulty because teens do not divulge difficulties. Case managers may misclassify a problem when they do not have the adequate information. When an essentially prevention-focused organization sponsors and houses a case management component, it may have to help its staff learn how to assess a youth's comprehensive needs.

Dissemination of the case management component has not gone beyond two of the demonstration sites that participated in the original Kellogg-funded project plus two other affiliates that decided to implement it on a very limited basis. Connections Advocacy is currently being implemented at Girls Incorporated affiliates in South Dakota and Birmingham, Alabama. Elements of the program exist in other affiliates that already provide some degree of counseling services and many of the other aspects to Teen Connections, including Orange County and Santa Barbara, California, and Memphis, Tennessee. Connections Advocacy allows these latter sites to add a case management component to their existing treatment services.

Involvement in Evaluation Activities

Teen Connections–Bronx participated in a national evaluation along with the three other Teen Connections demonstration sites. However, the Bronx Teen Connections site and one of the other demonstration sites had some difficulties with the independent evaluator conducting the national data collection effort. In 1992, the Bronx program reported that some clients were offended by specific questions on a form the youth had to complete (one of the questions asked the teens if they had bugs in their houses) and that the evaluator had made remarks within hearing range of participants that reflected a disrespectful attitude. (The evaluator was overheard commenting that the kids were "making babies in the school halls.") One of the other evaluation sites had similar experiences. The national program staff were made aware of these issues. Arrangements were made for these two programs to continue with the national evaluation, but for the evaluator to refrain from certain types of direct contact with the youth.

During its operations as a demonstration site, Teen Connections–Bronx performed basic record keeping and had access to data from a variety of sources, including case managers' information on referral reason and an assessment of risk indicators; intake forms, including client background information; and service referral forms, including information on referral type, provider, date of referral, and date of service (obtained from follow-up calls to the referral agency and by asking the youth directly). Monthly program summaries were sent directly to the Girls Incorporated national director.

When the research and demonstration phase ended at the end of 1993, an evaluation by an independent researcher contracted by the Kellogg Foundation reported mainly positive effects for the two central components of the program: Teens for Teens and Connections Advocacy. The Kellogg report on the research and demonstration effects concluded that Teens for Teens and Connections Advocacy are powerful strategies for assisting Girls Club affiliate agencies to go beyond primary prevention and to take an active role in the community linking services to improve the health of teenage girls.

Concluding Thoughts

The demise of Teen Connections in New York City raises an interesting lesson for comprehensive service integration because it highlights the importance of program context. Context may be defined as the community needs and how the existing human services system is structured to meet these needs. Efforts to coordinate and integrate services within a given community may be limited by the make-up of the service delivery system already in place and the intransigence of this system in the face of change. The weaknesses of the host agency in New York contributed to its lack of success because the host agency (Girls Club of New York) did not have a high degree of credibility or visibility as a key service provider or as a broker for the service delivery system. Through a combination of its own resource limitations (money and staff) and the administrative and managerial difficulties of the host agency, Teen Connections could not effectively act as the "mortar between bricks."

Finally, the experience of Teen Connections as a research and demonstration project is not unique. The evaluation was done by an outside evaluator and thus was not "owned" by the program, and when the demonstration period ended there were no funds available to maintain program operations (assuming the host organization was able to do so). Thus, the experience of all Teen Connections programs operated by Girls Incorporated illustrates an important limitation to innovative programs that begin as research and demonstration efforts: When the demonstration period ends, the program can no longer be sustained at a high level of involvement and eventually disappears or becomes diluted because of lack of funding and resource support.

8

The Belafonte-Tacolcy Center, Inc.

Overview

Belafonte-Tacolcy Center is among the most prevention-oriented of the programs we studied. Offering comprehensive services that span a wide developmental continuum from pre-school-aged children to young adults, the Center functions as a community center or "clubhouse," with additional programs provided in local schools. All phases of a youth's development are addressed through a mix of educational, counseling, recreational, vocational, and leadership training activities. Its programs primarily target the children and youth themselves and secondarily target parents, who participate in individual counseling, group meetings, and workshops.

The Belafonte-Tacolcy Center was founded in 1967 by a group of young men in Liberty City, an impoverished inner city of Miami, as a grassroots organization serving local-area youth. Originally known as The Advisory Committee of Liberty City Youth (TACOLCY), the name was changed to Belafonte-Tacolcy Center in 1969 to commemorate a donation to the new facility by singer-actor Harry Belafonte. In 1970 it incorporated as a private nonprofit organization. The city of Miami owns the present Tacolcy facility, which was built in 1969, and leases it indefinitely to Belafonte-Tacolcy Center. The history of Belafonte-Tacolcy reveals strong continuity between the initial cohorts of youth served by the Center and today's youth. Many of the program's current leaders and managers were themselves youth participants in Belafonte-Tacolcy when it first opened its doors.

Mission, Goals, and Objectives

The overall mission of Belafonte-Tacolcy is to provide "diversified services to children, youth, and young adults aged 2½ to 26 years that can allow them to become responsible, productive citizens" (Belafonte-Tacolcy Center, unpublished documents, n.d.). The goals the program has set to carry out this mission include increasing social functioning, building leadership skills, and fostering healthy adolescent development. Although Belafonte-Tacolcy Center's core mission has not changed significantly over the years,

117

new activities and programs have been added over time in response to community needs.

The original youth programs included recreational activities, enrichment groups, a summer youth employment program, youth leadership groups, and a cultural arts program. These are still the core activities at Belafonte-Tacolcy. Programs added later focus on preventing specific problems such as alcohol and drug abuse, academic failure, gang membership, HIV/AIDS, and youth unemployment, and on promoting child and adolescent development.

Belafonte-Tacolcy has added several program components for youth since 1981. The Community Outreach Intervention and Cultural Appreciation Program (COICAP) was added in that year as a school dropout and juvenile delinquency prevention program. The school-based Drug and Alcohol Abuse Prevention Program was developed at approximately the same time. Belafonte-Tacolcy worked with a number of other community agencies to start a Haitian Outreach Center in the late 1980s to provide outreach and on-site access to many services for newly arrived Haitian immigrants. The most recent program additions include a community-based HIV/AIDS awareness program (1989) and an Anti-Gang Program (1990).

Current Clientele

All children, youth, and their parents living in Liberty City are eligible for the programs and activities. Specific programs are geared toward various age groups as follows: day care is offered for 2½–5 year olds, after-school care is provided to children 6–13 years old, the Liberty City youth enrichment programs (including COICAP and other prevention modules) are targeted at youth from 6–18 years of age, and the Stay-In-School, the Outdoor Challenge, and the Youth Vocational Training and Employment Opportunities programs are aimed at youth 14 years of age and older.

The general profile of youth participating in Belafonte-Tacolcy programs mirrors the sociodemographic makeup of the Liberty City area: approximately 75% are African American, 20% are recent Haitian immigrants and refugees, and 5% are Hispanic. Most of these children and youth live in poor single-parent households and are exposed to open-air drug selling, neighborhood crack houses, high rates of criminal activity, and frequent violence. In general, Belafonte-Tacolcy considers all children living in Liberty City to be at risk and thus eligible for any Belafonte-Tacolcy programs.

Each component program of Belafonte-Tacolcy has its own target population within the general category of children and youth living in Liberty City. To participate in the COICAP program, youth must have been involved with the juvenile justice system or have displayed academic performance problems that indicate a high likelihood of dropping out of school. The Drug and Alcohol Abuse Prevention Program conducted in school classrooms involves the worker targeting an entire class that contains a high number of youth displaying poor school performance, behavioral problems, truancy, or prior drug involvement. Classrooms are identified by the school principal and teachers in conjunction with the Belafonte-Tacolcy worker. During the in-class workshop, the Belafonte-Tacolcy worker identifies individual children who require more intense preventive interventions. The Anti-Gang Program originally served mainly the children of former gang members, but slow recruitment led the program to expand to youth showing behavior problems in school (as identified by the school guidance counselor). The Health Enrichment Program featuring HIV/AIDS awareness goes to all youth attending Dade County schools located in the Liberty City area, as well as to parents and other members of the community through church groups and other street venues (e.g., beauty salons and barber shops).

Service Configuration

Specific program components are delivered at the Belafonte-Tacolcy Center and at a number of elementary, middle, and high schools. A variety of programs are aimed at younger children, including a meal program, day care and after-school care, and other child development enrichment activities. Also, a number of activities are aimed at older adolescents and young adults, including the Stay-in-School project, the Youth Vocational Training and Employment Opportunity Program, and adolescent development enrichment activities. Because the focus of this book is at-risk youth ages 10 to 14, we will deal primarily with activities geared toward this older group.

The basic model of all prevention activities at Belafonte-Tacolcy consists of a group workshop typically delivered within a classroom setting, in which the Belafonte-Tacolcy staff member presents a formal curriculum and at the same time identifies more serious problems in specific individuals. Those youth identified in the workshops as being at high risk are then offered more intensive services at Belafonte-Tacolcy, consisting of comprehensive needs assessment, academic tutoring, peer counseling, and parental support. The parent or youth may also be referred to outside services, including mental health centers, health crisis counseling centers, child welfare agencies, or other community-based groups. Belafonte-Tacolcy uses this basic model in the Community Outreach Intervention and Cultural Appreciation Program (COICAP), the Drug and Alcohol Abuse Prevention Program, the Anti-Gang Program, and the HIV/AIDS Health Enrichment Program. A variation of this basic model involves identifying the high-risk youth through their participation in recreational and sports development programs at Belafonte-Tacolcy and then referring these youth for comprehensive assessment and more intensive services if required.

The central and longest running prevention activity at Belafonte-Tacolcy is the Community Outreach Intervention and Cultural Appreciation Program (COICAP). This is a combined crime prevention and school dropout prevention program for youth 6–18 years of age. Most youth are referred by school counselors and teachers or the juvenile justice system, typically the courts. Some youth are also "walk-ins": They ask for help with school and after assessment become eligible for all program activities. COICAP offers an extensive psychosocial risk assessment, including a home visit, which is followed by an individualized treatment plan. Most plans include after-school educational and developmental workshops that emphasize building self-esteem; anxiety management; decision making; problem solving; and enhancing academic skills through tutoring, diagnostic assessment, monitoring progress, and working with school teachers. Finally, parents of COICAP youth become involved in parenting skills development workshops and family counseling, if appropriate. Youth in COICAP also participate in a variety of field trips, including Outdoor Challenge, a wilderness stress–challenge program.

The Drug and Alcohol Abuse Prevention Program is similar to COICAP but works with youth at risk for becoming involved in drugs. The program attempts to provide a comprehensive support system through a combination of school-based enrichment workshops, supervised recreational activities, educational tutoring–enrichment, individual counseling, and home visits. Belafonte-Tacolcy staff provide workshops on drug abuse prevention within the classrooms at various elementary and middle schools. Youth identified in these workshops by Belafonte-Tacolcy staff as requiring further assistance are then referred to the Center itself. There they may receive a more comprehensive assessment of needs and more intensive services and activities that follow the overall model of service delivery at Belafonte-Tacolcy (group and individual counseling, workshops in esteem building and refusal skills, academic tutoring, parenting skills development workshops and individual parental counseling, and referral to other agencies).

There are a variety of additional prevention and enrichment programs for youth in the 10 to 14 year age range. The Anti-Gang Program offers weekly developmental workshops to twenty 4th, 5th, and 6th grade classes in two primary schools. The workshops are geared to children of former gang members and children who "hang out" with older gang members, and they focus on building self-esteem, stress management, drug education, academic monitoring, individual counseling, parental involvement, and assessments.

The Belafonte-Tacolcy Health Enrichment Program provides HIV/AIDS education throughout the community (e.g., in schools, churches, beauty salons and barbershops, and other places where teens and young adults congregate). The core Health Enrichment Program consists of five 1-hour sessions presented to classrooms, church groups, or other assembled groups of youth or parents. The program is delivered through a variety of techniques, including videos, concerts, street outreach, lectures, music, role plays, and discussion groups. In school settings, Belafonte-Tacolcy staff provide a school-board-approved, in-class HIV/AIDS awareness curriculum to all students. Finally, Belafonte-Tacolcy operates a youth crisis telephone line, conducts an off-campus work-study program involving college students doing peer mentoring and tutoring, provides a summer youth employment and training program, and works with other agencies in the Haitian Outreach Center. Belafonte-Tacolcy also collaborates with other community agencies, including mental health centers, health crisis counseling centers, food banks, recreational centers, churches, and local private groups, such as the Private Industries Council.

The second executive director of Belafonte-Tacolcy, Otis Pitts, initiated the Tacolcy Economic Development Corporation (TEDC) following the 1968 race riots, which took place largely in the Liberty City area, where Belafonte-Tacolcy is situated. TEDC began with the goal of rebuilding the neighborhood and thereby enhancing the local economy. It continues to contribute to the maintenance and further development of the Liberty City area through large projects, such as building apartments and shopping centers. TEDC is an economic development program that creates jobs, improves neighborhood safety, and makes available more affordable housing. Belafonte-Tacolcy Center owns a shopping center developed by TEDC, and a portion of the profits get funneled back into the Center to support its youth programs.

Type and Make-Up of the Service Integration Network

Belafonte-Tacolcy is involved in three linkage networks. The first involves informal liaisons with other agencies in the Liberty City community. Second, Belafonte-Tacolcy has relatively well-developed links to the area schools through the Dade County School Board. Finally, Belafonte-Tacolcy is a partner with other agencies in two community development projects, the Haitian Outreach Center and the Tacolcy Economic Development Corporation.

Belafonte-Tacolcy has established informal ties to a number of agencies in the community, including mental health centers, health crisis centers, the state's Department of Social Services, food banks, recreational centers, the James E. Scott Community Association (a direct service agency), and the juvenile courts and juvenile justice departments. Staff also sit on a number of interagency councils within the Liberty City area, each of which addresses a specific community issue, such as hurricane relief, drug and alcohol abuse, mental health, and youth problems. These informal linkages come into play when staff note that a youth has a particular need that another agency can meet.

A highly developed set of links exists between Belafonte-Tacolcy and various elementary, middle, and high schools in the Liberty City area. These arrangements, formalized in written documents, involve drug abuse prevention, anti-gang, and health enrichment programs that Belafonte-Tacolcy delivers in school classrooms. In addition, youth already enrolled in the Stay-in-School Program may be released from classes for individual work on school grounds with a Belafonte-Tacolcy staff person. Belafonte-Tacolcy staff also frequently consult with school principals, vice-principals, guidance counselors, and teachers about individual youth.

Finally, Belafonte-Tacolcy Center participates in the Haitian Outreach

Center, a collaborative effort of the United Way, the Salvation Army, New Horizons, Legal Services of Greater Miami, and the Center for Haitian Studies. The Haitian Outreach Center is a comprehensive multiservice center that addresses many needs of Haitian immigrants, such as helping parents register their children for school, conducting workshops on how to deal with immigrant problems, and holding courses in English as a second language. The Salvation Army donates space, and United Way funds pay for staff salaries of workers outplaced from many community agencies. (Belafonte-Tacolcy has a full-time staff person at the Center.)

Belafonte-Tacolcy has an established plan for dealing with outside agencies that want to work with the Center, or that want to reach the youth at Belafonte-Tacolcy to fill in service gaps with new projects that will involve new funding. Once Belafonte-Tacolcy and the agency agree to work together to obtain funding and develop the new service, they draft and sign a written agreement. Acting on the agreement is understood to be contingent on receiving the funding to support the project. Funding sources for these collaborations typically consist of state or federal agencies with competitive grant programs; Belafonte-Tacolcy serves as the fiscal agent for grants resulting from successful applications. If a grant application is funded, a Belafonte-Tacolcy program manager and outside agency personnel establish a more polished version of the working concept and solidify working relationships between Center staff and an individual staff member at the other agency involved. During the past 5 years, Belafonte-Tacolcy program managers have followed this approach of gaining commitments from cooperating agencies before writing a grant application. In the past, Belafonte-Tacolcy sometimes received money for new programs without having specific agency commitments to cooperate. This informal process did not work because the agencies spent too much time during the grant period just setting up the arrangements before program services could begin. Now, agreements are formalized with the official in charge of each cooperating agency before funding applications are written.

Funding Sources

Belafonte-Tacolcy receives funds from local, state, and federal funding entities and from the United Way; it has an annual 1992 budget of $1.6 million. The breakdown by funding sources is 27% from federal agencies, 19% from state agencies, 38% from local sources, and 16% from the United Way. Approximately one third of local funds come from private donations. In the past several years, some major changes have occurred in the proportion of funds from each source. United Way funds have remained relatively constant over the past 5 years. But as a result of additional fundraising and new programs at Belafonte-Tacolcy, the United Way share of Belafonte-Tacolcy's budget has dropped from 48% 5 years ago to its present 16%. United Way funds have also fallen slightly in the past year (1% for all community agencies receiving funds) because of problems in the local economy. Over the last 5 years, an increasingly high proportion of program

funds in a greatly expanded total budget have come from short-term demonstration programs that provide support for a specified time period.

Update: 1996

Belafonte-Tacolcy has continued to move forward since we visited the
agency in 1992. As a result of the forces within the agency as well as
factors in the external interagency and larger policy environments, there
have been changes in management and administration, programming, interagency relationships, physical facilities, and evaluation activities over
the past 4 years.

Changes in Management and Administration

Strategic planning activities have been going on over the past year or so
and have featured joint meetings between all staff and the board of directors, which is a first for the agency. In the past, the board worked exclusively with the executive director and some selected administrative staff,
but this year the entire staff was included. The strategic planning activities also include four youth members to provide participant input into the
plan. Also plans are currently underway to develop a "youth seat" on the
board of directors so that youth continue to have a say in the agency's
direction. This is a relatively novel idea, but it is based on Belafonte-
Tacolcy's long history of providing a "career path" for its youth (several
active board members were participants in Belafonte-Tacolcy when they
were youths, 20–30 years ago).

Finally, in response to a request from the United Way, Belafonte-
Tacolcy reorganized its budget by eliminating or consolidating management positions in order to provide more programming activities.

Program Changes

Belafonte-Tacolcy no longer receives funding for the COICAP program because of an administrative difficulty in submitting a renewal application.
As a result of the funding reduction, Belafonte-Tacolcy is no longer hiring
youth from within the neighborhood as tutors and cannot operate the outdoor challenge–wilderness or peer mentoring components. However,
Belafonte-Tacolcy has been able to continue some key aspects of the COI-
CAP program using funds from United Way and the Metro Dade County
Community Block Grant. The COICAP program still provides intensive
counseling for identified youth, conducts field trips, and operates the
school-based prevention component.

Some changes in programs and services offered by Belafonte-Tacolcy
were spurred by shifts in federal, state, and local policies. First, the state
of Florida passed a law mandating community service as a requirement
for high school students to graduate. Furthermore, there was interest in

having university students perform community service as well, although this was not mandated by state law. At the same time, Belafonte-Tacolcy found that teachers in the inner city schools did not always not take into consideration the environment in which the children lived. Belafonte-Tacolcy wants to ensure that youth are both empowered and do not become penalized because of the environment in which they live. For example, a teacher gave a homework assignment, but there was not always a quiet place for the students to work, so the homework did not get done. In response to these trends, Belafonte-Tacolcy developed a peer tutorial program in which high school students help younger students on their homework assignments and college students help high school students to prepare for the Scholastic Aptitude Test (SAT). Florida International University (FIU) asked to work with Belafonte-Tacolcy. Over a series of meetings between Belafonte-Tacolcy and FIU, the SAT tutorial component was developed, and initial implementation began at the end of September 1996.

Another key change in Belafonte-Tacolcy programs was prompted by the new federal welfare law. State laws regarding welfare benefits, particularly those in Florida, have undergone some considerable restrictions in anticipation of the new federal law. For some time now, Belafonte-Tacolcy has been bombarded with requests by families needing jobs after the families went to the welfare office for recertification and found their benefits reduced. The message that their benefits will continue only for a limited duration of time, after which they must find employment, was clearly given, and families on welfare naturally went to Belafonte-Tacolcy for help. Belafonte-Tacolcy is trying to work with Jobs of Miami to refer parents to an agency that can help parents to find jobs, and it is also spending more time dealing with parents' needs. The problem is that parents want Belafonte-Tacolcy to provide these services because they trust the agency, but Belafonte-Tacolcy does not have the staff to deal with parents at the level they need the service. Belafonte-Tacolcy has been spending considerable time finding a partner agency that can provide preemployment, job search, and other employment-related services to parents at the Belafonte-Tacolcy facility. Thus far, Belafonte-Tacolcy has completed one interagency agreement with Jobs of Miami and will enter into more interagency agreements with Jobs of Miami as well as with other agencies. Although Jobs of Miami was happy to work out of the Belafonte-Tacolcy facility, eventually parents will have to go to the Jobs of Miami training site for the more intensive training and job readiness services. Belafonte-Tacolcy is working out a cooperative agreement with Jobs of Miami to share transportation for parents.

Changes in Interagency Relationships

Changes in interagency relationships occurred when Otis Pitts, the longtime and highly visible executive director of TEDC, left to take the post of deputy secretary at the U.S. Department of Housing and Urban Development (HUD) in the wake of Hurricane Andrew. The new executive director does not have as extensive a network in the community and is not as experienced in developing links with other agencies. There also has been a shift at TEDC toward concentrating on housing and urban development rather than on interagency collaboration. As a result, many of the key interagency relationships developed when Mr. Pitts was executive director of TEDC have been lost. Furthermore, TEDC is not as involved with Belafonte-Tacolcy as it was when we visited in 1992. At approximately the same time, Yvonne McCollough left Belafonte-Tacolcy and the agency went through a number of new executive directors, which only added to the increased distance between Belafonte-Tacolcy and TEDC. Ms. Sabrina Baker-Bouie was hired as executive director in March of 1996, so she is still relatively new. Lately the board of Belafonte-Tacolcy has been trying to rekindle its relationship with TEDC, and both agencies see the need to become reconnected. As one step, the Belafonte-Tacolcy board chairperson has written a letter to the TEDC board chairperson reminding him of the collaboration and asking if they could interchange board members. Currently, TEDC and Belafonte-Tacolcy are involved in several joint planning activities. For example, at the shopping center jointly owned by Belafonte-Tacolcy and TEDC, one of the largest tenants, a food store, wants to expand. Belafonte-Tacolcy has been working with TEDC on an expansion plan to give this store more space while at the same time providing some additional capacity for new youth projects, such as the joint Belafonte-Tacolcy/TEDC entrepreneurship program (discussed later).

The Miami Heat basketball team has entered into a partnership with Belafonte-Tacolcy in which Belafonte-Tacolcy will serve as a hub for any community program kicked off by the Heat. For example, a number of summer basketball camps and clinics are planned over the next year for a variety of age groups, and the Heat will coordinate these with Belafonte-Tacolcy and donate funds for the trophies and prizes. Finally, Belafonte-Tacolcy is receiving more funds from the city of Miami to operate recreational and sports programs, and the Summer Youth Employment Program operated by Belafonte-Tacolcy was among the largest in the area; it employed approximately 350 youth in the past summer.

Physical Facility Improvements

Over the years, the facility had fallen into disrepair, largely because of a lack of city funds with which to properly maintain it. This contributed to the bad feelings between Belafonte-Tacolcy and the surrounding neighborhood, who were beginning to perceive Belafonte-Tacolcy as "going downhill." Recently, the physical facilities have been transformed as a result of two factors: the United Way annual campaign kickoff and the federal "Weed and Seed" antidrug funding. Every year, to kickoff the United Way's annual campaign, one of the member agencies is chosen to undergo a large-scale face-lift using volunteers from all United Way agencies. This past year, Belafonte-Tacolcy was selected, and 2,000 volunteers worked to completely refurbish the existing facilities and to add a new library. When the city of Miami received federal "Weed and Seed" funds to reduce drug and alcohol abuse, crime, and violence, Belafonte-Tacolcy was selected as the safe haven for the Weed and Seed grant. This means that programs funded out of this grant will operate from Belafonte-Tacolcy, including the director and staff hired for the grant. The Weed and Seed director and the Belafonte-Tacolcy executive director have an informal arrangement that no program will operate out of Belafonte-Tacolcy without the mutual consent of both parties. The Weed and Seed grant will allow Belafonte-Tacolcy to add more programs (e.g., dance classes and outdoor camping), and more children will use the facilities, which will allow Belafonte-Tacolcy to rebuild its relationships with neighbors in the community (churches, businesses, etc.). The contribution by the United Way kickoff campaign in terms of refurbishing the facilities as well as the location of the Weed and Seed grant at Belafonte-Tacolcy has given the agency's image and credibility in the community a much-needed boost. Given the lack of resources elsewhere in the community, the larger service provider network and community report being pleased with its updated facilities and its expanded programming.

Plans for the Future

The program recently submitted a proposal to develop a youth entrepreneur center that would train high school graduates to operate a retail business. The proposed plan is for Belafonte-Tacolcy to open a store selling sneakers and t-shirts. Youth who work in the store receive on-the-job training through a local community college. The planned expansion of the shopping center will provide the space to open the storefront jointly operated by Belafonte-Tacolcy and the Tacolcy Economic Development Corporation. Additionally, a Narcotics Anonymous group holds weekly meetings in the evenings at the Belafonte-Tacolcy center to assist the families of youth who are affected by drug abuse.

Involvement in Evaluation Activities

Belafonte-Tacolcy lays the groundwork for future evaluation activities through its collection of program and client-monitoring data. Staff open files on individual children whenever a child participates in any of the recreation or prevention activities at the Center, whether located on site, at schools, or in the community. Client information includes family background data, assessment of needs and risk status, and some pre–post tests of drug knowledge or gang affiliation. Belafonte-Tacolcy monitors progress toward quarterly and annual goals through a monthly client service data report developed by the program director. This report specifies the number of services provided, the number of clients served, and the overall units (in hours) of service given each month. Programs also use a goal-oriented recording system to identify goals for each client (youth and parent or family) and specific objectives to achieve these goals. In addition, many of the recreational activity programs and the school-based workshops also keep records, primarily of attendance, to track a youth's participation across a set of Center-based and school-based programs and activities. There is some pre–post testing for classroom presentations and group activities, to see whether youth have moved in the desired direction with respect to skills and abilities, knowledge, and behaviors.

The board has appointed a program committee to monitor quarterly data-gathering activities for the purpose of preparing evaluation summaries for funders. Systematic formative evaluations are now required by each funding source. The executive director and a recently hired administrative assistant coordinate data-gathering activities while program staff maintain detailed records of client participation in center activities. The evaluation summaries provide basic information for the yearly evaluation conducted by a United Way allocations panel. This evaluation includes a site visit by the panel as well as studying the evaluation summaries prepared by the executive director.

Despite its ability to monitor program processes, Belafonte-Tacolcy is at a relatively early stage in its evaluation capability. The data currently collected allow for a monitoring function and a "formative" evaluation mechanism by being able to describe both client characteristics and service use. However, Belafonte-Tacolcy does not yet use a computerized management information system (MIS) for its recordkeeping and tracking of services, and this should be a first step toward more systematic evaluations. Without this additional capability, Belafonte-Tacolcy cannot obtain timely summaries and cannot perform data analyses to detect, for example, patterns in service use or changes in client risk and backgrounds. Furthermore, a true formative or process-oriented evaluation should build from the monitoring data by collecting additional information on community needs, staff perceptions of client changes, and service use and to identify potentially viable measures of effectiveness.

The program director indicated substantial enthusiasm and willingness to do more in-depth evaluation of the program and was particularly interested in assessing long-term effectiveness using a longitudinal design. She was willing to involve Belafonte-Tacolcy in a research and demonstration project even if it meant changing some of the program procedures to accommodate the research study. However, the program currently lacks the resources and capabilities to participate in more extensive evaluation research. Recently Belafonte-Tacolcy has initiated discussions with its part-time grant writer, who is also an evaluation specialist at the University of Miami, on ways to improve the evaluation capabilities. In general, Belafonte-Tacolcy has established a solid foundation of basic service and client monitoring, but it is not yet ready for more intensive formative or summative evaluation activities.

Concluding Thoughts

The Belafonte-Tacolcy Center distinguishes between prevention and treatment cases; many of the youth who enter through the prevention programs do so at one of two schools where Belafonte-Tacolcy maintains an active presence or by coming to the Center for recreational activities or team sports.

Belafonte-Tacolcy puts a stronger emphasis on comprehensiveness than on integration of services. Its strengths are that it is a long-standing, integral part of the community and that many generations of local youth have participated in its programs. This has led to a unique feature of a strongly comprehensive service integration strategy: Program clients develop a "career path" of participation in the program across many years. Youth may enter to participate in the social and recreational programs but eventually they can receive counseling, tutoring, and other benefits that will help them become successful as adolescents. Those who achieve the highest levels of success can stay with the Center by becoming involved as youth leaders, either through peer tutoring or by becoming involved in board activities and the direction of the Center. Finally, not only can youth gain social and educational skills by participating in Belafonte-Tacolcy, they can have a real opportunity to attain their economic goals through the strong community development components.

Another unique feature of Belafonte-Tacolcy is its mix of activities in both its own community center and at the schools. It conducts important prevention activities in the schools, and its presence there allows it to work with the schools on identifying youth who may be having academic difficulties early, so that more intensive programming can be offered. However, these links with the schools are not easy to develop. Belafonte-Tacolcy noted that when seeking funding for new services, it was important to have the service sites in agreement *before* the funding came through. Their experience has been that these negotiations can take a long time and may extend through a significant proportion of the grant period if they are not in place at the beginning. Although this has occurred in their work with schools, it is also a more general lesson when they become involved in collaborative efforts with other agencies and community groups.

The experience of Belafonte-Tacolcy in cooperating with other community services and programs demonstrates the importance of timing and money issues on the delivery of services. Sometimes cooperative arrangements have been developed for a specific project, which is funded for a limited period of time. Should that funding run out before new funding is found to replace it, Belafonte-Tacolcy will have to reduce or eliminate the program, even if it may eventually seek to start it up again when new funding arrives. Agency staff find these ups and downs extremely disruptive, and cooperative relationships may be lost for good if agency staff lose faith in the stability of program efforts. A vicious circle develops whereby fluctuations in funding affect the quality of such important items as physical facilities. When the facilities cannot be maintained at a reasonable level, members in the community and other agencies begin to view the program as deteriorating, which then reduces capital funding efforts and future program initiatives.

Like most prevention-oriented programs, Belafonte-Tacolcy has the willingness but little capacity for conducting evaluation research. Although there is strong anecdotal evidence attesting to its effectiveness, no studies have systematically studied the program. And no studies can do so given its current limited information system and lack of skills to conduct even formative evaluation studies. But long journeys begin with baby steps. Belafonte-Tacolcy should be given the opportunity to improve its management information system, including more systematic collection of information on clientele and program usage and the widespread use of computers to organize and summarize the data. This would be the beginning of a greater use of systematic feedback on program use that could guide more intensive evaluation efforts later on.

By offering a diverse program that enables youth to stay with the agency during their entire childhoods and adolescence, Belafonte-Tacolcy helps youth to become successful and thereby to avoid typical problems that occur for youth living in dangerous neighborhoods. Furthermore, by focusing not only on social and academic achievement but also on economic opportunity and community development, the program aims to make a difference in those very neighborhoods so as to reduce the levels of danger and its allure to the youth living in these communities.

9

Oasis Center

Overview

Nashville's Oasis Center is a private, nonprofit, community-based agency providing a comprehensive set of crisis services to teens and their families throughout the greater Nashville area. From its beginnings, the Center has focused its programs and activities on prevention and treatment (e.g., crisis counseling and school-based education to prevent drug and alcohol abuse). Its focus in 1992 was largely on helping teens as individuals rather than on serving whole families or a geographically concentrated community. Since 1992 the Center has added more family-focused programs. Oasis Center was originally conceived as a drop-in center to provide counseling and crisis intervention for clients of all ages. The Rap House opened in 1969 in response to concerns about drug use in the community and the incarceration of juvenile-status offenders in adult jails. A health clinic was added the following year, and a crisis shelter, Oasis House, opened in 1976. In the early 1980s, Oasis Center refocused its efforts from serving individuals of all ages to providing comprehensive services to meet the needs of teenagers and their families. By concentrating on teenagers, the Center could proactively serve adolescents at the point at which they are most likely to get "off track."

Current Mission, Goals, and Objectives

The Center's mission is to empower youth and their families to meet the demands of adolescence, primarily through the provision of youth-centered services. Its primary goal is "to provide comprehensive services to help teens and their families succeed." The Center's objectives include (a) providing teens with help for immediate problems, (b) helping teens to resolve their underlying problems, and (c) facilitating the teen's transition from adolescence to adulthood and preparing teens for the responsibilities of adulthood. In 1988, Oasis Center developed a 5-year plan that identified the following administrative and service-related long-range goals:

- Identifying and filling service gaps;
- Involving and serving minorities;

- Advocating for youth and family service needs at all levels;
- Continuing to use sound agency management;
- Diversifying the program's funding base;
- Obtaining permanent facilities; and
- Refining financial and data management systems.

Oasis Center periodically reassesses its goals and objectives and the services it provides in response to identified client and community needs. For instance, after an internal review revealed that Oasis Center's foster care services were not meeting the needs of the teenagers being placed, the Center phased out the program and redirected its energies toward home-based and independent-living services.

Oasis Center's previous executive director, Della Hughes, was well-informed about regional and national needs with regard to youth services and related issues and helped to focus the center's activities in its formative years (1979–1988). She was also instrumental in developing a strategic plan to provide comprehensive services to teenagers that involved changes in the composition of the board of directors and expanded fundraising capabilities. Oasis Center modified the role and membership of its board of directors from a loose network of social service providers to a board composed of community members committed to the Center's mission and with the influence necessary to promote fundraising opportunities within the community. The current board includes representatives from local businesses, educational institutions, the legal community, community volunteers, and a high school student representative.

Current Clientele

Oasis Center provides services to 13–21 year olds and their families, most of whom reside in urban Davidson County, Tennessee. More than 50% of the youth served are between 13 and 15 years old. Approximately 20% of program participants are African American, and almost 80% are White. The demographic profile of the client population is consistent with that of Nashville. Oasis Center programs served approximately 3,000 youth in 1991. This figure does not include more than 9,700 youth educated about Project Safe Place (discussed later) through school presentations and other publicity about Project Safe Place.

Clients may enter Oasis Center through any of its programs and services. In most cases, clients refer themselves into Oasis Center programs. They learn about the program through word of mouth, friends who have participated in Oasis Center programs (especially the Early Intervention Program located in schools), and Project Safe Place outreach activities. Project Safe Place participants refer youth to Oasis Center for services or to the Center's youth shelter for immediate care. Other referral sources have included counseling agencies, teachers, juvenile court, and state agencies having custody of a child.

Most Oasis Center programs focus on youth but may involve their families in services and treatment. On entering the service delivery system, youth are assigned a case manager who matches the youth and his or her family with needed services. Family members may receive crisis counseling or longer term counseling services to deal with a range of family issues (e.g., communication, parent–child relationships, drug and alcohol abuse). Families who have an adolescent at risk of out-of-home placement receive 6 months of intensive in-home services. Oasis Center also serves parents directly by offering parenting skills groups at the Center and workplace parenting programs.

Service Configuration

Many of Oasis Center's programs have evolved from needs identified during the course of service delivery. The Center currently offers a range of residential, educational, and vocational services, including an emergency shelter, extensive counseling services, family preservation and home-based services, sex abuse prevention, community outreach activities, school- and community-based group counseling (early intervention for drug and alcohol abuse prevention), youth opportunities programs, and life transitions programs. Clients may enter the service delivery system through any of these programs or services. All clients receive a detailed intake interview and assessment, at which time staff identify their service needs and develop an action plan. The intake and referral interview records referral source, presenting problems, and related information; information about the client's family and living situation; service history; and service plan. The Center's assessment form records the client's gender and ethnic group and gathers detailed information about the client's family, education, legal status, social and peer-related activities, general health, emotional and psychological state, and history of drug use.

Residential Services

The Center provides a short-term emergency residential shelter for youth ages 13–17, and a residential independent living program for youth ages 17–21. Although residents learn about the emergency shelter from a variety of sources (e.g., school, juvenile court, counseling agency), the most common form of entry into the shelter is through the Safe Place outreach program organized by Oasis. Residents receive temporary shelter; individual and group counseling; family counseling when appropriate; attend school, most often within the shelter; and participate in recreational activities. Shelter residents have included homeless youth, youth from families that are in crisis, and youth in the custody of a state agency, among others.

The independent living program provides a residence for older youth until they can establish themselves independently. It also provides non-residential services such as employment counseling and independent living skills training. Youth enter the independent living program through several Oasis service components, and also through referrals from outside agencies.

Community-Based Counseling

Counseling services include individual, group, and family counseling and group activities such as early intervention, alcohol and drug abuse prevention, and suicide prevention programs. The Center offers outpatient services to families on a sliding fee scale; services range in duration from 2 months to 2 years. Crisis walk-in services are available to individuals in need of immediate assistance when the residential shelter or clinical services component is unavailable.

The Early Intervention Program and other topic-specific groups run for 8–10 weeks and provide participants with the opportunity to practice group skills (e.g., teamwork, group interactions) and deal with common issues (e.g., sexual abuse, drug or alcohol abuse). Oasis Center also offers group sessions for interested parents.

Outreach Activities

Project Safe Place is a 24-hour outreach service for youth in crisis between the ages of 13 and 17. This national program is sponsored locally by Oasis Center. The Nashville community has designated certain businesses and public locations as "safe places" from which trained staff help youth to contact Oasis Center and arrange for services or transportation home or to the residential shelter, if necessary. Many youth enter the Oasis Center service system by referring themselves through Project Safe Place. The Project Safe Place headquarters and hotline is located in the shelter.

Youth Opportunities Program

This program includes a youth employment component for teens ages 16 to 19 and training in life skills and career planning to prepare teens who are in the custody of the Tennessee Department of Human Services for independent living.

Type and Make-Up of the Service Integration Network

Oasis Center facilitates a client's access to the services of community agencies and resources that have forged both formal and informal linkages with the center. Formal arrangements exist with a downtown Nashville health clinic to provide transportation and health care to residents of the emergency residential shelter and with the Nashville school system to accept credits from the school that Oasis Center runs in its youth shelter.

Most of Oasis Center's interagency relationships are informal and have developed through staff participation on community boards and committees. Oasis Center is a member of the Adolescent Services Network, a forum composed of many youth-serving agencies in Nashville that meets monthly to discuss issues relating to chronic runaways. The Center also meets with other emergency or crisis services agencies in an Emergency Services Network to deal with the needs of youth who have been neglected or abused by alcohol- or drug-abusing caregivers.

Oasis Center receives referrals from numerous agencies and provides information and referral to clients needing services not provided by the Center. For instance, Oasis Center refers parents of substance abusers to the Alcohol and Drug Abuse Council for services and maintains informal linkages with a local agency for suicide prevention or evaluation referrals.

Oasis Center interacts regularly with the juvenile court and the state Department of Human Services (DHS), which refer youth to the Center's shelter and other programs. Staff of the juvenile court and DHS perceive Oasis Center as responsive to the needs of youth and families and regularly refer youth to the Center for services, including emergency shelter, home-based services, counseling, independent living, and general equivalency diploma (GED) preparation services.

The linkages between Oasis Center and both juvenile court and DHS extend beyond referring clients to Oasis Center for services. Oasis Center has helped the juvenile court to develop a crisis intervention group in its detention facilities. Additionally, Oasis Center makes it a practice to refer youth to DHS on discovering physical or sexual abuse or if Oasis Center is unable to locate an emergency residential shelter resident's guardian.

Key representatives from these organizations have identified barriers and facilitators to interagency coordination. The barriers typically relate to the structure and focus of these government agencies. For instance, prior to 1990 the juvenile court was uninterested in taking a proactive approach to the treatment of juveniles appearing before the court. But a newly appointed judge has shown great interest in using the community resources available to at-risk youth. As a result, Oasis Center provided crisis intervention training to juvenile court staff, and regular interagency meetings began in 1990 between the Center, juvenile court, and DHS.

These agencies cite open communication across agencies as a key to successful coordination. As a result of regular interagency meetings, Oasis Center created a DHS liaison position to respond to its concerns that DHS did not act on emergencies in a timely manner. The liaison spends part of each week at DHS serving as an information source about Oasis Center's services and ensuring that needy youth do not fall through the cracks at DHS.

Funding Sources

Many Oasis Center programs were initially funded with federal discretionary money; the bulk of the Center's current funding comes from government grants and the United Way. In 1990–1991, Oasis Center's funding came from federal and state government grants (60%), the United Way (26%), private contributions (9%), and program service fees (5%). Every component of Oasis Center's programming receives financial support from several funding sources. This is a deliberate strategy adopted by the agency to assure that changes in funding sources, especially reductions or eliminations, do not completely wipe out any program component.

Update: 1996

Oasis Center sets its program goals in 5-year cycles. When we visited in 1992 the Center was in its last year of one cycle. During that cycle they achieved most of their long-range administrative and service-related goals (as described at the beginning of this chapter). The exception was their desire to diversify their funding base, which has moved up to be a top priority goal in the 1993–1998 5-year plan. New service-related goals in this plan include expanding the volunteer involvement in Oasis Center and developing a system for organizing volunteers, developing their community connections through youth involvement and advocacy, and strengthening their prevention and early intervention services to parents and youth, with a special emphasis on preadolescent youth. An additional goal is to develop a program evaluation system for the whole agency.

Oasis Center has added many new services since 1992, strengthening some of its existing program components and expanding and reorganizing others into whole programs of their own. The two areas that have "graduated" to program status are Youth Opportunities, which has become the Education Program, and transitional living services, which is now referred to as the Independent Living Program. Under the Education Program, Oasis Center has grouped its youth employment activities (previously called Youth Opportunities Program), the school program that operates in the youth shelter, a new learning center that includes a GED program, and a drug and alcohol safety program that used to be contracted out and has now been reincorporated into the services that Oasis offers under its own roof.

The independent living services have expanded into a significant new program. Still included is a group living facility staffed by Oasis personnel for youth who are gaining the skills to live on their own. Added to this base is a scattered-site apartment program available to youth who are ready to leave the group facility and to other youth from the community who need some help but do not need the level of supervision provided in the group facility. Youth in the apartment program have leases in their own names and do not have to leave their apartment when they are ready to leave the program. Oasis Center offers youth in the apartment program a wide array of supportive services and skill-building experiences, including maintaining an apartment and getting along with neighbors; vocational skills, getting a first job and a subsequent job, getting along with coworkers and supervisors; transportation; nutrition and budgeting; educational counseling, including options such as GED or high school completion, choosing a career path, help with school or training applications, and similar matters. Furthermore, the Center now offers the nonresidential aspects of its Independent Living Program to youth who do not live in its residential facilities.

Several new elements have been added to Oasis Center's shelter and counseling programs. Every Wednesday night Oasis holds an ongoing, multiple-family group therapy session for families currently involved with its shelter because of a youth in residence and families who have been involved in the past. Youth and family members all attend, and groups commonly run as large as 40–50 people. Oasis feels that this group has been very effective at helping families deal with each other. Some families keep coming for a very long time after their son or daughter has left the shelter. Some of these families have been trained as "family mentors" who can become guides and resources for families who are dealing with their problems for the first time. The goal is to have a family mentor for every new family, but they have not achieved this yet. Family mentors also cofacilitate the Wednesday night meetings.

In a similar vein, Oasis Center has been recruiting and training peer educators, who are teens who can talk with other teens about their problems and issues. Some peer educators are graduates of Oasis programs, but most are recruited from around the community. Approximately 20 are active at any given time and make at least a 6-month commitment to the program. Peer educators answer the Oasis crisis line three evenings a week, during which the line is called the "TeenLine." They also cofacilitate groups on HIV/AIDS and alcohol and drug prevention that Oasis holds both in their shelter and in the community.

Three new types of groups have been added to Oasis Center's topic-specific community-based counseling groups. These are (a) a group for 17 year olds called "Rites of Passage" that focuses on issues of becoming an adult, which includes a wilderness weekend experience; (b) a mother–daughter group that focuses on the nature of this relationship; and (c) a group for 13–17 year old boys who have witnessed their mother's battering, to help them choose another way to relate to the world and to their female partners. Another new service in this program area is the family retreat weekend. This is an intensive 3-day experience for families and youth, with follow-up services. The court orders families into the program and pays for it, as a diversion program for youth who have just had their first encounter with the juvenile justice system. Some shelter families also attend the retreat weekends after signing a voluntary agreement with the court. The weekend focuses on teaching ways of resolving or mediating conflict, family relations and the values each family member has for each other and the family as a unit, and other issues facing these families. The weekend is followed by home-based services to help link the families to longer term supports. In addition, Oasis Center has started an Alternative Spring Break Program involving community service and group dynamics. Last year, which was the program's first, one group worked in Nashville and one did community service in South Carolina. The program will be repeated in spring 1997.

Oasis Center is also focusing on doing more with volunteers and hopes the volunteer activities will grow into a program of their own that brings many more interconnections between Oasis Center and the community.

Street Outreach is a final new program at Oasis Center. Originally funded by a federal grant, the program places Center staff on the streets at places where runaway and homeless youth congregate. They make contact, talk with youth, discuss problems and issues, and offer services. The Center has already seen eight youth come into the shelter and off the streets as a result of these outreach efforts, and it hopes to see more. The program is now being supported by Center funds while a new federal grant is pending.

In addition to the networks and coalitions Oasis Center participated in during 1992, staff now also take part in the Nashville Violence Prevention Coalition and the Nashville Coalition for Youth. The staff liaison position that the Center once supported at DHS is no longer in place.

Involvement in Evaluation Activities

When we visited in 1992, Oasis Center was performing a variety of evaluations, the majority of which were process evaluations. Many of the grants operating at that time included a mandatory evaluation component. To meet these requirements, the Center produced computer-generated monthly data reports to track caseload, client disposition, and management. The Center has also participated in impact evaluations for specific service components when the funding source supporting them required it. In 1992, these programs included Home-Based Services, ELECT, and Independent Living. At that time, Oasis Center planned to incorporate outcome-based evaluation into its Early Intervention Program, with 90-day follow-ups to gather self-reported behaviors, attitudes, and knowledge related to the contents of the early intervention activities.

Since 1992, Oasis Center has significantly expanded its evaluation activities. During the past few years, staff have designed and implemented agencywide evaluation practices. The Center has a systemwide database that encompasses all of its programs, activities, and clients. The system includes recording of outcomes for all program areas within the agency, measured at program completion and at 3- and 6-month follow-up intervals. The system is not used on-line; agency staff still do mostly what they used to, although the specific paper forms have changed a little. Data are entered into the system by support staff hired for that purpose and by the residence staff during nighttime hours. An additional major effort at self-evaluation and external verification also occurred in 1996 when Oasis Center for the first time applied for and received accreditation by the Council on Accreditation of Services for Families and Children, Inc.

Concluding Thoughts

Oasis Center is a stable, multifocused youth-serving program with deep roots in its Nashville community. It supports many programs that could be replicated in other locations. However, perhaps the domain in which it can best serve as an example to other programs is its systematical approach to pursuing its own mission and modifying it in response to the changing needs of youth. Its staff and board regularly examine the Center's activities in relation to identified needs in two equally important ways: through collaborative interactions with other community agencies and actors and through reflecting on the needs of current clients and the ability of its programs to meet them. Using both of these mechanisms in a conscious effort, Oasis Center has continued to grow and change while maintaining its core programs and mission.

10

CHINS UP Youth and Family Services, Inc.

Overview

CHINS UP, an acronym for Children in Need of Supervision, constitutes one of the best examples in our study of how a single agency can have a broad impact on the service delivery network and, indeed, the entire community. By emphasizing comprehensive service integration for youth at risk, it serves as an example of how a treatment-oriented agency can become more preventive. CHINS UP has become a major player in its community by proactively identifying needs and developing programs to meet these needs. CHINS UP plays many roles; as initiator or facilitator of new programs, as "honest broker" filling gaps and bringing agencies together, and as innovator and builder of new ventures.

The system of services for youth in El Paso County—the community served by CHINS UP—includes an important example of services integration called Joint Initiatives, described earlier in Chapter 5. CHINS UP played an important role in the founding and development of Joint Initiatives and, in many ways, the two are inextricably connected. Although CHINS UP was the focus of our site visit, it is really the combination of CHINS UP and Joint Initiatives that constitutes the highly evolved form of service integration operating in Colorado Springs.

Mission, Goals, and Objectives

CHINS UP serves primarily youth ages 10 to 18 who are referred from the El Paso County Department of Social Services (DSS) or the juvenile court system because of juvenile delinquency or other status offenses or who are victims of physical or sexual abuse or family violence. The mission of CHINS UP is "to provide short-term residential care, therapeutic foster care, and treatment services for children and their families with the goal of supporting, preserving, and promoting the child's welfare, safety, and family relationships wherever possible" (Mission Statement, CHINS UP, n.d., p. 1). CHINS UP is an advocate for children and families and is a provider of a continuum of services for troubled youth primarily from El

Paso County, including Colorado Springs. The philosophy of CHINS UP is to collaborate with other agencies in the community and, through creativity and innovation, to integrate services in nontraditional ways.

The agency's history of growth testifies to the vigor and purpose with which CHINS UP follows its mission and objectives. The program began in 1974 after the community expressed a need for emergency shelter care for troubled and runaway youth. The agency started a shelter program consisting of eight beds for troubled boys and girls. In 1978, in response to needs identified in the community for alternative educational services for troubled youth, CHINS UP added a state-certified special education program for the shelter children. One year later, in 1979, CHINS UP began its Family Therapy Program, which focused on reuniting troubled youth with their families. In 1984, in response to the community's need for additional foster homes with a therapeutic component, CHINS UP initiated its Therapeutic Foster Care Program, which recruited, trained, supported, and provided services to 15 foster homes and more than 25 children. In 1990, CHINS UP began the El Paso County Family Preservation Program to expand local family preservation services. In 1991, CHINS UP was one of 10 statewide pilot programs that was awarded state funding under Colorado's new Alternatives to Incarceration program, known locally as Senate Bill 94, to provide an alternative to detention for youthful status offenders through a program called Detention Services for Juveniles (DSJ). Both the El Paso County Family Preservation Program and DSJ were developed by Joint Initiatives and won by CHINS UP through a competitive bidding process.

At the time of our initial visit in 1992, CHINS UP provided a continuum of preventive and treatment services for troubled youth, including emergency shelter and residential care, special education, therapeutic foster care, family therapy, family preservation, and alternatives to juvenile detention. As we found when we interviewed them in 1996, their core programs have become well-established, and they have branched into several new and interesting areas.

Current Clientele

The primary target group for most CHINS UP programs are youth (and their families) about to be placed in out-of-home settings or already institutionally involved (e.g., in detention, emergency shelter, or foster care). These youth and their families typically trigger intervention by El Paso County DSS or the Division of Youth Services (DYS) of the Colorado Department of Human Services as a result of several of the risk markers or problems identified in our theoretical model, including behavioral problems, juvenile crime, physical or sexual abuse, family violence, abandonment or running away, or family crises.

Relatively little distinction exists between the youth and families involved in each of the program components. The specific type of services offered to families and youth by CHINS UP depends on the referral source as well as on a comprehensive needs assessment conducted by CHINS UP. Many youth enter CHINS UP through the short-term residential shelter and later receive other services. El Paso County DSS typically refers youth to the residential shelter program for the following reasons: parent–child conflict, need for supervision, physical or sexual abuse, to await placement in a foster home, or because a youth has run away from his or her own home or a foster home. Other youth and families first come to the attention of CHINS UP through the El Paso County Family Preservation Program or DSJ. Sometimes youth initially involved in the El Paso County Family Preservation Program may later appear at the Zebulon Pike Detention Center because of criminal involvement and will then be assessed by the CHINS UP workers in this program.

The characteristics and backgrounds of youth and their families in each of the two core programs at CHINS UP, the Residential Shelter Program and the El Paso County Family Preservation Program, show great similarities. Youth in the residential shelter program are mainly White and between 13 and 16 years of age, whereas children in the El Paso County Family Preservation Program may range in age from birth to 18 years (although 36% of all children are 10–15 years old). Boys, primarily White, generally make up roughly two thirds of the youth participants, and most youth were living at home prior to coming to CHINS UP. Most families who participate in the El Paso County Family Preservation Program have annual incomes of less than $20,000, with 46% of all families earning less than $10,000; the family backgrounds of youth in other programs at CHINS UP are similar. The statistics are roughly similar in the other CHINS UP programs, although the proportion of youth from minority groups may be somewhat higher in the detention services program.

Most of the youth in the Residential Shelter Program were either living at home or were at the Zebulon Pike Detention Center prior to their stay in the shelter, whereas youth in the El Paso County Family Preservation Program lived in homes headed by single mothers or with both parents. Typically, youth in the residential shelter either return to their homes, transfer to another residential program, or run away from CHINS UP (after which the case is closed).

Service Configuration

The core program at CHINS UP is the short-term residential shelter for abandoned, runaway, and abused youth. This program is not a drop-in type of shelter; youth must be referred from the El Paso County DSS, DYS, the Colorado Springs Police Department, or private practitioners. Youth can stay for a maximum of 3 months, and the primary goal of the program is to determine long-term care arrangements for the youth, either returning the youth to parents or seeking alternative custody or foster care.

Youth in the residential program receive ongoing individual case assessments, medical attention, and health services provided through the Community Health Center, individual and group counseling, and transportation for emergencies. Experienced therapists and managers are on call 24 hours a day, 7 days a week. Residential shelter staff include a residential director, two case managers, and 35 full- and part-time counselors.

A key feature of the residential shelter is that although it is not a secure facility, there are strict rules for remaining in the shelter. Youth can and often do run away for periods of time, but they must return within 24 to 48 hours or else they are considered AWOL (away without official leave) and subject to sanctions on return. As long as the youth return (which most do), CHINS UP does not close the case file during these short runaway episodes. Another important feature of the residential shelter is its strictly enforced rule against any form of physical contact between the youth and staff or among the youth. This rule was enacted several years ago in response to concerns that both victims and perpetrators of physical and sexual abuse are often living in the shelter at the same time.

Approximately 30% of the youth in the residential shelter also receive problem-focused family therapy. In particular, youth who appear most likely to return to their family at the end of the shelter stay receive family therapy as long as the parents agree to participate. Therapy continues on an outpatient basis for 6 months after the youth returns to the family. The Family Therapy Program is staffed by a clinical director, two full-time family therapists, and six part-time contract therapists.

All shelter youth receive special educational services through a CHINS UP-based alternative school licensed by the Colorado Department of Education. The education program features certified special education, GED courses, and individualized instruction. Staff include one education director, two full-time teachers, and two teaching assistants. Finally, all shelter youth participate in a set of recreational and leisure activities designed to build self-esteem and to foster personal growth. These include educational tours, cultural events, physical activities and sports, guest lectures, and volunteer opportunities.

The Therapeutic Foster Care Program provides long-term therapeutic foster care for children from birth through 18 years of age who cannot stay in their own homes for a variety of reasons. DSS contracts with CHINS UP to recruit, train, license, and monitor foster homes. DSS usually refers youth from a short-term residential placement following a court-ordered removal from the home due to physical or sexual abuse. Some of the youth may be referred from the CHINS UP residential shelter. Youth may stay in a therapeutic foster home until they reach 18 years of age. CHINS UP provides therapeutic and supportive services to the foster parents, as well as respite care and recreational activities.

The El Paso County Family Preservation Program is a recent addition to CHINS UP and represents the preventive end of the continuum of services offered by CHINS UP. Through intensive in-home intervention on a short-term basis, the El Paso County Family Preservation Program strives to prevent unnecessary out-of-home placement of children and youth. This intensive, time-limited (4–6 weeks maximum) intervention makes available to the family a family specialist 24 hours a day, 7 days a week. This program closely follows the Homebuilders model currently operating in family preservation programs across the country (Kinney, Haapala, & Booth, 1991). In this model, the family specialist works with the family in its own home, using a goal-oriented strategy with limited objectives and a high level of collaboration with community agencies and institutions, including DSS, DYS, schools, food banks, and county welfare and mental health agencies. Referrals of families to this program come from the county DSS, DYS, and local school districts. The El Paso County Family Preservation Program staff include a program director, three family specialists, and an intern. Each family specialist handles only two family cases at any one time, permitting intensive interaction and attention over the 4- to 6-week period.

CHINS UP also operates the newly developed Detention Services for Juveniles (DSJ) program out of the Zebulon Pike Juvenile Detention Center. The program was initiated through Senate Bill 94 in order to reduce overcrowding at Zebulon Pike by finding alternatives to lock-up for first-time and status juvenile offenders. Youth arrested for a status or criminal charge and brought to Zebulon Pike at the preadjudicated stage are eligible for the program. While waiting to be locked up prior to their hearing, these youth undergo an assessment by a CHINS UP staff person working at the detention center. On the basis of the risk assessment, staff assign to each youth a specific level of risk and may recommend alternative release if the youth does not appear likely to be a risk to self or community. Alternative release strategies include any combination of electronic or passive monitoring, home confinement, daily telephone or face-to-face contacts, random electronic voice verification through telephone calls to the home, curfew, or release on a personal recognizance bond. A not-for-profit organization provides electronic monitoring and tracking and collaborates with CHINS UP staff.

Type and Make-Up of the Service Integration Network

CHINS UP collaborates with an extensive, varied, and well-organized network of agencies. Some of these agencies are partners in the programs it operates, whereas others become involved with individual cases through monthly multi-agency team meetings. Finally, CHINS UP collaborates with other agencies in the operation of Joint Initiatives.

CHINS UP works collaboratively with a variety of agencies in the course of its day-to-day operations. Its staff work off site, at the Zebulon Pike Detention Center, to operate the DSJ program. At this location, they cooperate with the courts, sheriff's office, the detention center, and a private security company that conducts the monitoring of released juveniles. CHINS UP staff who provide family preservation services work in the homes of the families as well as in the community at large, and their offices are located in a space separate from the CHINS UP central facility. The El Paso County Family Preservation Program workers at CHINS UP spend considerable time interacting with other agencies to meet the immediate needs of client families, including financial assistance, housing, emergency food, and the resolution of school problems.

Residential center youth receive medical services through the El Pomar Health Center several times a week. The Center sends a nurse practitioner to the shelter youth to provide routine physical examinations, sexually transmitted disease screening, birth control counseling, and prenatal care. Private practitioners who accept Medicaid conduct in-office eye and dental exams. CHINS UP also has an agreement with the local YMCA to provide the youth with a "ropes" course, an Outward Bound type of program designed to build self-esteem and teamwork. CHINS UP also has an ongoing contract with the Pikes Peak Mental Health Center to allow up to 3 youths to be seen by two licensed therapists once a week. Through another agreement with the local Job Training Partnership Act (JTPA) program, youth staying in the residential shelter can engage in part-time work or a preemployment training experience through the summer jobs program. Other special activities for residential shelter youth occur in collaboration with agencies in the community, such as workshops on sexually transmitted disease given by the El Paso County Department of Health and Environment, or a "scared straight" type of program provided at the Cañon City jail for CHINS UP youth.

In addition to these formal arrangements, staff from other agencies involved in a particular case attend a variety of meetings with CHINS UP staff. Youth at the shelter who are disruptive and violent are asked to leave, but their cases remain open, and a monthly meeting is held to discuss youth who have been disruptive with all agencies that serve these youth. The meeting helps to monitor these youths' behavior outside of the shelter. In addition, a multi-agency review team meets once a week to discuss a specific case and arrive at alternatives to a potential out-of-county foster care placement. The CHINS UP director of case management convenes the meetings with all agencies involved with the youth and family, including JTPA; the courts; the youth's attorney; the DSS caseworker; the DSS supervisor; and some treatment centers, such as Cheyenne-Mesa, a long-term residential facility, or an emergency shelter, Dale House.

Finally, CHINS UP played a major role in the development of Joint Initiatives and is actively involved as a member agency. More about the role CHINS UP played as well as the nature of Joint Initiatives in the county's service integration network is presented in Chapter 5.

Funding Sources

The bulk of CHINS UP funding comes from fees for services paid by El Paso County DSS or DYS, according to its audited financial report for fiscal year 1991; these account for 46% of total program support. Other sources of funds are as follows: 19% from foster care fees, 11% from aftercare services funded by a variety of state agencies, 8% from the El Paso

County DSS family preservation budget, and 8% from the El Paso County Department of Education for its alternative school. Smaller amounts of support come from United Way (3%), child nutrition, family therapy fees, the Colorado Trust, and independent contributions. Given the program's commitment to providing services to youth under public agency supervision, it is not surprising that the bulk of its support comes from fees for services that are either court-ordered or paid for by the county DSS office.

Update: 1996

Major changes have taken place at CHINS UP since our visit in 1992. For the most part, these changes mark a significant expansion of its services to cover the complete continuum of care from most restrictive to least restrictive environments for youth at risk. Along with these expansions, CHINS UP continues to enjoy unsurpassed support from the community and is involved in the network of services for youth and families in ways that clearly mark them as a mature comprehensive service integration organization.

Program Changes

In 1992 an elderly neighbor living next door to CHINS UP began renting her cottage for the foster care program. In January 1994 this neighbor, Salome Smith, died at the age of 94, and she had willed her entire property to CHINS UP, which consisted of the main house and the cottage, with no strings attached. Because the executive director of CHINS UP knew about her will, he organized a luncheon and press release to honor her before she died. After the will was probated, CHINS UP moved all of its administration department to the main house, now called "Salome House," whereas the foster care program continued to operate in the cottage, now called "Frank House" in honor of Ms. Smith's late husband.

In January of 1993, CHINS UP began One to One Mentoring, a mentoring program for youth ages 8–17 who are referred from the courts, probation, mental health, police, or schools. This program is currently serving 30–40 mentorships a year. The mentors are adult volunteers. Most recently the program received good cooperation from a local TV station, which ran an advertising spot once a week featuring one of the youth waiting for a mentor. It has also had good results recruiting adult volunteers from the community, whom they screen extensively.

In January 1994, CHINS UP began STAR, which is an acronym for Skills Transitions and Reality. The program, with a capacity of 12 youth, helps adjudicated delinquent youth become integrated back into the community after being paroled from a state secure institution. These youth have irritated the court and community to such a degree that they were committed to a state institution and now are reentering the community, which for most of them means they are being maintained at home. CHINS UP put together a comprehensive package of services with the aim of helping these youth stay at home and out of the courts. The services include alternative education, electronic monitoring and tracking, family preservation, and vocational and recreational programs. Funded by the state Division of Youth Corrections (DYC, formerly DYS), the program has been operating for 18 months.

CHINS UP staff have identified that drug and alcohol abuse is often the reason for a paroled youth's failure to successfully return to his or her community. To address this problem, CHINS UP hired a drug and alcohol counselor who assesses risk and actual involvement with drugs and substance abuse and then provides group and intervention services. CHINS UP connects the youth to vocational and educational services so that he or she can complete a GED and gain preemployment skills, and it also does extensive family preservation work to ensure that the youth can live with his or her own family in the community. When youth do complete their GED, CHINS UP links them with local community colleges for continuing education if this is the youth's goal. Finally, CHINS UP complements but does not supplant the parole officer's work. For example, these youth are not placed in the residential facility of CHINS UP, and drug testing (urinalysis) is left to the discretion of the parole officer.

In early 1995, the owner of a property next door to Salome House offered the property to CHINS UP at a significant discount (20%). CHINS UP bought the house and named it Lucy House, in honor of the previous owner's mother. Lucy House contains the El Paso County Family Preservation Program and the Therapeutic Foster Care Program (now called the Treatment Foster Care Program), as well as a female adolescent advocacy program. As a result of this improvement in working space, the three houses that are next door to CHINS UP's main building now are home to the following programs: Salome House for administration, Frank House for one-to-one mentoring and maintenance, and Lucy House for family preservation and treatment foster care.

In June 1996, CHINS UP kicked off its Youth Advocacy Program, funded by a 1-year grant from the U.S. Office of Juvenile Justice and Delinquency Prevention (OJJDP). The program is an outgrowth of a change in policy at the county detention center, in which the presiding juvenile judge placed a limit on the number of preadjudicated and adjudicated youth who can be locked up, in order to "force" the system to try to keep these youth in their community and away from the negative influence of other detention center residents. In the past, female chronic runaways were likely to be locked up if they continued to run away, and this led to their becoming more of a problem as they learned negative behavior while locked up. One of the key goals of interest to OJJDP is that these girls be weaned from the juvenile justice system and maintained in the community.

The OJJDP-funded program is aimed at helping chronic runaway girls in the juvenile system by offering intensive contact from a staff person who is available to an adolescent 24 hours a day, 7 days a week. The clinical director of CHINS UP supervises one full and one part-time staff. They obtain referrals from the courts, who help to identify the chronic runaways among the female delinquent population. Staff meet informally with the adolescent, they talk, they become involved in activities in the community, and a trusting relationship between the adolescent and the staff person develops. As a result, it is expected that if the delinquent youth were to run away from the shelter or foster care home, the staff person would be among the first contacted, and the goal for the staff would be to make sure the girl is safe and then, without using coercion, to try to change the conditions or the girl's perceptions about the conditions that led to her running away. Currently the program is operating at full capacity, serving 16 female adolescents. The girls stay in the program until they demonstrate a track record of not running away, although the criteria are flexible to ensure continuity in care for these youth. As part of the grant, an evaluation is being conducted. Baseline data are collected on the youth's record of running away, placement history, and background, and then specific goals are set for each youth to modify her runaway behavior.

In July 1996, with funding obtained through Title IV-A of the Social Security Act, CHINS UP collaborated with DYC and the El Paso County Department of Human Services (DHS, formerly DSS) to initiate a 2-year program for youth who are involved in corrections or who are receiving a combination of social services (parent–child counseling, abuse or neglect monitoring, or delinquency treatment) and probation. An important criterion is that the youth must be involved in both social services and probation, if they are not currently in the correctional system. Approximately 42 families are in the program, which uses a combination of family preservation intervention and an intensive in-home model to prevent out-of-home placement or to facilitate reintegration into the home. The funding stream specifies that the intensive services are provided for a maximum of 4 weeks. Thus, staff can only have two cases active at a time, and they spend approximately 12 to 15 hours per week with each case. There is a major evaluation component that is being conducted by the University of Southern Maine. The evaluation uses a control group of youth who are referred from the same sources (corrections and social services/probation). It is not clear which measures are being used or how long the evaluation will operate.

Perhaps the largest project CHINS UP is currently developing is a staff secure facility, which was a key program goal for Joint Initiatives. Colorado Springs has no such entity, nor does most of the rest of the state. This facility will differ from secure lock-up facilities such as the county detention center (it is less restrictive) and from the current CHINS UP shelter care program (it is more restrictive). Staff in a staff-secure facility prevent youth from running away through a highly intense program and physical restraint of those youth attempting to leave. There are more staff per resident to prevent a youth from running away, but in the end, if the youth is going to run, he or she can. CHINS UP has just completed a feasibility study commissioned through the Colorado Springs Non-Profit Center, an advocacy and service group for nonprofit agencies. The study concluded that CHINS UP can raise the necessary amount of money if the public sector (city and county) provides some additional funds. Foundations are also committed as long as there is public sector funding, particularly those foundations that donated to the original capital campaign in 1987. The staff-secure facility can be developed if CHINS UP meets a specific dollar objective, split 50% from foundations, 40% from the public sector, and 10% from private donations.

Not coincidentally, a building to house the facility has been located across the street from CHINS UP. The building was originally built as a business college in 1966 and has been vacant since 1993. CHINS UP bought the building at a considerable discount from the market value, and a capital campaign for the staff-secure facility, which will be housed in this building, will help to pay off the mortgage. Sometime later in 1997, CHINS UP will move its alternative education programs into the first floor of the building and then will refurbish the lower floor to build the 20-bed staff-secure facility. Its location across the street from CHINS UP is ideal because the facility already fits the zoning for the area and because the neighborhood surrounding CHINS UP has shown a high degree of support for the agency's mission. This level of support is rare because most communities display the NIMBY (Not in My Back Yard) phenomenon whenever a secure juvenile facility or any human service facility is planned to open in their neighborhoods. There are administrative efficiencies involved in locating the staff-secure facility across the street from CHINS UP. CHINS UP provides food service for one of the for-profit residential facilities in town (for a fee) and can do the same for this facility without building a new kitchen.

Changes in Funding

The creativity of CHINS UP in programming and property management is equaled by its adeptness at accessing various funding sources. For example, they have found creative ways of generating funds for programs, including the STAR program, from emergency assistance money funded under Title IV-A of the Social Security Act. This money is included in the block grant of AFDC funds transferred to the states, and the states can decide what to do with their welfare money because there will be almost no federal requirements on the funds, and they could spend none, some, or all of the block grant funds on emergency assistance. CHINS UP appears to be especially effective in obtaining this money to support its new programs (and with good justification because these programs are both cost-effective and fit the terms of the funding agreement).

CHINS UP's funding environment eased considerably in the past year because of a recent change in state laws. The state of Colorado agreed to settle a lawsuit brought against it by the Colorado Lawyers Committee for not doing enough for child welfare (24 other states were also sued on these grounds). Colorado did not want to contest the suit and therefore agreed to restructure its rates for grants to private nonprofit agencies for child welfare and foster care. The previous rate structure gave newer facilities higher fees than older facilities, including CHINS UP. The rate structure was revamped, allowing older facilities to upgrade and provide more treatment services. As a result, CHINS UP now receives twice as much state money for emergency and foster care placements. CHINS UP has used the increase to improve its facilities, increase staffing levels, provide more comprehensive treatment services, and attract higher quality foster homes. The program has gone from nine children in foster care placements in 1996 to 50 children in 1997.

Additional funds have also been made available through the state of Colorado's creative use of Medicaid funds. The community of providers for residential children's services convinced the state to designate these services as residential treatment centers, qualifying for Medicaid reimbursement under a rehabilitation option. As one of these facilities, CHINS UP gets double its previous daily rate for each Medicaid-eligible child in care. These additional funds have also been used to upgrade service by hiring more qualified staff and offering more treatment in addition to the program's shelter services.

Changes in Interagency Relationships

CHINS UP now has a complete continuum of care for troubled youth, from most restrictive to least restrictive environments as well as preventive and educational programming, with the exception of group homes and hospital beds. Its new goals focus on improving services. The program also remains closely tied to Joint Initiatives. The executive director for CHINS UP, Mr. Gerard Veneman, recently completed his 1-year stint as board chair for Joint Initiatives, and CHINS UP continues to be a key player in the planning and development of services by Joint Initiatives. It is noteworthy that DHS pulled out of Joint Initiatives while Mr. Veneman was chair of the Joint Initiatives board. CHINS UP in general, and Mr. Veneman in particular, still maintain an excellent working relationship with the director of DHS and consider DHS among their most important customers.

One of the potential improvements to services, with some accompanying risks, is the recent trend toward using managed care principles in child welfare and juvenile treatment services. According to Mr. Veneman, CHINS UP is ideally situated to use a managed care model because of the wide continuum of services that simplifies the contracting and because CHINS UP is already cost competitive. Philosophically, he is not fond of managed care but feels that there has to be greater accountability for outcomes and better cost containment, whether the human service system likes it or not.

Involvement in Evaluation Activities

CHINS UP has not had extensive experience with evaluation research, but it is highly motivated and, with a computerized information system capability, has laid a good groundwork for future evaluation research. CHINS UP uses a relatively comprehensive computerized information system to monitor its services and client characteristics. Each CHINS UP program component maintains extensive records on client characteristics, assessment of risk, family backgrounds, service participation, and case disposition and referral destinations. All information from the separate program components is entered into a computerized database that generates reports to summarize program participation by individual cases, hours of direct and indirect service provided, case file status, and dispositions. For example, they are able to report that the outpatient family therapy achieved a success rate of 76%, with success defined as the child remaining at home and continuing in school or working full- or part-time. They report that 90% of the target children in families served by the El Paso County Family Preservation Program remained at home with their families, despite the high risk of out-of-home placement for the target youth at program entry. They also report that the multi-agency review team has successfully reduced the number of out-of-county foster care placements of youth by 25% compared with the state average, which has shown a consistent increase during the same period. In addition, the information system is able to calculate the cost per unit of service provided to each youth in the program and identify which funds supported those services. This has potential utility in a cost-effectiveness component to an evaluation.

CHINS UP would like to do some longitudinal follow-up of the youth in the residential shelter and family preservation programs. However, limited time, resources, and staff expertise constrain the agency's evaluation activities.

It is noteworthy that CHINS UP maintains its interest and motivation for evaluation despite some prior negative experiences with outside evaluators. When we visited in 1992, the Detention Services for Juveniles was being assessed as part of a statewide evaluation of the programs funded through the state's Senate Bill 94 program. Conducted by a private contractor, the study ran into resistance from the DSJ workers, who perceived it as not meeting their needs, being overly intrusive and rigid, and not being done competently (especially the forms they are given to complete, which appeared to lack sufficient operational definitions). There were issues of who had control of the data, which stakeholders' needs were being met by the evaluation results, and overly high expectations for the results. In the 1996 interview we did not ask specifically about this evaluation, although we did ask about evaluation activities in general. Nothing was heard about the evaluation, which suggests it may have gone the way of many evaluations with good intentions but competing interests and goals; its findings may have been ignored, and the report may have subsequently been buried (although this is pure speculation on our part). Still, CHINS

UP remains highly motivated to carry out its own evaluation research activities.

Concluding Thoughts

CHINS UP will continue to operate in the forefront of collaborative service integration models, and it will continue to be creative, take risks, and change with the times. As Mr. Veneman said, "It is in the basic traditions of social work, there are real needs and there are few people in this business who will belly up to the bar and take the risks" (G. Veneman, personal communication, September 1996).

11 _____

Houston Communities in Schools

Overview

Houston Communities in Schools (CIS) is an excellent example of comprehensive service integration located within the school system. It is among the best developed of the school-based prevention programs because it offers a wide range of services to youth and it is focused both on primary prevention and on the identification and reduction of risk. Using the principle that the best place to reach younger adolescents is by going to where they spend most of their time—the school—the program provides an umbrella under which all social and related services are coordinated and available on the school premises. Furthermore, the Houston CIS demonstrates how local community agencies and businesses can focus on a single goal, reduction of school dropout, and work together to make a difference.

Houston CIS was initiated by Judge Wyatt Heard of the juvenile court in conjunction with the Houston Independent School District (HISD), the Chamber of Commerce, the Houston mayor, and various community and business leaders. It was the first Texas implementation of the national Cities in Schools program model, which was based on the late 1960s "street academies" for poor urban youth. The first site opened in 1979 at a middle school in Houston with a first year budget of $80,000 and two full-time paid employees (the executive director and the project manager at the school site). Originally named Houston Cities in Schools because of its affiliation with the national Cities in Schools organization, the Houston CIS left the national Cities in Schools organization in 1986 and became incorporated as "Communities in Schools." Since its incorporation, the program has been funded by public and private sources as well as in-kind contributions.

Over the years, new school sites were added as money became available and demand from principals grew. By the start of the 1989–1990 school year, the program had expanded to nine sites in elementary, middle, and high schools. Rapid expansion has continued since that time, and demand far exceeds the resources of CIS. In the 1992–1993 school year, Houston CIS operated at 18 Houston Independent School District schools and three schools in adjacent school districts.

Mission, Goals, and Objectives

Houston CIS defines its mission as coordinating services to at-risk youth and their families in such a way that the whole environment and circumstances of the youth and family are addressed. Its primary purpose is the prevention of school dropout among elementary, middle, and high school students who are at risk due to a variety of factors. The overall goals of the Houston CIS project are to decrease the dropout rate, decrease delinquency, prepare participants for adult work roles, improve school performance, improve school attendance, and increase the graduation rate.

To accomplish these goals, each CIS school site focuses on counseling, enrichment, and academics and also tries to increase parental involvement in school activities. Although CIS administrators note that its dropout prevention mission has not changed over the 12 years it has been in operation, methods for carrying out this mission and accomplishing its goals have recently shifted. CIS used to approach each new school site with a generic plan for developing the program at that school. When setting up a CIS program at a new school site now, CIS tries to develop a plan geared more specifically to the school in question. Thus the types of programs offered and services coordinated at each new school are tailored more toward the specific needs of the individual school.

Current Clientele

The potential clientele of CIS at any given school site includes all students at the school as well as their siblings, parents, and other family members, although the primary client is the student. Students or their parents become familiar with CIS at a school by word of mouth or during the initial registration period at the beginning of the school year. Parents also register their child for CIS so that they can get such benefits as clothing and food vouchers and participate in special activities geared for parents. CIS also gets student referrals from any school personnel (including teachers, the principal, or a guidance counselor) for reasons related to acting out behavior, crisis intervention, poor school performance, grades, or truancy.

For the purposes of defining levels of risk among students, CIS staff distinguish between caseload and noncaseload students. *Caseload* students are those at higher risk who generally require the more intensive, counseling-oriented services or ancillary family support services, whereas the *noncaseload* students are those who have immediate needs requiring crisis intervention or simply want to participate in the school clubs and enrichment activities sponsored by CIS. Caseload students usually come to CIS through referrals from a teacher, principal, or school guidance counselor, whereas noncaseload students are likely to be walk-ins. Caseload students usually have more than one presenting problem, and these may include school infractions, acting out, violent or delinquent behavior, physical or mental health problems, drug or alcohol abuse, physical or sexual abuse, attempted suicide, or family financial problems.

All students receive a risk assessment at a relatively early point in their contact with CIS. Throughout their membership in CIS, they continue to be monitored, and noncaseload students can become part of the caseload if they experience personal or family crises or their school performance declines. Consistent with the nonlabeling approach, CIS does not formally identify students as "caseload" or "noncaseload," and in general no stigma attaches to students who belong to CIS.

Wide variations exist in the sociodemographic makeup of the 21 CIS school sites and their surrounding communities. We visited two sites that illustrate this diversity. One, Edison Middle School, is located in a Hispanic community that has been termed "Little Mexico," whereas another, Key Middle School, is located in a low-income African American community. Despite the wide variations in community backgrounds, the common thread is that CIS chooses schools characterized by high numbers of students at risk of school dropout. Almost all students live in families with less than $12,000 per year for a family of five (at or below the poverty line), 60% live in single-parent homes or with grandparents, legal guardians, foster parents, or independently without supervision, and approximately one third come from families where Spanish is the predominant language spoken at home.

Service Configuration

CIS provides prevention, enrichment, assessment, diagnostic, short-term treatment, and case management activities to children and their families at selected school sites. CIS's 21 sites (as of 1992) differ in the types of services available to program participants; in general, services vary according to the specific needs of the school campus and its surrounding community. CIS is capable of providing participants with a range of services through on-site programs and referrals. Student participants and their families may receive support services, individual counseling, academic enhancement, crisis intervention, parent involvement, information and referral, social services, English as a second language (ESL), employment, and enrichment or recreational activities.

Most sites offer a wide range of activities and services. Each school has a CIS office that houses CIS staff and agency partners. Staff members assess students, match students with needed services, and monitor students' academic progress and use of these resources from within this office. After an initial assessment, the case manager channels the client into either a caseload or noncaseload track. Caseload clients require more in-depth attention through weekly meetings with a case manager. Noncaseload clients often receive crisis intervention services and typically participate in one or more of the after-school activities.

The CIS office has an open, nonjudgmental atmosphere that encourages all students in the school to belong to CIS. CIS actively discourages labeling of students and has successfully marketed itself to students and their families as a place to go for enrichment or recreational activities, to belong to a group, and to become more successful in school, thereby increasing both its accessibility and utilization.

In one site we visited in 1992, Edison Middle School adopted a "club" concept in order to introduce activities into a school that had been riddled by female gangs. A modeling club, ESL club, Mariachi club, and other after-school activities are some of the activities introduced by Edison's CIS program with the goal of building self-esteem. The CIS program at Edison has eight major components: (a) counseling, (b) academics, (c) enrichment, (d) career awareness, (e) health, (f) parent involvement/parent clubs, (g) employment and preemployment skills, and (h) social services.

Type and Make-Up of the Service Integration Network

CIS has established both formal and informal agreements with a range of agencies to provide services to both child and family. These services are provided either on site (at the school) or by way of referrals to outside agencies. Over time, CIS has recognized the need for more clearly defining each partner's roles and responsibilities. A "memorandum of understanding" is now used to detail the relationship and rules between CIS, its partner agencies, and a host school. The memorandum of understanding is drawn up at the beginning of the school year and formalizes the roles and responsibilities of the school and CIS staff. This helps CIS to tailor the offerings to the needs of the particular site and to ensure that CIS does not become overextended (as has happened in the past). The most common type of interagency collaboration involves sharing resources, specifically agency staff. Most agency staff members have offices at the school where they work with the other CIS staff to deal with client concerns.

Local school CIS programs have linkages with different agencies, depending on the perceived needs of the community. Typically, agencies with workers placed at the school sites include community youth services agencies, the state drug and alcohol prevention office, juvenile justice agencies, the city parks and recreation department, the state employment office, big brother/big sister programs, and child guidance and crisis counseling agencies. Also available at the typical CIS school are tutoring and mentoring activities provided by local college and high school students and parenting enrichment and parent-focused services, including advocacy, information, and referral. The program manager at each site and the central CIS office develop the linkages with each agency or service present at the site. The CIS office has a full-time staff person responsible for forging and maintaining agency linkages and providing support to CIS school sites in need of particular services.

At Edison Middle School, for instance, program participants have on-site access to a Community Youth Services crisis intervention worker from a local youth services agency, a drug counselor funded through the Texas Commission on Alcohol and Drug Abuse Prevention, two caseworkers (one is a volunteer from the Jesuit Volunteer Corps), and 40 tutors from the University of Houston.

Funding Sources

During its first 5 years, Houston CIS received funds primarily through private donors plus a small amount of initial support from the national Cities in Schools program. The first external grant came from the state's Department of Criminal Justice to conduct a dropout prevention program. During the early years, Houston CIS was supported by grants from the state's Departments of Criminal Justice and Education (Chapter 2 funds) and private funds. In 1985–1986 a statewide CIS office within the governor's office, supported by the Governor's Discretionary Fund, was created. State legislation in 1986 institutionalized the CIS program model as part of the Texas Employment Commission (TEC) and the Texas Youth Commission. In 1990 CIS started receiving compensatory education money diverted from school districts.

A host of local businesses, including oil, utility, and real estate companies, contributed funds during those early years. CIS established an interagency policy council comprising all agency partners as well as representatives from the school district and business and community leaders. Eleven agencies participated in the collaboration during the first year of operation, including the city health department, parks and recreation department, police, Depelchin Children's Center (serving teen mothers), the Houston Child Guidance Clinic, Big Brothers/Big Sisters, and Community Youth Services. Corporate office space was donated by Tenneco, a key business supporter of CIS. The state-level Communities in Schools organization also provides seed money to start new project sites.

During the 1991–1992 fiscal year, the program received 28% of its support from public sources, 31% of its support from private sources, and 40% of its support from in-kind contributions.

Update: 1996

As of June 1996, Houston CIS had 40 programs in 39 sites as well as 8 programs operating in satellite centers of the Harris County Juvenile Probation Department. According to data from the 1994–1995 school year, 18,045 students received services from Houston CIS, and retention rates for caseload students in the same year ranged from 89–100%, with middle and high school students averaging 95% retention in school.

The rapid expansion of CIS in schools over the past 4 years has brought about a host of changes that were required for the administration and management to keep up with the demand. As well, there were changes in the funding climate and the legislation that have an impact on CIS. Finally, as CIS expanded into more schools and more school districts, the types of services it offered were required to expand as well for CIS to meet more diverse local conditions and needs. To meet the challenges of offering new services, CIS forged linkages with a greater diversity of private and public partners. Thus, the changes that have occurred since our first visit in 1992 are in the areas of legislation and funding, administration and management, programs, and interagency linkages.

Changes in Legislation and Funding

Since our visit in 1992, a major shift occurred in the legislation under which CIS operated. The state CIS office was housed within the Texas Employment Commission (TEC) until June 1996, when new state legislation created the Texas Workforce Commission (TWC) under a section called "Youth Initiatives." The TWC was created to save money and reduce bureaucracy. All state workforce programs under the auspices of DHS, the Texas Employment Commission, and the Department of Education were merged into the legislative umbrella called TWC. But this was only one of two parallel funding streams. The second funding stream involved local block grants that were administered by the local workforce commissions. The overall intended effect of these two funding streams is to give local providers faster access to block-grant funds, create greater decentralization so that local areas can make decisions about where the funds are allocated, and ultimately allow local providers to respond more quickly to emerging problems and needs. These changes should result in greater communication between local providers and the funding sources, with reduced bureaucracy.

Because the legislation was signed into law in June 1996, it is too early, as of this writing, to tell whether the expected benefits will be realized and whether any negative, unintended consequences will take place. Clearly the law benefits CIS, which is seen as being an important local provider who can coordinate different agencies to solve local problems. The change would give CIS better communication with the state funders.

There has also been a shift in the funding climate, since 1992. Now many federal grants require local educational areas (LEAs) to have a partnership agreement with a CBO (community-based organization). Also, many foundations are looking for local partners and, where in the past they might have supported single-focused organizations, more collaborative arrangements between organizations are now being supported. CIS is often used as a local CBO that will bring together service providers from different systems.

In 1996, Tenneco was bought by El Paso Energy, and the full effects of this change are not fully known at the time of this writing. The CEO who initiated the school enrichment program was the former CEO of Tenneco, and he has continued to be actively involved, particularly in raising private funds. El Paso Energy has not made a physical move to Houston, and currently there is no ongoing participation by the new company, but some board members believe there will be good dialogue.

Federal welfare reform legislation (Personal Responsibility and Work Opportunity Reconciliation Act of 1996, P.L. 104–193) will affect CIS, but its full impact remains to be seen. There is a feeling that CIS may need to address parents' needs for employment and self-sufficiency. A series of planning meetings are being held as of this writing to understand the implications of federal welfare reform better. One idea is that CIS could make links with the current agency partners who deal with education, employment, and preemployment training to provide remediation, GED, and workforce development to parents so that they can be prepared for the world of work.

Changes in Management and Administration

In the past several years, CIS has made its planning process more standardized through a new planning committee. The planning committee is designed to help CIS decide which of many requests for new collaborative projects it will pursue and in which school districts. The CIS planning committee includes representatives from different service systems, such as the school districts, major agency partners, and universities.

CIS acts as a broker providing assistance with funding as well as entree into the schools for community-based organizations (CBOs) that want to provide a new service for youth at risk via the schools. But it is also careful to check potential partner agencies. CIS uses a number of criteria to determine the suitability of the agency or service provider as a partner. The partnering agency must have a proven track record, the key individuals must be known to CIS, and there must be demonstrated sincerity and a commitment to stay in the school for at least 3 years. In many cases, CIS tries to ensure that the CBO has 3 to 5 years of funding already committed to the project. CIS provides continuous monitoring of the agency partners to make sure that project goals and objectives are met and that services are provided according to plan.

When CIS is asked by schools to venture into new schools or new school districts, relatively strict guidelines developed by the CIS program planning committee are used. The guidelines became highly structured to assure that all schools and school districts would be treated fairly and that the community would see CIS as being objective in making decisions about where to begin new services. The criteria set forth by the program planning committee include funding, feeder pattern, longevity, and commitment. CIS makes use of the existing feeder pattern in school districts, where several elementary schools "feed" their graduating students to specific middle schools, which in turn feed their graduates to a specific high school. Depending on the size of a school district, there may be many feeder patterns, each operating in parallel. CIS has determined that the most effective use of its services occurs when it can engage the entire feeder network (i.e., when CIS can enter the elementary schools in one network and then also enter the middle and high schools from the same feeder pattern).

When a request comes in for expansion of the program to a new school, CIS studies the number of requests that have come from schools in the same feeder pattern. Typically there will be a "groundswell" of support for

CIS to become involved in a cluster of schools, so often a request from one school is followed by a request from another school in the same feeder pattern. CIS will also work with area superintendents to do some planning beforehand to see where the program can best intervene. In fact, the area school superintendents serve as guides and strategic planners to assist CIS in identifying the needs in particular schools or clusters of schools. CIS places higher priority on schools in a feeder network in which it already has a presence, before starting schools in new feeder networks.

CIS creates "vertical teams" that coordinate activities across all schools in the feeder network. Each vertical team has a relatively high degree of autonomy and reports to the CIS head office through a team leader. The vertical team approach allows CIS to gear its programs to meet the needs of a given school feeder network. Thus, the selection of new schools as CIS sites is determined by the feeder network in which the potential schools are located.

The planning process was created to ensure impartiality and objectivity because CIS's community image is critical to its success in working with various school districts, service systems, and community groups. CIS works hard to be above reproach in terms of favoritism or special interests. Previously, CIS found that a service expansion to a school feeder pattern serving students from predominantly one minority group was often accompanied by complaints from schools serving predominantly other racial subgroups. It makes sure that there are tangible policies in place to address all concerns and that the CIS board of directors includes parents and a diversity of schools that fully represent the composition of the city. As Cynthia Briggs, executive director, remarked, "The folks in this city don't listen to what you say, they watch what you do." So CIS consistently strives for broad-based support and objectivity in providing services and expanding into schools. As a result, CIS has gained unmatched credibility and widespread support over its 18-year existence, and this reputation is guarded zealously.

Program Changes

Since the 1992 visit, CIS has expanded services in a number of new directions. Two parent programs have been piloted and are being considered for expansion. The first, Padres Con Poder, is a 5-week parent empowerment program using interactive video vignettes to stimulate discussion about solving problems. The purpose of the program is to help parents deal with family themes, develop parenting skills, and solve problems, as well as to help them focus on community problems such as drugs and violence. Parents meet once a week for 5 or 6 weeks at the elementary school attended by their child. The second parent program, Cara y Corazon, was developed through an arrangement with Texas Community Services and takes place in a middle school. It consists of a 12-week parenting education program in which 2-hour sessions held once a week deal with Hispanic family values and problems affecting families, such as alcoholism and drug abuse, family violence, and dysfunctional families.

Another new program was initiated several years ago when a Request for Proposal was issued through the U.S. Office of Juvenile Justice and Delinquency Prevention, Department of Justice, seeking partnerships between juvenile probation and local community-based organizations (CBOs) for remedial assistance to adjudicated youth and to prevent more serious youth offenders from being removed from their communities and placed in long-term lock-up facilities. The announcement mandated that systems must work together to use funds targeted at juvenile delinquency more effectively. Houston CIS already had an ongoing relationship with the Harris County Juvenile Probation Department through well-established interagency meetings, and this facilitated a successful application for these funds to establish a joint program. The proposal was a collaborative effort between both agencies, and a working interagency agreement was developed as part of the proposal that spelled out the responsibilities of the respective parties. In its first few years, two probation officers were assigned to Houston CIS and shared office space with CIS at two middle schools. The current program consists of two components: (a) remedial education and pre-employment skills for adjudicated youth and (b) aptitude, diagnostic, and achievement testing as well as support services for serious youth offenders.

The first component of the joint CIS/Juvenile Probation program is to provide remedial education and employability skills to adjudicated youth so that they can obtain work skills and employment. These adjudicated youth may not necessarily be serious or repeat offenders. From January to June of 1996 (the most recent period for collecting data), the program worked with 796 youth through CIS offices in local middle and high schools. The second component of the CIS/Juvenile Probation program is to provide support services to the subset of adjudicated youth who are serious offenders. The focus of this effort is on youth offenders who have already been through court and for whom this is their last chance before being sent to youth villages (long-term lockup facilities). The program offers a holistic approach to supportive services by coordinating juvenile probation with local school systems and the Houston CIS. At the local schools, probation officers are mandated to see these youth on a daily basis, and the schools provide the facilities and support for this to happen. Schools also help probation officers to meet with parents and teachers on an as-needed basis to support the monitoring and maintenance of serious youth offenders in their own communities. Houston CIS pulls it all together by conducting aptitude and diagnostic testing of the participants and sharing offices in schools with juvenile probation workers. Thus, there is close, ongoing monitoring of the students as well as follow-through with teachers and parents.

On Saturdays, Juvenile Probation holds a special program called "Super Saturday," in which a variety of specialists come to a local school to work with youth and parents. The goal of these Saturdays is to bring together a variety of service providers to meet with the youth and their families and deal with all issues that they face. In many instances the chiefs of the agencies are present so that parents can see who is in charge.

Counseling services are contracted by Juvenile Probation to professionals in the community who do one-to-one and group sessions. Houston CIS provides additional diagnostic and assessment services as well as crisis counseling and information and referral. Many recreational activities hosted by CIS also occur during Super Saturday, and Houston CIS conducts occasional field trips as well as other enrichment activities. The schools make the facilities available, and teachers provide some remediation and tutorial assistance on these days. All of these activities are done to keep youth offenders who have already been in front of the court functioning in their communities and diverting them from further delinquency and incarceration. An important side benefit is that parents involved in the program have gained a different perspective on how the systems work because systems are coordinated and they know the specific individuals who help operate the system. Many of the key service systems for youth are coordinated on these Super Saturdays.

In 1996 CIS joined three existing programs with the goals of keeping high school students on grade level and increasing the overall graduation rate. The program partners are Move-It Math, Success for All, and Consistency Management. All four programs (including CIS) provide a comprehensive package of remediation and enrichment programs for high school students. Success for All is a reading enrichment program that complements the Move-It Math program, whereas Consistency Management focuses on school discipline and school behavior expectations (targeted at working with teachers and principals to improve the school's follow-up and consistency in dealing with student behavior problems). CIS provides social services, information and referral, crisis intervention, and parental involvement.

CIS's three-program partnership developed from the initiative of a single individual. A retired chief executive officer (CEO) from a large Houston company became concerned about the small number of students graduating from high school and entering postsecondary institutions. When he looked into the problem, he found that a relatively small percentage of boys graduated from high school. He then made it his mission to find innovative programs that could combat the high dropout rate, particularly for high school boys. After spending 1½ years roaming the country and searching for effective programs, he approached CIS and pulled in the three other programs that were based nationally and that he believed made a difference.

All of the funds are provided through private entities and were raised by the CEO who started the idea and brought the programs together. A clear decision was made to go after private donations because the CEO did not want strings attached and he wanted to make needed changes to maximize effectiveness "on the fly." The CEO raised the money but then made each principal in the participating school his or her own chief executive officer to spend the dollars as he or she chose. An important element to improve the chances of success was that the project would be initiated collaboratively in all schools within one specific feeder network, using the vertical team approach. Thus, grade-appropriate interventions by all agency partners were spread out through seven elementary schools feeding into one middle school, which fed into one high school. Focusing on all schools within a given feeder network ensures that students receive continuous intervention across all grades, even when they graduate to higher levels in different schools, thereby maintaining consistency of intervention and school values on graduation.

Also, CIS has piloted a number of special programs within the past year or two:

- Peer mediation training for high school students was initiated through a grant from Northwoods Presbyterian Church. Twenty-four students were trained to resolve conflict among students, with an adult observer present to ensure student safety. Within a relatively short period in the school semester following training, four conflict situations were resolved successfully by these trained mediators, and the program may be expanded within the next year using assistance from the Americorps program.

- With assistance from Serve Houston, Americorps volunteers provided after-school programs at several elementary schools. The volunteers assisted students with homework and study skills, tutorials, creative arts activities and instruction, and supervision for sports and recreation. The YMCA provided playground equipment and gave some additional training and field supervision.

- An anti-gang program was initiated through a grant from the mayor's Anti-Gang Office. The program was located in a middle school that seemed especially hard hit by gang activities. The program goals were as follows: (a) to intervene with students identified as being at risk of gang involvement, (b) to help students break free of a gang, and (c) to counter the influence of gangs on other students in the school. There are weekly "gatherings" to support belonging in a peer group alternative to gangs, and in this pilot project approximately 10 students in the one middle school are involved.

- A mental health program was field tested during the past summer at several elementary schools, with a grant from the Mental Health/Mental Retardation Authority (MHMR). Students identified as having mental health problems were given a clinical assessment and then participated in individual and group counseling provided by licensed therapists.

- A CIS technology education specialist, funded by the Texas Education Agency, worked with students at two high schools to teach preemployment skills as part of the business technology classes and helped students to find after-school jobs to help them stay in school.

- The Childress Foundation Academy implemented a new program in the 1995–1996 project year involving 125 incoming 9th grade students who had been identified as being at risk. The Academy functions as a "school-within-a-school" by occupying a separate wing of a high school staffed by four academic instructors. This group of students is followed as part of the Academy as they move through grade levels while new cohorts of at-risk students also join when they enter 9th grade. When the Academy students move to the 11th grade, they are then mainstreamed back into the host high school to finish their high school education. CIS provides support services to these students and monitors their progress as they move from the Academy to the larger school. The YMCA provided resources to create a "Teen Court" at the Academy, in which students trained as judges, jurors, attorneys, and bailiffs handle student infractions of Academy rules. Sentences are limited to community service; attending educational seminars, and in some cases, service on the Teen Court.

Changes in Interagency Relationships

CIS continues to expand its recruits from social services, businesses, and community groups to provide volunteer services or in-kind support in CIS school sites. A careful perusal of its most recent partners attests to the diversity of groups attracted to CIS, including Foster Grandparents, Interfaith Ministries, Houston Trial Lawyers' Foundation, The American Society for Civil Engineers, The Children's Museum, Baker and Botts law firm, University of Houston, Texas Southern University, University of St. Thomas, Houston Community College, Lyondell Petrochemical Company, and Bates Southwest advertising agency.

The support base for CIS in the community is further strengthened through the fledgling Friends of CIS (FOCIS), which is in its third year of operation. Membership in 1995 reached 150 volunteers who become personally involved with CIS students. The volunteers must undergo special training to tutor CIS students with reading problems and to work as a team providing coverage for all students in the program. FOCIS also organizes benefits to raise funds for CIS, such as theater benefits with a reception.

Involvement in Evaluation Activities

Central to any beginning work in evaluation is the careful monitoring of client background and service usage. Houston CIS has developed and maintains a sophisticated management information system (MIS) that features complex database software and a 20-terminal local area network (LAN). Two major upgrades of hardware have occurred since 1992 because of the increased requests for reports geared specifically for each funding source as well as external requests for data. The hardware was purchased out of general operating revenues. Technical assistance covering which hardware to buy and how to make it fill the program's needs was provided free by volunteers from the business community and by the vendors from whom the equipment was purchased.

Based at the Central CIS office, the MIS was designed to meet the reporting requirements of multiple funding sources, some of which require line-item budget justification as well as monitoring of service functions. The MIS produces reports that describe the amount and duration of CIS services provided by type of student, family background, or site. In addition, the MIS system records funding data and produces reports that estimate the cost per student contact hour, depending on the types of services provided. Sites receive monthly updates of services provided from this system. For example, the 1996 fact sheet reports that the cost per service hour of CIS is $17 and that the cost per student served is $222. Furthermore, for every dollar spent directly by CIS, another 60¢ is leveraged through partnerships with community agencies.

To obtain this level of information, there is an elaborate but well-designed reporting system that begins at each CIS site. With the use of vertical teams to manage clusters of CIS sites, the internal monitoring system was strengthened, from the perspective of both the field and the central office. Site staff are organized as vertical teams with site staff receiving paperwork and information and passing these along to a cluster leader. The cluster leader is the manager responsible for program accountability and monitoring for a cluster of schools in a given feeder area. The cluster leaders report to the director of field operations at the central office, who compiles data across all schools and teams.

School or agency personnel making a referral to CIS complete a CIS intake form at the time of the referral. Both caseload and noncaseload students must have a completed intake form. Within 2 weeks of the referral, a student assessment form is completed for caseload students, recording basic intake information, such as reasons for referral and presenting problems. A signed parent or guardian consent form is also obtained for all students. For caseload students, CIS holds a staffing meeting to determine services, assigns a CIS caseworker, and opens a folder on the student. Once the (caseload or noncaseload) student enrolls at CIS, a student activity record form tracks the services and activities received by the student or family members from CIS or an agency partner on site. Separate forms record participation of students in group or workshop activities; other forms record participation by CIS staff, school staff, parents, or other members of the community in CIS-run workshops or group sessions. A termination report is completed whenever a student terminates either from the caseload only or from all CIS activities. This report records a number of potential reasons for termination, including achieving goals or no longer requiring services, graduation, moving to another school, referral to another agency, alternative educational placement, expulsion, institutionalization, and dropping out from CIS. Students enrolled in CIS can stop receiving caseload services but can still remain in CIS to engage in the enrichment and recreational activities.

Program monitoring continues to be refined and is an important feature of CIS that suggests a high degree of readiness for more extensive evaluation efforts. There is a great deal of interest in evaluating the effectiveness of the program, in order to increase efforts at replicating the model in other school districts. Several external evaluation entities that the CEO put in place even before he began raising money are developing formative and summative evaluation studies. Evaluation is being conducted by the Houston Independent School District (HISD) and by the University of Houston School of Social Work, and these are being coordinated with the CIS's own evaluation group. A large number of outcomes are being measured, including grade point average, attendance, behavior, parental attitudes, and alternative methods of school discipline. One of the evaluation studies will be using a comparison feeder network of schools. An evaluation report by HISD showing initial results should be released sometime toward the end of 1996. CIS conducted a survey of participating school principals from the existing feeder pattern, and the respondents gave high praise to the program's services.

Concluding Thoughts

Three factors seem critical to the success of this model of comprehensive service integration. First, it is a school-based program in which a range of services for adolescents, from school counseling, to drug and alcohol abuse treatment, to juvenile delinquency, to health services, are held under one roof. Second, it was created and continues to be strongly guided by a partnership between public and private interests, including some major corporations located in the city of Houston. Private interests, including big business, see that they have a stake in what happens to adolescents in their communities and that, for future prosperity, they must make a commitment to improving schools. Finally, the program has reached a level of acceptance among school administrators and principals from a number of school districts that is almost unprecedented. Rather than closing their doors, school administrators welcome the "under one roof" notion and the tailoring of programs and services to the local conditions that seem to be a formula for success in working with school districts. Schools are often seen as being resistant to change because of the large, slow-moving bureaucracy, so it is intriguing to look at the universal acceptance and the high respect accorded to Houston CIS. That this has happened is not a coincidence and owes a great deal of credit to CIS's founding principles of paying attention to its reputation and credibility, working with local schools, and tailoring its approach to local conditions.

12 _____

I Have a Future

Overview

I Have a Future is an innovative, prevention-oriented program devoted to giving youth specific principles for living (e.g., the Nguzo Saba Seven Principles of Blackness) and teaching them the skills needed to abide by these principles. It serves youth living in two public housing projects in North Nashville, Tennessee, plus youth attending the high school serving these projects. It is organized around curricular modules related to prosocial behavior, family life education, and other topics; it also offers youth the opportunity to participate in stimulating activities, such as self-defense, computer skills, sports, and entrepreneurship, once they complete the core modules. The program is designed to keep youth involved during all of their adolescent years, from the age of 10, when they may join, until they graduate from high school.

Mission, Goals, and Objectives

I Have a Future has a mission: "To address the problems confronting poor African American youth through a comprehensive effort of prevention, addressed toward early pregnancy and childbearing, substance abuse, violence, and school failure" (I Have a Future "Fact Sheet," unpublished program document, n.d.). This mission is elaborated in goals related both to client outcomes and to program development. The program states as its goals that it intends "To develop a replicable community-based, life-enhancement program that promotes a significant reduction in the incidence of early pregnancy and childbearing and other harmful behaviors among high-risk male and female adolescents between the ages of 10 and 17" (I Have a Future "Fact Sheet," unpublished program document, n.d.).

The goals of I Have a Future have been extended to five specific objectives:

- To improve knowledge, attitudes, and behaviors related to personal health, human sexuality, drug and alcohol abuse, homicide and violence reduction and other factors which may place adolescents at risk.

- To provide greater access to, and increase utilization of, comprehensive adolescent health services and social services, including contraceptive availability.
- To improve socially adaptive/appropriate behaviors with particular focus on school achievement, pre-vocational skill development, and delinquency rates.
- To enhance the ability of high-risk adolescents to overcome environmental barriers in attaining the skills necessary to pursue meaningful employment and educational opportunities with the promise of upward mobility.
- To engender a more positive self-concept and constructive attitude toward community, family life, and the future through the use of the Nguzo Saba Principles. (I Have a Future "Fact Sheet," unpublished program document, n.d.)

I Have a Future has the additional program objective of involving adult members of its two housing project communities in activities that will support them and their children in resisting drug and alcohol dependency and taking greater control of their lives and circumstances.

Current Clientele

I Have a Future provides services to 10–17 year olds who live in either of two public housing projects in Nashville. Participants are spread relatively evenly over the age range, and 98% of them are African American; 51% are male. At any time, approximately 150 youth actively participate in services. More than 500 youth have come through the program since services began in 1988.

Most youth refer themselves to I Have a Future. They learn about the program through word of mouth, a friend or sibling in the program, or presentations made by the program in schools and community groups. Referrals also come from concerned parents, counselors, and social workers in schools. A few referrals come from juvenile court or probation, which send youth to participate in I Have a Future's conflict resolution module. Those who live in the projects sometimes stay on after their obligatory participation ends, but those from elsewhere have a difficult time getting to the program because transportation is only available while they are fulfilling their court obligation.

Every new participant signs a contract on entering I Have a Future. The contract commits the youth to have a physical examination within 60 days (available free of charge at the program site), participate in the 8-week module on prosocial behavior, participate in either the CHARM (Choosing How to Adorn and Refine Myself, for girls) or MATURE (Males Adorning, Thinking and Using Refined Energies, for boys) module, and participate in the 14-week family life education module. Participation in at least one of the modules must happen within the first 60 days; youth must complete the prosocial module before attending any other module.

Each youth discusses further ways to participate in I Have a Future once he or she has successfully completed the 60-day commitment.

Other I Have a Future participants include more than 250 adults from the two public housing projects (not necessarily parents of "Future" youth) who have participated in 4-week Parent Empowerment seminars. Approximately half of these parents have gone on to participate in the 12-week extended Parent Empowerment seminar offered by I Have a Future or to other chemical dependency or codependency support resources, such as Alcoholics Anonymous, Narcotics Anonymous, Al-Anon, Adult Children of Alcoholics, or individual substance abuse counseling. Some have become involved in local tenant councils, educational activities, the development of day care resources within the housing projects, and other activities on their own behalf or on behalf of their families and communities. Approximately 30 parents who have been through Parent Empowerment serve as recruiters, counselors, and trainers for this part of the program.

Service Configuration

I Have a Future organizes its services around curriculum modules delivered to small groups of youth, coupled with a thorough assessment, case management, and tracking system. In addition, the program offers primary health care on site.

The I Have a Future program began officially in 1987 as an adolescent pregnancy prevention program. Its original approach used case management and brokering of services, including brokering for some enrichment activities (e.g., karate, dance). Staff of various community agencies came to the community center in the housing projects where the program operates to deliver these services, while program staff provide primarily case management. The community center location was shared with many other programs and could not offer I Have a Future a space it could call its own and where the youth could feel a sense of ownership. Furthermore, it could not provide space for the health clinic part of the program. Also, the program did not control the contents of the services offered through these brokered arrangements and could not expect to integrate the value system it tries to convey to its users into all the services offered.

When the deputy director at the time of our 1992 visit, Dr. Lorraine Greene, joined the "Future" staff in February 1989, she helped to turn the program structure and emphasis toward an approach more culturally sensitive to the situation of African American youth, one that incorporates a clear value system into every element of the program and one that explicitly addresses the broad array of problems and prevention needs confronting youth. It was clear that to do this, program staff would have to be able to do more than case management: They would need the skills to run groups, convey values and principles, and actually provide many of the services that had previously been obtained through other agencies. At the same time, the Nashville-Davidson Housing Authority committed one housing unit in each housing project to be used as program space for I

Have a Future. The new approach thus combines case management with curriculum modules and activities for youth and parents taking place at sites completely under the control of the program (one large apartment in each of two public housing projects). Carnegie Corporation offered I Have a Future a technical assistance team to help develop the content of the different modules, which include family life education, preemployment, prosocial behavior, conflict resolution, and alcohol and drug abuse prevention. Each module teaches skills and then gives youth opportunities to practice the skills in different settings. Each also teaches youth how to think about and apply the Nguzo Saba Seven Principles of Blackness (unity, collective work and responsibility, purpose, self-determination, cooperative economics, creativity, and faith) in daily life situations. The program still accesses some services in the community, such as karate and dance classes.

Everyone is required to participate in three of the modules: prosocial behavior, family life education, and CHARM (for girls) or MATURE (for boys). Prosocial behavior covers such topics as how to behave in groups; decision-making and problem-solving skills, with a particular emphasis on alcohol and drug abuse prevention; and on respecting oneself and others. Youth must complete the prosocial behavior module before they can participate in other modules or activities. Family life education addresses the stereotypes and realities of family life and covers issues related to adolescent sexuality and prevention of teenage pregnancy and childbearing. CHARM and MATURE are ongoing modules for girls and boys, respectively. They address issues of grooming, dress, hygiene, and self-respecting behavior. These modules give boys and girls a chance to discuss things in same-sex groups that they might feel less comfortable discussing with the opposite-sex present. Youth in the program may attend CHARM and MATURE at any time.

After completing the initial required modules, youth may choose from among a variety of other modules and activities, including tutoring, self-defense, computer skills, preemployment, creative movement and dance, sports, art classes, outings, conflict resolution training and violence prevention, peer counseling, and entrepreneurship. The program is meant to accommodate youth staying as long as 7 years (coming in at 10 and staying until they graduate from high school), so there is always something new or different to do.

Case management begins with a thorough assessment within 2 weeks of a youth's program entry. Counselor and youth then discuss needs and preferences and how these can be met. Once finished with the initial required modules, youth may select activities or modules that appeal to them or the counselor may recommend certain activities on the basis of his or her assessment of the youth's circumstances. Any module may be repeated, and several modules are designed to be ongoing, with youth attending for as long and as often as they like (i.e., CHARM, MATURE, conflict resolution). Youth achievement within each module is assessed by pre- and posttesting using paper-and-pencil instruments. Every month, the counselor and youth meet to see how things are going; progress notes are written on every youth every month. Every 6 months there is a major reassessment of each youth in terms of achievement of past goals and setting of new ones.

Other activities involve opportunities for service. Youth may be selected as peer counselors, which are paid positions for 10–15 hours a week that give youth responsibility for monitoring program activities, giving speeches and presentations in the community, helping younger children with schoolwork, overseeing the latchkey program for 6–10 year olds, recording everyone's grades on school report card days, and similar duties. Youth who are not officially peer counselors may (and do) help others with schoolwork and offer other supports as appropriate. Most youth are in the Entrepreneur's Club, in which they learn business skills, operate a business of their own, and earn money.

Services to youth are complemented by programs for adult residents of the two housing projects where I Have a Future operates. The Parent Empowerment Program offers both 4-week and 12-week seminars for parents on issues of codependency and alcohol and drug abuse, such as self-esteem enhancement, dealing with depression, and other related matters. Some graduates of these programs receive additional training to become recruiters, peer counselors, and supports for first-time adult participants.

Type and Make-Up of the Service Integration Network

I Have a Future provides a summer JTPA program with federal funds on site through a contract with the city of Nashville. Tennessee State University provides educational enrichment workshops and tutoring on site to I Have a Future participants through another contract. Other interagency agreements with community agencies are for short-term resource sharing. For instance, for several years a local Catholic church operated parenting skills workshops that were part of the I Have a Future Parent Empowerment Program. I Have a Future is a member of the Alliance for African American Males, a consortium of community agencies. The Alliance occasionally refers youth to I Have a Future. I Have a Future also may have occasion to call on the services of other programs in the Alliance when participants need them.

The program would now have more collaborative activities if it had succeeded in getting funding for several projects. I Have a Future and several of the schools attended by program clients have written joint grant applications to support I Have a Future programming at school sites. I Have a Future staff now go to the local high school at least monthly to do special activities and also run some of the program's modules in the schools. Most of the participants are I Have a Future youth, but others may also participate. I Have a Future has enough of a presence in this school to be listed as a club in the school yearbook. There are plans for I Have a Future to develop and staff a health clinic in the school. The school has made space available; proposals to raise money to staff the clinic have not been funded, but I Have a Future and the school will keep trying. If it opens, this clinic will be available to all students, not just to I Have a Future participants.

In general, I Have a Future uses a variety of community resources and obtains referrals from a number of agencies. It also succeeds in providing a comprehensive program for at-risk youth that is geared to prevention and to life options and empowerment. If some recent fundraising activities had been successful, the program would now be involved in some more collaborative arrangements with several schools. But as things stand, I Have a Future does not do much in a service integration framework.

Funding Sources

I Have a Future receives 90% of its funding from private sources: the Carnegie Corporation, Bill and Camille Cosby (as individuals), the William and Flora Hewlett Foundation (for the entrepreneur's program), and the William T. Grant Foundation (for evaluation). Approximately 10% of program support comes from the Tennessee Department of Mental Health and Mental Retardation to fund the Parent Empowerment Program and the latchkey program. In addition, program space is donated by the Nashville-Davidson Housing Authority.

The program began as a demonstration with major support from the Carnegie Corporation. It was never funded up to the level of its original design, and it has been operating with many staff at half-time rather than at the full-time level originally planned. The program has recently been renewed by the Carnegie Corporation for another 2 years and by the Hewlett Foundation for 2 years. The amount of funding from the state of Tennessee is small but stable. But it is uncertain where the program will get the remaining part of its budget (approximately 40%) if the Cosby funding is not renewed. Program staff have written several unsuccessful grant proposals and are looking for additional sources of support.

Update: 1996

The mission, goals, and objectives of the program remain the same in 1996 as they were in 1992. The program's leadership has changed, from Dr. Lorraine Williams Greene, who was the deputy director in 1992, to Ms. Leslie McKnight as the current program coordinator. Dr. Greene maintains a relationship with the program and has responsibility for handling requests for descriptions of the program and for assistance in replicating it in other communities. We were referred to her as the appropriate person for this update, and the interview was conducted with her. Dr. Henry Foster has been the program's official director throughout the period. The program serves between 150 and 200 youth at any one time and has now served more than 850 youth over the course of its existence. It has a waiting list for membership at this time.

Shifts in Funding

I Have a Future has experienced some major and some minor changes in the years since 1992. The major changes have to do with funding levels and sources. In addition, several aspects of its service configuration have changed. Major grant support was running out when we visited the program in 1992. Some was renewed, and the program obtained some additional grant money over the years, succeeding in holding things together through the summer of 1995. Becoming a United Way-designated agency and receiving grants from United Way helped during the 1993–1995 period. In 1992 I Have a Future had three half-time and one full-time direct service staff. For several years thereafter, the program lost a half-time direct service position but was still able to maintain services with two half-time and one full-time staff. During that time the program suffered losses of administrative staff, until it was reduced to no administrators at all by the summer of 1995. During the 1995–1996 school year, the program was reduced to a skeleton crew of on-site staff supported by peer counselors, including some college students, so they were able to keep the physical program sites open at the two housing projects and continued to offer services at the high school. Funding came from state dollars that were the result of an initiative by African American state legislators, but the future availability of these funds is uncertain. During this same period, ironically, the program received continuing recognition as a unique and valuable model program, and many other communities sought help from program staff as they tried to replicate its approach and service configuration.

The fundamental problem was in obtaining funding for the core of the program. Spinoffs were relatively easy to fund, being new activities, but the basic services at the housing projects were much harder to maintain. The program's rather desperate funding situation, with threat of ultimate program closure, may have stimulated the Nashville Health Department to action. In 1996 the Nashville Health Department committed itself through public statements and active negotiations with Meharry Medical College to take over the program's funding and operations. The Health Department has plans to expand the program into other housing projects and operate it as a true public health model. Dr. Lorraine Greene was very happy about this development, feeling that it reflected the original purpose and vision for the program and would assure its continued existence, stability, and adherence to the basic program design.

Changes in Program Configuration

Programmatic changes concern activities with parents and the location of many services for youth. Soon after our visit in 1992, the parents involved in the Parent Empowerment Program decided that they wanted to do their own program, which they named "Parents of Worth." The new program received seed money from the state to do drug elimination work in their housing projects and also worked to get residents to bid on doing repairs, beautification, and other activities in the housing projects. I Have a Future staff supported Parents of Worth with letters as they tried to get financial support for their projects, and they also provided Parents of Worth members with training on conflict resolution and violence reduction under a contract from Parents of Worth. When the Centers for Disease Control (CDC) started its model teen pregnancy prevention projects, using the I Have a Future model as one option, a member of Parents of Worth accompanied Dr. Greene to Atlanta to provide technical assistance on replication to the new CDC grantees.

The plans underway in 1992 to develop a clinic at the local high school have come to fruition. The school did some minor renovations and then made available space in the school buildings to have a teen health clinic. I Have a Future provided staff for the clinic 3 days a week and was also able to refer youth back to its project-based sites for services they could not deliver on the school grounds. A good deal of program activity switched to the high school, but until mid-1996 the school-based program activities were not able to expand because of lack of staff. I Have a Future was also able to maintain some of its health services through a strong collaboration with the Tennessee State School of Nursing. Foundation funding helped create a project to develop an adolescent health promotion and disease prevention program. For approximately 4 years, nursing students rotated through the clinics at the I Have a Future sites, providing services and stretching the limited staff resources.

Involvement in Evaluation Activities

Because it was established as a demonstration, I Have a Future has been involved in evaluation and documentation of its activities since it began. Conducting these evaluation activities was part of the program's obligation under its demonstration funding; it received financial support from the William T. Grant Foundation specifically for evaluation.

The evaluation design for the original demonstration was developed by the staff of the Meharry Medical College who developed the program. These same staff developed the initial instrumentation. When the program shifted emphasis after Dr. Greene arrived, the new staff used the original instrumentation as a base and added components that assessed newly important program aspects (e.g., values orientation, issues related to sexuality, self-concept measures, and measures to assess the effects of many specific components of the program's curriculum modules). Staff made inquiries of knowledgeable people in assembling their current instrumentation but basically designed and developed their evaluation system themselves.

The first data collection effort was a community needs assessment that established the parameters of the program. Thereafter, the evaluation used a quasi-experimental pre–post design, comparing teens in two North Nashville housing projects where the program operates to teens in two East Nashville housing projects that do not have the program. As part of this evaluation, three annual waves of individual interviews with sampled teens were conducted, starting early in the program's history and continuing through 1991. The results based on these surveys have not yet been published; according to Dr. Greene, preliminary results indicate that the program has had a very positive impact on reducing teen pregnancies and helping youth avoid participation in other problem behaviors that are part of the program's prevention effort.

At the time of our 1992 visit, staff were involved in additional data collection as part of their ongoing work with youth. The staff administered a thorough assessment for each new participant and recorded the results, documented monthly progress in notes, and conducted a bi-annual review, reassessment, and update of each youth's service plan. This work has continued as well as possible given the difficult funding and staffing circumstances affecting the program in recent years. Finally, every youth participating in a module completes an assessment before and after participation, to document learning and attitude change.

Throughout the energy-consuming work of trying to keep the program afloat financially after 1992 while she was still deputy director, Dr. Greene managed to piece together several additional outcome-evaluation projects. With the help of an intern, she was able to find and re-interview 80 to 90 of the participants in the treatment sample from the program's demonstration evaluation, although she does not have any similar follow-up data on the comparison sample. She is currently working on doing the same for everyone who has gone through the entrepreneur program, many of whom are now in their later high school years or have graduated. She has data showing very good performance on high school graduation rates and the likelihood that those who graduated went on to postsecondary education. It is hoped that I Have a Future's data collection practices will return to their former strength once staff and activities have stabilized and full functioning is restored.

Concluding Thoughts

Two thoughts are paramount in relation to I Have a Future: the power of its program design and its funding problems. By concentrating its efforts on a small geographical base and trying to reach all youth within its two housing projects, I Have a Future offers these youth an alternative peer group and value system as a way to resist the drug/early pregnancy/school failure climate that prevails in their environment. The protection created by this alternative contributes to the success of the program's clients, even though they live under circumstances that work strongly against their performing well in school, staying free of drugs and pregnancy, and gaining a view of the larger world that offers them opportunities for future growth and self-sufficiency.

The fluctuating financial fortunes of I Have a Future epitomize the fate of many model demonstration programs. Foundation funding gets them started, but they often have a very hard time achieving stable local support once foundation funding ends, even when they clearly work well and do the job they were designed to do. Program services get diluted; staff are stretched so thin they cannot offer the same concentrated attention to each youth. Even when a program is very strong, well-conceived, and well-operationalized, and has strong evaluation results, all of which characterize I Have a Future, survival is not assured. It is difficult or impossible to raise stable local funding to keep the program in operation as originally conceived, or at all.

The quality of this program and its unique characteristics have been recognized nationally, as attested to by interest in replication and sponsorship as a model program by the Centers for Disease Control and Prevention. But "all politics is local," and I Have a Future nearly died due to the lack of local interest and commitment. The I Have a Future story has a happy ending, but getting there was a struggle, and the end was by no means assured.

13 _____

Garfield Youth Services

Overview

Garfield Youth Services (GYS) provides services and supportive activities for all youth in Garfield County, Colorado, a rural county on the western slope of the Rocky Mountains. Its core focus is on prevention and services related to alcohol or drug abuse, and more recently on youthful criminal behavior. However, GYS has always seen its role as serving all youth in the county, not just the "bad kids." This commitment shapes its approach to local agencies, activities, and residents. Its strong prevention orientation leads it to offer a broad range of activities tailored to the needs of the main communities in the county. GYS also is a catalyst for developing supports for youth throughout the county, working with every local agency to accomplish this goal without consideration of turf or whether a new service or activity eventually will be offered by GYS or some other agency.

Mission, Goals, and Objectives

GYS states its mission as to provide "opportunities for ALL YOUTH to be responsible, contributing members of society and working with their families toward this end. Through prevention, advocacy and direct services, GYS strives to enhance the quality of life in our communities" (GYS, unpublished program document, n.d.). GYS also has specific written goals and objectives to make this mission statement more explicit. These goals and objectives are more short-term than the mission statement and frequently pertain to goals and objectives for specific new undertakings. The entire history and development of GYS indicate that the "all youth" part of the mission statement is taken very seriously in the development of specific goals and objectives. A great deal of the agency's prevention work has developed from thinking about how to reach and serve all youth, all parents, and all families. Yet GYS does not strive to be all things to youth; its major focus is in alcohol and drug prevention work, treatment issues stemming from the alcohol and drug involvement of youth, and youth involved with the criminal justice system, often as a result of alcohol or drug use. GYS has decided not to expand in a major way to include services related to adolescent pregnancy (either prevention or care), reasoning that the activities of other community resources were already adequate to handle the need. However, GYS does provide group sessions on these topics in areas of the county that have no prevention resources.

Current Clientele

GYS sees youth clients and their parents for treatment services (crisis intervention, case management, and restitution), youth and adults for school-based prevention services, youth and adults for community-based short-term groups on various topics, and youth and adults in the Pals (mentoring) Program. Of their new service clients (758 youth) for FY 1992, 59% were male and 41% were female; 39% were 16 or older, 49% were ages 10–15, and 12% were younger than 10. GYS also handled 239 alternative-sentencing clients and 25 restitution clients, and it ran groups for 304 participants. School-based prevention interventions reached almost 3,000 youth (not necessarily unduplicated) and approximately 750 parents, and 115 teachers attended training sessions. Several hundred youth attended short-term groups located in the community. The Pals Program made 52 new matches, with many more youth, teens, and adults participating as ongoing junior, teen, and senior Pals.

Service Configuration

GYS has an extensive range of both prevention and treatment services. Prevention services include school-based presentations to youth and to parents, presentations to community groups, and the Pals Program. The program offers parents and adult community members groups for stepparents, parenting the young child, powerful parenting, being a new parent, parent support, and bridging the gap (for parents and adolescents together). It offers Project ChARLIE (Chemical Abuse Resolution Lies in Education), an early intervention program, to elementary school classes. It conducts drug and alcohol awareness classes, prevention classes, and refusal-skills classes in middle and high schools. In the community, it runs groups for youth on family change, self-esteem, drug and alcohol awareness, children of alcoholics, theft/petty theft, death and loss, communication skills, prevention of teenage pregnancy and STDs, sexuality education, defensive driving classes, young men's issues, young women's issues, social skills, and feelings. The Pals Program involves adult and teen community members as mentors for more than 100 youth; GYS also schedules monthly activities for Pals who have a match (a mentor) and for youth on the Pals waiting list who have not yet been matched.

GYS' system of 10 active host homes bridges the gap between prevention and treatment services. These homes serve as the community's youth shelter, providing a temporary emergency residence until a permanent arrangement can be developed for youth who cannot or will not stay in their own homes. GYS developed these homes when it became apparent that an occasional need arose for youth emergency shelter but that not enough demand existed to justify setting up a full-time shelter. GYS trains the host-home families, places youth in the homes when necessary, and supervises the placement.

In the treatment area, GYS offers crisis intervention counseling to youth referred by police departments, the courts, the district attorney, probation, the schools, the departments of social services and mental health, the Division of Youth Services of the state Department of Institutions, parents, friends, and self-referral. The crisis team produced the most referrals from any single agency (33%), but 34% came from all the courts combined. Counseling typically lasts 4–6 weeks and can be renewed if necessary. A recent addition to GYS's treatment options is case management through the community evaluation team (CET), which is supported by a grant from a new state program (Colorado's Alternatives to Incarceration program, known as Senate Bill 94) to reduce detention placements and youth commitments to the state Department of Institutions. This team is described later, in relation to the service integration network in Garfield County.

In some instances GYS has identified service needs and acted to fill them. It is more common, however, for community agencies, such as the schools, courts, and social services, to approach GYS to supply services to youth that the agencies themselves cannot provide with existing resources. GYS has become more selective in deciding what to take on and what to pass over. The board and staff of GYS routinely refer to their mission statement and agency purpose in deciding whether to expand in a new direction.

Along with its efforts throughout its history to be perceived as an agency for all youth, GYS has stressed the importance of having all members of the community care about and work toward improving the chances of all youth to have a successful life. GYS has demonstrated its willingness to work with the entire community to this end. In a rural area characterized by distinct regional differences in orientation and resources, this inclusive and cooperative approach has been both absolutely necessary and highly effective.

GYS director Debbie Wilde is articulate about the unique aspects of developing services in a rural area where before GYS there were virtually no services for youth. First, there are no turf battles to fight, because no other agencies already have a claim on a particular type of service. Second, the community recognizes all new services as needed and welcome. Third, the welcome new services receive depends on the program's ability to develop the new service with the full cooperation of each local community at every step. Wilde stresses how GYS presents and interprets each new program in ways that each local community will understand, including changing the program name slightly if that seems important to community acceptance. Wilde notes the importance of developing community members' sense of responsibility for "our children and youth" and encouraging their participation and involvement rather than leaving things to some official agency. For instance, when community members blamed the schools for not doing enough to prevent youth behavior problems, GYS offered alcohol and drug prevention programs to the schools and training for the teachers. GYS then helped the schools respond to the community by saying, "This [GYS program] is what we [the schools] are doing, what are you [the community] doing?" Wilde believes that this approach helped reverse the attitude that youth were someone else's problem and began to get community people thinking about their role in supporting all youth.

Type and Make-Up of the Service Integration Network

GYS is part of a service integration network in both a "back-end" and a "front-end" way. By "back-end," we refer to the typical image of service integration, in which a program with a client can access services for that client through a formal network with other providers. The most straightforward instance of this for GYS is the CET, a multiagency team involving GYS, mental health and social services, the courts, schools, and other relevant agencies as necessary. The team meets regularly for 3 hours and handles six clients or families in each meeting. Youth often attend, and parents attend in approximately 90% of the cases. The outcome of each meeting is a service plan involving two or more agencies, to which the youth, parents, and relevant agencies agree. Staff say this team approach cuts the time needed to arrange the elements of a service package from several days to half an hour. In addition, agencies that have committed themselves during team meetings to provide or arrange for certain services follow through more quickly than they did before the team began to function.

But the more interesting aspect of service integration in Garfield County is at the "front end." When government agencies in the county (schools, courts, social services, police) identify a service need for youth that they cannot fulfill, they turn to GYS. GYS will consider developing the service and will discuss how the new service will relate to existing agencies, whether GYS is the right place for the service, and other relevant issues. GYS also identifies unmet needs through calls to the hotline it runs. Often in its history, GYS has developed the service; in other cases, the process has resulted in the task being taken on by other agencies. Regardless of which occurs, over the years GYS has become the "mortar" or "glue" that holds the system together. It is seen by both public agencies and private citizens as "the place for youth" in the county. According to GYS's director, in a rural county where there are no services to start with, practically anything is welcome and service development is a cooperative enterprise. We think this cooperative development of services needed in the community is an important aspect of service integration that is often overlooked in the focus on improving the process of serving clients already in the system. We discuss it further in Chapter 15.

Funding Sources

GYS is paid by some local government agencies to deliver services (e.g., by the schools to do some prevention workshops and by the Department of Social Services to handle early intervention with first-time referrals), but almost half of its funding comes from state and federal contracts to provide services that local agencies cannot offer with their own resources. Of its FY 1992–1993 projected budget, GYS received support from the following sources:

State contracts	19%
Federal contracts	27%
Garfield County government agencies	10%
Other counties	4%
Garfield County schools	2%
Drug-free schools	8%
In-kind rent	4%
Foundations	7%
United Way	6%
Contributions	5%
Operating revenue	7%
Other	<1%

for the following services:

Drug and alcohol prevention	24%
Drug and alcohol intervention	6%
Diversion	8%
Drug and alcohol offenders	11%
Victim services	7%
Runaway youth	14%
Case management	21%
Management/general	4%
Fundraising	5%

Update: 1996

The mission and focus of GYS remains the same in 1996 as it was in 1992: to serve all of the youth in the community. The need for the types of services and activities provided through GYS has gained increasing recognition in the surrounding community, and the agency is now working with groups in several neighboring counties to bring its vision of supports for youth to a broader constituency. Within Garfield County, GYS's commitment to "do what is necessary" within its mission has led to new program areas and funding streams as community concerns have changed.

Changes in Service Configuration

The two biggest changes in the community context have been (a) an increasing public concern with safety in public schools, accompanied by increasing use of suspension and expulsion and (b) an influx of immigrants from Mexico and other parts of Latin America into the community, which until very recently was overwhelmingly White. The "safe schools" movement produced many youth who were out of school with no supervision and nothing to do, which in turn produced a serious concern with the solution itself: removing youth from school without providing any alternative activities or supervision. In their usual approach to newly defined community issues as the "mortar" holding the system together, GYS worked with school officials, parents, youth, and other concerned parties to identify appropriate solutions and then to obtain funding for a new program within the agency. Through the new program, GYS provides supervision for out-of-school youth. This program has given the agency official reasons to be in contact with youth at younger ages than was previously possible, because school problems usually precede direct involvement with the courts (court referrals were GYS's earlier first point of contact with youth). In doing assessments and family interviews for these younger youth, GYS is finding all the same problems that are familiar among the court-involved youth. GYS feels that the new program gives the agency a chance to intervene earlier, that their efforts are better for both the family and the youth, and that they may be preventing future trouble that would involve the courts. In addition to this program, Colorado has responded to juvenile crime by putting more money into community prevention efforts, and GYS has received funding to work with juvenile offenders, including pre-placement assessment and family involvement, and in-community electronic monitoring as an alternative to incarceration.

The influx of Spanish-speaking immigrants, both legal and undocumented, many of whom have little command of English, has affected both the program and staffing at GYS and the types of problems present in the community. GYS and other local agencies have had to assure the presence of bilingual staff and board members, both because of need and because funders are requiring them to do so. In addition, language and culture issues are posing problems within the community as youth from different cultures clash with each other (including encounters between youth from the different Latin cultures, as well as encounters between Latin and Anglo youth) and as Latin youth who want to be "American" come into conflict with their parents in the same ways that the first American-born generations have always clashed with their foreign-born parents. GYS has been trying to work on these cultural issues in many ways. It has encouraged parents of children and youth in each school classroom to get to know each other, to establish phone trees so the parents can know what their children are doing and can offer each other both moral and practical support, and to work on cross-cultural understanding. One interesting mechanism they are using is the development and distribution of "community norms and expectations" for how youth should behave. One example is curfew guidelines, suggesting to parents what appropriate bedtimes and study times should be for elementary, middle school, and high school aged children. These guidelines have helped both long-time and newer residents to structure their children's afternoon and evening time and have helped parents feel that they have some support and back-up for imposing this structure.

A final area in which GYS has refined and developed its goals and programming is in the area of parenting classes. The agency has dropped its classes for new parents and has increased its focus on children in middle schools and their parents. They now offer classes for both youth and parents in how to handle conflict situations other than by resorting to violence and have groups for what they call the "'tween years" (approximately 10–13 years old) to help youth of this age make the transition from childhood to adolescence smoothly and without getting into trouble. Both GYS and the school system personnel with whom they work have begun to realize that as early as second or third grade they can identify many of the children who are likely to be in trouble later on. They do not know yet how they should begin to make the connections and structure services for these children, but they are beginning to work on the issue in the same way that they have worked on developing other new program elements: They proceed slowly and carefully, involving all interested parties, and maintaining a focus on their primary mission and commitment to serve all youth in the county.

Expanding Service Integration

Services for youth in Garfield County continue to become more comprehensive and more integrated through the expanded workings of the CET. This team was quite new when we first visited GYS in 1992. Since that time, the team approach has worked extremely well with respect to direct client service. In addition, the CET has been the basis for an expanded effort at coordination and policy development involving the CET agencies at multiple levels. The heads of the agencies composing the CET had begun meeting to do some long-range planning and to make policy decisions about service implementation. It then became apparent that decisions made at this level were not necessarily filtering down to the caseworker level, where they could manifest themselves in changed casework practice with youth. Gradually representatives of caseworkers from the different agencies began to be invited to the policy meetings, so that decisions could incorporate practical issues of implementation, could therefore be translated more directly into practice, and could be explained at the casework level by people who had participated in the decision making.

Shifts in Funding

GYS's funding base has shifted to include a higher proportion of criminal justice sources, reflecting some changed public emphases and the increased availability of funding for community prevention in the area of youth crime. Because most of the new money comes from the state, the proportion of GYS's budget supported by state funding has gone from 19% in 1992 to 33% in 1996. Federal funds are down as a proportion of revenue (from 27% to 21%), as are county funds (from 10% to 5%). Donations are up from 5% to 11%.

GYS has greatly increased its ability to obtain unrestricted donations from the community as a result of excellent public relations and some innovative funding strategies. Hiring a public relations person seemed an extravagance when GYS did it approximately 5 years ago. But having such a person on staff has greatly increased the program's visibility in the community through publicity, brochures, newspaper and other media stories, and representation at many community events. The public relations effort is directed toward assuring that everyone in the county knows what GYS does, who it serves (all youth, regardless of income or issues), how it works, and its successes with youth. GYS's fundraising strategies depend heavily for their success on the program's good reputation built by the public relations activities. In 1989 the program held a Catch a Calf contest, followed in 1990 by a Cow Patty Catch. Their first annual Kiss a Pig contest, in 1991, raised $2,700. This is an event held in conjunction with the Garfield County Fair. In the weeks before the event, contestants collect as much money as they can for youth programs in the county. The contestant who collects the most money gets the privilege of kissing a pig or piglet in front of all their friends and neighbors. The event draws standing-room only crowds, having raised $28,000 in 1995 and an unprecedented $49,000 in 1996. These resources give GYS flexibility in obtaining grants with matching requirements and in providing some of the communitywide preventive activities that may not meet the criteria for categorical funding.

Involvement in Evaluation Activities

The evaluation capacity and activities of GYS have been quite stable from our 1992 site visit to the time of this writing. Program staff do not see GYS as able to conduct an outcome evaluation on their own, but they would welcome assistance in conducting evaluations of both their treatment and prevention activities if the evaluation could be designed to reflect the scope of their program activities and impacts on clients and community. GYS staff have long been involved in a number of data-related activities that could form part of an evaluation framework, including the following:

- Program staff produce computerized program statistics on client age, sex, residence, and ethnicity; number of clients served and reason for referral to each type of treatment service; and number of presentations, number of attendees, and location for each type of prevention activity.
- Crisis intervention clients fill out an assessment survey at intake

on behaviors, attitudes, and feelings in the areas of family, physical or sexual abuse, drug or alcohol abuse, self-esteem, mental health, behavior, life skills, peers, perception of future, school, and community. Staff use this assessment to identify issues to explore in counseling. Clients complete the same assessment at termination, and staff compare the composite scores derived from each administration. The expectation is that the scores will decrease significantly. If they do not, or if they go up, staff offer additional counseling.

- Participants are asked to provide written feedback for all large-group prevention activities. In school presentations, both students and teacher complete an evaluation form. In parenting groups and other community presentations, the participants complete an evaluation form. In both instances, this feedback is limited to feelings about the session and how it went. Only a few of these activities use pre–post testing to assess changes in the knowledge or attitudes that were the target of the prevention effort.

Concluding Thoughts

Garfield Youth Services was the only rural program we visited. It exemplifies some of the strategies that may be necessary in rural areas to develop effective and comprehensive services for youth. Its staff and directorship are stable, its vision is clear, its familiarity with its communities is intense, and trust levels are high (in part as a result of GYS's own efforts). Along with the Center for Family Life described in Chapter 14, GYS is an excellent example of "reverse service integration," where, as a result of a program's work to assure that all services are available in a community, it often becomes the source of those services. Thus it *receives* referrals from many agencies rather than relying on an extensive network of services to which it refers its own clients.

14 ⸻⸻⸻⸻⸻⸻⸻⸻⸻⸻⸻⸻

Center for Family Life

Overview

The Center for Family Life is a community-based prevention and treatment program in Sunset Park, a Brooklyn, New York, neighborhood. Preventive activities and services for teens are concentrated in three after-school centers that maintain afternoon, evening, and weekend hours. Youth employment services are also offered in the summertime, and counseling services for youth or for youth and families are available from the Center. Opened in 1978, the Center provides a broad spectrum of services aimed at reducing poverty, child abuse, and neglect through activities that reduce the isolation of parents and children and develop their skills and ability to help themselves. The Center also works toward improving the lives of families and children through community-building activities. In 1980, staff of the Center for Family Life were instrumental in starting the Human Services Cabinet to organize community resources around the issues faced by children and families. The Cabinet remains a dynamic part of the community's efforts to serve itself.

Mission, Goals, and Objectives

The mission of the Center for Family Life is to provide an integrated and full range of personal and social services to sustain children and families in their own homes, to "counter the forces of marginalization and disequilibrium which impact on families," to buffer the negative influences of the environment on children, youth, and families that lead to delinquency, and to provide alternatives to foster care or institutionalization (Center for Family Life, unpublished program documents, n.d.). The Center meets this mission by providing a broad spectrum of recreational, enrichment, supportive, and counseling services to children, youth, and families living in the Sunset Park neighborhood. A further goal is to make changes not only at the individual and family levels but also at the community level. The aim is to help the community develop, through its own efforts, the services and activities it has identified as needed. The Center emphasizes empowering community members to address community needs collectively and sees itself as a combination of settlement house, child guidance clinic, and community center that holds to the principles of providing a broad continuum of services in a non-labeling, nonstigmatizing, and noncategorical fashion. Its objectives are to foster access to normalizing opportunities, build competence, resolve conflicts and crises in families, change the underlying environmental conditions affecting family and community life, and engage in inter-organizational planning and exchange to promote collaboration of all human service agencies in the community.

The Center for Family Life was established as a replication of a successful community outreach program called the *Family Reception Center* (started in 1972 in the adjacent Brooklyn neighborhood of Park Slope). The prime catalysts behind replicating the model were two nuns from the Sisters of the Good Shepherd Order, Sister Mary Paul and Sister Mary Geraldine. Both remain today as the director of clinical services and center director, respectively, at the Center for Family Life. The sisters worked at the Family Reception Center and had first-hand knowledge of the needs in Sunset Park, which ranked among the most impoverished of all neighborhoods in New York City. Foundation grants were secured to cover the costs of site renovation at an ideally suited central location in Sunset Park, and the Center for Family Life officially opened in November 1978 to provide intensive family-centered services.

Current Clientele

Center programs serve children and youth (from birth to 18 years old) and their families. Any resident of the Sunset Park community is eligible to participate in the open-enrollment programs, because these enrichment and prevention services define risk according to the antecedent condition of living in the Sunset Park neighborhood. This is an area with a high rate of poverty, overcrowding, intrafamilial disruptions, and social isolation reinforced by language and cultural differences. In its 1992 annual report, the Center described the race/ethnicity of children and youth in the open-enrollment programs as follows: 81% are Hispanic, 8.9% African American, 3.7% Asian, 2.6% White, and 4% come from other ethnic groups. Slightly more male than female children participate in the programs (55% male), and 50% of all children are between the ages of 10 and 15 years, with the remainder split almost equally between those less than 10 years of age and those 16 to 20 years old.

Families, children, and youth initially come to the Center in either of two ways: as family-counseling clients or as participants in the Center's open-enrollment programs. Families who enter as registered counseling clients receive intensive short- or long-term counseling for family crises in order to reduce the risk of serious long-term problems or family break-up. These families can either seek services themselves or be referred from the district Department of Social Services, New York City's Administration for Children's Services (formerly the Child Welfare Administration, a public agency), school guidance counselors, or school principals. Families, children, and youth who come to the Center as open-enrollment participants generally have not been referred by an outside agency or service provider and typically do not have identified service needs but simply want to participate in the Center's enrichment and recreational programs. Any resident in the Sunset Park community is eligible to participate in the open-enrollment programs.

The Center has established two criteria for eligibility for its counseling services, based on its desire to make itself accessible to community families as a generic family support agency without the formal screening processes and potential stigma families might feel in applying for government programs. The two criteria are that the family reside within the Sunset Park neighborhood and that the household unit include at least one child under the age of 18 or a pregnant woman. Families receiving counseling and intensive counseling services are generally those whose children are considered at significant risk for removal from the home because of a variety of intrafamilial or environmental problems.

Under the terms of the Center's contract with the city's Administration for Children's Services (ACS), authorized by New York's Child Welfare Reform Act, the program is obligated to serve at least 29 families in any month (and 55 families over the year) who are directly referred by ACS because of documented neglect or abuse. In addition, the contract obligates the Center to serve a minimum of 187 additional families in any month who either refer themselves or are referred from any other source. Originally ACS funded the Center's counseling services to meet three goals of the Child Welfare Reform Act: to prevent foster care placement of children in those instances in which the risks can be managed within the home and community ("unnecessary" foster care); to facilitate the return of children already placed in foster care; and to avert the return of children to out-of-home placements (recidivism). The Center for Family Life augments these legal mandates with its own broader goals for counseling services. The Center approaches all presenting problems of children and youth through a family focus; it directly provides or arranges for a range of therapeutic interventions to meet the needs of the whole family, which in many instances it assesses as underlying the particular problem exhibited by a child or youth.

Service Configuration

Since its inception the program has provided both treatment and prevention services. It initially emphasized treatment-oriented individual and group casework services for families in crisis through its family counseling program, which continues to operate. In response to community needs, the Center for Family Life began enhancing its prevention components over a 10-year period. In 1981 an employment services program for adults was initiated through federal funding from Comprehensive Employment and Training Act (CETA) and Job Training Partnership Act (JTPA) and operated in the Bush Terminal area of Brooklyn. An after-school program and Teen Evening Center was initiated in one local elementary school in 1980–1981, followed by a similar afternoon program and Teen Evening Center at a second school (P.S. 314) in 1983. In 1991 an after-school center was opened at a middle school to complete the current service array in three schools. The two Teen Evening Centers and three after-school programs, in three schools, become summer day camp programs in July and August of every year.

Also in 1980 the Center initiated its storefront Thrift Shop, Advocacy Clinic, and Emergency Food Program in collaboration with other community agencies; these programs moved to their present storefront site in February 1989. In 1983–1984 the teen programs were expanded to include a Counselor-in-Training Program that developed youth leadership and mentoring capabilities among younger adolescents, who were later hired to assist the after-school program for the younger children. In 1989 the Center for Family Life took over the community's Summer Youth Employment Program when that program was about to be terminated. In 1991 the Center for Family Life successfully obtained a grant through a Dewitt-Wallace/Reader's Digest School Partners Project to develop its third school-based arts enrichment and after-school center program, the first to be situated in a local middle school rather than an elementary school.

The Center offers families in the family counseling program a wide range of support and counseling services and activities. Comprehensive assessment and evaluation services assist in developing an individualized treatment plan for the family. The Center offers short- and long-term counseling using individual, group, or family sessions as appropriate to the particular family. The counseling services may involve more than one method of therapy and may include as many family members as required. As adjuncts to the counseling, families also participate in family life education and discussion groups, women's support groups, and therapeutic activity groups for children and teens. There is also an in-home aid and support service provided through its Foster Grandparent Program, in which elderly men and women, supported by the Center's professional counselors, visit the home and give support to parents and families in crises. Families receiving counseling services can also obtain medical, legal, vocational, social, and religious assistance through other community agencies and services. Families also receive extensive help in assessing and remedying their children's school problems and learning disabilities. For these activities, Center staff work with school-based support teams and share evaluation and planning duties with school personnel in developing an individualized educational plan to move the child or youth toward participation in mainstream classrooms. Families requiring emergency food or clothing have access to the Thrift Shop, Advocacy Clinic, and Emergency Food Program. The Center also supports and licenses a small number of satellite foster family homes that provide care for neighborhood children in instances of serious crises, so that children and youth do not need to be removed from their own neighborhood, schools, friends, and other close ties. Keeping the child in the neighborhood also facilitates more intensive services aimed toward family reunification, thereby preventing long-term out-of-home placements.

Both counseling and open-enrollment families have access to a broad array of preventive and enrichment activities. The Center provides comprehensive, enriched school-age child care and extended day activity programs on site at two elementary schools in the community. Programs include dance, drama, arts and crafts, sports, cooking, and homework help, as well as activities for parents. The after-school programs at the elementary schools involve teenage counselors and counselors-in-training as leaders and mentors for the younger children.

Counseling and open-enrollment families can also take advantage of the Teen Evening Centers (open two evenings per week at each of two public schools), which offer a range of recreational and enrichment activities as well as specific preventive and teen leadership programs. At a third (middle) school, Center staff operate an arts enrichment program in a number of classrooms and an extensive after-school program consisting of a learning center and activities in theater, dance, visual arts, and other arts. The highlight of each of these three school-based programs is a schoolwide theatrical performance at the end of the year for the school and community, in which all youth who participate during the year take part.

The Infant/Toddler/Parent Program provides early stimulation and group play for infants and toddlers 6 months to 3 years of age. Children are supervised by early childhood teachers while mothers meet in an adjacent room in group sessions as a support to each other in resolving personal and parenting needs. Parent workshops and community forums on a variety of topics are organized at nearby public schools and other sites during the school year. Workshops are held in three languages: English, Spanish, and Chinese. Finally, the Parent Advisory Council was created to provide policy and planning advice to the Center.

All families also have access to two employment training programs. One is for adults and is designed primarily for parents. It operates all year and provides counseling, job search assistance, and job placement for adult men and women. The second employment-oriented program is the Summer Youth Employment Program, funded by the city's Department of Employment. The money for both of these programs is JTPA money coming through city agencies. The Center recruits all teens for the program from among youth ages 14 to 21, places them with cooperating nonprofit organizations in and near Sunset Park, and offers the youths concurrent workshops throughout the summer on sexuality issues, career planning, and multicultural relations. Approximately 40 organizations accept teens from the Summer Youth Employment Program each year; each participating agency maintains records of the youth's attendance on the job and provides job coaching and guidance to prepare the youth for future labor market participation. More than 700 youth participate during each summer.

Type and Make-Up of the Service Integration Network

The Center for Family Life engages in widescale, comprehensive, and well-planned service integration efforts that take staff and resources directly into the community. Its service integration network operates both in-house, off site at other agencies, and through informal arrangements with other agencies and organizations. Its in-house service integration involves accepting referrals for counseling services from child welfare and social service agencies, the courts, and the school system. In addition, it operates workshops and family life enrichment groups for counseling and open-enrollment families at its central building.

The bulk of its programs are delivered off site at other agencies, particularly in local schools. The After-School Care Program operates in two elementary schools and one middle school in the community. The Arts Enrichment Program is conducted by a Center for Family Life staff person in several classrooms at a local middle school. This staff person also sits on a sub-committee of the school's site-based management committee, which deals with the coordination of services by community agencies at the middle school. The Teen Centers are run at two public schools, two evenings a week at each site, for a total of four evenings weekly, by Center for Family Life staff and teen leadership volunteers and counselors. In addition, Center for Family Life caseworkers meet regularly with the guidance counselors and school staff to initiate and monitor individualized service plans for students with academic or behavioral problems.

In general, the Center eschews formal agreements with the schools or any other collaborating agencies in favor of more informal arrangements. Center staff meet with school personnel to plan activities and programs that meet the school's needs and that can be operated within school guidelines. Their experience has been that the local schools have so many needs that they welcome all of the programs that the Center has proposed and, without formal written agreements, will provide Center staff with direct access to children and youth in the classrooms as well as outside of school hours. This level of cooperation with the schools has been achieved because the Center and the schools work together to do a great deal of mutual planning before actually launching any new program. The planning assures that the programs will meet the needs as perceived by both school and Center staff.

Three other collaborative efforts exemplify the highly developed cooperative ventures in which the Center and other local agencies participate without benefit of formal written agreements. The first of these is the Thrift Shop, Advocacy Clinic, and Emergency Food Program that the Center operates in conjunction with many other community groups, churches, and not-for-profit agencies. Before this program began in 1980, the Center and other agencies had identified a need for this particular set of services and for an easily accessible, informal, and non-stigmatizing mechanism for delivering them. The collaborating agencies each contribute goods and services to these programs, which are available at a storefront location. The emergency food bank, for instance, is stocked through periodic food drives (and sometimes through direct purchase). When a client family of any of the participating agencies needs food, the agency gives the family a voucher, which the family takes directly to the food bank and exchanges for groceries. Now in its 12th year, the program flourishes without benefit of any written commitments among agencies.

The Center operates the Summer Youth Employment Program under a contract with the city. The Center must locate and work with approximately 40 nonprofit agencies, each of which provides summer jobs for one or more youth. Each of these host agencies must complete a written application to participate in the program. The application states the number of youth the agency will accept and the number and types of assignment available (e.g., clerical, advocacy). Other than these agency applications, there are no other formal agreements between the host agencies and the Center for Family Life. Under the program, the Center recruits, screens, and places the youth in agencies and offers a variety of support activities during the summer. The host agencies supervise and work with each youth to develop positive attitudes and habits that will lead toward future labor force participation.

The third informal but highly collaborative arrangement in which the Center participates is the Human Services Cabinet. In 1980 the Center for Family Life was a prime mover behind the Cabinet's formation. The Cabinet includes representatives from approximately 60 public and voluntary agencies and community groups in the Sunset Park area. The Cabinet is an arm of Community District Board Number 7. New York City is divided into 59 community districts, each administered by a board that is part of the city's governance structure. The Community District Boards are intended to bring resolution of local matters under more control by local community members. The Human Services Cabinet is designed to coordinate services and to plan for communitywide events within Community District Number 7 and also to initiate timely responses to emerging neighborhood issues affecting families and children. All agencies and organizations operating in the district can become members of the Cabinet, and to date more than 60 of them participate. There are no formal documents of membership, nor are there formal decision-making processes. The Center for Family Life often acts as both opinion leader and catalyst for planning within the Cabinet.

The Human Services Cabinet has evolved over the 12 years of its existence. Agencies are usually represented by their directors or high-level staff. The Cabinet produced a resource directory of the 60 or more agencies in the district to improve interagency referrals. It is a forum for discussing issues that affect the whole district and its agencies. Member agencies are beginning to work on joint grant applications to meet needs identified through the Cabinet. It makes recommendations to the Youth Committee of the Community District Board, which has some resources to allocate. In recent years, allocations have begun to reflect the recommendations of the Cabinet. The Cabinet tries to increase the comprehensiveness of services and activities in the community by identifying needs and working together to develop plans to meet those needs.

Funding Sources

The Center obtains nearly 70% of its funding from the public sector and relies on grants and contributions from foundations, corporations, and individuals for the remaining 30%. Staff philosophically oppose receiving public funds from categorical or single-problem funding streams. The treatment services provided by the Center, in the form of counseling and casework, are relatively well-funded, whereas the more prevention-oriented open-enrollment programs appear to suffer from unstable and inadequate funding.

Approximately one half of the Center's budget goes toward support of the counseling and casework services. The Center receives the bulk of its funds for these programs from ACS (a combination of city and state funds). The New York City Department of Employment funds the Summer Youth Employment Program and the Adult Employment Services Program, although a portion of the adult program's funds come from JTPA. Together these public agencies supply approximately three quarters of the funding for the employment programs; the rest of the funding is private. Finally, the New York City Department of Youth Services provides one half of the funds required to operate all school-based services, including the after-school program. The New York City Department of Youth Services has a private match requirement.

Of the Center's many programs, the school-based prevention and enrichment-oriented programs (after-school programs and Teen Evening Centers) are the biggest, serving more than 2,000 children and youth annually. They are also the most vulnerable to funding cuts because they rely most heavily on support from foundations and private donors (public sources supply only approximately half of their annual operating expenses). These private sources are more likely than public programs to change their priorities, to limit each grantee to only a few years of support, or to require new services in exchange for continued support. A host of foundations provide funds to support Center activities, including the Foundation for Child Development, the Morgan Guaranty Trust Company Foundation, the Robin Hood Foundation, and the Tiger Foundation. IBM has donated computer hardware and software.

Update: 1996

Since 1992, the Center for Family Life has pursued its mission to serve the Sunset Park neighborhood with expansions of existing services and some new service configurations.

Service Expansions

The Center has run after-school, evening teen center, and summer programs at P.S. 314 for many years. Approximately 2 years ago, this school became a Beacon School, with the Center as its lead agency. The idea of a "Beacon School" is that the school should become a true community center, where many agencies can offer programs and where representatives from many community stakeholders can feel at home and make their voices heard. As part of its work at the Beacon School and with its children and families, the Center has greatly expanded the services and activities it offers at P.S. 314. Hours have been expanded both during the week and on weekends. Many more community agencies offer programs in the school, with the Center coordinating times and places. ACS supports the Center to provide intensive counseling services to 45 additional families per month who live in the immediate neighborhood of the school or whose children attend the school. Many more community stakeholders and parents, from different ethnic groups, have become active participants in the school, fulfilling a concept of the school as a community center that has been in the minds of Center staff since the Center's inception. The additional counseling responsibilities bring the average number of families seen in a month to approximately 260; annually the number of families receiving counseling services is approximately 450.

As of July 1995, the Center lost its JTPA funding for its adult employment services program, and it has been maintaining the program with private support since that time. Support has come from the Center's normal fundraising activities and from foundation grants. Although the loss of JTPA funds placed a serious financial burden on the Center to maintain the program, Sister Mary Paul says that the "staff virtually applauded" when the Center lost its JTPA funds. The feeling at the Center was that JTPA's performance standards were too rigid and too simplistic given the types of people that the Center wanted to help. Most of their clients and potential clients have one or more issues that limit their ability to get a job immediately, such as limited English proficiency, no work history, long-term welfare dependency, and few job skills. The Center sometimes had trouble meeting JTPA performance standards and were sometimes chided by JTPA administrators for working with people "who were not promising." Running the program with private money has allowed the Center to take the clients whom they consider to need help the most, whom JTPA would not touch, and to do what is necessary for them. This can include helping clients get voluntary positions to learn skills and gain experience, helping them to improve their English, getting them treatment for depression, working on life organization skills, or arranging for child care. In making the decision to keep the Adult Employment Services Program going despite loss of federal funds, the Center felt very strongly that getting someone into a job of which that person could be proud was critical from a therapeutic standpoint. They had seen so many people "get attached to their own competence" for the first time in their lives and seen the successful handling of a job contribute to helping clients make major changes affecting their lives and well-being. Center staff felt it was essential to keep the Adult Employment Services Program running, even without JTPA funds, because it was an ingredient so essential in achieving the ultimate goals of family counseling: success and self-sufficiency. The Center has had great success in helping its very disadvantaged clientele move into competitive employment and also in keeping them on the job.

The Center's budget has shifted slightly toward less public and more private funding (65/35 instead of 70/30 public and private). The proportion of its budget that goes to its different activities has remained about the same, with the intensive counseling services taking up approximately half of the budget.

Increasing Visibility

Finally, the Center for Family Life is attracting a good deal of attention as a model for other communities. The Center has had increasing numbers of visitors from other cities and states who are interested in how it has created the network of services, activities, and supports now available in the Sunset Park community. An example of a Center activity that has attracted outside attention is its Neighborhood Foster Care Program. The program has been replicated in a number of states and communities, and more are interested (New York City is making it the model for most of the city's foster care). The Center's program has only 15 foster families and hardly ever has more than 25 children placed with these families at any one time. By taking a broad and flexible approach to risk management, the Center is able to keep more children at home so that children go to foster care homes only when it is really necessary. When this happens, because the children are still in the neighborhood and because of the intensive and broad array of services at the Center's disposal, CFL is able to work with families to get children back home very quickly and with very low recidivism (return to foster care). Since 1988, when the program started, its rate of adoptions (termination of parental rights) has been approximately 10%, which is very low in comparison with other New York City neighborhoods. This program's experience also suggests the effectiveness of the Center's intensive approach to working with children and their families. The effectiveness of the Center's Neighborhood Foster Care Program is borne out by statistics maintained by the Administration for Children's Services (ACS) comparing Sunset Park with other neighborhoods on foster care and other child welfare benchmarks.

Involvement in Evaluation Activities

The Center for Family Life has always maintained extensive records for its counseling families, as required by the ACS. Detailed statistics are kept on every case and aggregated each month in a report to ACS. At the end of the year the program director aggregates the statistics for program use in annual progress reports and program planning.

Documentation appears weakest in tracking clients and services in the prevention or open-enrollment programs. Because of its interest in documenting the impact of the Center's prevention efforts, the Foundation for Child Development helped the Center set up a database to track child and parent use of prevention programs, especially the after-school programs, Teen Evening Centers, and the Parent Council. Only since 1990 has the program been able to generate a list of unduplicated cases for various programs; the list goes to the Department of Youth Services (the funding source for the after-school programs).

In a program with as many interrelating components as this one, it is not surprising that staff have difficulty accounting for all of the services provided by the Center. Staff have concerns both about the amount of time it takes to document service activity fully and to aggregate the data and about possible underreporting of service delivery in some program components. For example, they suspect that the use of food vouchers at the Thrift Shop and Emergency Food Bank is underreported. In 1992 the Center was just starting to computerize its records; staff were using manual spreadsheets to record service use and had to aggregate much of the raw data by hand.

In 1992 the Center for Family Life did not conduct extensive evaluation research, but Center staff were involved in some evaluation activities, including the following:

- The ACS conducts a yearly quality assurance review that consists of a site visit and selected case reviews. The ACS official reads selected case records, evaluates the action taken, and determines whether it meets performance standards.
- The Center conducts an annual client satisfaction inquiry, sending client satisfaction questionnaires to all families that have ended their counseling during that year plus a sample of open cases. The questionnaires are anonymous and include self-addressed and stamped return envelopes. Results are used to review and improve service delivery.
- The Foundation for Child Development funded an evaluation of the Center's adult employment program to look at child and family issues related to a parent's employment. The foundation was interested in learning about the impact of the welfare-to-work transition on the children of the household and on family functioning. By late 1992, when we visited, the Center had completed intake assessments of the entire sample of 150 parents and children.
- The Center also participated in an assessment of how its work is perceived by the larger community of Sunset Park. This evaluation was carried out by a researcher engaged by the Surdna Foundation.

The staff of the Center for Family Life were eager at the time of our visit to participate in a comprehensive impact research project with an appropriate design and adequate staff support. Staff had some concerns about evaluation research, including the lack of reimbursement for staff time spent on evaluation activities, and hesitancy about using evaluation designs in which outcome measurement is either simplistic or makes questionable claims given the data available. Nevertheless, they were and remain very interested in participating in research based on a solid design and employing evaluators trained in social work research and in measuring the impacts on children and families of a very complex array of services and activities.

At the time of our visit, the Center was one of eight finalists in the Annie E. Casey Foundation's search for four family-support programs to participate in a national evaluation study. It was selected and has been involved for several years in this massive evaluation effort. The project involves programs following different models or structures, all of which showed evidence of repeated effectiveness in developing services, involving the community, and creating an environment of cooperative enterprise. Several reports have been published so far by the research team from Columbia University School of Social Work, and more are coming. The Center staff believes that this evaluation effort has shown a full appreciation of the complexity of their endeavor and that it has focused on important elements of the Center's position in its community.

Since our 1992 visit, the Center also has made a major investment in software and data collection to understand and account for clients' patterns of service use. Staff want to know who uses which services and in what order. They want to move toward the capacity to analyze the effectiveness and efficiency of each service type and also to be able to do cost-effectiveness analysis. To this end, they have bought a software package that is specifically designed to focus on the family as the unit of analysis. The Center is the first program to try to use this software package in a very complex program environment, and it has hired a programmer to develop significant modifications and additions to make the basic software reflect the Center's array of services. Their new software has the ability to record all of the services and activities received by each individual and also to connect each individual to a family unit. All the data on families and individuals for a number of years back have now been entered into this program, and the Center is looking forward to the results of analysis. Questions the Center will be able to address with these data include the following:

- The density of services to each family;
- The number of individuals in a family who get services and who do not get services;
- How people flow through the system (e.g., do people come through the open-enrollment programs first and then access specialized services when they need them, or do people come into the counseling program first and then find themselves able to run their own lives better as they learn about and start to use the open-enrollment programs?); and
- Whether one route is more effective than another in helping people.

Concluding Thoughts

The Center for Family Life has created a remarkable network of community services and support for families and youth in one of New York City's poorest neighborhoods. Data collected by city agencies attest to the program's effectiveness in stemming some of the worst consequences of extremely poor urban environments. Its focus on a geographical area of "manageable" proportions has allowed it to meet evolving community needs in ways that involve more and more community members. Along with Garfield Youth Services, described in Chapter 13, the Center for Family Life serves as the mortar or glue of the community system, holding together the array of local services and activities available for families and youth and stimulating the development of new ones. It is a catalyst for change and collaborative action. The Center's accomplishments are the result of its founders' long-term commitment to the neighborhood, clarity and consistency of vision, and insistence that its programs be participatory, nonstigmatizing, and empowering.

Part III

Cross-Cutting Issues

15

Service Integration and Other Cross-Cutting Issues

The research reported in this book highlights the many different types of programs that exist to serve youth. The previous nine chapters described in depth each program we visited, revealing that the programs operate in many settings and vary greatly in the degree to which they focus on prevention and enrichment activities or on treatment, services, and dealing with youth already involved in problem behaviors. Some of the programs are small and fairly tightly focused on one particular problem, issue, target group, or restricted age range; but many are broader, up to and including programs that try to make a difference for all or most children and youth, or for all the residents of entire neighborhoods, regardless of age.

In addition to understanding how each program worked, our project examined both common themes and major differences across programs to gain an understanding of program choices that may lead in distinctly different directions. Our project focused on programs serving younger adolescents (10–14 year olds) because few other efforts had concentrated on this age range and because we considered this group important if primary prevention or youth development was a goal. However, we do not want to forget that these programs work with youth who have already been shaped by community opportunities and institutions, so we will also try to understand these programs in their larger community context. This chapter distills the most important lessons to be learned from cross-program analysis, looking at the scope and variety of service activity, service integration, client participation and risk levels, program choices on key issues such as target age group and prevention or treatment focus, and community and cultural context.

Scope and Variety of Service Activity

The experiences of the diverse programs we studied show that there is no one model for effective integration of services for youth. Our nine programs offer a very wide variety of services through their own auspices and make an even greater variety of services available to their clients through either normal referral procedures or through special arrangements. Before examining the structure of service integration at each program, we present an overview of where the nine programs fit on a treatment–prevention continuum, the breadth or narrowness of their problem focus, and the variety of their service offerings. These characterizations are rough but do provide a sense of this set of programs in relation to each other. We then examine service integration structures for these same programs. As will become clear, no simple one-to-one relationship exists among a program's orientation toward treatment or prevention, its problem focus, its service variety, and its service integration structure.

Prevention–Treatment Continuum

The nine programs we visited can be arrayed on a prevention–treatment continuum, which is illustrated in Figure 15.1. Two of the nine programs concentrate almost entirely on the treatment end of this continuum: CHINS UP and Oasis Center. In the middle of the continuum are three programs that provide a balance of activities: Garfield Youth Services, Center for Family Life in Sunset Park, and Houston Communities in Schools. Their programs reflect their ongoing commitment to respond to unmet needs with additional program components cooperatively developed with other agencies and tailored to the community. At the prevention end of the continuum are four of our nine programs: Belafonte-Tacolcy, Big Brothers/Big Sisters, I Have a Future, and Bronx Teen Connections.

All seven of the programs that have significant preventive components strive to create an alternative, protective environment for their participants, with alternative norms and peers to support them. Sometimes that alternative is as simple as supplying a mentor to act as friend and role model. Some of our programs try to create such an environment, but many of their clients do not participate in it, so the effect is weakened. Others succeed very well in giving teens real alternatives. Thus, even within these few programs, we see variations in the degree to which the programs are trying to, and are able to, create alternative protective environments to counter the negative environments in which their clients live and to help

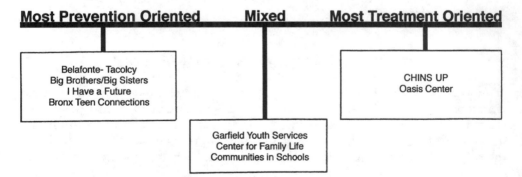

Figure 15.1. A prevention–treatment continuum.

them succeed in institutions such as the schools, where they rarely get the individual attention they need. Their success in creating an alternative environment reflects in part the strength of each program's philosophical orientation toward its target, whether it is trying to affect a whole community or trying to help individuals in a community. Those with a community focus have done very well in affecting their entire community; considering that this is a very difficult goal to achieve, we were impressed by their success.

Problem Focus

Some programs define their focus very narrowly, dealing with only one or two problems or issues; others see their primary mission as affording access to a broad range of services and meeting a broad range of needs. As a consequence, their assessment procedures differ, as does the structure of their service and referral networks. Our nine programs can be arrayed on a continuum reflecting this narrowness or breadth of problem focus, as shown in Figure 15.2.

Five programs have a fairly defined focus, although the focus differs across programs. Bronx Teen Connections concentrates on health and pregnancy prevention, Garfield Youth Services and Belafonte-Tacolcy focus mostly on prevention of substance abuse, Oasis Center is primarily oriented toward mental health and prevention of substance abuse, and Big Brothers/Big Sisters does only mentoring. Somewhere in the middle of this spectrum is CHINS UP. The programs with the broadest scope are I Have a Future, Center for Family Life, and Houston Communities in Schools. The first two of these programs have an intense community focus, seeking to create a world within the larger environment that offers enough attractions to help clients withstand the stresses of the neighborhood, cope successfully with school and other community institutions, and build toward the future. Whatever it takes to succeed at this goal is an appropriate activity for the program. Both programs involve youth, their families, and other community members. Both offer youth a broad range of developmental and preventive activities, from sports and other recreation, to tutoring, to opportunities to assume responsibility within the program. Nei-

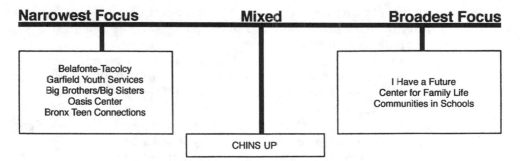

Figure 15.2. A continuum of program breadth of focus.

ther is particularly treatment-oriented in terms of serving youth. Houston Communities in Schools is organized quite differently from the first two comprehensive programs, but it also addresses a broad range of youth needs.

Breadth of Service Offerings

Service breadth refers to the variety of services and activities a program offers (e.g., health, education, or substance abuse), whether in the prevention or the treatment domain, and also to whom the program offers the services (e.g., to youth, to their parents or whole family, or other community members). Almost all of the programs we visited *could* arrange for a particular client to receive a particular service that is not offered by the program if the need were pressing. We focus here on the programs' main activities, those into which they put most of their effort and toward which their program structure is geared.

Table 15.1 displays the programs' service offerings, ordering the programs from left to right according to the breadth or variety of services they offer. This ordering also roughly corresponds to the programs' practice at the time of our visit of offering services exclusively or almost exclusively to youth (Teen Connections; Big Brothers/Big Sisters; Oasis Center, and to a lesser extent, I Have a Future). To the right in Table 15.1 are the programs that offer the most variety and to the most types of participants.

Service Integration

When we began this investigation, we followed the usage in the literature, in which *service integration* refers to procedures and structures that help several service agencies coordinate their efforts to address the full range of service needs presented by youth and families in an efficient and holistic manner. We believed that several key characteristics should be present in such a service integration system for at-risk youth. These included the following:

- An approach to helping at-risk youth that sees each youth as an individual but also as part of a family, a neighborhood, and a community that may be influenced to reduce the risk that a youth will participate in problem behaviors or experience risk outcomes.
- A comprehensive, individualized assessment at or near the point of intake that is conducted for each youth and family to identify the full range of his or her individual and family service needs.
- A coordinated service plan that, based on the needs identified, is developed to ensure that all needs are addressed in an efficient fashion by the program or programs best suited for the task.
- Institutionalized interagency linkages that ensure that service referrals result in actual service delivery. This may entail an inter-

Table 15.1. Services Provided by Programs

Service/Program	TC	BS	Oa	CFL	CIS	Fu	BT	CU	GY
Alcohol/drug: prevention									
Programs at agency	Y	Y				Y,C	Y		
Programs/work in schools			Y		Y		Y		Y,C
Programs/work in community							Y		Y,C
Alcohol/drug: treatment			Y					Y,P	Y,P
Education									
On-site school			Y				Y		
Tutoring				Y,C	Y	Y	Y		
English as a second language				Y,C	P		Y,C		
Socialization/mentoring	Y	Y				Y	Y		Y
Employment/training				Y,C	Y,P	Y	Y,P	Y	
Mental health									
Counseling/therapy			Y	Y,P	Y,P	Y,P	Y	Y,P	Y,P
Crisis hotline/safe place			Y						Y,C
Housing									
On-site shelter/host homes			Y					Y	Y
Assistance to find housing				P			P		
Help getting public benefits				P			P	Y,P	P
Health									
Primary health care	Y		Y			Y,C		Y	
Health-related prevention: pregnancy, STDs, etc.	Y	Y				Y			Y
Social services									
Foster care/independent living			Y	Y				Y	
Family preservation/crisis intervention				Y,P				Y,P	Y,P
Other				Y,P	Y	Y	Y,P	Y	
Criminal justice system (CJS)									
Detention alternatives							Y	Y	Y
CJS referrals for service			Y	Y		Y	Y	Y	Y
Other related to juvenile justice			Y	Y	Y		Y	Y	Y
Recreation									
Sports, arts, writing, entrepreneur club, special trips/activities	Y	Y		Y	Y	Y	Y	Y	Y

Note. Table covers only services the program provides itself, in any location, or services available to program clients through explicit contractual arrangements. Does not include services that may be offered through referral. TC = Teen Connections, Bronx; BS = Big Brothers/Big Sisters, Miami; Oa = Oasis Center, Nashville; CFL = Center for Family Life, Brooklyn; CIS = Communities in Schools, Houston; Fu = I Have a Future, Nashville; BT = Belafonte-Tacolcy, Miami; CU = CHINS UP, Colorado Springs; GY = Garfield Youth Services, Glenwood Springs, CO; Y = offered to youth; P = offered to parents of youth receiving services; C = offered to members of community, who may be parents, but not necessarily of youth served by program.

agency case management function, colocation of services at a single
site, or sharing of other resources among programs.
- Follow-up on service referrals to ensure that services are delivered
  in an appropriate manner and that the program coordination structures are functioning effectively.

In hindsight, the clear implication of these five criteria is that a program has clients who need services (as opposed to activities or enrichment); that the services are available from some agencies other than the
program; that various barriers, including categorical funding, single-focus
agencies, conflicting eligibility criteria, and cumbersome application processes, make it difficult for program clients to get these other services from
other agencies; and that interagency cooperation of several kinds will work
to reduce those barriers and get the clients what they need.

These criteria are all driven by an assumption that clients have problems and that the problems need fixing. They all assume something re-
sembling a case management approach to helping people, and except for
the first criterion, they are not particularly relevant to programs whose
major approach to helping youth is prevention- and activity-oriented, or
community-oriented.

Equally important, the criteria ignore the potential relevance to service integration of program development to strengthen a community's
ability to support all of its youth. Several of the programs we visited do
not appear to make extensive use of networks for referring their clients
elsewhere. They do access these networks when appropriate, sometimes
even using formal service integration mechanisms such as multi-agency
teams. However, these programs have made major investments in *developing* service components that other community agencies have identified
as unmet needs. They are thus a referral source *for* government agencies,
accepting as clients those youth whom government agencies do not have
the resources to assist, filling in gaps in community services, and working
cooperatively with networks of agencies to assure that appropriate resources are available. Important elements of these programs often are recreational, cultural, artistic, entrepreneurial, and community service activities to children and youth when they are young enough for the activities
to help them avoid trouble and develop healthy habits and values. In a
very real sense, these programs are the mortar that connects the whole
community of youth-serving agencies and activities. It seems important to
us to include a discussion of these capacity-building efforts under the rubric of service integration. Without such a discussion, the significant investments of some programs in program and community development in
response to community need could be overlooked, even though these efforts
may be more important than formal service integration in certain communities in promoting youth development. Although not usually thought
of as service integration, it seems to us that programs with this attitude
and history are the very essence of a service system that truly meets the
needs of youth in its community.

Scope and Variety of Service Integration Agencies and Arrangements

Table 15.2 provides a quick way to examine which types of programs and activities are included in the service integration networks of the nine programs we visited and the particular mechanisms through which they and the index program interact. Included, along with typical programs, are activities not necessarily associated with a formal public service system, such as efforts to prevent alcohol and drug abuse, socialization and mentoring activities, and recreational activities. The columns of Table 15.2 indicate whether services are part of the program itself or are made available through several mechanisms that may be part of a service integration network.

Obviously the most common approach for many services is for the program staff to provide the service directly. Mental health, criminal justice, and health agencies are the external agencies most likely to be involved in the formal service integration arrangements depicted in Columns 2 and 3, by sending a representative either to the program or to a multi-agency team. All but one of our nine programs could access mental

Table 15.2.   Service Integration Networks and Arrangements

Service	In-house staff	On-site other agency	Off-site formal, other agency	Off-site, formal, program does	Off-site, in-formal	Volunteer, mentor, or business community
Alcohol/drug-related	5	2		1	2	1
School-related	4	4		2	1	1
Tutoring, socialization, or mentoring	7	3	2	1		3
Employment/training	3	3	2	1	1	
Mental health	6	3	5		3	
Housing/shelter	4	1	3	1	1	1
Income maintenance	3	2	3		1	
Health	5	2	4		3	1
Social services—CPS/ OH/FC	3	1	4		2	
Other	4	3	2		1	
Criminal justice	3	3	4	1	1	1
Recreation/extra	6	3			1	3

Note.   Table entries are the number of programs (out of 9) that offer a particular service through a particular mechanism. Column 1 = service delivery by regular program staff (not service integration); Column 2 = colocation at the program site (staff from other agencies come to the program); Column 3 = formal arrangement between the program and other agencies to provide the service; Column 4 = program has formal arrangement to provide its own services at another site, to the clients of the host program; Column 5 = arrangements with other agencies that are frequent and relatively easy, but not formal; Column 6 = types of volunteer arrangements that expand service options. CPS = Child Protective Services; OH = Out of Home Placement; FC = foster care.

health services through a formal mechanism, and all but two had formal ties to criminal justice agencies (usually the courts). Although it may not seem to some readers that the courts should be considered a service agency, our programs sometimes could use the courts to require that another agency provide or pay for needed services (e.g., the juvenile court judge can tell DHS to pay for mental health care for a youth under DHS custody who is a program client). The courts can also require a youth and his or her parents to attend counseling and other services as a condition of probation and can place a youth in shelter or transfer custody of a youth from his or her parent(s) to the state, so they may exert considerable leverage over youth and even their families in particular aspects of program participation. The services least likely to be accessed through arrangements beyond the program were alcohol and drug prevention activities (in part because this was the specialty of many of these programs), recreation activities (again, a focus of many programs), and housing.

The informal arrangements shown in Column 4 are something more than normal referral procedures, which are not included in Table 15.2. They are consciously worked out relationships with a personal element. In many instances caseworkers in the program and the referral agency know each other and have developed an understanding for working together. The program caseworkers have deliberately sought these relationships to improve their clients' chances of getting needed services. Insofar as they are more common than formal service integration arrangements and they often work to facilitate service delivery, they should get some credit. But because they depend on personal relationships, the program's ability to help clients access services breaks down if the relationship sours or if one or the other party to it leaves. Many programs have found themselves having to rebuild their entire referral network from the ground up when a key staff person leaves. These types of informal relationships and arrangements are no substitute in the long term for formal commitments. However, some informal arrangements (e.g., those between Oasis and a number of its referral agencies) involve agency heads rather than caseworkers. These arrangements tend to be more stable and consistent in the face of personnel changes than ones dependent on caseworkers.

The finding that our programs use the arrangements in Columns 4, 5, and 6 less extensively than either performing the service themselves or operating through formal mechanisms is not likely to generalize to other youth-serving programs. Because we selected the programs because of their involvement in formal referral and service delivery mechanisms, their pattern of service delivery is most likely to favor formal arrangements.

Sharing Clients and Information

One of the biggest barriers to interagency cooperation can be requirements for treating information about clients with confidentiality. In part because the formal service integration arrangements used by the programs we visited involve either colocation or multi-agency teams, the several agencies involved often serve the same client and usually need to share information. Most of the programs have worked out successful arrangements for release of information as needed, usually on a case-by-case basis. For instance, in the Garfield County multi-agency team, the agency bringing the youth for teaming obtains signed releases from the youth and parents to share relevant information with the agencies that will attend. Once a plan is developed, additional releases are obtained to allow only those agencies that have responsibilities to fulfill under the plan to share relevant information. An agency that is a member of the multi-agency team but not part of a particular client's plan will not know anything more about the client than what was shared at the meeting. The releases are only for the length of the plan and only for the information relevant to immediate treatment needs; they are not general releases or permission to share information beyond the framework of the multi-agency team and the specific plan. Houston Communities in Schools has an arrangement under which a parental consent form is obtained for each youth participating in the program. This form spells out how information will be released to the various case teams. The consent form was developed to handle issues that had arisen with respect to confidentiality in the early days of the program.

On the other hand, programs that do not have formal linkages but rather rely on informal arrangements did mention that information sharing was a continuing problem. Even when they are trying to get help for a specific client, they have to talk in generalities. Another problem that arises with the less formal arrangements is that information that could be shared is not shared because there is no feedback mechanism to assure that a referring person ever hears what happened with a referral. An example among our nine programs is Belafonte-Tacolcy, in which participants in one program component may not know about other components offered by the same program in which they might be interested. Belafonte-Tacolcy has no in-house centralized database to identify all the activities a given youth receives. Furthermore, linkages in the schools with counselors and social workers often result in a youth being referred to Belafonte-Tacolcy for services without feedback to the school counselor about what happened.

Perceived Impacts or Benefits of Service Integration

The programs with service integration arrangements in place and working well include CHINS UP, Garfield Youth Services, Houston Communities in Schools, Center for Family Life, and one component of Oasis Center. Program staff members and representatives of other agencies in the community all credit these arrangements with helping them accomplish more, get more appropriate services to clients, and ensure that each participating agency follows through on its commitments with greater speed and thoroughness. They say that service integration also greatly reduces the likelihood that youth will fall through the cracks. Another common perception is that the improved communication reduces the number of times that program staff ask an agency for something that the agency cannot do or in a way that the agency cannot handle. So service integration has produced more appropriate requests for service, with the requests framed and accompanied by documentation in a way that helps agencies to respond promptly and positively.

The two Colorado programs cite some concrete numbers to bolster their perceptions of the impact of service integration. Garfield Youth Services has reduced by half the number of children and youth placed in detention (and therefore out of county, because the county has no detention facility) and has reduced the time in detention of the remaining youth by 77%. CHINS UP and Joint Initiatives can also point to substantial reductions in out-of-county placement (30% the first year, now stable at 45%), in-county placement in foster care (through the Family Preservation Program), improved foster care services (through the Therapeutic Foster Care Program), and streamlined service delivery through several multi-agency teams.

Staff of the Center for Family Life add another perceived benefit: more stable staffing patterns. Center for Family Life staff feel that because of their community-building philosophy, staff get "hooked" on seeing what happens and making things get better. Their core staff has been with the program for a very long time. The schools also perceive that they get greater respect with the presence of Center for Family Life programs in their buildings, and they report that youth do better in school and are happier as a result. (No specific data are available.)

On the other hand, the staff at more than one program we visited expressed some reservations about formal arrangements and did not have many formal linkages. These program staff believed that formal arrangements reduced the program's flexibility in finding just the right service or agency for their clients. They were reluctant to commit to one or a few agencies because they did not want to limit their options.

Difficulties Encountered With Service Integration and Approaches Taken

Service integration efforts face many barriers, including professional training and orientation, administrative procedures, eligibility rules, and the categorical nature of funding. Service agency staff typically are trained in rather narrow, specialized traditions, such as mental health or criminal justice services, and may not feel comfortable dealing with other issues or working within an interagency framework. Single-focus programs encourage this disciplinary insularity. Administrative and bureaucratic procedures often obstruct service integration efforts. Agencies may insist on following their own intake and case-processing procedures. Confidentiality requirements may limit an agency's ability to share information about clients with a service integration team. Categorical funding from government agencies, foundations, or other institutions also perpetuates single-issue programs. As long as legislatures and funders structure programs to address specific issue areas, single-issue programs will continue to provide services and have difficulty making their services available to populations not specified by their mandate.

Any change from the status quo, no matter how well-intentioned or needed, encounters difficulties as it is implemented. Many of the problems noted in past experience and research with service integration were mentioned during our site visits, along with a variety of approaches taken to diffuse them.

Turf Issues

"Turf issues" was one of the most frequently mentioned difficulties. These can exist between agencies, between program staff and staff of an agency with which they want to work, and between ethnic groups. Sometimes these issues reflect a desire to keep control over a problem area, sometimes they reflect different expectations that cooperating agencies might have for a program to which they all contribute, and sometimes they reflect different approaches to solving the same problem. Agency-to-agency issues mentioned during site visits included the following:

- Several agencies competing for the same dollars to develop similar programs.
- Agencies with control over some of the same youth (e.g., juvenile court and DHS) failing to agree about the best approach, either for specific youth or for whole groups of youth with similar problems, and therefore not being willing to commit resources to the case or cases.
- Agencies with different goals for the program, some of which are contradictory. For example, in CHINS UP's Detention Services for Juveniles (DSJ), courts want youth to show up for hearings and not reoffend; the district attorney wants to know that the community is safe; Division of Youth Services (which runs the detention center) wants fewer youth in the center (which operated at close to 300% capacity before DSJ began and now runs at around 150% capacity).

These are potentially serious issues that the programs have handled in several ways, all of which involve ongoing communication, patience, and creativity. In the DSJ case, the program makes daily decisions that establish a precarious balance among the different agencies' goals, keeps a close watch on the youth it releases, and hopes for the best. The juvenile court/ DHS conflict was resolved primarily by a change in personnel; a new chief judge had a different attitude toward interagency cooperation, and the two agencies and the program now have a good working relationship. The agencies involved in competitive struggles for money recognize that they have to change their approach once one agency gets a grant or contract for a new service. Their lines of communication are open enough that they cooperate with the new program so the community gets the services, but relations are sometimes touchy because issues of competition may surface at any time.

Other agency-to-program and program-to-agency issues revealed during site visits include the following:

- Disciplinary differences in approach that engender hostility or distrust (e.g., social workers from Center for Family Life coming into schools to run an after-school program that teachers thought they should run. This problem had both turf and discipline aspects; the social workers and the educators had different approaches to dealing with children).
- Some key person in an agency feeling threatened by a program person with more extensive credentials or experience.
- Program staff coming into a school at the busiest times of the school year and expecting school staff to help them and showing no flexibility or understanding of school procedures, schedules, or needs (in the perception of the school staff).

Ethnic tensions were also mentioned by one program. These were described as jealousy and contention over the distribution of resources and concern about whether agencies affiliated with and serving particular ethnic groups would get their own resources or would have to be under the control of agencies affiliated with different ethnic groups.

In general, programs and agencies address these problems by pursuing the maximum level of openness and communication, often coupled with pragmatic help. For example, the social workers from the Center for Family Life came into the schools during the school day, helped teachers with audiovisual equipment and special activities, and tried to convince teachers of the benefits to children of the after-school program. In addition, they added an academic (tutoring) component to the after-school program, which gave the teachers a role to play that used their own training and experience. These approaches worked to improve cooperation. Houston Communities in Schools deals with person-to-person turf issues by developing memoranda of understanding that spell out the separate and complementary roles and responsibilities of the CIS staff person and the school personnel.

Several programs mentioned the timing of efforts and the need for up-front negotiations to assure successful cooperative activities. Both Belafonte-Tacolcy and Houston Communities in Schools noted the importance of having the school principal on board before bringing new services into a school. Belafonte-Tacolcy also noted that when seeking funding for new services, it was important to have the service sites in agreement before the funding came through. Their experience has been that these negotiations can take a long time and may extend through a significant proportion of the grant period if they are not in place at the beginning.

Belafonte-Tacolcy also mentioned another way that timing and money issues affected cooperation and service delivery. Sometimes cooperative arrangements have been developed for a specific project, which is funded for a limited period of time. Should that funding run out before new funding is found to replace it, the youth-serving program will have to reduce or eliminate the program, even if it may eventually seek to start it up again when new funding arrives. Agency staff find these ups and downs extremely disruptive, and cooperative relationships may be lost for good if agency staff lose faith in the stability of program efforts.

Finally, several different programs mentioned the effects of interactions within an agency on service integration. Their comments indicate that successful service integration and interagency cooperation depends on having the commitment of both agency directors and line workers. Programs that have tried service integration with either one but not both have run into difficulties. If the service integration effort is developed primarily at the line-worker level without the support of the agency director, the line workers risk not being able to summon their agencies' resources when cases require them. Alternatively, if the service integration effort starts at the top, no amount of agency director commitment can produce better service delivery if the line workers either have not heard about it or do not like it. The agency directors we spoke to during visits to several programs voiced their recognition of having to do some training and reorientation with their line workers to make the new system work. Other programs include people at every level in negotiations for new cooperative arrangements; nothing goes forward until all agree—agency heads, supervisors, and line workers alike. For instance, Garfield County (where Garfield Youth Services is located) has evolved a planning group that initially included only agency heads. Gradually these group members began bringing mid-level managers and line workers to the meetings so that issues could be discussed, difficulties resolved, and decisions made all at the same time and with commitment and understanding from every level.

Program Choices and Trade-Offs

Programs continuously face choices of direction and focus as they grow and evolve. These choices shape a program's content and structure of service delivery and ultimately its anticipated program outcomes. This section summarizes our findings about the major choices and trade-offs faced by the programs now and in the past.

Essential program choices are typically based on philosophical considerations, practical considerations, or both. A program's orientation toward prevention or treatment is perhaps its most basic decision. From this decision many other things follow, including the age of youth with whom the program intervenes, what the program offers to its participants, whether or not the program treats youth holistically or maintains a narrow problem focus, and how broadly the program casts its net to include in its activities adults in addition to youth.

Orientation Toward Prevention or Treatment

A program can focus on "fixing" youth who are already in trouble. If it makes this choice, it will probably be dealing with older youth and will probably concentrate on treatment or service delivery. Alternatively, a program can focus on helping youth avoid getting into trouble in the first place. Within this approach there are still differences of orientation, mainly revolving around whether the program sees itself primarily as keeping youth away from something bad or primarily as helping youth achieve something good; the difference is that between a prevention and a youth development approach. Both prevention and youth development approaches are likely to concentrate their efforts on the younger end of the adolescent age spectrum (10–15 year olds rather than 16–19 year olds) and to offer a wide variety of activities and chances for participation other than treatment. Both are also more likely than a treatment-oriented program to view youth holistically and to extend program involvement beyond individual youth to their families, friends, and other members of the community. However, a program based on a youth development philosophy is probably more likely to make these latter choices than is a strictly prevention-oriented program.

Choice of Target Age Group

In many of the programs we visited, the decision about which age groups to target was integrally tied to the program's focus on prevention versus treatment. In an effort to reach youth who will benefit most from preventive services and activities, programs such as Houston Communities in Schools and Garfield Youth Services have expanded their targeted age range to include younger clients. Other programs always included children as well as youth. Houston Communities in Schools has responded to an increase in the magnitude of problems experienced by younger children by increasing its presence in middle and elementary schools. By adopting a pattern in which youth participate in CIS in elementary, middle, and high school, they hope to intervene at an early stage in the child's development and maintain contact with the youth for a longer period of time to prevent future difficulties. Garfield Youth Services also expanded the targeted age group for some of its preventive services, and CHINS UP included all children under age 18 in its Family Preservation Program caseload. The Center for Family Life has always considered all children in neighborhood families part of its mission, and I Have a Future offers activities for all school-age children by including a latch-key program for 6–9 year olds. The younger the age of interest, the more preventive is the mix of services and activities that these programs offer. Services for older teens in these programs include a more even balance between prevention and treatment. For programs that extended their initial age targeting to include younger children, the motivation came from a recognition that because problems are rooted in early childhood experience, prevention activities need to reach younger and younger children in order to be effective.

Decisions about the age range of clients have been central for other programs as well. A key turning point in Oasis Center's development was its decision to refocus its efforts from serving individuals of all ages to providing comprehensive services to meet the needs of teenagers. This decision influenced the types of programs and services offered to clients over the years and reflected both philosophical and pragmatic concerns.

The trade-off evident when programs choose to target one age group is that they exclude youth of other ages who potentially need services. Because some programs do not want to lose contact with youth as they get older, they deliberately structure their activities to promote continued participation of clients over time. Belafonte-Tacolcy accommodates youth until the age of 26, and I Have a Future provides programs for youth between the ages of 10 to 17 plus a latchkey program for 6–10 year olds. These programs thus chose a structure that incorporates two critical preventive elements identified in Chapter 3: start early and stay involved with youth for many years.

Striking a Balance Between Services / Treatment and Activities

Of the programs we visited, those most oriented toward youth development or prevention had a higher ratio of activities and participatory events to services than did the more treatment-oriented programs. Prevention is typically introduced in the form of activities, although it may include more structured services, whereas treatment is usually limited to the provision of specific services. Prevention, and especially youth development, may include recreational or group activities geared toward building self-esteem (e.g., Belafonte-Tacolcy, Houston Communities in Schools); specialized groups (e.g., Oasis Center); structured curriculum modules geared to developing the skills of goal setting, planning, assertiveness, or conflict management, mentoring/role modeling (e.g., I Have a Future, Bronx Teen Connections); and work-oriented skills (e.g., I Have a Future's Entrepreneur's Club). Treatment usually involves interaction with a case worker or social worker who facilitates a client's acquisition of needed treatment (such as counseling, social services) or provides it directly.

Regardless of treatment or prevention orientation, programs retain much flexibility in how they structure their offerings. Big Brothers/Big Sisters, for instance, has intentionally chosen to limit itself to prevention and to pursue this end solely through its role modeling (mentoring) program. The trade-off inherent in limiting its services to role modeling is the recognition that staff need to build relationships with community agencies to ensure the availability of a network of service providers and to train mentors to recognize when their little brother or sister may need these services. Houston Communities in Schools, on the other hand, offers "one-stop shopping" for many different prevention, enrichment, and treatment activities and services at each participating school.

A focus on prevention or treatment also influences the nature of and potential obstacles to evaluating a program. Prevention activities do not lend themselves to as rigorous an evaluation as do treatment interventions. Case files and records are typically maintained for clients receiving treatment services, and these data can be used to assess the impact of treatment. Some prevention programs require clients to participate in a well-defined set of activities (e.g., I Have a Future's mandated curriculum modules), which makes it easier to evaluate client participation and other program impacts. However, many programs do not regularly track participants in prevention activities, and specifications concerning who constitutes a client are less well defined. As a result, measuring the potential impact of these interventions may be more difficult. To do prevention components justice, evaluators would have to develop specific strategies appropriate for handling prevention activities, to be used in conjunction with more typical treatment-oriented evaluation methods.

Within whatever prevention or treatment mission an agency adopts, it still needs some way to assess what aspects of the program a client might need. Some programs have a specific definition of risk that guides their decisions about how a particular youth will participate in the program. When we visited programs, we were interested to learn how a program's definition of risk helps the program shape the specific activities or services it will offer a youth. We were also interested in how thoroughly a program's working definition of risk incorporates the elements in the conceptual framework presented in Chapter 4, where we suggested that youth be considered high risk if they have at least one risk antecedent condition or risk marker and also display at least one risk behavior.

Most of the programs visited use some type of working definition of risk, but wide differences exist in the specificity of these definitions. Furthermore, different service components of the same program often focus on different aspects of risk. Programs that provide mainly treatment services, such as CHINS UP and Oasis Center, tend to focus primarily on the youth and his or her presenting problems at intake. Risk is defined predominantly by the presence of system markers (e.g., out-of-home placement or poor school performance) and problem behaviors (e.g., drug use, juvenile delinquency, or family conflict), which is consistent with the empirical research on risk. For example, CHINS UP will not allow youth runaways into its shelter unless they have had prior involvement with the courts, juvenile justice, or child welfare. So potential clients must be at a quite high level of risk before they can enter the program. Once in, however, levels of risk do not determine what types of service the youth will receive from CHINS UP, except in Detention Services for Juveniles. Youth in Oasis Center's treatment component are not formally classified by risk factors, but a detailed intake interview and assessment provides information useful for identifying service needs and developing an action plan to meet those needs.

In the more exclusively prevention-oriented programs, such as I Have a Future, Big Brothers/Big Sisters, and Bronx Teen Connections, risk is defined less according to already existing problems or system markers and more according to antecedent risk conditions, such as the neighborhood (in the case of I Have a Future) or the family environment (in the case of

Big Brothers/Big Sisters and Bronx Teen Connections). This approach means that the level of risk is equal for all program participants and does not determine the receipt of specific services. The prevention activities in Bronx Teen Connections, Big Brothers/Big Sisters, and I Have a Future are open to almost any youth who meets the entry criteria. But these programs do identify different risk levels through their assessment processes, which may lead to the offer of additional services. In addition, Bronx Teen Connections has learned over the years that it has to screen out teens at very high risk because the program is not equipped to handle these youth.

The programs that offer both prevention and treatment components use their risk assessment to distinguish between youth at high risk and those at lower risk. The mixed-approach programs identify high risk primarily by whether the youth exhibits any risk behaviors or risk markers, including violence, truancy from school, drug or alcohol abuse, and police or juvenile court involvement. Youth considered to be at high risk are offered treatment services, whereas all others are offered the preventive or enrichment programs. High-risk youth may still continue to participate in the program's prevention aspects if they want to do so.

These programs offer youth at low or moderate risk their most basic prevention programs. For most programs, low risk means that the youth live in specific antecedent conditions, such as poverty, single-parent households, or neighborhoods characterized by drug use or violence. For moderate risk, they may also display some of the common risk markers, such as poor school performance or involvement with child welfare services. These lower risk youth may participate in all prevention activities along with the more high-risk program clients.

To summarize, many programs use explicit risk assessment techniques to determine which program services to offer youth. Many of the programs, especially those with a major focus on prevention, consider that the neighborhood and family conditions of youth put everyone in the program's vicinity at risk, so the program will welcome the participation of all youth in the neighborhood in its recreational, educational, and cultural activities. Sometimes there also are gradations within the prevention component, as when a youth judged to be very vulnerable is offered a mentor even though she or he has not yet begun to participate in specific risky behaviors. Usually, the presence of specific problem behaviors triggers treatment or counseling, which is the more intense and focused of the service offerings in these programs. Thus the programs we visited use both explicit and implicit risk criteria in deciding whether to accept a youth into the program and what aspects of the program to offer.

Extending the Program to Serve Youth, Family, or Neighborhood

Although all of the programs visited for this project ultimately serve at-risk youth, their efforts may be focused at the individual, family, or community level and on younger children and adults as well as youth. Their choice of level and age inclusiveness is usually driven by the focus of their mission on youth development, prevention, or treatment. Overall, the programs we visited can be classified as follows:

- Serving youth almost exclusively (Bronx Teen Connections).
- Focusing primarily on child or youth clients but involving families in program activities to varying degrees (5 programs: Oasis Center, CHINS UP, Big Brothers/Big Sisters, Houston Communities in Schools, and Belafonte-Tacolcy). Age ranges for primary clients among these programs run from elementary school age (CIS) to young adulthood (26 for Belafonte-Tacolcy).
- Having broader orientations (I Have a Future, Center for Family Life, and Garfield Youth Services). They are oriented strongly toward serving youth, their families, and the surrounding community. In fact, GYS and the Center for Family Life expend considerable effort to maintain a public image as serving the entire community.

The programs that have chosen to tailor their services toward youth may still recognize the importance of including the family in some facets of service delivery. Some programs simply include family members in a child's treatment plan; others view the treatment of a child holistically and direct services toward all facets of the child's environment, including parents and family. Still others see the family as the focal point of service (e.g., CHINS UP's Family Preservation Program or the Center for Family Life's counseling services).

It seems quite clear that programs with a strong treatment orientation are most likely to focus narrowly on specific youth. It would be quite unusual to find a neighborhood orientation in a program focused heavily on treatment; this approach is much more likely to be found in prevention-oriented programs. Family involvement may be found in programs with either orientation (or both), but the actual types of family involvement are likely to be different. In treatment-oriented programs that involve families, the program will most likely involve the family in addressing the specific treatment issues arising with the youth who is the client. In prevention-oriented programs, adult community members may be involved in program activities even if they are not parents of specific youth in the program, and more activities may be planned for the participation of entire families.

In some cases, a program's services may not fully reflect its program goals or objectives. Assuming that the program still endorses its stated mission and goals, exploring the lack of fit between a program's goals and services is one way to evaluate the extent to which its goals are met. Two examples will illustrate this point. From the inception of Bronx Teen Connections, a key objective of its case management component has been the involvement of significant others of the youth receiving services. This objective was reintroduced during the third year of the demonstration by the program's funders, who felt that the present service structure did not actively include immediate family members in case management. One result of recent strategic planning at Oasis Center was the introduction of a new goal: advocating for youth and family service needs at all levels. This new goal has shifted the program's orientation from adolescents to both adolescents and their families in the time between our visit in 1992 and our follow-up in 1996.

In some programs, participants can keep coming for years. Sometimes their participation is very intense, and sometimes it tapers off to one or two visits a month or less, but the program still considers the participants to be program clients. In other programs, formal attachment to the program (being a program client) is clear, intense, and brief—usually only until the client's immediate problem is resolved. In addition, some programs offer activities and services to youth, their families, and other community members who may never formally enroll in the program. The more a program focuses on youth as primary clients, the clearer program attachment usually is. Conversely, programs directing significant effort toward families and community often encourage several varieties of participation in addition to being a formal client.

Most of the programs we visited define their clientele very broadly. They see people as their clients when they participate in any aspect of program services and activities, and these often involve a broad spectrum of program components spanning prevention and treatment modalities. Because of the mix of treatment and preventive services these programs offer, many youth, families, or other individuals may come in contact with the program in some way that an outsider looking at the program might not think of as being a client. Examples might be youth attending a school assembly presentation put on by the program or parents coming to the program for "Family Night."

Because the array of services and activities available to youth and other community members is so complex, it is sometimes difficult to tell who is a program client and who is not, or where significant program impact on individuals could be expected versus a more diffuse influence on the norms and expectations of the community. Often on site visits we got the feeling that if we were to limit our attention only to the program's involvement with the youth who could be considered formally enrolled, we would miss some of the more ephemeral but critical aspects of the program's importance to its community. The implications of this issue for evaluation are discussed further in Chapter 16.

A characteristic that appears typical of many comprehensive program efforts is that youth and families can enter the program without necessarily being identified as needing a specific service. This is especially true for the more comprehensive service delivery programs that provide both prevention and treatment services. A "club" approach, in which any youth in the school or community can apply or register with the program, means that youth and families are not stigmatized for joining the program. In fact, many of these programs emphasized during our site visits that they do not believe in identifying clients on the basis of presenting problems or dysfunctions. Furthermore, just as youth and others can be attached to these programs without having an identified service need, they can also receive specific services without being identified as a formal client. Finally, variability across programs is to be expected, but often there may be as much variation within programs as there is across programs. Sometimes even the programs themselves have trouble keeping track of participants as they move among the various program components.

Community and Cultural Context

Programs providing services to at-risk youth exist in a variety of settings, and locales may serve a culturally diverse mix of youth. It is important to understand the influence of community and cultural issues on the design, operation, and likely institutionalization of these programs. Overall, our nine programs serve clients from a range of racial and ethnic backgrounds. Some programs primarily serve clients from one racial or ethnic group (I Have a Future, African Americans; Belafonte-Tacolcy, African Americans; Garfield Youth Services, Whites). Others have more of a mix, although the client population reflects the predominant racial or cultural group of the community served by the program (Oasis Center, 80% White and 20% African American; Center for Family Life, 80% Hispanic, with a growing Asian community; Bronx Teen Connections, 80% African American, 20% Hispanic). Still other programs serve a diverse clientele (Big Brothers/Big Sisters, 50% African American, 25% Hispanic, 20% White; CHINS UP, 60% white, 14% African American, 12% Hispanic, and others; and Communities in Schools, 51% African American, 45% Hispanic, 4% White, and others). Although Houston Communities in Schools serves a diverse population throughout its 21-school system in Houston, the clientele at a given school tends to be homogenous. Big Brothers/Big Sisters faces intercultural issues that influence delivery of services, especially among their diverse Hispanic clientele. Additionally, one of our programs is located in a rural area and serves many small towns with different attitudes toward services.

This section explores the impact of cultural issues on the following program elements: (a) program philosophy or curriculum, (b) service delivery, (c) staffing, and (d) community perceptions and program ownership.

Program Philosophy

A program's philosophy guides its goals and objectives and ultimately its structure and operation. The philosophy or long-range strategic plan of three of the nine programs reflect cultural considerations. I Have a Future adopted a program orientation that is culturally sensitive to its African American clientele. By incorporating the Nguzo Saba Seven Principles of Blackness (unity, collective work and responsibility, purpose, self-determination, cooperative economics, creativity, and faith) into its curriculum modules, the program tries to instill more positive self-concept and constructive attitude toward community, family life, and the future.

Part of Oasis Center's current 5-year strategic plan includes the goal of involving and serving minorities. The Center's staff is almost exclusively White, although approximately 20% of program participants are African American. In line with the themes of "empowerment" and "opportunity" that are popular within the community, the Center plans to focus on multicultural diversity and to recruit a more culturally diverse staff.

Garfield Youth Services maintains a philosophy of serving all county youth, and in that effort exerts itself to offer programming that will appeal to youth and their families, especially those who are not "in trouble." The program also sees its role as being a spokesperson for youth interests, and it recently opposed selling beer at a countywide event meant to attract youth, on the grounds that it set an example counter to the program's drug and alcohol prevention message.

Service Delivery

Service delivery is the program element most frequently influenced by cultural considerations. Cultural issues affect the types of services offered and the process of delivering services in the majority of the programs we visited. In some instances, the needs of specific ethnic groups within a community have influenced the range of services provided by a program. To illustrate, Miami's Belafonte-Tacolcy Center collaborated with other agencies to create a comprehensive multiservice center to meet the needs of the community's rapidly growing Haitian immigrant population. When the Center for Family Life experienced an influx of Chinese immigrants, it provided English language services and modified some of its programs to accommodate non-English, non-Spanish speaking participants. The Parent Council meetings currently take place in three languages: English, Spanish, and Chinese.

Cultural issues also play a role in the service needs and issues identified by the different communities participating in the Houston Communities in Schools program. Located in Houston's "Little Mexico," the CIS program at Edison Middle School has addressed the lack of English language fluency among parents, illegal immigration, and ineligibility for the employment opportunities provided at the site. At Key Middle School, many of the CIS program activities focus on developing youth leadership groups and providing academic enrichment in response to a perceived lack of positive role models promoting academic achievement and discipline within the low-income, largely African American community.

Cultural awareness is also important during the course of service delivery. At Big Brothers/Big Sisters, social workers must be sensitive to potential conflicts inherent in intercultural matches. To illustrate, Big Brothers/Big Sisters program staff report that in Miami members of other Latin American groups tend to envy Cubans. Staff have found that this leads to lower rates of success for matches between a Cuban and an individual from another Latin American country. The program has found that matching non–African American Blacks (e.g., Haitians) with Hispanic participants is not typically an issue, but pairing an African American volunteer or child with an Hispanic volunteer or child tends to be problematic. In addition, program participants from the different Latin American countries may have different values and expectations that influence their participation in these types of programs.

Programs based in or providing services to rural settings, such as Garfield Youth Services, experience a different set of service delivery issues relevant to understanding the program's approach and success. Most rural areas sorely lack the resources and services needed to assist at-risk youth. When GYS was created, for instance, there were no services available to at-risk youth in the catchment area, and any services they provided met a need. However, GYS has found it important to be extremely sensitive to the language and values of each small community in the county it serves. This sensitivity extends to tailoring program advertising, references to the program, and content of services to the area involved. The benefits are that no part of the county feels neglected and community members and public officials from every region of the county actively support the program.

Staffing

The diversity of a program's clientele is also considered when programs make staff selections and specify staffing requirements. Those programs that serve a multicultural clientele have identified a need or have attempted to ensure that their staff reflects this diversity. Minority staff members not only bridge language barriers that might limit a client's access to services (e.g., Chinese social workers for the Center for Family Life) but may also serve as role models to minority clients. Houston CIS staff reflects the racial and ethnic composition of its clients. The program also attempts to recruit "agency partners" and volunteers that reflect its client composition. The lack of male African American volunteers at Big Brothers/Big Sisters has become a major focus of recent marketing and recruiting initiatives. The program spent more than $30,000 several years ago to recruit male African Americans through ads and flyers targeting minority-owned businesses, churches, African American fraternities, and a popular African American newspaper, but the return was negligible. The lack of male African American volunteers prolongs the waiting period for African American boys who wish to be matched with them.

I Have a Future went through an interesting transition to ensure that its staff met the cultural needs of the program's clients. The project originally followed a brokering model, assessing needs and referring youth for services and recreational activities to agencies outside of the housing projects in which the program was located. The project's 1992 deputy director felt that these service providers did not fully comprehend the unique needs and complex situation of these African American residents of housing projects. In reaction, she got the Public Housing Authority's commitment of one housing unit in each of the two housing projects served by the program and moved services into these units. The program activities also changed, toward curriculum modules on needed topics to be implemented by an almost exclusively African American staff.

Some programs favor multicultural staffing to highlight their cultural awareness and sensitivity. For example, both Big Brothers/Big Sisters and Belafonte-Tacolcy Center strive for a culturally diverse board that is knowledgeable about community issues and needs. CHINS UP makes sure that its residential shelter staff include African American and Hispanic individuals to reflect the ethnic composition of the youth residents. Conversely, Bronx Teen Connections severed ties with the national Teen Connections demonstration's independent evaluator, who was perceived to be insensitive to the culture of its program participants and upset youth with the types of questions asked. Of the four sites that make up the national Teen Connections demonstration, people at two sites had this reaction to this particular evaluator.

Community Perceptions and Program Ownership

Communities want to feel that their needs and interests will be met by the programs housed within their community. A community's perception of local programs and feeling of ownership are important to the programs' long-term viability. In our sample of programs, numerous factors influenced these perceptions and ultimately the sense of community ownership. One situation is a program whose board (or management) does not represent the community's predominant racial, cultural, or socioeconomic status (e.g., Bronx Teen Connections). Communities may not have a sense of ownership in these programs if they perceive that their needs or interests will not be adequately represented. To facilitate community ownership, some programs hire past program participants and other community members as staff (e.g., Center for Family Life, Belafonte-Tacolcy). Garfield Youth Services has taken a different approach to meeting the needs of the diverse communities within its rural catchment area. To ensure a program's success, its programming and approach is tailored to accommodate character differences among these communities. These modifications may be as simple as altering program names in recognition of community sensitivities.

A community's perceptions may also directly affect program participation or success. Misperceptions about the racial, cultural, and socioeconomic background of program participants affect some Dade County community members' willingness to participate as volunteers in Big Brothers/ Big Sisters. A segment of older volunteers for the Intergenerational Match Program were hesitant to serve as mentors because they perceived that the youth the program serves were of low socioeconomic status, "bad" children from poor neighborhoods. The program applied marketing strategies to clear up this misconception. In Colorado Springs, the community's perception that the area's juvenile justice system is racially biased (in favor of Whites) initially made CHINS UP's Detention Services for Juveniles program a risky venture. The community did not overwhelmingly support the program's monitored release of juvenile delinquents. As a result, CHINS UP risked negative publicity and loss of community support if the released juveniles were to reoffend while waiting for trial on the earlier charge. However, because great care was taken to honor these sensitivities, the program has worked out well, and in 1996 it was enjoying strong community support.

Another aspect of community support and ownership is the interactions of community members and institutions with the program as it tries to meet community needs. The most creative of our nine programs had both the skill and commitment to work with community members to identify needs not currently being met and to develop new services and activities that enhanced the total offerings of the community. In addition to organizing for integrated service delivery, they worked with the community to develop a broad array of resources to support children and youth.

Concluding Thoughts

This chapter's examination of many cross-cutting program issues makes clear the importance of visiting a variety of programs and examining how different programs approach the same issues. Having made these comparisons, some important consistencies across programs stand out, as do the critical program choices that have led to quite different client and service mixes and arrangements. The diversity of the program configurations we found in these nine programs attests to the creativity and determination with which program staff seek to meet the needs of their youthful clients. The record of success assembled by many of the programs suggests that their comprehensive approach, flexible attitudes, and in some instances long-term involvement with youth may be the keys to making a difference for high-risk young people. These programs' diversity combined with their demonstrated impacts also indicate that a wide variety of approaches can make a difference for youth. However, whichever approach a program selects must respond to the complex life circumstances facing the youth and bring a consistent philosophy to bear on these circumstances. In this broader context, service integration efforts designed to facilitate service delivery across service systems and funding streams can help.

Service Integration

We have seen that some of the programs we visited for this project have gone quite far in the direction of establishing fully operational systems of integrated services. It should be equally clear that others have not or do not see the need to create extensive formal structures to support the cross-agency access that they feel they have.

As the findings discussed in this chapter make clear, the "classic" service integration model is primarily appropriate for programs with a substantial or exclusive treatment focus. It is not as relevant for prevention programs, although it can be adapted to accommodate the more service-oriented aspects of these programs. Yet prevention programs often have a need to access particular services when staff notice that a youth participating in recreational, mentoring, educational, or artistic activities is beginning to get into difficulties that could lead to risky behavior. Prevention programs need a systematic way to flag these youth while "prevention" is still the right word to apply. They also need mechanisms to assure that youth get the services they need, even though most of the youth in the program do not need these services most of the time.

We also found several examples of programs that serve as the glue or mortar holding the diverse elements of a service system together, fill gaps in services when there is a need, and basically promote the smoother and more appropriate functioning of the system and of services for youth. If this type of activity has been noted before in relation to service integration efforts, not much has been made of it, or at least we have not seen it described or appreciated elsewhere. We were quite impressed by the magnitude of the achievements possible over the years for a program with the dedication to fill this role in a community, and we think that this aspect of service integration deserves more attention than it has received so far.

Trade-Offs and Choices

The selection of youth development, prevention, treatment, or some combination of these appears to be the most fundamental decision affecting program configuration. It drives most other choices, including the age group to target, the mix of services and activities to offer, and how broad a net to cast outward from youth as primary clients to family, friends, and community. The programs that seemed to us most exciting and innovative were those found on the development and prevention end of the continuum. However, the same characteristics that make these programs exciting may also make them extremely difficult to evaluate. This is especially true if one is interested in assessing some of the more global aspects of their influence, such as changes in the environment of whole neighborhoods. We discuss these issues further in Chapter 16.

Community and Cultural Context

It is clear that cultural issues affect many aspects of program operations. The programs we visited very consciously made their activities culturally appropriate and accommodated the cultural sensitivity of their youth participants. This was sometimes quite difficult to do, but for different reasons. Some programs faced a multicultural environment where everyone was highly sensitized to racial and cultural differences; other programs had one group heavily in the majority and had some difficulty meeting the needs of the few minority clients they served. But all programs grappled to a greater or lesser extent with cultural issues and found that they were often better able to reach and help youth when they were able to provide culturally appropriate programming, staff, and volunteers.

When we asked ourselves what we had learned about the cultural context of our programs and how that cultural context influenced decisions about clients, staff, services and activities, and presence in the community, we saw that our programs wrestle with cultural issues in virtually every aspect of their existence. They try to maintain a staff that reflects the cultural backgrounds of their clients, try to adjust their programming to the neighborhood and community cultures they serve, develop programming specifically to enhance certain cultural identities and strengths among their clients, and try to help newcomers and outsiders to respect and appreciate the cultural diversity of their clientele and community.

From an evaluation perspective, the cultural context of program activities is critical. It might seem that one could study the impact of particular service offerings or particular inter-agency arrangements independently of the cultural context in which they operate. But the experience of visiting these programs has convinced us that one must also understand how a particular technique, service, or activity is understood by clients and the larger community before one can judge whether it is fair to expect it to have an impact. A good multiprogram evaluation of even the simplest activity or service offering would do well to document the meanings of that activity for the program's clients, their families, and associates as part of understanding how and why the activity works or fails to achieve its promise.

16

Evaluating Programs Offering Integrated Services and Activities to Youth

In this chapter, we discuss special issues in evaluating comprehensive service integration programs. Even treatment-oriented programs may have difficulties documenting short-term impact. Programs oriented toward prevention and youth development will have even more difficulty because their effects usually cannot be detected in the short term. When one adds the special characteristics of programs trying to offer comprehensive and integrated services to the problems of evaluating treatment, prevention, and development effects, the difficulties can be great indeed. Yet programs of great promise often cannot get the support they need to continue to serve youth without having clear evidence for effectiveness. In this chapter, we focus on several aspects of evaluations that, in our experience, pose the greatest challenges for youth-serving programs, and we offer some suggestions for how programs might make certain decisions about their evaluation design that will maximize the usefulness of the evaluation effort.

We begin with a discussion of what one might want to know about youth-serving programs that use service integration or community-based approaches. We continue with a look at special issues that are of particular importance to this type of program and conclude by examining program evaluability, including a program's readiness, willingness, and capability to conduct an evaluation.

What Program Impacts Are Important?

A program's stated goals are the starting point for identifying appropriate outcomes to measure. Once these goals are identified, the evaluator and program staff can determine the most meaningful, available, and feasible measures in the particular evaluation setting.

Measuring the attainment of some goals is easy. If a program tries to keep youth in school until the end of each school year, this is an easily observable outcome. If the program tries to assure that teenagers bear

healthy babies, the birth of a full-term normal-weight baby without physical or mental abnormalities is a clear measure of success. Both of these
outcomes affect a public system; the school or the hospital records the
outcome, and the evaluation can access the system records.

However, efforts to use existing secondary source data, such as school
records, reports from participating service agencies, or arrest records, as
indicators of program impacts may be complicated by privacy regulations.
Confidentiality agreements within and between agencies that restrict
evaluator access may limit the utility of these data sources for evaluation
purposes. How the lead agency defines its agreements with the other member agencies concerning shared information may affect the availability of
secondary data sources. If data on individual clients is prohibited, the
recording agency may still be able to provide aggregate data against a list
of program clients (e.g., reporting the percentage of listed youth with full-
term, normal-weight babies).

Other goals have clear outcomes conceptually, but these outcomes may
not generate accurate system markers. For instance, programs trying to
prevent substance use or criminal behavior have a conceptually clear outcome: The youth either engages in the behavior or does not. But many
youth may engage in the behavior without getting caught, and some youth
who use drugs or commit crimes relatively infrequently may get caught
on the rare occasions when they do so. Public systems are poor recorders
of these outcomes. In addition, youth may or may not be willing to tell an
evaluator what they have been doing or may not be able to recount their
activities accurately. If we could observe the youth at all times, we would
know whether program outcomes were achieved. But no evaluation will
ever reach this level of surveillance. For some outcomes one can make
random observations (e.g., random urine tests for drug use), but most
youth-serving programs probably would consider such observations
unacceptably intrusive and disruptive of the program and its relationship
with clients. Furthermore, because one can only randomly observe those
clients one can contact, it is critical that the evaluation take steps to
assure excellent continuing contact with all program and comparison
youth.

Measuring Individual Outcomes

Programs may try to affect their clients' knowledge, attitudes, or behavior
with respect to a wide range of topics. Prevention programs usually target
particular behaviors associated with risk (e.g., not using drugs, not smoking, abstinence from sexual activity). They may try to change the behavior
directly, but usually they will also try to change knowledge about the risks
associated with the behavior and attitudes toward the behavior as a means
to effect behavior change. Knowledge and attitudes are typically measured
with paper-and-pencil instruments; often these are administered immediately after an intervention, and the results are compared with responses

before the intervention. The important extension of this methodology to assessment in some follow-up period is less often done, but much research indicates that the effects of short interventions aimed at knowledge and attitudes often wear off relatively quickly and rarely affect behavior (Zimbardo & Leippe, 1991).

Changes in behavior are important to measure, whether the program is primarily a prevention or a treatment program. The nature of the behaviors may be more complex in treatment programs (e.g., counseling a youth and his or her parents may attempt to change long-ingrained habits of interaction and communication), but measuring the presence or absence and increase or decrease of behaviors is usually an essential element of program evaluations. Self-reports (through interviews or questionnaires) and system markers of behavior (e.g., school, agency, court records) are common evaluation tools.

Some program objectives may not be clear conceptually and therefore will be difficult to measure. Many programs try to increase youth self-esteem or to promote growth or leadership ability, but these terms are hard to define. Some of these goals do not have readily available standardized measures with sound psychometric properties. This is the case, for example, with measures of the quality of parent–adolescent interaction (Howrigan, 1988). For other topics, such as self-esteem, measures are either short (therefore easy to use) and global (therefore harder to affect) or detailed (giving information about many specific aspects of self-esteem, and therefore more likely to register change) but long (therefore difficult to use). Although measures for many psychological characteristics exist, many do not have norms or else lack norms specifically for youth, so one would not be able to say that the youth of a particular program score as high or higher than, say, 70% of youth in the nation. If one *could* find and use scales with national norms that matched one or more program objectives, the norms would provide a natural "comparison" group. In recent years several adolescent health behavior surveys have been developed and widely used, including the Minnesota Student Survey (Minnesota Planning Agency, 1996) and the Centers for Disease Control and Prevention's Youth Risk Behavior Survey that is being used in at least some school districts in every state (Youth Risk Behavior National Survey, n.d.). Any youth program evaluation would do well to adopt questions and techniques from these surveys for behaviors relevant to program goals.

What happens all too often is that evaluations fall back on measures that are available or feasible rather than measures that are meaningful in evaluating these programs. This is a documented shortcoming of many previous evaluations of innovative programs for children and youth, dating back to the early evaluations of Head Start. Despite the mandate of Head Start to influence a broad range of outcomes, including children's health status and parents' community involvement, more than half of Head Start effectiveness studies have focused primarily on children's IQ scores (Hauser-Cram & Shonkoff, 1988).

Measuring Behaviors Prevented

Trying to measure things that did not happen (successful prevention) poses many difficulties, not least of which is that a comparison is required to show what would have happened without the program (for a more detailed discussion of evaluating teen pregnancy prevention programs, see Card, 1988, and Moore, Sugland, et al., 1995; for school-based programs, see Trutko, Chessen, & Stapleton, 1994). Sometimes evaluators try to measure prevention indirectly, by assessing increases in skills or competencies that are hoped to inoculate the recipient against risk conditions (Bloom, 1979). Others use survey responses of the target population; if these also are done on a population not experiencing the intervention, comparisons can be made to see whether the intervention group shows less of the behavior than the comparison group. One of our programs (I Have a Future) used this approach for the outcomes of pregnancy and drug use prevention; published evaluations have also done so (see, e.g., Zabin, Hirsch, Smith, Streett, & Hardy, 1986). At least one state routinely uses a standard instrument to survey 9th and 12th graders to see whether prevention goals are being achieved (Minnesota Planning Agency, 1996).

Sometimes an evaluation uses a population rate of something that registers as a marker in some social agency's data system (e.g., citywide drug arrests for youth; citywide teen birth rates), even if the intervention has been addressed only to a very small proportion of the whole population, such as one neighborhood. For example, a primary prevention program might be assessed by measuring citywide or countywide arrests of juveniles, or teen birth rates, or total school dropout rates, but perhaps the program operated in only one community representing only 5% of the youth in the city. This practice is clearly an unfair measure of program impact, because it is very unlikely that the program could have affected a whole community. If at all possible, the evaluation should seek system data at the neighborhood level, to assess the impact on the population actually reached by the program. Among our nine programs, the Center for Family Life, whose target neighborhood is a New York City community planning district, routinely receives reports from city agencies on a variety of child welfare indicators (e.g., rates of reported child abuse, foster care use, and termination of parental rights) for its own and other planning districts, so it can chart its own progress in relation to districts without similar programs.

Measuring System Change

Documentation of comprehensive service integration programs should include an assessment of the effectiveness or efficiency of the referral network and the extent to which it is a stable creation of the program. Many youth-serving programs rely heavily on informal interinstitutional linkages with existing service agencies; other linkages are formal and explicit.

The literature on interagency cooperation discusses the nature of social agency "service boundaries" and their "permeability" or "rigidity." Of course, agency rigidity may be merely a reflection of the rigidity of their funding sources or the benefit programs they administer, and programs have no choice about following the rules associated with the funding streams. Overly rigid agencies or benefit programs maintain many restrictions on client eligibility, despite official participation in an integrated network. These restrictions have been associated with clients' not receiving services from the referral agency, despite making contact. The Office of Technology Assessment (1991) has identified this factor as a major impediment to traditional service delivery for at-risk youth; it is also a prime reason for attempting service integration, whose purpose is to increase permeability.

Service integration may work in any of a variety of formats. If the program design is one in which youth enter through any of several coequal agencies in a network, each of which retains "their" youth as primary clients and provides case management services for accessing the services of the other agencies, there could be as many images of "the program" as there are agencies in the network. Because each may have a somewhat different emphasis, youth who are clients of one program may receive a very different set of services from that received by youth who are clients of another agency. Another model, more common than the one just described, is a central youth-serving agency that provides an array of activities and services itself and also establishes interagency linkages for the services or entitlements it cannot offer or needs only rarely. Both of these models could be evaluated for the effects of service integration on the ease, frequency, volume, speed, and other aspects of service delivery. But for the first model, it might not make much sense to ask about the effects of "the program" on all of the youth served by agencies in the network.

The ability of agencies in a service integration network to work out more flexible and "permeable" boundaries will certainly affect service delivery and will probably also affect client outcomes. Evaluations of service integration programs should document how the networked agencies developed more flexible procedures (if they did) and describe the changes in agency flexibility that resulted. Gomby and Larson (1992) have suggested a variety of indicators that can be used to document the system and its service delivery effects (parentheses ours):

System changes:

- Memoranda of understanding between agencies (should increase);
- Waivers to use funding streams in innovative ways (should increase);
- Steering committee with multi-agency representation (should be one);
- Frequency of meetings among participating agencies (should increase);

Service delivery effects:

- New, simpler forms;
- Number of contacts clients have with multiple agencies (should increase);
- Time spent waiting for services (should decrease);
- Referral patterns (should become more creative and appropriate);
- Services delivered to one agency's clients by other agencies (should increase but also should be more appropriate);
- Services used by participants (should increase and also should be appropriate to participants' needs);
- Services offered by participating agencies. (Agencies might fill in gaps in service system, might alter their service mix to avoid duplication, or might drop a service if it becomes clear that another agency is more effective at providing it.)

To these we might add the following system effects:

- Increased personal contacts and comfort of agency staff across service systems (e.g., among education, juvenile justice, mental health, income maintenance);
- Increased knowledge among case managers of services available;
- Complete inventory and reference book of services available in the community, their eligibility criteria, and how to apply;
- Extent to which agencies use colocation of staff, staff exchange programs, multi-agency teaming;
- Changes in allocation of financial resources in the system away from ineffective activities and toward effective ones.

The first two additional indicators of system effects would require questionnaire or survey assessment. The last three additional indicators may be documented from existing records (e.g., the reference book will exist, the staffing patterns will be documented through memos and agreements, budgets will reflect shifts in funding). It would be a quite remarkable achievement if a program were to accomplish shifts in financial resources toward more effective interventions after documenting which approaches were effective and which were not.

It may be important to document what is missing from the service integration package in any given program, either because it is completely unavailable in the community or because the core program could not or has not yet developed a relationship with the appropriate agencies. For example, at-risk youth probably would not benefit from an employment-oriented peer support program unless jobs appropriate to the youth were available in the community. This issue was confronted by Halpern and Larner (cited in Halpern, 1986) in the Child Survival/Fair Start initiative, in which the effectiveness of a program for migrant workers was adversely affected by the lack of medical resources to treat conditions once these were identified by the program.

Finally, the specific configuration of service integration in one community is probably impossible to replicate in other locations. Not only may specific services differ, but the personal relations necessary to get a network started will certainly differ. Therefore, it is critical to document the spirit and process of network development, as distinct from the service components, because the process is what other communities must replicate to achieve a network that fits their needs.

Comprehensiveness and service integration are not the same thing. A program can be comprehensive by providing all needed services itself, without relying on any interagency collaboration. A program can be integrated (i.e., use collaborative arrangements) and not comprehensive. A program can rely on service integration as its mechanism to become comprehensive. A program's definition of *comprehensive* may differ from the evaluator's or funder's definition. We think it is important for any evaluation in this area to try to sort out the effects on clients of comprehensiveness from those of service integration, as well as the effects of service integration on the comprehensiveness experienced by clients.

The most likely service integration impacts that affect clients are improvements in the ease, frequency, volume, speed, and accessibility of services not available through the core program. It may also happen that the client gets one or more services that he or she would not have received at all without service integration. Then we would want to assess the impact of faster, easier service receipt and also the impact of a different, enhanced service mix. It could be that speed and ease mean that the situation the client faces does not have a chance to deteriorate beyond hope. Or, because the program can "deliver" when needed, the client keeps coming to the program and participating in enhancement activities. It should also be relatively easy to tell whether service integration increased comprehensiveness (assuming that service delivery was recorded accurately and fully). However, if the services would not have been available without service integration, then the effects of service integration and comprehensiveness would be confounded and the evaluation would not be able to identify independent effects for these program characteristics.

Evaluators and program staff should discuss and develop realistic expectations of the specific nature of increased comprehensiveness they anticipate from service integration, as well as of the effects they expect that are not related to enhanced comprehensiveness. Once these effects are identified, the evaluators can develop mutually acceptable ways to measure them, including observational or qualitative approaches. Ultimately the decision may be that it is too difficult to separate out the effects of service integration on comprehensiveness and service integration independently of comprehensiveness unless one is doing a multisite evaluation of programs that vary systematically in their degrees of each.

Measuring Community Impacts

Comprehensive service integration programs for at-risk youth feature a wide range of potential program goals, including changes to the participants, the families of participants, and participant peer groups and changes in interagency linkages and the larger community environment. Although measures exist for youth skills (particularly school performance), social skills, and "problem behaviors," proven assessment instruments become scarcer as one moves farther away from youth and their concrete behaviors as the focus of measurement. A "catch-22" situation may arise, where programs use narrow outcome measures to assess complex, ecologically oriented programs, simply because there are so few valid and reliable alternatives (Weiss, 1988). But the measures chosen do not reflect most of the effort of the program or its intended effects.

If the program is designed to change a whole community, then the appropriate measurement will be at the community level. Schinke, Orlandi, and Cole (1992) have provided an excellent example of measuring the community impact of introducing Boys and Girls Clubs with specific antidrug programming into public housing projects. They looked at changes in substance abuse, parental involvement, and general neighborhood disorganization. Substance abuse was measured by counting discarded containers and drug paraphernalia found on project grounds; parental involvement was measured by participation in tenant associations, youth organizations, and schools; general neighborhood disorganization was measured by vandalism and graffiti in unoccupied housing units. Parental involvement increased and the other indicators decreased in housing projects that had Clubs; housing projects with Clubs also fared better on each measure than comparison projects without clubs. The results led to widespread entree into Public Housing Authority projects for the Boys and Girls Clubs, which now operate more than 100 clubs on housing project grounds.

It is not easy to develop methodologies to measure community change. A recent project supported by the Assistant Secretary for Planning and Evaluation of the U.S. Department of Health and Human Services is attempting to do so. The Aspen Institute is currently working to develop a theoretical approach to evaluating comprehensive community change initiatives. Thus far, publications focus on articulating the theoretical bases for actions to change communities (Connell, Kubisch, Schorr, & Weiss, 1995). The elements of the theories proposed may become the core of future evaluations. Another activity, the National Neighborhood Indicators Project (Urban Institute, 1996b) is working to develop neighborhood-level social indicators in cities around the country. The data from this project could afford statistics against which to compare one's own neighborhood performance in the presence of community change efforts. The results of these projects may contribute to better evaluations of community change in the future.

Issues for Multisite Evaluations

Multisite evaluations pose their own problems for selecting outcomes to measure. Outside evaluators may impose common outcome categories on all programs in a multisite evaluation, but this common set of outcomes may not reflect significant aspects of each program in the evaluation. To some extent, the selection of outcome measures might need to be specific to each program site because at least some of the program goals will be highly site-specific.

Even programs with the same nominal goals may prefer different indicators of goal attainment. These differences may be a function of the way the program has been implemented at the given site or they may stem from differences in decision-making processes at different program sites. For example, some sites might not allow evaluators to use some measures that they consider overly intrusive, but other sites may have no problem with the measures. The result may be a great deal of intersite variability with respect to which program goals are included in the evaluation, whether major program goals are left out for some sites, the nature of the relationship between the program and the evaluation, and the selection of specific measures to operationalize the program goals. These differences across sites may serve as barriers to cross-site comparisons of program effectiveness, particularly if these sites must coordinate with a national evaluation team whose main goal is to assess overall program outcomes.

Another major issue affecting the results of multisite evaluations is differences in client risk levels. As discussed in more detail next, it is essential that any evaluation, most especially a multisite one, gather data about client risk levels so that analyses can adjust results to account for client differences at each site. An additional problem for multisite evaluations is the pattern of client attachment and departure from the program. When some programs try to attract youth for extended periods of years but others consider their task done in a period of 4–6 weeks, the impacts of the programs are likely to be so different that one probably would not want to include them in the same evaluation even if nominally they have some of the same goals.

Specific Issues Important to Service Integration Programs Serving Youth

All program evaluations face issues of selection bias, identifying appropriate control or comparison groups, and conducting follow-up data collection without creating bias due to differential attrition, to name just a few. Standard evaluation texts discuss these issues, and we do not repeat this basic information here (see., e.g., Burt & Resnick, 1992; Harrell, 1996; Hatry, Blair, Fisk, & Kimmel, 1987; Mark & Cook, 1984; Martin & Kettner, 1996; Mohr, 1995; Patton, 1990; Rossi & Freeman, 1993), although we do briefly summarize these issues for the reader. In this section we concentrate on issues of particular importance to evaluations of youth-serving programs that involve treatment, prevention, and youth development elements, including whom the program wants to include as a participant or client for evaluation purposes, the importance of taking into account (potentially different) client risk levels, and difficulties in documenting service delivery and other process aspects of the programs.

Defining the Participant and the Unit of Analysis

Some programs have a clear way of knowing when someone becomes a client and when someone stops being a client. A formal intake procedure marks the entry point. Completing the full intervention marks exit from the program. However, many programs have some trouble deciding when someone has really become a client or when someone has stopped being a client, because the nature of their involvement with the program may change very gradually over time. When conducting an evaluation, one expects to describe the program's effects on its participants. Therefore program staff and evaluators together must think through what it means for someone to be a program client or participant and who should be included as a participant in the evaluation.

Defining a client by intake status. Most programs have some clearly identifiable intake procedures. A simple approach would be to define youth who have gone through these procedures as program clients; those who have not begun or completed the procedures would not be considered clients and therefore would be excluded from evaluation.

However, the process of attachment to a program can be vague. If a youth has one or two phone conversations with program staff or even pays the program one or two visits, but this occurs without benefit of formal intake and several months before the youth begins to attend program activities regularly, when did that youth become a client? What if the program staff spend a lot of time (say, up to half of one of its two staff members' time) talking to and advising youth who never attend regularly—are these youth clients? Is it fair to expect the program to affect their lives, as is implied by including them in an outcome evaluation? On the other hand, is it fair to exclude these youth from an evaluation, even if there may be more of them in raw numbers than youth who attend regularly? How does the program get "credit" for them?

A more difficult issue is what to do with youth and others, such as parents, who benefit from a program's prevention activities without ever going through an intake procedure. A program may reach many youth and adults through classroom or community presentations, without maintaining a list of participants. One option for evaluations is simply to count the number of such people reached, or the number of presentations made. Another option is to conduct pre–post surveys of the nonclient participants' knowledge, attitudes, and behaviors that the program is trying to change. Yet a third alternative is to try to assess communitywide impacts by surveying the general public for knowledge about the program; perceptions of its impact; and most important, community members' knowledge, attitudes, and behaviors with respect to the prevention topic. An ultimate impact measure would be communitywide rates for the behaviors in question (e.g., pregnancy rates, high school completion rates, drug arrest rates), although such a measure would be fair only if the program had taken on the task of trying to change a whole community's behavior and if the rates could reflect the particular geographic area targeted by the program.

Defining a client by exit or completion status. A standard evaluation approach is to assume that some standard service package is "the program" and to begin measuring program impact from the time clients complete "the program." But this approach entails some significant drawbacks for many programs serving at-risk youth.

Programs for at-risk youth typically are flexible in their service provision and do not penalize youth who do not come consistently or do not participate in some program components. This program orientation has important implications for designing an appropriate evaluation. Irregular program attendance may simply be a fact of life for at-risk youth, because many lead relatively chaotic lives (or their parents do). Doing anything regularly may be difficult for them. Even if the youth are consistent attenders, the program may not have a set of core services, or its "core" may include only a small proportion of the service and activity options the program makes available to youth.

One source of this trouble, common to many youth-serving agencies, may be that the program tries to operate as a club, membership organization, or family. Once attached, users or members are encouraged to stay around for years, perhaps changing roles as they grow older (e.g., becoming mentors themselves), perhaps coming around less but still dropping by on occasion. There is no set intervention or group of services that everyone receives, nor is there a level of performance that, once achieved, is considered completion.

The issue of when a client has left the program is not unique to programs operating as clubs. Programs of many other types also have difficulty specifying what they consider to be "program completion," and many approaches may be taken. Some programs will have a well-defined set of core services or activities that participants are expected to complete. Those who do so can be considered program graduates (although they still may not leave). Other programs may have a status or role (such as counselor or peer mentor) which, if attained, means a youth has graduated from the program's basic activities to a different level. An evaluation might consider such youth to be finished with the program. When programs have neither a well-defined set of services nor a marker for graduation, it may be hard to tell who has finished. For these programs, one would want to structure follow-up in terms of time since program entry rather than in terms of time since finishing the program.

At-risk youth may stop coming to a program at some early point because they do not feel it meets their needs, because of problems related to accessibility, or because they do not get along with program staff. If an evaluation defines program participation at a specified minimum level of involvement, then the probability of selection biases is increased. That is, if the intervention group is defined as those who received the full program intervention, they are likely to differ from those who drop out. Any differences observed by the evaluation might then be a function of initial group differences (self-selection) rather than of the actual intervention. A good evaluation design would need to correct for these potential biases.

   Handling "clients by association." **Boyfriends and girlfriends.** Problems similar to those faced with the infrequent participant arise in considering individuals whose contact with the program is peripheral to that of a primary client. In adolescent pregnancy programs, this issue frequently arises for boys and sometimes for family members also. Some programs only address the service needs of boys if they are the boyfriends of the girls who are the program's primary clients; they do not consider the boys to be clients in their own right. Other programs help teenage boys whether or not their girlfriends are in the program and do count them as clients. These programs may spend equal amounts of time helping boys, but if the evaluators use the program's definition of a client, the latter programs' efforts will "register" in an evaluation, whereas those of the former programs will not.

   Parents and family members. Parallel problems arise in deciding how an evaluation should handle services to families. Many programs try to get parents involved, often as adjunct "staff" or as coaches trying to reinforce the program's values for their own children. Service integration programs may address family needs directly because the family's situation is adversely affecting the youth in the program. For example, programs may help parents get drug treatment, or housing, or income supports, or job training, or parenting skills training to reduce abusive behavior. In such cases, who should be considered the client? If the family is the primary client (as is the case in one of the sites we visited), then the situation is reversed. We must ask whether each child should also be considered a separate client, even if a given child may not participate in program activities.

   Neighborhood or community as "client." Even further from the standard service delivery model is the situation in which a program is trying to change conditions in a whole neighborhood. If a program's target is a whole neighborhood, it may not be appropriate at all to use an evaluation design based on the experiences of individuals who are in direct contact with the program. Rather, some type of community rate (probably collected by public agencies), neighborhood survey, or other aggregated data in which a random sample of neighborhood residents respond to questions measuring important outcomes may be more appropriate. Such a survey could also assess changes (increases) in parental and other adult participation in PTAs, tenant councils, and chemical dependency treatment or prevention programs and other signs that the community's adults are taking on more neighborhood responsibilities. It is also possible to use observations and unobtrusive measures, as Schinke et al. (1992) did in counting the number of crack vials and needles found on streets or the number of shooting incidents around the neighborhood in an evaluation of a program designed to reduce drug involvement among youth in housing projects. (Both decreased after the program began operating.)

Implications. There are no right answers to the question of Who is a client?, but it is a key question. If only one program is involved in an evaluation, the answers for that evaluation should be negotiated between the evaluators and program staff until both are satisfied that the program will be fairly represented by the clients or users included in the evaluation. If an evaluation covers a number of programs, even more negotiation will be necessary to reach a definition of program entry and program exit that all can agree on and that does not seriously misrepresent some of the programs involved. Furthermore, the evaluation design may have to be somewhat flexible to accommodate program differences. These agreements may include different classes of clients (e.g., youth, families as a whole, boyfriends and girlfriends, or siblings who are not primary clients themselves, etc).

A solution to the problem of identifying program clients is to divide the evaluation design into several components. For the fully participating clients, standard and thorough evaluation procedures would be applied. For prevention clients, such as those reached through classroom outreach, or for "clients by association," the evaluation can design an approach that is appropriate to their level of involvement and probable program impact. The same can be done for neighborhood impact. The critical point is to recognize when designing the evaluation is that it may not be appropriate to treat all persons in contact with the program identically for evaluation purposes and that the design should be adjusted accordingly. The design can be structured to accommodate different approaches for each major way that clients come into contact with the program.

If the definitions finally negotiated do omit some significant numbers of youth or other people who have had program contact, the evaluators should develop some way to reflect this level of effort even if these people will not be included in formal follow-ups and impact assessments. Often simple counts will do, along with an assessment of how much time the program commits to this type of contact. For example, in the multisite evaluation of adolescent pregnancy programs funded by the Department of Health and Human Services' Office of Adolescent Pregnancy Programs (Burt, Kimmich, Goldmuntz, & Sonenstein, 1984), programs reported both the number of nonclient counseling and referral calls they handled and the number of hours they devoted to this effort. Often these calls were from pregnant teenagers who were not sure that the program was right for them; program staff spent a good deal of time talking with them until they decided but had "nothing to show for it" if the teen decided not to join the program as a new client. With these "nonclient" data, programs were able to show funders that their support was being used to serve the community in ways that complemented service delivery to formal clients. Of course, if a significant proportion of program effort goes into these activities, an evaluation that focuses on outcomes for the more intensive program services may not actually assess significant aspects of the program's impact.

A further implication of the foregoing is that the package of services offered by youth-serving programs with a prevention youth development focus is usually too multifaceted and too flexible for an evaluation to use "program exit" or "program completion" as the point at which impact evaluation begins. For these programs, it seems much more appropriate to use the point of program entry as the time to begin. This decision, of course, has its own implications for the thoroughness with which service delivery must be measured.

Differences in Client Risk Levels That May Affect Services Received and Evaluation Plans

Programs for youth may serve a very wide age range (10–19, and sometimes both younger and older). Youth of different ages within this range are likely to have very different needs and to experience very different risk probabilities. Youth programs are quite likely to offer some combination of preventive activities and treatment services and may also facilitate access to housing, income maintenance, and other concrete services for the families of youth in the program. Because of the age range of interest, it is likely that programs will serve some youth whose situations are only moderately risky alongside others who are already in serious trouble. As a result, activities and services offered to youth are likely to differ widely. Some programs may attempt to serve all youth; others will specialize in a particular age group or in youth engaging in a particular type of problem behavior. Cross-program evaluations and evaluations of programs serving a wide range of ages and risk levels need to decide how to incorporate and understand the effects of this diversity.

Effects of risk level on selection into a program. A client's risk level may affect which program a client enters. Youth at low risk may enter youth development or prevention programs where activities are the primary focus, whereas youth at higher risk (or youth who are already in trouble) may enter or be placed in case management or treatment programs.

The biases involved in the effects of risk on selection into a program must be faced in any multiprogram evaluation. Such evaluations need to ensure that the programs included in the evaluation all are serving youth with roughly similar risk levels or else that the design includes enough programs serving youth at different risk levels so that researchers can analyze differences within and between programs grouped by the average risk level of their clients.

Effects of risk level on mix of services received. A client's risk level may affect which service components of a comprehensive program he or she is offered. The biases involved in the effects of risk on service delivery within programs are faced by every evaluation. The inconsistencies of program delivery (which the program sees as flexibility) offer a number of opportunities as well as challenges for evaluators. An evaluator can examine the process by which programs determine who needs what—programs may appropriately offer a different mix of services to different youth. An important evaluation question is, How do programs determine who needs what?

In programs that emphasize activities over services, as many youth-serving programs do, some service needs may be overlooked. In any program, a youth is only likely to be referred for services if a staff person has become aware that the youth has some service need. In heavily activity-oriented programs, routine and comprehensive needs assessments may not be done. For instance, in mentoring programs, a youth's mentor may not make a systematic effort to identify new service needs as they arise, even if a program staff person has conducted an initial needs assessment. Therefore service delivery may look erratic in these programs. An important evaluation issue in the context of programs set up this way is whether the program misses many existing service needs. It might also be important to address what happens to youth when their needs are not met. Either of these evaluation options requires the evaluator to conduct needs assessments for all clients. Although such evaluation activities may be seen as disruptive to the program, they have been obtained in some instances through negotiation. For these needs assessments to happen, the program or the program funder must care about whether the program identifies and addresses most of its clients' needs.

No evaluation should make the assumption that an organization delivers "a program" similarly for all clients, regardless of risk level. Therefore every evaluation, including those for youth-serving programs, has to plan to collect measures of initial client risk status (also sometimes called *client difficulty*). These data will be used in outcome analyses to qualify any observed results, either by analyzing results separately for different risk groups or by entering initial risk level as a covariate or control variable in regression, analysis of variance, or other statistical treatments. The former is a safer approach because the latter assumes that risk can be measured as a continuum and that the continuum is linear. In reality, risk may be multidimensional, bi- or multimodal, and quite nonlinear.

Client risk levels may be used in analysis to understand or qualify evaluation results. Study participants who show improvements may have a relatively low risk level. The program may only have helped those with some preexisting competencies and skills. In other cases, the program may have been most helpful to those who were the least functional when they entered the program. For example, Project Redirection used initial risk level information (e.g., whether in school or dropout; AFDC [Aid to Families with Dependent Children] recipient or not) and participation levels (months of active program participation) to understand which teenagers benefited most from the program. The analysis indicated that those teens who benefited most were those who faced the greatest obstacles to self-sufficiency at program entry (Polit, Quint, & Riccio, 1988). In either case, recognizing the impact of client risk levels and planning the evaluation so they are available for use in regression or other multivariate analysis will increase the accuracy of interpretation. In some cases using client risk levels can prevent researchers from drawing false conclusions, as would have happened if the Project Redirection researchers had stopped their analysis when results showed no effects for all clients taken together. The real impact of the program was only visible when clients were grouped by risk level.

Implications. It is crucial that multiprogram evaluations plan for the high probability that client risk levels will differ among programs. It is almost as likely that single-program evaluations will encounter clients with very different risk levels. Evaluators must develop designs that can assess the effects of varying risk levels on outcomes of interest. This means that programs being evaluated must have record-keeping procedures (and preferably a management information system) capable of recording both the problems of youth at risk who are actual clients and the types and amount of services each youth receives (Jacobs, 1988). The quantification of risk is a new and highly experimental enterprise. Until measures of risk achieve acceptable levels of reliability and validity (Wells, Fluke, Downing, & Brown, 1989), recording risk levels will not be simple. We would approach this by having programs record at intake the presence in a youth's background of factors (antecedents, markers, problem behaviors, risk outcomes) included in the risk model described in Chapter 4. Then the evaluation will have the information and can use the variables as controls in any combination where needed in the analysis. Furthermore, using multiple measures of risk to create a composite score reduces measurement error and yields better results.

To have sufficient statistical power to detect differences in outcomes among youth with different levels of risk, an evaluation must have planned for a sample large enough to include subgroups of adequate size. For many of these programs, it may take longer than expected to assemble the required sample and subsample sizes. Longer evaluations may be more costly and will certainly take longer to produce results.

Documenting Service Delivery

Early in an evaluation project of comprehensive service integration efforts, researchers will identify the services available in the network, the existence and nature of the links between program components, and the program's expectations (hypotheses) for how these components will affect client outcomes. This set of clear predictions tells the evaluator what elements of system functioning must be documented to trace program impact, and it lets the evaluator distinguish between intended and unintended program benefits.

A "black box" evaluation (Cronbach et al., 1980) is one that assumes that the treatment group gets "the program," that the control group does not get "the program," and that the evaluator knows what "the program" is without having to measure actual program delivery. This type of outcome evaluation is not able to identify which program components are most effective under what kinds of local conditions. Rather than asking the question of whether a program "works," we should be asking how it works, what components are the "active ingredients," under what conditions, and for whom (Weiss, 1983). Not knowing these specifics makes it harder to recommend future applications of a demonstration program or to translate results into broader policy directions.

In reality it is the very rare program that is delivered virtually identically to every participant. It is our belief that no agency actually delivers "the program on paper" to each one of its clients. Even the most carefully structured and precisely defined program will not be able to treat every client exactly the same way. Most programs do not attempt such uniformity, and many consider it contrary to their philosophy. Even curriculum-based interventions vary from teacher to teacher, although all children in a single classroom presumably are exposed to the same input (if they are not absent and if they are paying attention). The best approach to documenting each possible program configuration is to be sure the evaluation obtains data on actual service delivery, including participation in activities, for each client and each activity or service. A management information system will facilitate this type of data collection. At the very least, a manual method of recording client participation or service receipt must be in place and must be used.

Another problem involves documenting services provided by agencies other than the program on which the evaluation is focused. It is relatively common for programs to refer their clients to other agencies for needed services without having any system in place to get feedback from the referral agencies as to the client's actual receipt of services. In these programs there is no one file that contains all the information about a given client's receipt of services. Programs may even resist the need to know whether clients got the services for which they were referred. They see their responsibility as making the referral; and the client has the responsibility to follow through. It is critical that the evaluators of service integration projects develop arrangements to get feedback from referral agencies about the actual delivery of services, as this is one of the fundamental mechanisms through which the program is supposed to work. If it is not known whether clients are receiving services, it is not known whether the program is functioning as intended. If it is not functioning as intended, it cannot have the impact that is expected.

Even case management programs, which specialize in service delivery by referrals and accessing community resources, may find it difficult to record all client contacts and services received. It is even more difficult to get programs whose major focus is growth-enhancing activities or recreation to record participation. Their emphasis is on keeping the youth involved, not on solving a particular problem in a relatively short time period. Evaluation is especially challenging if services and activities are handled by different people (e.g., a mentor does enjoyable activities with youth but sends the youth to a case manager if specific services are needed).

Participation in activities can be recorded with a daily sign-in log or similar mechanism, which will not capture precise levels of participation, but the program staff probably will be less inconvenienced than if a more precise mechanism is required, and data recording the number of days a month the youth attended the program can serve as a proxy for detailed participation records. If the program has some staff who handle service assessments and referrals, these staff should record the actual services delivered to youth.

It is essential that service integration efforts maintain accurate records of service delivery in order to do justice to a program offering comprehensive services (where most clients will not get many services, but any client can get a service if needed). When contemplating doing an evaluation, researchers should examine the program's current practices and future ability to record service delivery on a client-by-client basis. To provide maximum flexibility in analysis and adequately represent the program as delivered to clients, it is important to have, or to develop, a systematic method for recording who got what services and who participated in what activities. If the program also relies on interagency collaboration to supply some or many program services, documentation of service delivery on a client-by-client basis should be a core component of any evaluation for formative purposes as well as for outcome analysis.

Evaluation planners should consider augmenting quantitative records of service delivery with qualitative and observational methods, which make interpretations of quantitative results more valid. For example, the quantitative data from an evaluation of an early childhood intervention to prevent school failure (Travers, Nauta, & Irwin, 1981) showed no improvements in the children's cognitive abilities. This finding suggested that the cognitive stimulation curricula, delivered via home visits, was not effective. However, qualitative techniques showed that home visitors often were not able to deliver the planned curriculum because they had to help the parents deal with more concrete living problems, such as housing evictions, physical safety, and financial problems. In effect, the program never happened, so it could not show any effects.

Comparison or Control Groups

To demonstrate that a program made a difference, outcomes for program participants or communities must be compared with something, either with outcomes for some comparison group of nonparticipants (or another whole community) or with the participants' preprogram behaviors to serve as their own controls. Own-control designs work best when participants have exhibited a stable characteristic over a number of years (e.g., average annual days of hospitalization), and that stability would be expected to continue if the program does not intervene to change it. These designs are not a good choice for youth, because youth are in too much flux for any preprogram characteristics to be stable or to be expected to stay stable during the measurement period in the absence of the program.

This leaves various comparison or control group options. Figure 16.1, taken from Harrell (1996), gives a quick overview of design choices, taking account of the opportunities and circumstances in which programs find themselves. Harrell has provided an easy-to-understand discussion of design options, and the reader can also consult any standard evaluation text for discussions of the trade-offs among aspects of internal and external validity, practicality, and compatibility with program and community values.

Reducing Attrition at Follow-up

Any evaluation with a goal of learning whether a program makes a long-term difference for clients involves the problem of staff having to contact all of the program's participants at some follow-up time, such as 1 year after program entry. Researchers often cannot find a significant number of participants in this follow-up effort, and this problem is known as *attrition from follow-up*. Initial sample sizes must be large enough to assure that the final follow-up sample will have enough respondents to test hypotheses even with expected attrition. Follow-up methods must assure, to the extent possible, that people lost to follow-up do not differ in important ways from the people for whom data were collected. At the very least, biases introduced by attrition should be examined. Maintaining contact with both treatment and control or comparison groups at follow-up is essential for results to be credible. Often too few resources or too little ingenuity are put into this effort, particularly if the follow-up is left to program staff to do in addition to their regular duties rather than assigned to people whose only job it is to complete follow-ups. Many longitudinal investigations provide interesting case studies of methods for reducing attrition at follow-up.

Program Evaluability

Readiness for Summative Evaluation

Evaluators often speak of two forms of evaluation: formative and summative. A *formative* evaluation tries to provide a program with feedback about its implementation or procedures so the program can identify its strengths and weaknesses, build on the former, and work to correct the latter. *Summative* evaluation tries to assess whether the program has met its goals for affecting the lives of its clients. For example, youth programs might be trying to promote school completion; abstinence from drugs, alcohol, or sexual behavior; lawfulness; development of business and entrepreneurial skills; or a sense of investment and pride in one's community.

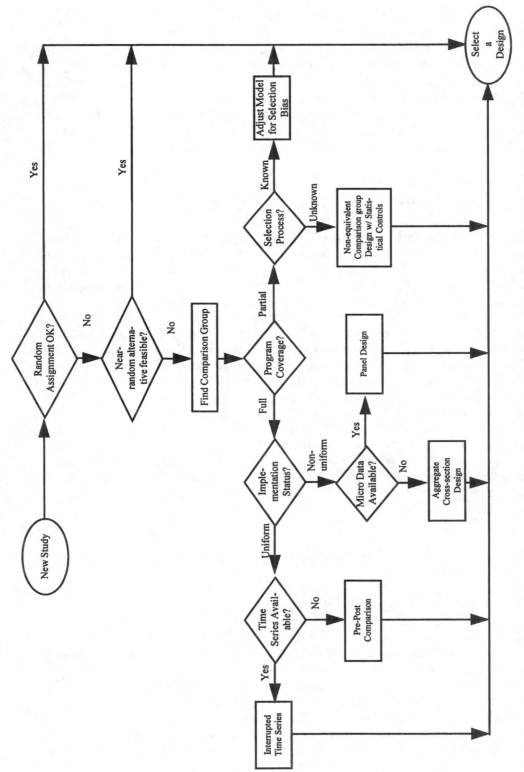

Figure 16.1. Decision tree for selecting impact evaluation designs. From A. Harrell, 1996, *Evaluation Strategies for Human Services Programs: A Guide for Policymakers and Providers* (p. 18). Washington, DC: Urban Institute Press. Reprinted with permission.

A summative evaluation would indicate how well the program has succeeded in helping its clients to achieve these outcomes.

Most programs, whatever their stage of development, can benefit from formative evaluation efforts, including assessments of program implementation and service delivery processes. But not all programs are ready for summative or impact evaluation, and it is summative evaluation that we focus on here. There is some question as to whether many comprehensive service integration programs for at-risk youth are ready, because this is a relatively new and developing type of program. Those that have been in stable operation for 10 years or longer are certainly ready. Others that are just beginning to assemble their network and negotiate interagency agreements probably are not ready. Mark and Cook (1984) have maintained that the major weakness of past summative evaluations has been the premature use of experimentation. One needs extensive prior knowledge of program operation to conduct a valid summative evaluation, including knowledge that the treatment is well developed; that it will be implemented as planned; that measures are available, appropriate, and well developed; and that the "ecology" of the program is well understood (Mark & Cook, 1984). It can do more harm than good to evaluate a program that does not meet these criteria.

Typically, one begins any potential evaluation endeavor with an evaluability assessment (Schmidt, Horst, Scanlon, & Wholey, 1975; Wholey & Newcomer, 1989). During the evaluability assessment process, researchers identify the expected short-, medium-, and long-term goals of the program; the program components that are designed to produce the desired outcomes; the assumptions underlying the connection between program inputs and outcomes; and whether outcomes are measurable (Ruttman, 1984). Understanding the community context in which the program operates is also important, including the preprogram allocation of human, organizational, and financial resources in the community and how the program fits into these arrangements. Then one can examine whether the program tried, and if it tried whether it succeeded, in changing these arrangements and to what effect.

Certain circumstances might render a full-scale summative evaluation of a program unreasonable. The program might be very new, undergoing major reorganization, or experiencing widespread staffing changes. The program might not have the ability, or the willingness, to record the types and amounts of data that a full-scale evaluation would require. The program might be stable and have a good record-keeping system but lack a clearly articulated set of goals for clients or reasons for offering the services they do. Or they may have goals for which no reasonable measures exist. If the reason for funding an evaluation is to identify the effects of programs that conform to a certain model, it is important to assess whether each program under consideration actually fits the model. In the case of service integration programs, one would want to assess whether the program as it actually operates has service linkages that are so fragile, casual, or opportunistic as to lead to the conclusion that the program did not really represent a service integration effort. In addition, one would want to know whether other programs in the service network will cooperate in collecting data on services and activities actually used by youth.

Finally, evaluation resources must be adequate and timetables must be long enough to allow the true impacts of the program to be observed. For most youth-serving programs, and most especially the preventive ones, one should not expect to see statistically significant changes on major outcome variables for a number of years. One might, however, look for shifts in the right direction that only reach statistical significance after several years, as happened in the evaluation of the Quantum Opportunities Program (Hahn, 1995).

Willingness and Capability

Willingness refers to the attitudes, perceptions, and beliefs that staff communicate about the potential utility of an evaluation study and their motivation to help carry one out. In particular, one would be interested in identifying any possible negative attitudes toward evaluation research as well as expectations for gaining benefits from an evaluation. *Capability* refers to the resources that programs already have in place that either enhance or constrain the potential for conducting an impact or outcome evaluation, including staffing patterns, resources, and informational systems. Finally, an important factor affecting both capability and willingness is the program's history of participating in evaluation efforts, because this experience will contribute toward existing capabilities as well as to positive or negative staff and management attitudes about the experience.

The programs visited during the research project illustrate how programs may appear on the dimensions of willingness and capability. As might be expected, the programs differed widely in terms of both willingness and capability. Generally, those with the highest levels of capability were also those with more positive attitudes toward evaluation, although there were some cases in which the two dimensions did not correspond exactly.

Willingness. At the time of our visits, most of the programs showed an interest in doing more evaluation research and assessing program outcomes in particular. Seven programs expressed a high degree of interest in doing more evaluation. When expressing such interest, many executive directors specifically indicated that they wanted to do some form of longitudinal follow-up of their clients, feeling that what happens to clients years later is an indicator of the program's success. The enthusiasm of some program staff was related to earlier positive experiences with evaluation studies. Staff at the remaining programs may not have had experience with outcome evaluations, but they did have to report some types of data from their information systems and had conducted process evaluation studies. Individuals at some of these programs were enthusiastic but somewhat naive about evaluation. The staff were highly motivated to do anything that would be required of them but felt they would need technical assistance, and at that point they had not been successful in finding any. At the time of our visits, these programs had not received any financial support to pursue development of an evaluation system, even though funders had suggested they do more evaluation. Subsequently, several of them did have special data systems or evaluation projects underway.

Capability. The programs we visited could be grouped into low-, moderate-, and high-capability levels on the basis of their existing resources, research experience, and level of documentation at the time of our visits. The low-capability programs appeared to lack the existing resources required for an evaluation study. In these programs, either staff were not knowledgeable about evaluation research, few concrete resources existed to support an evaluation, or both.

Information systems in these programs were at a relatively primitive level. Although some information was collected through documentation of client backgrounds, monitoring of service utilization, and in some cases client goals, little of this was systematically aggregated, with the exception of the information required by funding sources. Information systems at these programs were not computerized, and it was not always clear how information was aggregated for reports. There did not appear to be one central unit or department responsible for putting the information together.

These programs also had some trouble tracking the involvement of outside agencies, which would be an important component of documentation for service integration types of programs. Once a referral was made to another agency or another agency provided services to a client, there often was not much feedback or recording of the extent of the services received.

Some programs were at the mid-level of evaluation capability at the time of our visits. At a minimum, these programs maintained some form of computerized database system in which service and client statistics were input regularly. These systems were used to generate reports for funding sources and provided feedback to program staff on client flow rates, intakes and terminations, and client backgrounds. Typically, this capability also involved having staff whose job responsibilities included updating the database regularly by entering new forms as they were completed. These programs kept extensive records on what services clients received, the length of stay of clients in the program, client backgrounds and assessment of risk, and information about the involvement of outside agency partners in either the referral or service provision processes. Some programs still relied on the executive director to analyze the service statistics, but generally top management was supported by volunteers and staff who completed the forms and did the initial tabulation of the information.

The moderate-capability programs were also distinguished from the lower levels of capability by their ability to use the documented information for the purposes of planning and internal evaluation. For example, one program had in place a system whereby risk assessment data were collected at two time intervals over a period of 4–6 weeks, at the beginning and end of short-term crisis counseling (for the treatment clients). Although this information was used only to inform counseling decisions, having the system in place gave the program a higher capability for evaluation than some other programs.

Another characteristic of the moderate-capability programs is that they had relatively well-formulated and sometimes quite specific plans for improving their evaluation capability. One program had already collected client outcome data from some of its program components, and it planned to incorporate outcome-based evaluation into others, including a 90-day follow-up after clients completed an early intervention program. Another program had plans to expand its respondent base for a mail survey to gather information on youth, parent, and volunteer experiences with the program and the satisfactions they derived from participating in it.

Despite such well-articulated evaluation plans, this group of programs had some reservations about the potential trade-off between the costs and benefits of an evaluation study. Some were concerned that because evaluation research activities were usually covered under agency overhead, they must be funded by indirect rather than direct service funds. Yet funders were reluctant to provide more money for administrative overhead, and as a nonprofit agency, the program felt continually pressured to reduce overhead costs. Thus although the interest was high, there was a sense that the resources available for evaluation were insufficient and that real obstacles existed to future evaluation research that would need to be overcome. Other programs in this group articulated similar concerns, although not as directly.

Finally, several programs had high levels of capability, including highly sophisticated computerized management information systems. They also had staff specifically assigned to do the data entry, compilation, and generation of summary statistics to give top-level management current information ready for analysis. One program had a very sophisticated level of documentation, with a research director and staff responsible for the design and operation of a relatively complete computerized management information system. A manual outlined all of the documentation forms and provided well-specified steps for completing the forms and sending them to the central office for data entry. All staff were given a once-a-year training and update in the use of the information system, and project managers were responsible for checking the accuracy of forms before sending them to the central office. All programs had extensively documented all aspects of their activities, including the prevention activities, and included data on their interactions with affiliated agencies when program clients received services from these affiliates.

The high-capability programs usually had conducted some form of evaluation research in the past or were doing so at the time of our visits. The evaluation studies were generally small scale and primarily used internally to identify targets for planning and service utilization. The most established form of an evaluation system included pre–post assessments of a youth's participation in each program module, tracked service delivery over time, and has used a quasi-experimental design with a comparison group to assess outcomes. These programs tracked important data on service delivery and client participation, satisfaction, and outcome. They collected a wide range of information from youth, staff, and affiliated agencies. One program also had a variety of mechanisms already in place that would assist an outcome evaluation, including a 1-year follow-up of all youth in one of its program components; goal attainment scaling conducted by front-line staff; and a set of outcomes at termination from a program, including the youth's disposition when he or she left the agency.

An interesting finding among the high-capability programs was that they maintained excellent documentation and information systems as well as a high level of readiness despite some negative experiences with prior evaluation research. For example, one program was part of a statewide evaluation of state-funded programs offering alternatives to placing juveniles in detention facilities. The program staff were substantially dissatisfied with this evaluation; they perceived it as not meeting their needs, being overly intrusive and rigid, and not being competently performed (especially the forms they were given to complete, which appeared lacking in sufficient operational definitions). The evaluation also suffered from conflicting expectations between the various stakeholders in the evaluation results. The staff were concerned that the evaluation findings could negatively affect the program if the results did not match the overly high expectations of these stakeholders. The solution, which appeared to be characteristic of all high-capability programs, involved implementing their own documentation and information system so they could maintain control over the site-specific data and how it would be used.

The staff at all high-capability programs had high hopes for future evaluations and specifically wanted to track both prevention and treatment clients after they left the program. Programs offering services at more than one location also wanted to conduct a comparison between sites to identify planning issues specific to how the program was delivered at each site. This type of comparison was particularly germane to one program that operated in 21 sites. All of these programs clearly indicated that any costs accrued from doing evaluation research were more than compensated for by the benefits of the information obtained.

Who Should Conduct Evaluations?

The experience of many evaluation efforts suggests that, in addition to their regular duties, program staff should not be expected to conduct the evaluation or collect significant amounts of data for it. They do not have the time, and they will always place a higher priority on responding to the needs of clients than on systematic data collection, which is appropriate to the staff's role.

This means that the evaluators (those who do the actual work of evaluation) should be outsiders. But outsiders may not really understand the program or be responsive to its needs and concerns. Two of the programs we visited gave examples of how evaluation can go wrong from the perspective of the program staff. Staff at both programs had had experiences with evaluators that left them feeling the evaluators were not sensitive to the concerns of their clients or were not able to reflect the complexity of client experiences in the program. One program worked with an evaluator for the national demonstration program of which they were a part. The evaluator imposed record-keeping forms that seemed inappropriate or offensive to the youth. The program staff also felt that the evaluator was not sensitive enough to the African American youth population that made up the program's clientele. The program was continuing to participate in the national evaluation, after making some adjustments in the way the evaluator dealt with the program and its clients.

The staff at the second program did not want an evaluation to oversimplify or misrepresent the complexity of the program or of clients' experiences in it. The program had had one experience with evaluation that staff felt was not an adequate reflection of the program; in particular they felt that its rather cut-and-dried approach to outcome evaluation did not do justice to either their services or the benefits their clients derived from the program.

For an evaluation to be a good one, an outside evaluator needs to take the time to get to know the program and work carefully with the program staff to develop mutually agreeable arrangements. Furthermore, evaluation funders need to allow enough resources to provide researchers to get to know the program (Quinn, 1992). The effect will be to have an "insider's" outside evaluation, which is likely to be more valuable to insiders and outsiders alike. The resulting evaluation design and products will be well worth the effort in terms of program good will and in terms of a qualitative and quantitative documentation of program activities and impacts.

Evaluators and Program Staff Working Together

From the program perspective, the best evaluations are those that do not disrupt program activities, do not place a heavy burden on program staff, and reflect the program and its goals in a positive light. Although evaluators may place major emphasis on numbers and types of services (e.g., to demonstrate comprehensiveness or to show the effects of service integration), programs may feel this emphasis does not reflect their overarching purpose of youth development, growth enhancement, or leadership training (Pittman & Cahill, 1992).

Because most youth-serving programs do not evaluate themselves, the claims they make to their communities about program impact may be exaggerated. Individuals running such programs may fear evaluation, because they fear the data will not support their claims. It is critical for evaluators to work with program staff until they understand the possible benefits of evaluation and are prepared to support the evaluation effort.

Working with program staff until they are satisfied with evaluation plans is relatively easy when only one program is involved and that program has hired the evaluator. For evaluations imposed from outside, the situation is sometimes more difficult. It reaches maximum difficulty in multisite evaluations. Multisite evaluations usually occur when a foundation or federal funder provides financial support and cooperation with the evaluation is a condition of receiving project money. Often the funder, not the program, specifies the goals and outcomes to be examined. This situation needs to be handled very delicately to avoid alienating the staff at the programs involved, because each program may have a different service configuration and interpret success in its own way. Occasionally a youth-serving organization with many affiliates will undertake its own evaluation, as did the Boys and Girls Clubs of America (Schinke et al., 1992), Girls Incorporated and Big Brothers/Big Sisters of America (described in Quinn, 1992). The Center for Substance Abuse Prevention (HHS) funded the first two evaluations, and foundations funded the third through the evaluator Public/Private Ventures, Inc. In these three cases, the parent national organization controlled the evaluation and took pains to structure the work to be compatible with national and local goals and with the workload and operating procedures of local affiliates.

For an evaluator, there is a significant difference between a situation where a program funder has required an evaluation and one where an evaluation is requested by a parent organization. In the former situation, the evaluator ultimately answers to the program funder, whereas in the latter the evaluator answers to the program. Evaluators involved in the first type of evaluation should try to shape their behavior as if they were involved in the second type, if they want to gain the greatest degree of cooperation from the programs. This may take some diplomatic negotiating, to simultaneously remain responsive to the funders' questions.

Quinn (1992) has detailed many suggestions for maximizing the mutual satisfaction of programs and evaluators. These include the following:

- Include planning for evaluation as an integral part of planning for the program itself;
- Help program staff understand in nontechnical ways the different types of evaluation, their purposes, and what they can do for programs;
- Involve staff in decisions about what level of evaluation to conduct, in specifying important program outcomes and in defining measures of success that make sense to the program;
- Recognize and work with the "daily life" of a program, including potential difficulties with random or quasi-experimental design, the flow and flexibility of program activities, and youth participation, and plan the evaluation accordingly; and
- Include in the evaluation design plans to document the community context, service system context, and other contexts in which the program operates, so program staff see that the evaluators understand the program and will be able to present it accurately to the outside world.

Evaluators who follow this advice will produce evaluations that are more useful for both the program and the sponsor.

Concluding Thoughts

Programs addressing school dropout, teenage pregnancy and parenting, substance abuse, and delinquency have certain characteristics that are specific to their problem focus, yet analyses of many evaluations (Dryfoos, 1990; Office of Technology Assessment, 1991; Resnick, Burt, Newmark, & Reilly, 1992) have noted a surprising number of program elements of success that recur in evaluation after evaluation regardless of program focus. Successful youth-serving programs, those that evaluations have shown to make a difference for youth, are those that:

- Identify at-risk youth early and intervene early;
- Provide long-term and consistent intervention, with age-appropriate content changing over the years;
- Provide individualized attention and instruction, including intensive counseling as needed;
- Make comprehensive services available to youth, as needed, through on-site provision, colocation, or case management support;
- Include an emphasis on growth, skills enhancement, life options, and vocational orientation;
- Develop and use multiple channels of influence, including communitywide support and effort (e.g., media, church, parents/families, neighborhood prevention campaigns); and
- Provide a safe and stable physical environment for the program.

Obviously programs serving youth should heed these findings, and evaluators should be sure to include them in evaluation designs. This will make the designs more complex than simple summative statistics, but only by including these mechanisms of program operation as part of the design whose impact must be documented will an evaluation do justice to what makes the programs work.

Twenty years of evaluation studies focusing on service integration efforts also has revealed some common findings that future evaluators should heed (Kusserow, 1991a, 1991b). These evaluations were mostly concerned with treatment-oriented programs. They show that service integration efforts for these types of programs have indeed made services more accessible to clients and more responsive to their needs. Specifically, these efforts have enabled clients to obtain and benefit from services that they otherwise would not have received. Both the specific benefits and the general level of impact of service integration depended on the commitment and communication levels of agency staff in all linkage agencies and on institutional support and agreement from the participating agencies.

Kusserow (1991a, 1991b) has concluded, however, that service integration efforts usually have not been sustainable over the long run, because the underlying systems never really change. Therefore the interagency connections tend to atrophy unless carefully nurtured over time. He has listed six barriers commonly encountered by service integration efforts that limit the degree of system change that can be achieved:

- Size and complexity of the human services system;
- Professionalization, specialization, and bureaucratization;
- Limited influence of integrators;
- Weak constituency for service integration;
- Funding limitations; and
- Insufficient knowledge.

Service integration efforts to help at-risk youth also face these barriers. The programs visited for this project can offer some additional insights into the sustainability of service integration efforts. It seems clear to us that service integration works best when there is some entity committed to "the long haul." Several of our programs are approaching their 20th year, still with the same vision and the same commitment to developing activities and services for youth, maintaining those that already exist, and involving every element of their local community in the process. Some operate almost completely with formal interagency agreements, some operate almost completely without them, and some follow a mixed approach. The technical details of the network and the identity of its members in each case are less important than the existence of the committed agency and its continued ability to bring the community together to address its needs.

Anyone potentially interested in evaluating a program for at-risk youth might begin by exploring a number of the issues explored in this chapter. The history and community context of the program will be particularly important to understand because it will help determine the scope of a potential evaluation. One would also want to understand as much as possible about existing service integration linkages and arrangements, how these came about, and what the program staff think the linkages do for their clients. Given the importance of program goals in determining what outcomes to measure, one would want to talk with program and community informants at length to understand what the program is trying to do and how it sees its present approach as advancing those goals for its clients. In addition to a focus on potential evaluability, it would be important to catch the "gestalt" of the program and understand the choices faced by programs that try to serve at-risk youth. One would also explore program goals and program approaches in order to understand what program staff think youth need and how they feel they have to go about attracting and supporting youth.

The potential evaluator should be interested to learn whether the programs have participated in any evaluations or whether they have thought about evaluation. Staff attitudes toward evaluation should be assessed, and discussions should address what an evaluation would have to look like in order to be compatible with their program operations. It is important to examine any record-keeping systems they may have and to look at the mechanisms they have developed for recording participation and tracking client service needs and service receipt. It is also important to discuss the issues of how "clients" are defined and how the programs try to affect families and neighborhoods, if they do. Finally, if comprehensiveness is a focus, one would examine what the programs mean by "comprehensive" and the various routes they have taken to achieve access to services for their clients.

17

Financing Integrated Service Programs

Our review of nine youth-serving programs across the country raises a set of fundamental issues, most of which are likely to become more urgent in the near future. One significant issue is how to sustain funding for integrated service programs in an era of decreasing social service funding, resistance to new or higher taxes, managed care, results-based accountability, and devolution of responsibility for major social service programs from the federal to the state and local levels. Although some state and local governments are pioneering creative approaches to funding services for children and families, others may be constrained from doing so. Another critical issue is the role of nongovernmental funders in the new social service landscape. Although the nongovernmental players in this arena have traditionally been nonprofit organizations, corporations, and foundations, it may be necessary to develop new partnerships among these players in order to generate the support required to maintain a social safety net for vulnerable youth and their families. This chapter outlines some of the challenges related to financing social service programs and describes some of the innovative approaches that are being tried at the state and local levels.

Challenges

The central financing challenge for social service programs is to obtain funding that is sufficient and flexible enough to meet the complex needs of individual clients, their families, and the community at large. We will accept the challenge of finding sufficient funding as a given and describe four additional issues that are currently facing service providers at the local level. These are the devolution of federal programs to the state and local levels, centralization and fragmentation of funding streams, managed care, and time-limited funding. These are the challenges that now or will soon beset all social service programs.

The Impact of Devolution

The 1996 federal welfare reform law (Personal Responsibility and Work Opportunity Reconciliation Act of 1996, P.L. 104-193) represents a dramatic shift in responsibility for social service program from the federal to the state level. Although the welfare reform legislation focused primarily on ending the entitlement to welfare (AFDC) and delegating the responsibility for welfare-to-work programs to the states, it also made changes in a number of other social support programs that include children among their beneficiaries (SSI, food stamps and Title XX; U.S. Department of Health and Human Services, 1996b). These changes included a significant reduction in funding for Title XX, which states use to fund a wide range of social service programs for children and families. The fact that the legislation ended legal immigrants' entitlement to AFDC and food stamps means that states with large populations of legal immigrants have a significant new financial responsibility. On the positive side, states will have increased authority for the design and administration of social service programs related to welfare (Orland, Danegger, & Foley, 1995).

There are a number of reasons why states and local governments will find it difficult to take on the additional burdens created by welfare reform. States are facing a number of constraints in raising revenue for education and social service programs, including rising school enrollments, slower economic growth, and hostility to raising taxes (Cutler et al., 1995). Local governments will face many of the same problems. It is highly unlikely that nonprofit charitable and religious organizations will be able to fill the gaps in funding left by reduced federal and state dollars, despite the claims of the politicians who engineered the devolution process. It is also unlikely that private foundations and corporate philanthropy will be able to take on the role that the federal agencies have had, especially because their traditional role has been to provide seed or demonstration money rather than operational program dollars.

The ultimate test of devolution will be the impact on low-income children and their families. Several large foundations, including the Annie E. Casey Foundation, the Kellogg Foundation, the Henry J. Kaiser Family Foundation, and others are funding the Urban Institute to conduct a major multiyear study to determine the impact of devolution on children and families nationally and on a state-by-state basis. The study, called Assessing the New Federalism, will focus on the effect of changes in government programs and fiscal policies in the areas of health care, income security, job training, child welfare, and social services through the construction of a 50-state database containing indicators of significant changes in policy, funding, program participation rates, and key outcomes; intensive case studies of 13 states (including a detailed analysis of state spending on children); and a detailed household survey of the same subset of states (Urban Institute, 1996a). A number of other foundations, nonprofit research and advocacy organizations, and HHS are also funding studies of how welfare reform will affect children and families.

Centralization and Fragmentation

Many experts consider the structure of the current system for financing social services to be the most significant barrier to the development of prevention-oriented, community-based support systems for children and families (Farrow & Bruner, 1993; Gardner, 1994). Its fragmented and categorical funding streams, focus on process rather than outcome, and treatment rather than prevention have stood in the way of developing services that are locally controlled, prevention-focused, and oriented to the family as a unit (Gardner, 1994; Orland et al., 1995). Although there is some movement at the federal and state levels toward decentralized funding and an outcome rather than a process orientation, much of the social service delivery system is still structured in the traditional way.

It is too soon to tell whether decategorization will move beyond the federal welfare reform and a few state experiments. While the drama unfolds, most programs will continue to juggle numerous funding streams in order to keep their programs afloat (Burt et al., 1992; Dryfoos, 1994; interview with S. Kazanjian, 1996[1]). Dryfoos (1994) has noted that it is preferable for service providers to develop a comprehensive program design first and then seek funding for it, rather than "chasing dollars" and forcing the program to fit the restrictions imposed by the funding source (Dryfoos, 1994). It would also be better if service providers could tailor funding streams to fit families' needs, rather than fitting families' needs to available resources (Farrow & Bruner, 1993). In reality, most service providers must chase service dollars and match up their clients' needs with the categorical, problem-oriented funding available to them.

Managed Care

Another critical factor in the financing of social services is managed care, the movement to contain costs and improve access to and quality of health care. In managed care systems, providers agree to provide specific services for clearly identified populations at a prenegotiated rate over a certain period of time. Managed care can be used to contain costs by limiting access to services or by limiting the array of services available to clients (Stroul, 1996). It can also be used to improve access to care for people living in underserved areas, improve the quality of care through standardized protocols, and emphasize prevention over treatment. Although the ideal managed care system provides the right amount of services to the people who need them, some managed care systems have emphasized cost containment over quality of care (Feig & McCullough, in press).

Managed care can affect services for at-risk children and youth in two ways: The agencies that fund services through Medicaid may be required to use managed care providers for their clients, and social service admin-

---

[1]Steven Kazanjian, Greater Germantown Housing Development Corporation, August 6, 1996.

istrators at the state or local level may adopt managed care approaches to funding or delivering services (Feig & McCullough, in press). At the federal level, Medicaid reform is being debated and will have a significant impact on a number of children and families, especially those that rely on Medicaid to pay for mental health services. Some states have received waivers from HHS to alter their Medicaid systems to include managed care components, and by 1985 almost 40% of all Medicaid recipients were enrolled in managed care plans (Feig & McCullough, in press).

Managed care may have some advantages for social service programs, especially those that are attempting to create a holistic and integrated service system. Most managed care plans involve capitation, the payment to a provider agency of a flat amount of money per month or year to cover each individual enrolled in the system. The provider organization must meet all of these individuals' needs and pay for any services that go beyond the capitated rate. This may actually facilitate comprehensive or "wrap-around" services, because the funds follow the individual and service providers can do whatever is necessary to serve the adult or child in their care (Stroul, 1996). On the negative side, some managed care plans may limit access to services, such as counseling or substance abuse treatment, for children and families who need these services on a long-term basis (Feig & McCullough, in press). Although managed care clearly has the potential to improve social service delivery systems, it is too early to gauge its impact on low-income children and families.

Time-Limited Funding

Private citizens, corporations, and foundations have funded social services for children and families in a more flexible, comprehensive, and integrated fashion than is possible with government programs. The flexibility of these nongovernmental funders is due in large part to the absence of mandated eligibility and reporting requirements (Orland et al., 1995). Although this type of funding has obvious benefits, it is typically limited in both time and amount. Funding arrangements can take the form of "seed money" to get a project through a planning and early implementation phase or can specify a project period that typically lasts between 3 and 5 years. Private funders tend to support time-limited demonstration projects to advance knowledge in the field and are typically less interested in underwriting the operating costs of a program over many years (interview with S. Kazanjian, 1996; Orland et al., 1995). This means that even projects that benefit initially from generous corporate or foundation support can be left scrambling for critical operational dollars to maintain their programs, even when evaluation results document positive program impact (interview with S. Kazanjian, 1996).

Although federal funds were once an excellent source of operational and program support, many federal demonstration programs that supported youth-serving projects have recently experienced downsizing or been eliminated altogether. An example is the High Risk Youth Demonstration Program that was funded by HHS's Center for Substance Abuse Prevention from the 1980s through the mid-1990s. This program supported the development of community-based coalitions for comprehensive substance abuse prevention but lost all funding in 1996. That same year Congress ended funding for HHS's Youth Gang Drug Prevention Program and the Drug Abuse Prevention Program for Runaway and Homeless Youth. The new Community Schools Program, a comprehensive community-based program authorized by the Violent Crime Control and Law Enforcement Act of 1994, has received only a fraction of its authorization and was almost eliminated in 1996. The devolution of many federal responsibilities to the states, funding cuts in remaining programs, and the overall emphasis on government "reinvention" have deterred most federal agencies from launching long-term demonstration projects.

Innovative Approaches

The 1996 federal welfare reform will put increased pressure on states and localities to identify new ways to fund social services, but some local governments have been experimenting with innovative financing for a number of years. Although there are many creative techniques that policymakers and social service providers can use to stretch existing dollars, make funding streams more flexible, and even generate new sources of funds, we have room here to discuss only a few in any depth. In this chapter we briefly describe the creative use of Medicaid dollars, the establishment of special taxing districts and children's services councils, the pooling of existing funding streams, waivers of federal regulations and requirements, and redeployment and refinancing techniques.

One approach that will not be discussed at any length here, but is worth a brief mention, is the creation of a "children's budget" at the city government level. Examples of this approach are the referenda recently approved by voters in San Francisco and Oakland, California, to earmark a percentage of each city's tax revenue for children's services. In both cities this has created a permanent funding stream for children's programming that can only be altered by a future referendum (interview with A. White, 1997[2]). Other examples are the use of sales taxes, dedicated municipal taxes, cigarette taxes, and income taxes to fund schools, public libraries, and other services that benefit children and families (Kyle, 1997).

Orland et al. (1995) have noted that the effectiveness of innovative financing strategies may depend in part on preparing social service providers who will be sharing more flexible but reduced resources for the challenges of collaboration. They have noted that investments in training social service providers to work collaboratively will be critical to the success of these financing mechanisms. It will also be important to improve management systems for the design, budgeting, and evaluation of services

---

[2]Amos White, East Bay Asian Youth Center, Oakland, California, January 7, 1997.

and develop flexible, outcomes-oriented funding mechanisms with built-in incentives for interagency collaboration. The New Beginnings initiative, described in detail in Chapter 5, is a good example of institutionalizing collaboration through staff training and revamped financing arrangements.

Special Taxing Districts and Children's Services Councils

One way to provide a guaranteed stream of funding devoted to services for children is to create a special taxing district. Special taxing districts are independent, limited-purpose local government units that are separate both legally and fiscally from general purpose local governments. They are created to provide services that are not being supplied by existing governmental structures (Porter, 1991). Most special districts have been used to plan and finance the infrastructure of American cities, and they are typically used for specific purposes, such as fire protection, housing, and community development (Porter, 1991). Special taxing districts for children, however, have been tried only in the state of Florida.

Although most special districts are located completely within one county, some serve larger areas. Examples of these larger, multijurisdictional, special districts are the Southern California Metropolitan Water District in Los Angeles (which covers 6 counties), the Washington Metropolitan Area Transit Authority (8 counties), and the Nebraska Public Power District (75 counties). Special taxing districts now make up one third of all local government entities and are the most rapidly growing form of government in the United States (Porter, 1991). According to the Census Bureau, this rapid growth reflects an increased public demand for specialized services that cannot otherwise be provided by local governments and allows a concentration of effort in service provision that is not otherwise possible (Porter, 1991).

Pinellas County, Florida, pioneered the use of special taxing districts to guarantee funding for children's services in 1944. The district was the "brainchild" of a county juvenile court judge and a local attorney who were frustrated by the lack of social services for children who came before the court. As a result of their efforts, the Florida legislature approved a Juvenile Welfare Board Act that gave the county the power to create a special district for children and levy a tax to fund children's services, subject to a local referendum. In 1946, voters in Pinellas County approved the Board and its taxing authority (Porter, 1991). In 1991, the Pinellas County Juvenile Welfare Board had a $14 million budget and arranged for more than 80,000 children to receive services through 70 programs delivered by more than 40 agencies under contract to the Board. Since its inception, the Board has served as a leading advocacy agency for children in the county and facilitated the planning and coordination of efforts by numerous private and public agencies in the county that serve children (interview with

J. Levine, 1997[3]; Porter, 1991). It also monitors and evaluates funded programs (interview with J. Levine, 1997).

For almost 40 years, Pinellas County was the only county in the nation with a special taxing district for children. During the last 11 years, however, this approach to guaranteeing funding for children's programs has spread throughout the state of Florida. In 1986, children's advocates in Palm Beach County pushed for and won passage of the Florida Juvenile Welfare Services Law (Florida Statute 125.091). The law allows every county in the state of Florida to create special taxing districts for children. In that same year, Palm Beach County voters approved a referendum to create such a district in their county (Porter, 1991). The Children's Services Council of Palm Beach County currently plans, coordinates, funds, and evaluates children's programs throughout the county. It is governed by a nine-member board that includes the superintendent of schools, the administrator of the state Division of Health and Rehabilitative Services, a member of the county commission, and a member of the school board, as well as five at-large members appointed by the governor. As in Pinellas County, the council will exist in perpetuity and provide a constant stream of funding for children's services in the county unless it is discontinued by another referendum (Porter, 1991).

Since the 1986 legislation, five additional counties in Florida have established children's services councils. Although each county is governed by state requirements concerning needs assessments, notices of hearings, and distribution of funds, each council has unique features. As in Pinellas County, the children's services council has become the catalyst for child advocacy within the county and serves as the community-level body that brings all players in the field of services for children together (interview with J. Levine, 1997). It has also provided a forum, through an association of children's services councils, for sharing information about evaluation methodologies. To children's advocates, this coordinated planning, evaluation, and advocacy function is the best feature of the children's services council model (interview with J. Levine, 1997).

The Florida children's services councils are an example of a structural change leading to integration of planning, service delivery, advocacy, and evaluation. What was envisioned as a means of guaranteeing a perpetual local funding stream for children's services has become a powerful engine for advocacy and change on the state and local levels. Some observers have expressed concern that dedicated funds could be used to supplant, rather than supplement, local funds now supporting services for children and families or justify cuts in such programs on the state level. This does not appear to be the case in Florida thus far. In 1990, voters in Pinellas County approved a higher property tax rate to increase funding for the children's council (interview with J. Levine, 1997). This level of support is unusual in the general anti-tax environment of the 1990s, but perhaps even more so because the largest degree of support for the councils is in the precincts with the highest percentage of older voters. Support from state agencies

---

[3]Jack Levine, Florida Center for Children and Youth, Tallahassee, Florida, May 2, 1997.

and private philanthropies for children's services has actually increased since the growth of the children's councils. Jack Levine of the Florida Center for Children and Youth (a statewide advocacy group) believes this is due to several factors: increased media attention and public awareness of children's issues, the councils' identification of particular needs, and the councils' efficient administration of program funds (interview with J. Levine, 1997).

Pooled Funds and Waivers

Although it is not a new approach to funding social services, combining funds from different discretionary funding streams can be an effective way to gain flexibility to fund comprehensive services or to institute methods of integrating services for children. Combining discrete funding streams, or decategorization, can occur at the federal or state level (where it is typically referred to as *block granting*) or at the county or local level (where it is often described as *pooled funding*). Often the activity occurs on two levels: Funds are officially combined at the higher level of government (federal or state) and used in a flexible manner at the lower level of government (state or local). Pooled funding can occur through legislation, demonstration, or waiver of regulations.

Service providers and policymakers express different points of view about the merits of this approach. Some see decategorization as positive because it fosters an emphasis on local priorities, outcomes rather than inputs or process, developmental rather than deficit-driven approaches, and linkage of social services to economic and physical development in poor neighborhoods (Gardner, 1994). Another oft-cited benefit is the reduction in reporting, evaluation, and other administrative requirements. On the negative side, some believe that the greater discretion awarded states and communities under block grants will make accountability for outcomes more difficult (Gardner, 1994). Although advocates insist that decategorization is not a substitute for resources but rather a way of getting more from existing resources, pooled funds have often been linked with funding cuts. Coupling block grants with funding cuts was a centerpiece of the Reagan administration's block grant policy in the 1980s, and the 1996 federal welfare reform law included cuts in the Social Services Block Grant program. In this era of downsized government, service providers may have no choice but to work collaboratively and creatively within a pooled funding structure.

There are some good examples of states and localities that use pooled funds to encourage collaboration among service providers, which is an example of funding mechanisms driving program management (Cutler et al., 1995). These initiatives include the Kentucky KIDS program and A.B. 1741 legislation in California, both of which we described in Chapter 5. On the county level, the Joint Initiatives effort undertaken in El Paso County, Colorado, is an example of pooling funds to improve social services for children. Joint Initiatives involves a large number of county-level youth-serving agencies, both public and private, that each have committed significant staff and financial resources to a joint planning effort. This collaboration is successful in its advocacy and program planning efforts despite the departure of the county social services agency from the partnership. Joint Initiatives is profiled in Chapter 5.

Another approach to altering the existing funding structure to meet the needs of local programs involves getting a funder to waive major rules and regulations. Waivers can be initiated by the government agency, in a deliberate attempt to give service providers increased flexibility and autonomy. An example of state-initiated waivers as deliberate policymaking is California's A.B. 1741 legislation described in Chapter 5. Alternatively, programs or agencies (local or state) can apply to funding agencies for waivers of specific rules or regulations that will enable them to have more autonomy in the design and operation of their programs. An example of this second type of waiver is the welfare reform waivers that the majority of states have recently obtained for their own welfare reform experiments. Some of these waivers will enable states to postpone the effect of the federal welfare reform on their operations for a number of years; others give some states permission to impose even more restrictive conditions on receiving welfare than those stipulated in federal legislation.

Redeployment and Refinancing

In response to limited dollars for social services and pressure to demonstrate efficiency in program operations (both to obtain additional funds and justify existing funds), a number of states and localities have begun to use the strategies of redeployment and refinancing. *Redeployment* typically refers to a reallocation of resources based on information about a program's effectiveness in meeting certain outcomes (Gardner, 1994). Often this means a redirection of funds away from crisis-oriented, restrictive, or expensive types of care to prevention-oriented and home-based services (Farrow & Bruner, 1993). In some parts of the country, this technique has been combined with pooled funding and delegation of authority from state-to community-level agencies, but these approaches do not have to be combined to be effective. *Refinancing* refers to the use of federal entitlement dollars to fund existing and new services, which then frees up dollars previously spent on those services for other purposes, such as expanding and strengthening related programs (Farrow & Bruner, 1993; Gardner, 1994). Social service program administrators must have a plan for the use of refinanced dollars to avoid having these funds used for deficit reduction or other state priorities (Farrow & Bruner, 1993).

States and local governments have developed some creative techniques for funding their social services programs for children. These efforts are part of the answer to the first question posed at the beginning of this chapter. Through decategorization, new dedicated funding streams for children, and redeployment and refinancing strategies, some state and local governments are finding new ways to sustain social services for this population in the face of decreasing federal supports and elimination of federal entitlement programs. Although most of these approaches are still quite localized, as the realities of the welfare reform legislation and federal funding cuts begin to take effect, these practices may spread to other parts of the country. Although the role of the nongovernmental sector in this new scenario cannot be predicted with certainty, many organizations in the nonprofit sector have made clear that they are unable to fill the gaps left by cuts in federal funds. It is likely that creative approaches to generating and utilizing funds will have to be undertaken and new partnerships between states, localities, nonprofit organizations, foundations, and corporations forged if we are to sustain a minimum safety net for our nation's most vulnerable children.

Part IV _____

Conclusion

18

An Idea Whose Time Has Come: Conclusions and Recommendations

This chapter will discuss the key themes that emerged from our study and offer guidance for expanding service integration approaches into other communities. The preceding chapters presented the rationale supporting the utility of a comprehensive service integration approach; reviewed the history of service integration efforts; outlined current or recent service integration activities at the federal, state, and local levels; and described nine programs that have developed effective methods of working with at-risk youth. We discussed the key cross-cutting issues, identified the elements of exemplary programs, and reviewed the issues involved in evaluating and funding these programs. This chapter summarizes the major themes that emerge from the book as a whole, discusses the dynamic nature of service integration programs, and reviews the critical ingredients for the development, replication, and expansion of effective youth programs and service integration efforts.

Emerging Themes

The lessons that emerge from the history of service integration efforts are particularly relevant today, as funding and control of social services shifts from the federal to the state and local levels. As in previous years, the flexibility that characterizes block grant mechanisms is accompanied by reductions in funding. This new "extreme federalism" produces a Catch-22 situation: Although there is an increased need for collaboration and integration to stretch limited resources further on the local level, the reduction in funds available to statewide and local programs makes it less likely that any collaboration will be effective. In effect, local agencies are being asked to do more with fewer resources. To maximize their effectiveness, social service agencies focused on youth must develop in new directions. Instead of simply "tinkering" with their systems to make them more efficient, youth-serving organizations on the state and local levels may now need to make systemic changes. They may need to go beyond service integration approaches and address issues of flexibility, financing, and communitywide supports for children and youth.

Many youth experts, both practitioners and researchers alike, believe that the best way to overcome the fragmented and categorical nature of youth services is to develop an integrated service delivery system that addresses the complex, interrelated needs of adolescents and their families. Most are convinced that a flexible, community-driven funding stream is an essential element of such a system. Another critical element is a positive youth development focus, which begins with a view of young people as assets to their schools, families, and communities. The shift in thinking over the last decade toward the ecological model of child development has done much to alert practitioners, researchers, and policymakers to key contextual factors that make a difference in the lives of youth at risk. The best programs see a youth holistically and strive to provide supports to youth and their families at each point along the prevention–treatment continuum and beginning at ever younger ages. Our search for examples of agencies with these attributes led to the nine programs described in the preceding chapters.

It is not a coincidence that the movement of some innovative programs toward comprehensive service integration has occurred at the same time that scientific research and theories on adolescent development and problem behavior have reached a significant watershed. We suggest that three recent trends in the literature—the ecological movement in child development, the findings about long-term effects of early intervention programs for infants and children, and the recognition of the overlap among risk factors—point to the need for a new theoretical framework to address the challenges of creating positive outcomes for young people. A new framework must integrate existing notions of risk with a positive youth development approach to help service providers, parents, teachers, and others identify vulnerable youth so that supports can be strengthened and negative outcomes averted.

The conceptual framework we present in this book suggests that the multiple problems developed by some adolescents may be detected earlier, sometimes even in early childhood, by looking at a convergence of antecedent conditions and system markers. The framework acknowledges the importance of protective factors within an individual or within a youth's peer group, family, or community. In the absence of sufficient protective factors, there is an increased likelihood that youth who live under specific antecedent conditions and who experience any of the system markers we have identified will experience negative outcomes. The framework predicts that if problems are already evident, the lack of an effective intervention or environmental response creates a near-certainty that negative outcomes will occur in the future.

The implications of this conceptual framework are clear. By pinpointing antecedent conditions and system markers that occur early, when negative outcomes are a probability but not a certainty, parents, teachers, and agency staff could act more quickly to bolster young people's strengths, reinforce the protective factors in their environment, and counteract the negative ones. The fragmentary, single-issue, problem-oriented system of services that is still the dominant model does not foster this type of early intervention. To change the existing model of adult and agency interaction with youth at risk, we must consider the multiple pathways that lead toward potential problems during adolescence, act before problems occur, sustain social supports over a significant period of time, and consider the various protective and risk factors that are present in a young person's environment. This requires thinking in terms of childhood as well as adolescence, and in terms of interaction with each of the ecological levels of development, including the peer group, the family, and various actors and institutions in the local community.

Among the most important findings of this book are the key factors that make for effective programs, with effectiveness being defined in qualitative terms. These factors generally are the product of the fit between program components and local conditions in a particular community. Programs were successful when they were able to identify local needs, work with others in the community to develop viable strategies for meeting these needs, and then help to bridge the many gaps in services that existed because of traditional single-focus methods of meeting service needs. Effective programs serve as the "mortar" that binds the individual service "bricks" together to create a larger and stronger system that can support the varied and interrelated needs of young people.

We also highlighted the barriers faced by agencies or communities that wish to develop more comprehensive and integrated service systems for youth. These barriers include narrow staff training that undermines an interdisciplinary and collaborative perspective, administrative and bureaucratic procedures that obstruct service integration efforts, and the continued prevalence of categorical funding that focuses on preventing or ameliorating narrowly defined problems within relatively short time frames. The programs featured in this book overcame or eliminated these barriers by taking a holistic, long-term perspective rooted in the concepts of positive youth development.

Our programs provide valuable lessons to service providers and policymakers alike. One of the most important lessons is that service integration is not an adequate goal, given that it often involves trying to fit a youth or family into program requirements or piecing together several narrowly tailored, problem-oriented programs. The strongest programs we observed took a more holistic view of youth as individuals operating within the context of peer groups, schools, families, and communities and viewed these different environments as playing a role in reducing risk and building strengths and competencies in young people. They focused their activities on actually changing the environments in which youth live to make them more supportive, rather than merely working within existing resource constraints.

The Dynamic Nature of Comprehensive Service Integration

This book demonstrates that innovative services for at-risk youth are dynamic entities that grow and change over time in response to a variety of factors, which include the funding and policy environment; the needs of the youth, their families, and their communities; and the responses of other agencies within the same delivery system. This book could be viewed as a historical document that provides snapshot descriptions of nine programs at two different time periods. By the time this book is published, the programs will have changed and evolved to be different from the way they are presented here. The book describes both the origins of a new class of innovative program and their evolution over a 4-year period. We describe the directions these programs have taken and suggest some some approaches that may be appropriate for other communities. By comparing the programs in 1992 and 1996, we identify trends over time in the development of comprehensive service integration programs for youth at risk.

In most programs, the 1996 update revealed a consolidation of approaches and a greater entrenchment within the community. By 1996 the agencies had generally strengthened their original service goals and orientation and made conscious decisions to expand services around their unique points of strength on the prevention–treatment continuum. For example, if a program provided mainly treatment-oriented services in 1992, the update in 1996 revealed an expansion into prevention-oriented services. Similarly, if a program had strengths more along the prevention end of the continuum, these were bolstered in 1996 by adding programs for youth who already need more intensive interventions, thereby broadening the range of services and clientele. Over the 4 years, the most successful of these programs in fact became more comprehensive and holistic in their approach to youth. They began to embody the positive youth development approach or expanded their existing use of that approach.

In the remainder of this chapter, we present some trends that emerge from our study of the nine exemplary programs. We identify the critical conditions that must be in place if agencies and communities are to create more supportive environments for young people. Finally, we summarize the key factors that can empower individuals, agencies, and communities to undertake this challenging task.

Program Trends

Several trends emerge from our study of the nine programs. These trends indicate evolutionary shifts as comprehensive service integration efforts take hold in a given community or agency and may provide important lessons for replications of these approaches.

First, most programs are making a conceptual shift in their approach to adolescents, from a deficit model toward a positive youth development model. Although local, state, and federal initiatives have been ahead of the literature in this area, there is a growing body of empirical and theoretical work on this subject. In addition, policymakers and foundations are including positive youth development concepts in their funding announcements and exploring methods of measuring progress toward achieving positive outcomes for young people. Still, more progress is needed so that positive youth development concepts will be more fully incorporated into the existing framework of services for adolescents and their families. For example, much more effort could be expended in educating federal and state legislators and program and funding decision makers about the benefits of investing in positive youth development approaches. In addition, we still have much to learn about where the social service dollars are flowing and whether or not they are making a positive difference for young people.

Another trend is the devolution of funding social programs from federal to state and local responsibility and the implications of this shift. The 1996 federal welfare reform legislation (Personal Responsibility and Work Opportunity Reconciliation Act of 1996) could be the first of many legislative efforts to reduce the federal role in sustaining this country's social safety net. Insofar as devolution leads to greater decategorization of funding for youth services, this trend could give state and local policymakers and community service providers much-needed flexibility. However, further devolution may be coupled with reduced funding for youth services, which will force social service agencies to scramble for financial support.

The 1996 welfare reform legislation eliminated a number of entitlements and may lead the way to more block grants or stricter eligibility requirements for federally funded youth services. As we go to press, block grants for employment and training programs (which include several youth programs) and juvenile justice programs are being debated in Congress. Welfare reform will be the test case for the combined impact of block granting former entitlements, funding cuts and limitations, and eligibility restrictions for social programs. A number of research studies will document the effects of this significant change on our nation's most vulnerable children and youth.

Most of the programs in our study survived despite enormous odds. We describe several success stories that involve private funders and local government agencies picking up the slack left by state and federal funding cutbacks. These multifocus programs generally survive by putting together a package of different funding streams, although this means they must cope with the multiple and sometimes conflicting requirements generated by each funding source. Survival is also correlated to the strength of the programs' connections to the surrounding community. Exemplary programs work hard to develop strong community ties that they can call on for support when faced with funding cuts or other emergencies.

Another factor in the survival of these programs is that they did not give up on partnerships and interagency cooperation when they were faced with an imminent loss of funds. They developed greater cooperation strategies and partnerships with other agencies so their clients continued to receive services even when staff and activities had to be reduced. This is an important benefit of a service integration approach in periods of reduced funding. In traditional service configurations, when funds are reduced there is a tendency for programs or agencies to compete for scarce resources rather than to increase interagency collaboration. A zero-sum game develops in which a few agencies who are successful competitors survive or even thrive, but the overall system is adversely affected because other agencies close their doors and needs in the communities may go unnoticed. The best programs build partnerships that help all constituent agencies survive stressful times.

Another trend can be observed in the service changes that programs made from 1992 to 1996. Programs differed in the degree to which their service configurations in 1996 demonstrated a coherent vision and sense of purpose. Programs with a greater sense of coherence and purpose made changes in ways that broadened their range of activities along the prevention–treatment continuum or they modified their services to achieve greater fit with their mission statement. Other programs appear to have added "service appendages" that follow a patchwork design. Although these new services may meet local needs, they are not clearly related to the program's 1992 mission statement. The differences between programs that have grown coherently and those that have grown in a patchwork fashion may be a function of the current funding climate rather than internal leadership and administration issues. Some agencies have the relative luxury of developing a comprehensive program design first and obtaining funding for this program, whereas others have had to "chase dollars" and thereby provide new services because of shifts in the funds. In general, programs that have followed a coherent vision and sense of purpose are a more stable presence in their communities and a more consistent source of help for youth and families in need.

Finally, a trend across the nine programs is that their evaluation capabilities have increased but still lag behind their service provision capabilities and changes. Although most programs have incorporated some comprehensive monitoring functions to track participant needs, cases, and program activities, they have shown little interest in conducting or participating in rigorous evaluation studies. In today's outcome and results-based environment, programs must have the capability and willingness to engage in properly conducted evaluations in order to survive. Programs of this genre must also demonstrate cost-effectiveness or risk having integration be seen as an expensive add-on rather than a method of streamlining services and reducing costs. A few programs have been asked to participate in cross-site evaluation studies, but this is still the exception rather than the rule. In general, these programs need to work toward greater readiness for evaluation, so that when technical assistance and funds become available to demonstrate their effectiveness, they can seize the opportunity. Participation in evaluation studies will be critical in the competition with other programs for limited social service funding.

Recommendations

Conditions for Replicating Integrated Service Systems

The programs presented in this book faced a variety of problems in their early development and in maintaining long-term viability. The discussion thus far has suggested that many of these programs are mature enough in their development to warrant larger scale replication in other communities or regions. A key orientation of this book is toward looking at multiple ecological contexts when considering youth development. That same orientation is useful when examining the conditions under which comprehensive service integration programs can be replicated or expanded.

To be effective and long-lasting, change must take place at different ecological levels. We identify three ecological levels that must be addressed when considering replication or expansion of programs and services toward the innovative models presented in this book. The first level, the individual agency, is closest to the youth and families. At this level, changes are evolutionary rather than revolutionary. They involve shifts in practices and perspective that existing local youth-serving agencies can make when they decide to become the mortar that binds the bricks of prevention and treatment services in their local communities. The second level, the local service system, is the network of services involving all constituent agencies that provide prevention or treatment services for adolescents within an identified local jurisdiction, such as a town, city, or county. At this level, changes tend to be more revolutionary than evolutionary because the methods by which agencies interact to meet local needs must be reorganized, which involves systemic change. The third level, the policy system, involves the larger state and federal entities whose policy and funding actions either enable or constrain the provision of services for at-risk youth at the local system and the individual program levels. Changes at this level tend to be evolutionary simply because of the size and complexity of the systems that need to be changed.

At each of the three levels in which program innovations take place, different issues are more or less salient. In general, the following issues are important when determining the replication of comprehensive service integration strategies:

- Defining goals and objectives,
- Identifying the target population,
- Identifying the services to be offered,
- Establishing mechanisms for service delivery,
- Establishing service location,
- Identifying administrative factors,
- Addressing staffing issues,
- Settling funding issues,
- Planning evaluation, and
- Institutionalizing change.

These issues will be discussed within the three ecological contexts: the individual program, the local system, and the policy system. This discussion will identify some of the critical ingredients for the development, replication, and expansion of effective youth programs.

Factors on the individual-program level. At the individual-program level, there appear to be two critical ingredients: the ability to fill the gaps within a given service delivery network and the ability to maintain a holistic youth development perspective. Programs were successful when they were able to identify local needs, work with others in the community to develop viable strategies for meeting these needs, and then help to bridge the many gaps in services that existed because of traditional single-focus methods of meeting service needs. The best programs serve as the glue or mortar that holds the diverse elements of a service system together, fills gaps in services when there is a need, and promotes the smoother and more appropriate functioning of the system. They were most effective at these tasks when they operated with a view of youth as assets to the community who were deserving of support and encouragement on their journey to adulthood.

A program's goals should be based on a local community needs assessment and an assessment of services and activities already available, whether formal or informal. If the full range of stakeholders is included in the planning process, then this assessment should articulate the full range of needs in the community and the ability of the existing system to address those needs. Efforts should be made to solicit input and build support from as many of the partners as possible. Outside consultants can also be brought in to share their expertise. In addition, goals should be tailored to a clearly defined target population.

There is no definitive profile of youth or families who would benefit from these program innovations. It is clear, however, that youth who are not currently being served should be part of the target population for a service integration effort. This includes youth who have or are at risk of having multiple problems, such as substance abuse and mental health problems, homelessness, numerous health problems, and being adjudicated as delinquent. It also includes youth from families where parents abuse alcohol or drugs or where children are being neglected or abused. An equally important target group are families with no obvious problems other than limited resources but whose neighborhood poses a constant threat to their children's safety and health. Among the practical issues involved in defining the target population are what age range to focus on, whether to serve all youth or merely those who are at highest risk, and whether to include younger children in the program's focus.

A comprehensive approach involves a child- and family-centered orientation in which the range of each family's needs are identified and the services address the family's unique situation. This contrasts with a problem-centered approach, in which an agency addresses only the specific problems it is prepared to handle on its own. A comprehensive approach requires considerable variety in the breadth and depth of activities available and flexibility in the way that youth and their families participate. Successful youth service programs are marked by their common emphasis on client empowerment rather than on narrowly defined services from public agencies. However, individual programs must also have community "clout," which is the ability to get clients the services they need that come from other agencies in the community. This book demonstrates that for programs to be effective with youth, they must have a high degree of credibility in the community and with other agencies and they must be able to remain objective and above the influence of special interests or community groups.

Agencies that evolve into comprehensive service integration programs must be willing to operate in the gray area of the boundaries maintained by constituent agencies within a larger service delivery network (or even in the boundaries maintained across service delivery networks). Boundaries are defined as the overlapping jurisdictions of existing traditionally configured programs, in which catchment areas are defined, clients are exchanged, and turf issues are fought. When gray areas develop at the boundaries, the needs of some youth and families go unmet. To be successful, a program must be able to operate in this gray area as an honest broker, as a support to help other agencies become better coordinated, and as a problem-solver that identifies and tackles emerging problems in the community.

Agencies must make a number of decisions regarding the type of services they offer when they move toward a comprehensive service integration model. Comprehensiveness implies breadth of services, but there are opposing views on what constitutes adequate breadth. In one view, a minimum of two specific types of services in each of the three broad categories of education, health, and social services should be offered for the program to be considered truly comprehensive (Morrill & Gerry, 1990). Others argue that basic life skills, such as critical thinking, problem solving, decision making, social skills (e.g., constructive assertiveness), and use of social support systems, should be the program's focus (Hechinger, 1992). Still another view is that bringing the youth and family what they need, even if it comprises only one or two services, is a truly comprehensive approach.

The location of a service integration effort depends in large part on the presence of a dynamic person who is willing to take the lead in developing and running the program and on the nature and location of the funding sources. Integrated services can be delivered through school-based or school-linked sites, in community sites such as churches or community centers, through mobile arrangements, and by home visits. Many programs use school and community sites as their primary locations, although many community-based programs also offer services and activities in school settings. School-based programs have the potential to reach large numbers of youth and have a well-established organizational structure and niche in the community, but they may not be as accessible to families or to youth and families who are alienated from the educational system, such as high-risk dropout youth. They also may further stress an overburdened educational system, be restricted in which services they can provide (e.g., family planning services), and be constrained by rigid organizational rules. Community-based programs may avoid these problems but face issues of limited access for youth and families living in high-crime and gang-infested neighborhoods.

Discussions of comprehensive service integration often involve debates about where services should be delivered. Some programs aspire to on-site "one-stop-shopping," whereas others function as a link between clients and a very broad spectrum of services and activities, none of which is offered on site. The debate about service concentration usually involves trade-offs among the relative benefits of ease of access, youth learning to negotiate the systems themselves, and the potential to waste agency time and scatter resources on some services that may be used infrequently. Most programs fall somewhere between these two extremes.

When agencies move toward a comprehensive service integration approach, agency staff must change. Support for the integration model and willingness to adopt new roles are crucial at all staff levels. In most cases, existing staff must be trained to work effectively within an integrated model. Training should be sensitive to staff concerns such as "turf" issues, different professional orientations, and new jargon. When hiring new staff, agencies should select individuals who can establish trusting, respectful relationships with youth and families; span professional boundaries and specializations to address clients' needs; and work with the system, whatever their type or level of professional training (Sonenstein et al., 1991). One feature of the exemplary programs we studied was the ability of the key staff to see the strengths and resiliencies of the youth and families they served. Many of these programs also had staff who mirrored the racial and ethnic diversity of their clientele or who were sensitive to ethnic, racial, and gender issues.

Finally, individual programs must develop their capability to conduct or participate in evaluations of their service integration efforts. One of the most important steps is developing a computerized management information system that routinely monitors agency activities, including attendance and services provided to each participant, and features sophisticated case background and tracking capabilities. This book summarizes many of the evaluation issues specific to youth-serving programs that come up when developing a systematic evaluation design. It also describes publications that offer step-by-step guidance and technical assistance for conducting evaluations for particular types of youth-serving programs.

Factors on the local-system level. As the first concrete step in the planning process, the partners involved should work toward agreement on a common set of goals and objectives. To the extent possible, long-term commitment to the integration effort should be built in from the planning stage. One effective method for encouraging long-term commitment is through an independent interagency advisory group chaired by someone from a different agency every year to help minimize turf battles and forge a common purpose for the variety of service integration partners. Another method involves diversion of a portion of each partner's funds to support the integration effort, so each partner has an important stake in assuring success of the integrated approach.

To be a credible model of service integration, the agencies involved should have institutionalized linkages that establish the mechanisms for sharing resources. These mechanisms may include colocating in a single facility; sharing staff, financial resources, or information; and agreeing to provide services to referred people. An agency that provides needs assessments, service referrals, and referral follow-ups must be able to give referral agencies the information it has about a client's needs. Many agencies have confidentiality policies that prohibit the disclosure of client information between service agencies and sometimes even within different divisions of a single agency. For service integration to work, agencies must find ways to adjust these confidentiality policies and still protect sensitive information about clients. Gaining the informed consent of clients to share information with agency personnel who will be providing the referral service is one approach that has worked in some places. But even this may require changes in laws or rules.

Another factor at the local-system level is the sufficiency of funds for individual agencies and the presence of funding sources that offer incentives for interagency partnerships. Insufficient resources induce competitiveness between service programs and undermine collaborative efforts. Many local funding sources require partnerships between agencies for new initiatives and, in some cases, may even be responsible for bringing agencies together to cooperate. However, funding is also a key issue at the larger policy-system level because it is the availability of these funds that will support or detract from local system efforts to become more integrated.

An important factor at the local-system level is whether any changes created by service integration in the component agencies' functioning and interrelationships become institutionalized and take on a life of their own. Kusserow's (1991a, 1991b) summary of 20 years of service integration activities noted that although service integration efforts had made services more accessible to clients, it had done little to change the fragmented nature of the system itself. This suggests that efforts to create more supportive environments for at-risk youth must include a system-change component that goes beyond rearranging the service delivery system.

It is very important that service integration efforts rest on more than seed funding and strong personalities or leadership. Such factors are likely to be transitory. A program depending on these factors is likely to collapse when the funding expires and the individuals depart. Pooling at least a portion of each agency's core funding to support integration activities is a systemic change that can be crucial for assuring the survival of the integrated service network. This practice may assure adequate resources to continue the integrated approach after start-up funding expires. It also may solidify the commitment of participating agencies by their very tangible stake in the service integration structure.

Factors on the policy-system level. For service integration to work best, funding should be flexible and sufficient. Federal and state funding sources should be redesigned to blend together funds from multiple sources that historically have rigid categorical boundaries, to provide adequate and coherent funding for service programs that address multiple areas of need. This is unlikely to happen, however, especially in an atmosphere of decreasing government involvement in social services. Even where system change has been a primary component of demonstrations with significant funding to support it, as in the Robert Wood Johnson Foundation programs for the severely mentally ill or the Annie E. Casey Foundation New Futures projects for improving outcomes for at-risk youth, only modest system change has been achieved. The New Futures effort is discussed in Chapter 5. Most service integration efforts do not invest sufficient resources to stimulate system change and cannot be expected to do so.

Private funding is sometimes available, but usually it is not adequate to serve as the single source of funding for an entire integration effort. Although some widely respected service integration efforts have successfully combined public and private funds (e.g., New Beginnings in San Diego), this approach is still fairly unusual. The need to match funds from various sources that may be concerned with different issues may sometimes produce uncoordinated, funding-driven programming as well as an excessive administrative and development burden.

At the larger policy-system level, an important factor enabling the development of comprehensive service integration programs is evidence supporting effectiveness. We have few valid and reliable evaluations that test the effectiveness of programs and identify program components that appear to contribute to program success. Experts cite a lack of funding as a major barrier to evaluation efforts, because many categorical programs devote a small percentage of total resources to evaluation. Most serious evaluations are funded either by the federal government or by foundations and often involve special demonstration efforts rather than "normal" programs operating in a variety of environments.

Experience has shown that programs that look good as demonstrations often are diluted on replication. This phenomenon suggests that evaluation results are used to justify program dissemination or replication but are not reviewed in enough detail to assure that critical aspects of programs actually appear in replication. Experts have noted that evaluation results are rarely used to make decisions about continued program structure or funding, especially for programs that are mass-marketed and packaged for schools and teachers. Information on cost effectiveness, the level of spending, and the distribution of funds for youth programs on the local level is crucially needed. Evaluations can justify requests for additional program support.

Where postdemonstration funding is inadequate to sustain the integrated approach, the availability of evaluation data documenting the innovative processes and beneficial outcomes resulting from the use of an integrated approach can be instrumental in securing continuation funding. Policymakers, funders, and potential funders can make better-informed decisions on how to allocate limited resources when information is available to document implementation procedures, service costs, and cost savings. Even more desirable is information showing the impact of the integrated approach on program participants, component agencies, the social service system, and the overall level of funding for youth programs.

Looking to the Future

In the current climate of devolving federal responsibility for social programs to states and localities, greater understanding of the interconnect-
edness of problems in adolescence, focus on positive youth development,
and demands for increased accountability for program effectiveness, comprehensive service integration is one concept whose time has come. Efforts
at replicating aspects of the nine exemplary programs described in this
volume will require changes at three ecological levels: the individual
agency, the local service system, and the larger policy system. There are
a set of critical ingredients at each of these levels that will enable comprehensive service integration efforts to take root and reach sustainability
in different communities. One of these critical ingredients is a positive
youth development focus that sees the family, the school, the neighborhood, and the community institutions as players in creating a support
system for youth.

At the individual-agency level, an agency must be well-established
and credible, it must identify needs and take the initiative to fill those
needs, it must build coalitions and be inclusive of all key players in the
community, and it must maintain a reputation for objectivity and competence. Agencies that fit the "bricks and mortar" analogy are those that
meet these conditions and have a long-term presence in the community;
work at different ecological levels, including child, peer group, family,
neighborhood, and community; are effective at obtaining funding to support programs; have a clear sense of mission and purpose to guide their
growth; and generally have a strong and charismatic leader who can articulate the mission and goals to other agency personnel and stimulate
movement toward interagency cooperation.

At the local service system level, there must be strong incentives either from funders or the community to develop partnership arrangements.
There must also be agencies that can serve as catalysts in the community
for greater interagency coordination. There should be a thorough assessment of all the resources allocated to youth-related programs (including
schools, health, and employment services) in the community, which should
be followed by a serious consideration of which efforts are effective and
which are wasteful, and reallocation of resources should be on the table
for discussion. In addition, there should be institutionalized linkages that
establish the mechanisms for sharing resources, and agencies should demonstrate their commitment to sustained integration by pooling at least a
portion of each agency's core funding. Finally, a particularly useful model
for developing greater integration of services within a local network of
providers is through an independent interagency advisory group chaired
by someone from a different agency every year to help minimize turf battles and forge a common purpose for the variety of service integration
partners.

At the larger policy-system level, state and federal policies must explicitly encourage and support local service integration initiatives. However, the methods for accomplishing this end are fraught with problems.

In the abstract, it would appear that streamlined and flexible funding should enable agencies to provide supportive environments for youth. In practice, we do not believe that pooled funding will always be the best approach because it is so often coupled with funding cuts. Potential alternative solutions may lie in the methods used by the nine programs featured in this book or in some of the innovations being pioneered on the city and county levels. These efforts include funders requiring collaboration among different systems or groups of agencies, and using local referenda to create permanent and flexible streams of funding for children's services.

Additionally, state and federal governments can encourage and support multisite evaluations to identify key program processes and their link to positive client and community outcomes. With support for a holistic approach to the challenges faced by young people, flexible and adequate funding streams, and support for rigorous evaluation of such efforts, more youth-serving programs may be able to fulfill the promise held out by the nine programs featured here. But supportive communities for youth will not be created just by funding programs. Healthy communities for young people are created through the active involvement and sustained commitment of all of the individuals and institutions that make up an adolescent's world.

Appendix _____

Cities and Counties That Include Empowerment Zone (EZ)/Enterprise Community (EC) Areas

ALABAMA
Birmingham (U-EC)
Chambers County (R-EC)
Green and Sumter counties (R-EC)

ARIZONA
Chocise, Santa Cruz, and Yuma counties (R-EC)
Phoenix (U-EC)

ARKANSAS
Cross, Lee, Monroe, and St. Francis counties (R-EC)
Little Rock/Pulaski County (U-EC)
Mississippi County (R-EC)

CALIFORNIA
Imperial County (R-EC)
Los Angeles—South Central/ Huntington Park (U-EC)
Los Angeles (U-Supplemental EZ)[1]

Oakland (U-Enhanced EC)
San Diego (U-EC)
San Francisco (U-EC)
Watsonville/Santa Cruz County (R-EC)

COLORADO
Denver (U-EC)

CONNECTICUT
Bridgeport (U-EC)
New Haven (U-EC)

DELAWARE
Wilmington (U-EC)

DISTRICT OF COLUMBIA (U-EC)

FLORIDA
Jackson County (R-EC)
Miami/Dade County (U-EC)
Tampa (U-EC)

GEORGIA
Albany (U-EC)
Atlanta (U-EZ)
Burke, Hancock, Jefferson, McDuffie, Taliaferro, and Warren counties (R-EC)
Crisp and Dooley counties (R-EC)

ILLINOIS
Chicago (U-EZ)
East St. Louis (U-EC)
Springfield (U-EC)

R-EC = Rural Enterprise Community; R-EZ = Rural Empowerment Zone; U-EC = Urban Enterprise Community; U-EZ = Urban Empowerment Zone; U-Enhanced EC = Urban Enhanced, Enterprise Community, (The HHS grant to these localities was supplemented with HUD funds); and U-Supplemental EZ = Urban Supplemental, Empowerment Zone, (The HHS grant to these localities was supplemented with HUD funds).

[1] HHS did not award funds for the Los Angeles Supplemental Empowerment Zone; HUD contributed the entire amount of funding for this zone.

INDIANA
Indianapolis (U-EC)

IOWA
Des Moines (U-EC)

KANSAS
Kansas City (U-Enhanced EC)
    with Kansas City, MO

KENTUCKY
Clinton, Jackson, and Wayne
    counties (R-EZ)
Louisville (U-EC)
McCreary County (R-EC) with
    Scott County, TN

LOUISIANA
Catahoula, Concordia, Franklin,
    Morehouse, and Tensas parishes
    (R-EC)
Madison Parish (R-EC)
New Orleans (U-EC)
Ouachita Parish (U-EC)

MASSACHUSETTS
Boston (U-Enhanced EC)
Lowell (U-EC)
Springfield (U-EC)

MARYLAND
Baltimore (U-EZ)

MICHIGAN
Detroit (U-EZ)
Flint (U-EC)
Lake County (R-EC)
Muskegon (U-EC)

MINNESOTA
Minneapolis (U-EC)
St. Paul (U-EC)

MISSISSIPPI
Bolivar, Holmes, Humphreys,
    Sunflower, and Leflore counties
    (R-EZ)
Jackson (U-EC)
Panola, Quitman, and Tallahatchie
    counties (R-EC)

MISSOURI
Kansas City (U-Enhanced EC)
    with Kansas City, KS
Mississippi County (R-EC)
St. Louis (U-EC)

NEBRASKA
Omaha (U-EC)

NEVADA
Las Vegas/Clark County (U-EC)

NEW HAMPSHIRE
Manchester (U-EC)

NEW JERSEY
Camden (U-EZ) with Philadelphia,
    PA
Newark (U-EC)

NEW MEXICO
Albuquerque (U-EC)
Mora, Taos, and Rio Ariba counties
    (R-EC)

NEW YORK
Albany, Schenectady, and Troy
    (U-EC)
Buffalo (U-EC)
Newburgh (U-EC)
New York City—Harlem/Bronx
    (EZ)
Rochester (U-EC)

NORTH CAROLINA
Charlotte (U-EC)
Halifax, Edgecombe, and Wilson
    counties (R-EC)
Robeson County (R-EC)

OHIO
Akron (U-EC)
Cleveland (U-Enhanced EC)
Columbus (U-EC)
Scioto County (R-EC)

OKLAHOMA
Choctaw and McCurtain counties
  (R-EC)
Oklahoma City (U-EC)

OREGON
Josephine County (R-EC)
Portland (U-EC)

PENNSYLVANIA
Lock Haven/Clinton County (R-EC)
Harrisburg (U-EC)
Philadelphia (U-EZ) with Camden,
  NJ
Pittsburgh (U-EC)

RHODE ISLAND
Providence (U-EC)

SOUTH CAROLINA
Charleston (U-EC)
Williamsburg County (R-EC)

SOUTH DAKOTA
Beadle and Spink counties (R-EC)

TENNESSEE
Fayette and Haywood counties
  (R-EC)
Memphis (U-EC)
Nashville (U-EC)

Scott County (R-EC) with
  McCreary County, KY

TEXAS
Cameron, Hidalgo, Starr, and
  Willacy counties (R-EZ)
Dallas (U-EC)
El Paso (U-EC)
Houston (U-EC)
San Antonio (U-EC)
Waco (U-EC)

UTAH
Ogden (U-EC)

VERMONT
Burlington (U-EC)

VIRGINIA
Accomac and Northampton
  counties (R-EC)
Norfolk (U-EC)

WASHINGTON
Lower Yakima County (R-EC)
Seattle (U-EC)
Tacoma (U-EC)

WEST VIRGINIA
Braxton, Clay, Fayette, Nicholas,
  and Roane counties (R-EC)
Huntington (U-EC)
McDowell County (R-EC)

WISCONSIN
Milwaukee (U-EC)

References

Adams, G. R., Gulotta, T., & Clancy, M. A. (1985). Homeless adolescents: A descriptive study of similarities and differences between runaways and thrownaways. *Adolescence, 79,* 715–724.

Adelson, J. (1979). Adolescence and the generalization gap. *Psychology Today, 12,* 33–37.

Agranoff, R. (1991). Human services integration: Past and present challenges in public administration. *Public Administration Review, 51*(6), 533–542.

Alan Guttmacher Institute. (1994). *Sex and America's teenagers.* New York: Author.

Allen, J. P., Leadbeater, B. J., & Aber, J. L. (1994). The development of problem behavior syndromes in at-risk adolescents. *Developmental Psychology, 30,* 323–342.

Annie E. Casey Foundation. (1995a). *Focus: A report from the Annie E. Casey Foundation.* Baltimore: Author.

Annie E. Casey Foundation. (1995b). *Request for proposals to evaluate the New Jersey school-based youth services program.* Baltimore: Author.

Annie E. Casey Foundation. (1995c). *The path of most resistance: Reflections on lessons learned from new futures.* Baltimore: Author.

Arnett, J., & Balle-Jensen, L. (1993). Cultural bases of risk behavior: Danish adolescents. *Child Development, 64,* 1842–1855.

Bane, M. J., & Ellwood, D. (1989). One fifth of the nation's children: Why are they poor? *Science, 245,* 1047–1053.

Barker, G. (1996). *Integrated service models for youth: Focus on the international experience.* Unpublished paper prepared for the Colombian government as part of the preparation of the Child and Youth Development Project submitted to the World Bank, Human Resources Division, Country Department III, Latin America and the Caribbean Region.

Barnett, W. S. (1995). Long-term effects of early childhood programs on cognitive and school outcomes. *The Future of Children, 5*(3), 25–50.

Baruch, R., & Stutman, S. (1994). *Strategies for fostering resilience.* Washington, DC: Institute for Mental Health Initiatives.

Baumrind, D. (1991). Parenting styles and adolescent development. In J. Brooks-Gunn, R. Lerner, & A. C. Petersen (Eds.), *The encyclopedia of adolescence* (Vol. II, pp. 746–758). New York: Garland Press.

Belsky, J. (1981). Early human experience: A family perspective. *Developmental Psychology, 17,* 3–23.

Berreuta-Clement, J., Schweinhard, L., Barnett, W., Epstein, A., & Weikert, D. (1984). *Changed lives: The effects of the Perry Preschool Program on youths through age 19.* (Monographs of the High/Scope Educational Research Foundation, No. 8). Ypsilanti, MI: High/Scope Press.

Bloom, B. (1979). Prevention of mental disorders: Recent advances in theory and practice. *Community Mental Health, 15,* 179–190.

Botvin, D. (1986). Substance abuse prevention research: Recent developments and future directions. *Journal of School Health, 56,* 369–386.

Botvin, D. (1990). Substance abuse prevention: Theory, practice and effectiveness. In M. Tonry & J. Q. Wilson (Eds.), *Drugs and crime* (pp. 461–519). Chicago: University of Chicago Press.

Bretherton, I. (1985). Attachment theory: Retrospect and prospect. *Monographs of the Society for Research on Child Development, 50*(1, Serial No. 209).

Bronfenbrenner, U. (1979). *The ecology of human development: Experiments by nature and design.* Cambridge, MA: Harvard University Press.

Brown, S. S., & Eisenberg, L. (Eds.). (1995). *The best intentions: Unintended pregnancy and the well-being of children and families.* Washington, DC: National Academy Press.

Brown, J. E., & Horowitz, J. E. (1993). Deviance and deviants: Why adolescent substance use prevention programs do not work. *Evaluation Review, 17*(5), 529–555.

Bruno, R. R., & Adams, A. (1994). *Current population reports, population characteristics, school enrollment-social and economic characteristics of students: October 1993*. P20-479. Washington, DC: U.S. Department of Commerce, Bureau of the Census.

Bulcroft, R. A. (1991). The value of physical change in adolescence: Consequences for the parent-adolescent exchange relationship. *Journal of Youth and Adolescence, 20,* 89–105.

Burt, M. R., & Cohen, B. E. (1989). *America's homeless: Numbers, characteristics, and the programs that serve them*. Washington, DC: Urban Institute Press.

Burt, M. R., Kimmich, M., Goldmuntz, J., & Sonenstein, F. L. (1984). *Helping pregnant adolescents: Outcomes and costs of service delivery*. Washington, DC: Urban Institute.

Burt, M. R., & Resnick, G. (1992). *Youth at risk: Evaluation issues*. Washington, DC: U.S. Department of Health and Human Services.

Burt, M. R., Resnick, G., & Matheson, N. (1992). *Comprehensive service integration programs for at-risk youth*. Washington, DC: U.S. Department of Health and Human Services.

Bynum, J. E., & Thompson, W. E. (1995). *Juvenile delinquency: A sociological approach* (3rd ed.). Needham Heights, MA: Allyn & Bacon.

Card, J. J. (1988). *Evaluating and monitoring programs for pregnant and parenting teens*. Palo Alto, CA: Data Archive on Adolescent Pregnancy and Pregnancy Prevention.

Carnegie Council on Adolescent Development. (1989). *Turning points: Preparing American youth for the 21st century*. New York: Author.

Catalano, R., & Dooley, D. (1980). Economic change in primary prevention. In R. H. Price, R. F. Ketterer, B. C. Bader, & J. Monahan (Eds.), *Prevention in mental health: Research, policy and practice*. Mill Valley, CA: Sage.

Center for the Study of Social Policy. (1995). *Building new futures for at-risk youth: Findings from a five year, multi-site evaluation*. Washington, DC: Author.

Centers for Disease Control. (1991, October 11). Weapon carrying among high school students—United States, 1990. *Morbidity and Mortality Weekly Report, 40,* 681–684.

Centers for Disease Control. (1992). Physical fighting among high school students—United States, 1990. *Morbidity and Mortality Weekly Report, 41,* 91.

Centers for Disease Control. (1995a, March 24). *Morbidity and mortality weekly report: Youth risk behavior surveillance—United States, 1993, 44,* SS-1. Atlanta: Centers for Disease Control, U.S. Department of Health and Human Services.

Centers for Disease Control. (1995b). *Sexually transmitted disease surveillance 1994. September, 1995*. Atlanta: Centers for Disease Control, Department of Health and Human Services.

Centers for Disease Control. (1996). *The HIV/AIDS surveillance report: U.S. HIV and AIDS cases reported through June 1996, 8*(1). Washington, DC: U.S. Department of Health and Human Services.

Centers for Disease Control, National Center for Health Statistics. (1994). *Vital and Health Statistics* (Series 10, No. 190). Washington, DC: Department of Health and Human Services.

Chaplin, D., & Merryman, A. (1996). *Criminal behavior and victimization among disadvantaged youth*. Washington, DC: Urban Institute.

Child Welfare League of America. (1996). *Child Abuse and Neglect: A Look at the States*. Washington, DC.

Clark-Lempers, D. S., Lempers, J. D., & Ho, C. (1991). Early, middle and late adolescents' perceptions of their relationships with significant others. *Journal of Adolescent Research, 6,* 296–315.

Cloninger, C. R., Sigvardsson, S., & Bohman, M. (1988). Childhood personality predicts alcohol abuse in young adults. *Alcoholism, 12,* 494–503.

Connell, J. P., & Aber, J. L. (with Walker, G.). (1995). In J. P. Connell, A. C. Kubisch, L. B. Schorr, & E. H. Weiss (Eds.), *New approaches to evaluating community initiatives: Concepts, methods and contexts*. Washington, DC: The Aspen Institute Roundtable on Comprehensive Community Initiatives for Children and Families.

Connell, J. P., Kubisch, A. C., Schorr, L. B., & Weiss, E. H. (Eds.). (1995). *New approaches to evaluating community initiatives: Concepts, methods and contexts*. Washington, DC: The Aspen Institute Roundtable on Comprehensive Community Initiatives for Children and Families.

Council on Scientific Affairs. American Medical Association. 1992. Violence against women: Relevance for medical practitioners, *JAMA, 267*(23), 3184–3189.

Crockenberg, S. G. (1981). Infant irritability, mother responsiveness and social support influences on the security of infant mother attachment. *Child Development, 49,* 466–478.

Cronbach, L. J., & Associates. (1980). *Toward reform of program evaluation.* San Francisco: Jossey-Bass.

Cutler, I., Tan, A., & Downs, L. (1995). *State investments in education and other children's services: Case studies of financing innovations.* Washington, DC: The Finance Project.

D'Angelo, L. J., Getson, P. R., Luban, N. L. C., & Gayle, H. D. (1991). Human immunodeficiency virus infection in urban adolescents: Can we predict who is at risk? *Pediatrics, 88*(5), 982–986.

Dishion, T., & Andrews, D. W. (1995). Preventing escalation in problem behaviors with high-risk young adolescents: Immediate and 1-year outcomes. *Journal of Consulting and Clinical Psychology, 63,* 538–548.

Dryfoos, J. G. (1990). *Adolescents at risk.* New York: Oxford University Press.

Dryfoos, J. (1994). *Full service schools: A revolution in health and social services for children, youth and families.* San Francisco: Jossey-Bass.

Dutton, D. G. (1988). *The domestic assault of women: Psychological and criminological perspectives.* Toronto: Allen & Bacon.

Edelman, P. B., & Radin, B. A. (1991). *Serving children and families effectively: How the past can help chart the future.* Washington, DC: Education and Human Services Consortium.

Elliott, D. S., Ageton, S. S., Huizinga, D., Knowles, B. A., & Canter, R. J. (1983). *The prevalence and incidence of delinquent behavior: 1976–1980, National Youth Survey Report No. 26.* Boulder, CO: Behavioral Research Institute.

Elliott, D. S., Dunford, F. W., & Huizinga, D. (1987). The identification and prediction of career offenders utilizing self reported and official data. In J. D. Burchard & S. N. Burchard (Eds.), *Primary prevention of psycho-pathology, Vol 10: Prevention of delinquent behavior* (pp. 90–121). Mill Valley, CA: Sage.

Elliott, D. S., Huizinga, D., & Menard, S. (1989). *Multiple Problem Youth: Delinquency, Substance Use and Mental Health Problems.* New York: Springer-Verlag.

Emans, S. J., Grace, E., Woods, E. R., Smith, D. E., Klein, K., & Merola, J. (1987). Adolescents' compliance with the use of oral contraceptives. *Journal of the American Medical Association, 257,* 3377–3381.

Epstein, N. B., Bishop, D. S., & Baldwin, L. M. (1982). McMaster model of family functioning: A view of the normal family. In F. Walsh (Ed.), *Normal family processes* (pp. 115–141). New York: Guilford Press.

Erikson, E. H. (1968). *Identity: Youth and crisis.* New York: Norton.

Family Impact Seminar. (1990, June 8). *Keeping troubled families together: Promising programs and statewide reform.* Panel discussion by E. Cole, K. Nelson, B. Purcell, F. Farrow, & T. Ooms, Seminar on Family Centered Social Policy: The Emerging Agenda, American Association for Marriage and Family Therapy, Washington, DC.

Fanshel, D., Finch, S. J., & Grundy, J. F. (1990). *Foster children in life course perspective.* New York: Columbia University Press.

Farrington, D. P. (1983). Offending from 10 to 25 years of age. In K. T. Dusen & S. A. Mednick (Eds.), *Prospective studies of crime and delinquency* (pp. 17–38). Boston: Kluwer Nijhoff.

Farrow, F., & Bruner, C. (1993). *Getting to the bottom line: State and community strategies for financing comprehensive service systems.* New York: National Center for Service Integration Information Clearinghouse.

Fasick, F. A. (1994). On the "invention" of adolescence. *Journal of Early Adolescence, 14,* 6–23.

Federal Bureau of Investigation. (1994). *Uniform crime reports for the United States: 1993.* Washington, DC: U.S. Government Printing Office.

Feig, L., & McCullough, C. (in press). The role of child welfare. In M. Haack & P. Budetti (Eds.), *Drug dependent women and their children: Public policy and public health.* New York: Springer.

Feldman, R. A., Stiffman, A. R., & Jung, K. G. (1987). *Children at risk: In the web of parental mental illness*. New Brunswick, NJ: Rutgers University Press.

Fergusson, D. M., Horwood, L. J., & Lynskey, M. (1994). The childhoods of multiple problem adolescents: A 15-year longitudinal study. *Journal of Child Psychology and Psychiatry, 35,* 1123–1140.

Finkelhor, D., Hotaling, G., & Sedlak, A. (1990). *Missing, abducted, runaway, and thrown-away children in America. First report: Numbers and characteristics*. Conducted for the U.S. Department of Justice, Office of Juvenile Justice and Delinquency Prevention by the University of New Hampshire and Westat, Inc. (Cooperative Agreement #87-MC-CX-K069).

Fishman, M., & Dolson, J. (1987). *The evolution of human services integration: A federal perspective*. Unpublished manuscript, Department of Health and Human Services.

Flanagan, C. A. (1990). Change in family work status: Effects on parent-adolescent decision-making. *Child Development, 61,* 163–177.

Frieden, B. J., & Kaplan, M. (1975). *The Politics of neglect: Urban aid from model cities to revenue sharing*. Cambridge: MIT Press.

Galambos, N. L., & Almeida, D. M. (1992, November). Does parent-adolescent conflict increase in early adolescence? *Journal of Marriage and the Family, 54,* 737–747.

Gambone, M. A., & Arbreton, A. J. A. (1997). *Safe havens: The contributions of youth organizations in healthy adolescent development*. Philadelphia: Public/Private Ventures.

Garbarino, J., Schellenbach, C. J., & Sebes, J. M. (1986). *Troubled youth, troubled families: Understanding families at risk for adolescent maltreatment*. New York: Aldine.

Garbarino, J., & Sherman, D. (1980). High-risk neighborhoods and high-risk families: The human ecology of child maltreatment. *Child Development, 51,* 188–198.

Gardner, S. (1994). *Reform options for the intergovernmental funding system: Decategorization policy issues*. Washington, DC: The Finance Project.

Garmezy, N. (1991). Resiliency and vulnerability to adverse developmental outcomes associated with poverty. *American Behavioral Scientist, 34*(4), 416–430.

Garmezy, N., Masten, A. S., & Tellegen, A. (1984). The study of stress and competence in children: A building block for developmental psychopathology. *Child Development, 55,* 97–111.

General Accounting Office. (1989). *Children and youth: About 68,000 homeless and 186,000 in shared housing at any given time*. PEMD 89 14. Washington, DC: U.S. Government Printing Office.

General Accounting Office. (1995). *Child welfare: Complex needs strain capacity to provide services*. Washington, DC: GAO/HEHS-95-208.

Gibbs, J. T., Brunswick, A. F., Conner, M. E., Dembo, R., Larson, T. E., Reed, R. J., & Solomon, B. (1988). *Young, black, and male in America: An endangered species*. Dover, MA: Auburn House.

Ginzberg, E., Berliner, H. S., & Ostow, M. (1988). *Young people at risk: Is prevention possible?* London: Westview Press.

Gomby, D., & Larson, C. (1992). Evaluation of school-linked services. *The Future of Children: School-linked Services, 2*(1), 68–84.

Gottfredson, G. D. (1984). *Effective school battery: User's manual*. Odessa, FL: Psychological Assessment Resources.

Gottfredson, G. D., & Gottfredson, D. C. (1992, November). *Development and applications of theoretical measures for evaluating drug and delinquency prevention programs*. Paper presented at the annual meeting of the American Society of Criminology, New Orleans, LA.

Gottfredson, M. R., & Hirschi, T. (1990). *A general theory of crime*. Stanford, CA: Stanford University Press.

Grotevant, H. D., & Cooper, C. R. (1986). Patterns of interaction in family relationships and the development of identity exploration in adolescence. *Child Development, 56*(2), 415–428.

Hahn, A. (1995). *Evaluation of the Quantum Opportunities Program (QOP): Did the program work?* Waltham, MA: Brandeis University, Heller School, Center for Human Resources.

Halpern, R. (1986). Community-based support for high risk youth and families. *Social Policy, 17*(1), 17–18, 47–50.

Hamburg, D. A., & Takanishi, R. (1989). Preparing for life: The critical transition of adolescence. *American Psychologist, 44,* 825–827.

Harlap, S., Kost, K., & Forrest, J. D. (1991). *Preventing pregnancy, protecting health: A new look at birth control choices in the United States.* New York: Alan Guttmacher Institute.

Harrell, A. (with Burt, M. R., Hatry, H., Rossman, S., Roth, J., & Sabol, W.). (1996). *Evaluation strategies for human services programs: A guide for policymakers and providers.* Washington, DC: Urban Institute.

Hatry, H. P., Blair, L., Fisk, D., & Kimmel, W. (1987). *Practical program analysis for state and local governments* (2nd ed.). Washington, DC: Urban Institute Press.

Hauser-Cram, P., & Shonkoff, J. P. (1988). Rethinking the assessment of child focused outcomes. In H. Weiss & F. Jacobs (Eds.), *Evaluating family programs.* Hawthorne, NY: Aldine.

Hawkins, J. D., Catalano, R. F., & Miller, J. Y. (1992). Risk and protective factors for alcohol and other drug problems in adolescence and early adulthood: Implications for substance abuse prevention. *Psychological Bulletin, 112,* 64–102.

Hawkins, J. D., Jenson, J. M., Catalano, R. F., & Lishner, D. M. (1988, June). Delinquency and drug abuse: Implications for social services. *Social Service Review, 62,* 258–284.

Hayes, C. (Ed.). (1987). *Risking the future: Adolescent sexuality, pregnancy, and childbearing.* Washington, DC: National Academy Press.

Hechinger, F. M. (1992). *Fateful choices: Healthy youth for the 21st century.* New York: Carnegie Corporation.

Hogan, D. P., Astone, N. M., & Kitagawa, E. M. (1985). The impact of social status, family structure and neighborhood on the fertility of black adolescents. *Family Planning Perspectives, 17,* 165–169.

Howrigan, G. A. (1988). Evaluating parent-child interaction outcomes of family support and education programs. In H. Weiss & F. Jacobs (Eds.), *Evaluating family programs* (pp. 95–130). Hawthorne, NY: Aldine.

Huizinga, D., & Elliott, D. S. (1986). Reassuring the reliability and validity of self-report measures. *Journal of Quantitative Criminology, 2*(4), 293–327.

Illback, R. (1994). Poverty and the crisis in children's services: The need for services integration. *Journal of Clinical Child Psychology 23*(4), 413–424.

Illback, R. (1996). *Kentucky family resource and youth services centers: Summary of evaluation findings.* Louisville, KY: REACH of Louisville.

Jacobs, F. (1988). The five-tiered approach to evaluation: Context and implementation. In H. Weiss & F. Jacobs (Eds.), *Evaluating family programs* (pp. 37–68). Hawthorne, NY: Aldine.

Jargowsky, P., & Bane, M. J. (1990). Neighborhood poverty: Basic questions. Paper H-90-3. Cambridge, MA: Harvard University, Kennedy School of Government.

Jaynes, G., & Williams, R. (Eds.). (1989). *A common destiny: Blacks and American society.* Washington, DC: National Academy Press.

Jessor, R. (1987). Risky driving and adolescent problem behavior: An extension of problem behavior theory. *Alcohol, Drugs and Driving, 3,* 1–11.

Kagan, S. (1993). *Integrating human services: Understanding the past to shape the future.* New Haven, CT: Yale University Press.

Kagan, S., Goffin, S., Golub, S., & Pritchard, E. (1995). *Toward systemic reform: Service integration for young children and their families.* Falls Church, VA: National Center for Service Integration.

Kahn, A. J., & Kamerman, S. B. (1992). *Integrating services integration: An overview of initiatives, issues and possibilities.* New York: Columbia University, National Center for Children in Poverty.

Kentucky Cabinet for Families and Children. (1996). *Kentucky Family Resource and Youth Services Initiative fact sheet.* Frankfurt, KY: Author.

Kinney, J., Haapala, D., & Booth, C. (1991). *Keeping families together: The Homebuilders model.* Hawthorne, NY: Aldine-De Gruyter.

Knaul, F. M., & Flórez, C. E. (1996). Targeting youth: Empirical evidence, conceptual issues and rationales. Washington, DC: Unpublished paper prepared for the World Bank, Human Resources Division, Country Department III, Latin America and the Caribbean Region.

Knowlton, R. B., & Tetelman, E. H. (1994). Educators respond to New Jersey's one-stop shopping program. In R. A. Levin (Ed.), *Greater than the sum: Professionals in a comprehensive services model* (pp. 103–114). [Teacher Education Monograph No. 17]. Chicago: University of Illinois at Chicago.

Knox, V., & Bane, M. J. (1994). Child support and schooling. In I. Garfinkel, S. McLanahan, & P. Robins (Eds.), *Child support and child well-being* (pp. 241–256). Washington, DC: Urban Institute.

Kreppner, K., & Lerner, R. M. (Eds.). (1989). *Family systems and life span development.* Hillsdale, NJ: Erlbaum.

Kumpfer, K. L. (1989). Prevention of alcohol and drug abuse: A critical review of risk factors and prevention strategies. In D. Shaffer, I. Phillips, & N. B. Enzer (Eds.), *Prevention of mental disorders, alcohol, and other drug use in children and adolescents.* Rockville, MD: U.S. Department of Health and Human Services, Office for Substance Abuse Prevention.

Kusserow, R. (1991a). *Services integration: A twenty-year retrospective.* Washington, DC: U.S. Department of Health and Human Services, Office of the Inspector General.

Kusserow, R. (1991b). *Services integration for families and children in crisis* (OEI-09-90-00890). Washington, DC: U.S. Department of Health and Human Services, Office of the Inspector General.

Kyle, J. (1997). Financing municipal policies and programs for children and youth. In J. Kyle (Ed.), *New directions for cities, families and children.* Washington, DC: National League of Cities.

Lamb, M. (1981). *The role of the father in child development* (2nd ed.). New York: Wiley.

Lavery, B., Siegel, A. W., Cousins, J. H., & Rubovits, D. S. (1993). Adolescent risk-taking: An analysis of problem behaviors in problem children. *Journal of Experimental Child Psychology, 55,* 277–294.

Lerman, R. I. (1996). *Employment and earnings patterns by poverty status, age, sex and high school dropout status.* Washington, DC: Urban Institute.

Lerner, R. M. (Ed.). (1993). *Early adolescence: Perspectives on research, policy, and intervention.* Hillsdale, NJ: Erlbaum.

Lorion, R. P., Price, R. H., & Eaton, W. W. (1989). The prevention of child and adolescent disorders: From theory to research. In D. Shaffer, I. Phillips, & N. B. Enzer (Eds.), *Prevention of mental disorders, alcohol, and other drug use in children and adolescents* (pp. 55–96). Rockville, MD: U.S. Department of Health and Human Services, Office for Substance Abuse Prevention.

Maguire, K., & Pastore, A. L. (Eds.). (1994). *Sourcebook of criminal justice statistics: 1993.* Washington, DC: U.S. Government Printing Office.

Majors, R., & Billson, J. M. (1993). *Cool pose: The dilemma of black manhood in America.* New York: Touchstone Books.

Marcia, J. (1987). The identity status approach to the study of ego identity development. In T. Honess & K. Yardley (Eds.), *Self and identity: Perspectives across the lifespan* (pp. 161–171). London: Routledge and Kegan Paul.

Mark, M. M., & Cook, T. D. (1984). Design of randomized experiments and quasi-experiments. In L. Ruttman (Ed.), *Evaluation research methods: A basic guide.* Mill Valley, CA: Sage.

Martin, L. L., & Kettner, P. M. (1996). *Measuring the performance of human service programs.* Mill Valley, CA: Sage.

McGroder, S. M., Crouter, A. C., & Kordesh, R. (1994). *Schools and communities: Emerging collaborations for serving adolescents and their families.* Harrisburg: Pennsylvania State University, Department of Human Development and Families Studies and Graduate School of Public Policy and Administration.

Melaville, A. I., & Blank, M. J. (1991). *What it takes: Structuring interagency partnerships to connect children and families with comprehensive services.* Washington, DC: Education and Human Services Consortium.

Miller, D., & Lin, E. (1988). Children in sheltered homeless families: Reported health status and use of health services. *Pediatrics, 81,* 668–673.

Minnesota Planning Agency. (1996). *1996 children's services report card.* St. Paul, Author.

Minuchin, S. (1977). *Families and family therapy*. Cambridge, MA: Harvard University Press.

Mohr, L. B. (1995). *Impact analysis for program evaluation*. Mill Valley, CA: Sage.

Moore, K. A., Miller, B. C., Glei, D., & Morrison, D. R. (1995). *Adolescent sex, contraception, and childbearing: A review of recent research*. Washington, DC: Child Trends.

Moore, K. A., Nord, C. W., & Peterson, J. L. (1989). Nonvoluntary sexual activity among adolescents. *Family Planning Perspectives, 21*(3), 110–114.

Moore, K. A., & Peterson, J. L. (1989). *The consequences of teenage pregnancy* (Report No. 89-9). Final report to National Institutes for Child and Human Development and the Office of the Assistant Secretary for Planning and Evaluation, Department of Health and Human Services. Washington, DC: U.S. Department of Health and Human Services, Office of the Assistant Secretary for Planning and Evaluation.

Moore, K. A., Simms, M. C., & Betsey, C. L. (1986). *Choice and circumstance: Racial differences in adolescent sexuality and fertility*. New Brunswick, NJ: Transaction Books.

Moore, K. A., Sugland, B., Blumenthal, C., Glei, D., & Snyder, N. (1995). *Adolescent pregnancy prevention programs: Interventions and evaluations*. Washington, DC: Child Trends.

Moos, R. H., & Moos, B. S. (1976). A typology of family social environments. *Family Process, 15*, 357–371.

Morrill, W. A., & Gerry, M. H. (1990). *Integration and coordination of services for school-aged children: Toward a definition of American experience and experimentation*. Unpublished manuscript.

Mulvey, E. P., Arthur, M. W., & Reppucci, N. D. (1990, March). *Review of programs for the prevention and treatment of delinquency*. Washington, DC: U.S. Congress, Office of Technology Assessment.

National Center for Health Statistics. (1990). *Unpublished 1988 data from the National Health Interview Survey*. Hyattsville, MD: National Center for Health Statistics, Centers for Disease Control, Department of Health and Human Services.

National Center for Health Statistics. (1991, December 12). Advance report of final natality statistics: 1989. *Monthly Vital Statistics Report, 40*(8).

National Center on Child Abuse and Neglect. (1996). *Child maltreatment 1994: Reports from the states to the National Center on Child Abuse and Neglect*. Washington, DC: Administration for Children and Families, Department of Health and Human Services.

National Commission on Children. (1991). *Beyond rhetoric: A new American agenda for children and families*. Washington, DC: National Commission on Children.

National Network for Youth. (1991). *To whom do they belong?: Runaway, homeless and other youth in high-risk situations in the 1990s*. Washington, DC: Author.

National Performance Review. (1993a). *From red tape to results: Creating a government that works better and costs less*. (GPO Publication No. S/N 040-000-00592-7). Washington, DC: U.S. Government Printing Office.

National Performance Review. (1993b). *From red tape to results: Creating a government that works better and costs less, Strengthening the partnership in intergovernmental service delivery* (accompanying report of the National Performance Review). Washington, DC: U.S. Government Printing Office.

National Research Council. (1993). *Losing generations*. Washington, DC: National Academy of Sciences.

Offer, D., Ostrov, E., & Howard, K. I. (1989). Adolescence: What is normal? *American Journal of Diseases of Children, 143*, 731–736.

Offer, D., & Schonert-Reichl, K. A. (1992). Debunking the myths of adolescence: Findings from recent research. *Journal of American Academy of Child and Adolescent Psychiatry, 31*, 1003–1014.

Office for Substance Abuse Prevention. (1989). *Prevention plus II: Tools for creating and sustaining drug-free communities*. Washington, DC: Department of Health and Human Services, Alcohol, Drug Abuse and Mental Health Administration.

Office of the Assistant Secretary for Planning and Evaluation (OASPE). (1996). *Trends in the well-being of America's children and youth: 1996*. Washington, DC: Department of Health and Human Services.

Office of Juvenile Justice Programs. (1995). *Delinquency prevention works*. Washington, DC: U.S. Department of Justice.

Office of Technology Assessment. (1991). *Adolescent health* (Vols. 1–3). Washington, DC: U.S. Government Printing Office.

Oliveri, M. E., & Reiss, D. (1981). A theory-based empirical classification of family problem-solving behavior. *Family Process, 20,* 409–418.

Olson, D. H., McCubbin, H. I., Barnes, H. L., Larsen, A. S., Muxen, M. J., & Wilson, M. A. (1983). *Families,* Mill Valley, CA: Sage.

Ooms, T., & Owen, T. (1991). *Promoting adolescent health and wellbeing through school-linked multi-service, family-sensitive programs*. Washington, DC: Family Impact Seminar.

Orland, M. E., Danegger, A. E., & Foley, E. (1995). *Creating more comprehensive, community-based support systems: The critical role of finance*. Washington, DC: The Finance Project.

Osgood, D. W., O'Malley, P. M., Bachman, J. G., & Johnston, L. D. (1989). Time trends and age trends in arrests and self-reported illegal behavior. *Criminology, 27,* 389–417.

Paternoster, R., & Mazarolle, P. (1994). General strain theory and delinquency: A replication and extension. *Journal of Research in Crime and Delinquency, 31*(3), 235–263.

Patterson, G. R. (1976). The aggressive child: Victim and architect of a coercive system. In L. A. Hamerlynck, L. C. Handy, & E. J. Mash (Eds.), *Behavior modification and families: I. Theory and research* (pp. 267–316). New York: Brunner-Mazell.

Patton, M. Q. (1990). *Qualitative evaluation and research methods* (2nd ed.). Mill Valley, CA: Sage.

Pelcovitz, D., Kaplan, S., Samit, C., Krieger, R., & Cornelius, D. (1984). Adolescent abuse: Family structure and implications for treatment. *Journal of Child Psychiatry, 23,* 85–90.

Pence, A. R. (Ed.). (1988). *Ecological research with children and families: From concepts to methodology*. New York: Teachers College Press.

Peterson, G., Bovbjerg, R., Davis, B., Davis, W., Durman, E., & Gullo, T. A. (1986). *The Reagan block grants: What have we learned?* Washington, DC: Urban Institute Press.

Pittman, K., & Cahill, M. (1992). *Getting beyond the C's: The role of comprehensive programs, case management services and coordinated community planning in the development of supportive environments for youth*. Washington, DC: Academy of Educational Development, Center for Youth Development and Policy Research.

Pittman, K., O'Brien, R., & Kimball, M. (1993). *Youth development and resiliency research: Making connections to substance abuse prevention*. Washington, DC: Academy for Educational Development, Center for Youth Development and Policy Research.

Pittman, K., & Zeldin, S. (1992). *Evaluating youth development in programs and communities: The need for an integrated framework and collaborative strategy*. Washington, DC: Center for Youth Development and Policy Research.

Pleck, J. H., Sonenstein, F. L., & Ku, L. (1993). Changes in adolescent males' use of and attitudes toward condoms, 1988–1991. *Family Planning Perspectives, 25*(3), 106–110.

Pleck, J. H., Sonenstein, F. L., Ku, L., & Burbridge, L. C. (in press). Risk and protective influences on early adolescent risk markers in males. *Journal of Early Adolescence*.

Polit, D. F., Quint, J. D., & Riccio, J. A. (1988). *The challenge of serving teenage mothers*. New York: Manpower Demonstration Research Corporation.

Porter, P. J. (1991). *Special taxing districts for children: A powerful idea from Florida*. Boston: Harvard University, Division of Health Policy Research and Education.

Public/Private Ventures, Inc. (1994, December). *Community change for youth development: Research design*. Philadelphia: Author.

Public/Private Ventures, Inc. (1994, November). *Revised draft summary of the initiative*. Philadelphia: Author.

Public/Private Ventures, Inc. (1995, January). *Quarterly report to U.S. Department of Health and Human Services*. Philadelphia: Author.

Quinn, J. (1992). *Report on the consultation on evaluation of youth development programs*. Washington, DC: Carnegie Council on Adolescent Development.

Ramey, C. T., & Ramey, S. L. (1992). Effective early intervention. *Mental Retardation, 30,* 337–345.

Reid, J. (1986). Social interactional patterns in families of abused and nonabused children. In C. Waxler & M. Radke-Yarrow (Eds.), *Social and biological origins of altruism and aggression: Biological and social origins* (pp. 238–255). Cambridge, MA: Cambridge Press.

Resnick, G., & Giambo, P. (1996). *Evaluation of HIV policy in the job corps: Final report.* Unpublished report submitted to the Medical Office, National Office of the Job Corps, Department of Labor. Rockville, MD: Westat.

Resnick, G., Burt, M. R., Newmark, L., & Reilly, L. (1992). *Youth at risk: Definitions, prevalence, and approaches to service delivery.* Washington, DC: U.S. Department of Health and Human Services.

Resnick, M. D., Chambliss, S. A., & Blum, R. W. (1993). Health and risk behaviors of urban adolescent males involved in pregnancy. *Families in Society: The Journal of Contemporary Human Services, 74*, 366–374.

Resnick, M. D., Harris, L. J., & Blum, R. W. (1993). The impact of caring and connectedness on adolescent health and well-being. *Journal of Paediatrics and Child Health, 29* (Suppl. 1), S3–S9.

Ricketts, E. R., & Sawhill, I. V. (1988). Defining and measuring the underclass. *Journal of Policy Analysis and Management, 7*, 316–325.

Robert Wood Johnson Foundation. (1996). *Securing the health and safety of urban children: A Robert Wood Johnson Foundation initiative.* Princeton, NJ: Author.

Ross, D. G. (1972). *G. Stanley Hall: The psychologist as prophet.* Chicago: University of Chicago Press.

Rossi, P., & Freeman, H. E. (1993). *Evaluation: A systematic approach* (5th ed.). Mill Valley, CA: Sage.

Rotheram-Borus, M. J., Koopman, C., & Ehrhardt, A. A. (1991). Homeless youths and HIV infection. *American Psychologist, 46*, 1188–1197.

Rutter, M. (1979). Protective factors in children's responses to stress and disadvantage. In M. W. Kent & J. E. Rolf (Eds.), *Primary prevention of psychopathology* (Vol. 3). Hanover, NH: University Press of New England.

Rutter, M. (1985). Resilience in the face of adversity: Protective factors and resistance to psychiatric disorders. *British Journal of Psychiatry, 147*, 598–611.

Rutter, M. (1987). Psychosocial resilience and protective mechanisms. *American Journal of Orthopsychiatry, 57*(3), 316–331.

Rutter, M., & Rutter, M. (1993). *Developing minds: Challenge and continuity across the life span.* New York: Basic Books.

Ruttman, L. (1984). Evaluability assessment. In L. Ruttman (Ed.), *Evaluation research methods: A basic guide.* Mill Valley, CA: Sage.

St. Louis, M. E., Conway, G. A., Hayman, C. R., Miller, C., Petersen, L. R., & Dondero, T. J. (1991). Human immunodeficiency virus infection in disadvantaged adolescents. *Journal of the American Medical Association, 266*(17), 2387–2391.

Sameroff, A. J., & Fiese, B. H. (1989). Transactional regulation and early interaction. In S. J. Meisels & J. P. Shonkoff (Eds.), *Early intervention: A handbook of theory, practice and analysis.* Cambridge, England: Cambridge University Press.

Santrock, J. W. (1991). *Adolescence* (4th ed.). Dubuque, IA: William C. Brown.

Schinke, S. P., Orlandi, M. A., & Cole, K. C. (1992). Boys and Girls Clubs in public housing developments: Prevention services for youth at risk. *Journal of Community Psychology, 20* [OSAP Special issue], 116–127.

Schmidt, R. E., Horst, P., Scanlon, J. W., & Wholey, J. S. (1975). *Assessment of evaluability and rapid feedback evaluation.* Washington, DC: Urban Institute.

Schorr, L. B., & Schorr, D. (1988). *Within our reach: Breaking the cycle of disadvantage.* New York: Doubleday.

Schweinhart, L. J., Barnes, H. V., & Weikart, D. P. (1993). *Significant benefits: The High/Scope Perry Preschool study through age 27* (Monographs of the High/Scope Educational Research Foundation, No. 10). Ypsilanti, MI: High/Scope Press.

Sedlak, A. J. (1991). *National incidence and prevalence of child abuse and neglect: 1988, revised.* Rockville, MD: Westat.

Sedlak, A. J., & Broadhurst, D. D. (1996). *Third national incidence study of child abuse and neglect: Final report.* Washington, DC: National Center on Child Abuse and Neglect, U.S. Department of Health and Human Services.

Seitz, V., Apfel, N. H., & Rosenbaum, L. K. (1991). Effects of an intervention program for pregnant adolescents: Educational outcomes at two years postpartum. *American Journal of Community Psychology, 19,* 911–930.

Seitz, V., Rosenbaum, C. K., & Apfel, N. H. (1985). Effects of family support intervention: A ten-year follow-up. *Child Development, 56,* 376–391.

Smetana, J. G. (1988). Concepts of self and social convention: Adolescents' and parents' reasoning about hypothetical and actual family conflicts. In M. R. Gunnar & W. A. Collins (Eds.), *Minnesota Symposium on Child Psychology: Vol. 21. Development during the transition to adolescence.* Hillsdale, NJ: Erlbaum.

Smetana, J. G. (1994). Parenting styles and beliefs about parental authority. In J. G. Smetana (Ed.), *New directions for child development: No. 66. Belief about parenting: Origins and developmental implications* (pp. 21–36). San Francisco: Jossey-Bass.

Smetana, J. G. (1995). Parenting styles and conceptions of parental authority during adolescence. *Child Development, 66,* 299–316.

Smetana, J. G., & Asquith, P. (1994). Adolescents' and parents' conceptions of parental authority and adolescent autonomy. *Child Development, 65,* 1147–1162.

Smith, T. M., Perie, M., Alsalam, N., Mahoney, R. P., Bae, Y., & Young, B. A. (1995). *The condition of education 1995,* Office of Educational Research and Improvement, U.S. Department of Education. Washington, DC: National Center for Educational Statistics (NCES 95-273).

Sonenstein, F. L., Ku, L., Juffras, J., & Cohen, B. (1991). *Promising prevention programs for children.* Alexandria, VA: United Way of America.

Sonenstein, F. L., Lindberg, L. D., Stewart, K., & Pernas, M. (1996, November). *Current knowledge regarding male involvement in adolescent pregnancy prevention.* Paper presented at 1996 annual meeting of the American Public Health Association, New Orleans.

Springer, J. F., Phillips, J. L., Phillips, L., Cannady, L. P., & Kerst-Harris, E. (1992). CODA: A creative therapy program for children in families affected by abuse of alcohol or other drugs. *Journal of Community Psychology, 20* [OSAP Special Issue], 55–74.

Sroufe, L. A., & Rutter, M. (1984). The domain of developmental psychopathology. *Child Development, 55,* 17–29.

Steinberg, L. D. (1981). Transformation in family relations at puberty. *Developmental Psychology, 17,* 833–840.

Steinberg, L. D. (1988). Reciprocal relation between parent-child distance and pubertal maturation. *Developmental Psychology, 24,* 122–128.

Steinberg, L. D., Mounts, N. S., Lamborn, S. D., & Dornbusch, S. M. (1991). Authoritative parenting and adolescent adjustment across varied ecological niches. *Journal of Research on Adolescence, 1,* 19–36.

Straus, M., & Gelles, R. (1986). Societal change and change in family violence from 1975–1985 as revealed in two national surveys. *Journal of Marriage and the Family, 48,* 465–479.

Stroul, B. (1996). *Managed care and children's mental health: Summary of the May 1995 state managed care meeting.* Washington, DC: Georgetown University Child Development Center, National Technical Assistance Center for Children's Mental Health.

Substance Abuse and Mental Health Services Administration. (1996). *Preliminary estimates from the 1995 National Household Survey on Drug Abuse.* Advance Report Number 18. Washington, DC: Office of Applied Studies.

Tanner, J. M. (1972). Sequence, tempo and individual variation in growth and development of boys and girls aged twelve to sixteen. In J. Kagan & R. Coles (Eds.), *Twelve to sixteen: Early adolescence* (pp. 1–24). New York: Norton.

Tatara, T. (1994). *A comparison of child substitute care exit rates among three different racial/ethnic groups in 12 states, Fy 84 to Fy 90* (Research Note No. 10). Washington, DC: American Public Welfare Association.

Thompson, J. J. (1995). Annie E. Casey Foundation's New Futures: Urban youth policy reform effort earns weak reviews. *Youth Today 4*(6), 30–31, 48.

Thorne, C. R., & DeBlassie, K. K. (1985). Adolescent substance abuse. *Adolescence, 20*(78), 335–347.

Tracy, P. E., Wolfgang, M. E., & Figlio, R. M. (1990). *Delinquency careers in two birth cohorts.* New York: Plenum Press.

Travers, J., Nauta, M. J., & Irwin, N. (1981). *The culture of a social program: An ethnographic study of the child and family resource program—Summary volume.* Cambridge, MA: Abt Associates.

Trutko, J., Chessen, S., & Stapleton, D. (1994). *Evaluation design for the turning points program: Final report.* Arlington, VA: James Bell Associates.

University of Michigan. (1995, December 11). Drug use rises again in 1995 among American teens. *Press release, news and information services.* Ann Arbor: Author.

U.S. Department of Commerce, Bureau of the Census. (1990). *Census of the Population and Housing 1990* (Summary Tape File 3, Tables P-117, P-119, P-120). Washington, DC: U.S. Government Printing Office.

U.S. Department of Commerce, Bureau of the Census. (1993). *Current population reports: Consumer income* (Series P-60, No. 188, Table 8). Washington, DC: U.S. Government Printing Office.

U.S. Department of Health and Human Services. (1996a). *Overview—Empowerment zone/ enterprise community initiative.* Washington, DC: U.S. Department of Health and Human Services, Office of the Assistant Secretary for Planning and Evaluation.

U.S. Department of Health and Human Services. (1996b). *Summary of provisions: Personal responsibility and work opportunity reconciliation act of 1996 (H.R. 3734).* Washington, DC: U.S. Department of Health and Human Services, Office of the Assistant Secretary for Planning and Evaluation.

U.S. Department of Housing and Urban Development and U.S. Department of Agriculture. (1994). *Building communities: Together (empowerment zones and enterprise communities application guide).* Washington, DC: President's Community Enterprise Board.

Urban Institute. (1996a). *Assessing the new federalism: Project description.* Washington, DC: Author.

Urban Institute. (1996b). *Democratizing information: First year report of the National Neighborhood Indicators Project.* Washington, DC: Author.

Ventura, S. J., Taffel, S. M., Mosher, W. D., Wilson, J. B., & Henshaw, S. (1995, May 25). Trends in pregnancies and pregnancy rates: Estimates for the United States, 1980–1992. *Monthly Vital Statistics Report, 43*(11S).

Wagner, M., & Golan, S. (1996, April). *California's Healthy Start school-linked services initiatives: Summary of evaluation findings.* Menlo Park, CA: SRI International.

Wasik, B. H., Ramey, C. T., Bryant, D. M., & Sparling, J. J. (1990). A longitudinal study of two early intervention strategies: Project CARE. *Child Development, 61,* 1682–1696.

Weiss, C. (1983). Ideology, interests, and information: The basis of policy positions. In D. Callahan & B. Jennings (Eds.), *Ethics, the social sciences, and policy analysis* (pp. 213–245). New York: Plenum Press.

Weiss, H. B. (1988). Family support and education programs: Working through ecological theories of human development. In H. Weiss & F. Jacobs (Eds.), *Evaluating family programs* (pp. 3–36). Hawthorne, NY: Aldine.

Wells, S. J., Fluke, J. D., Downing, J. D., & Brown, C. H. (1989). *Final report: Screening in child protective services.* Washington, DC: American Bar Association.

Welte, J. W., & Barnes, G. M. (1985). Alcohol: The gateway to other drug use among secondary school students. *Journal of Youth and Adolescence, 14,* 487–498.

Werner, E. E. (1986). Vulnerability and resiliency in children at risk for delinquency: A longitudinal study from birth to young adulthood. In J. Burchard & S. Burchard (Eds.), *Prevention of delinquent behavior* (pp. 16–43). Thousand Oaks, CA: Sage.

Werner, E. E. (1988). Individual differences, universal needs: A 30-year study of resilient high risk infants. *Zero to three: Bulletin of the National Center for Clinical Infant Programs,* 8(4), 1–5.

Werner, E. E. (1989). High-risk children in young adulthood: A longitudinal study from birth to 32 years. *American Journal of Orthopsychiatry, 59*(1), 72–81.

Werner, E. E., & Smith, R. S. (1992). *Overcoming the odds: High risk children from birth to adulthood.* Ithaca, NY: Cornell University Press.

West, D. J. (1982). *Delinquency, its roots, careers and prospects.* London: Heinemann Educational.

West, D. J., & Farrington, D. P. (1973). *Who becomes delinquent?* London: Heinemann Educational.

Whalen, S. P., & Wynn, J. R. (1995). Enhancing primary services for youth through an infrastructure of social services. Special Issue: Creating supportive communities for adolescent development: Challenges to scholars. *Journal of Adolescent Research, 10*(1), 88–110.

White, K. M., Speisman, J. C., & Costos, D. (1983). Young adults and their parents: Individuation to mutuality. In H. D. Grotevant & C. R. Cooper (Eds.), *Adolescent development in the family: New directions for child development* (pp. 61–76). San Francisco: Jossey-Bass.

Wholey, J. S., & Newcomer, K. B. (1989). *Improving government performance: Evaluation strategies for strengthening public agencies and programs.* San Francisco: Jossey-Bass.

William T. Grant Foundation. (1988). *The forgotten half: Pathways to success for America's youth and young families.* Washington, DC: The William T. Grant Commission on Work, Family and Citizenship.

Wilson, W. J. (1987). *The truly disadvantaged: The inner city, the underclass, and public policy.* Chicago: University of Chicago Press.

Wolin, S. J., & Wolin, S. (1993). *The resilient self: How survivors of troubled families rise above adversity.* New York: Villard Books.

World Health Organization. (1989). *Announcement: The health of youth, technical discussions May 1989.* Geneva, Switzerland: Author.

Wozniak, R. H., & Fischer, K. W. (Eds.). (1993). *Development in context: Acting and thinking in specific environments.* Hillsdale, NJ: Erlbaum.

Yankelovich, D. (1974). *The new morality: A profile of American youth in the 1970s.* New York: McGraw-Hill.

Yoshikawa, H. (1995). Long-term outcomes of early childhood programs on social outcomes and delinquency. *The Future of Children, 5*(3), 51–75.

Young, A. M. (1983). Youth labor force marked turning point in 1982. *Monthly Labor Review, 106*(8), 29–34.

Youniss, J., & Ketterlinus, R. D. (1987). Communication and connectedness in mother- and father-adolescent relationships. *Journal of Youth and Adolescence, 16*(3), 265–280.

Youniss, J., & Smollar, J. (1985). *Adolescent relations with mothers, fathers, and friends.* Chicago: University of Chicago Press.

Youth Risk Behavior National Survey. (n.d.). U.S. Department of Health and Human Services, Centers for Disease Control and Prevention. Retrieved from World Wide Web: http://www.cdc.gov/nccdphp/dash/yrbs/ov.htm.

Zabin, L. S., Hirsch, M. B., Smith, E. A., Streett, R., & Hardy, J. B. (1986). Evaluation of a pregnancy prevention program for urban teenagers. *Family Planning Perspectives, 18*(3), 119–126.

Zimbardo, P. G., & Leippe, M. R. (1991). *The psychology of attitude change and social influence* (3rd ed.). New York: McGraw-Hill.

Zuckerman, M. (1979). *Sensation seeking: Beyond the optimum level of arousal.* Hillsdale, NJ: Erlbaum.

Zuckerman, M., Eysenck, S. B. G., & Eysenck, H. J. (1978). Sensation seeking in England and America: Cross-cultural, age and sex comparisons. *Journal of Consulting and Clinical Psychology, 46,* 39–149.

Index

About the Authors

Martha R. Burt is a Principal Research Associate at the Urban Institute in Washington, DC. She received her PhD in Sociology from the University of Wisconsin–Madison, and she has more than 20 years of experience with policy and evaluation research in a wide variety of areas. Much of her work has had a youth focus, including the areas of teenage pregnancy and parenting; runaway and homeless youth; and recently, rationales for investing in youth for the Pan American Health Organization. As Director of the Urban Institute's Social Services Research Program, Dr. Burt has had the opportunity to work in many arenas. She has directed major projects on homelessness, including analysis of two national surveys. She has also participated in projects concerning violence against women, covering rape attitudes, rape victim services, recovery from rape, and sexual harassment. Currently, she directs a national evaluation of projects funded under the Violence Against Women Act (1994). She has also been involved in research and policy analysis regarding programs for severely mentally ill persons, hunger and social service needs of elderly persons, and child welfare issues. She is the author of numerous articles and reports, as well as several previous books, including *Over the Edge: The Growth of Homelessness in the 1980s* (1992) and *Private Crisis, Public Cost: Policy Perspectives on Teenage Childbearing* (1982).

Gary Resnick is a developmental psychologist with a background that combines program evaluation, child development, and social policy research. He holds an MSW from the University of Toronto and a PhD in Applied Developmental Psychology from Tufts University in Boston. After receiving his doctorate in 1989, Dr. Resnick was an Assistant Professor in Family and Child Development at Auburn University, specializing in adolescent social development. Since 1991, he has been a Senior Study Director at Westat, Inc., a private employee-owned research company in Rockville, Maryland. At Westat, he has evaluated HIV risk and drug use among National Job Corps enrollees; conducted a longitudinal study of 10-year social development among Israeli kibbutz children; studied stress and satisfaction among couples in the military; and codeveloped an automated administration and scoring package for the Separation Anxiety Test, a measure of attachment for early adolescents. He is Associate Project Director of the Head Start Family and Child Experience Survey (FACES), a longitudinal study of program quality and child outcomes among a national sample of Head Start children. He has published journal articles and presented papers at national and international conferences in the areas of child abuse prevention, the effects of divorce on children's social development, evaluation research methods, the measurement of attachment in adolescence, and youth at risk.

Emily R. Novick received her BA from Barnard College at Columbia University in New York City and her MPP from the University of California, Berkeley. She has worked in the area of social policy for children and families since 1984 for nonprofit organizations, for federal agencies, and on Capitol Hill. In her current position as social science analyst in the Office of the Secretary at the U.S. Department of Health and Human Services, Ms. Novick directs research projects and conducts policy analyses on the prevention of high-risk behavior among adolescents and on the promotion of positive youth development. Current projects involve analyzing new national data on abusive intimate relationships among adolescents, staffing a national initiative on youth substance abuse prevention, and managing a website on adolescent issues. Ms. Novick also recently coproduced a nationally broadcast satellite video conference on youth development principles and programs for federal Empowerment Zones and Enterprise Communities. Ms. Novick lives in Silver Spring, Maryland with her husband David and daughters Lily and Rachel.